THE WATCHDOG

THE WATCHDOG

STEVE DRUMMOND

THE WATCHDOG

HOW THE TRUMAN COMMITTEE
BATTLED CORRUPTION AND
HELPED WIN WORLD WAR TWO

HANOVER
SQUARE
PRESS

HANOVER
SQUARE
PRESS™

Recycling programs
for this product may
not exist in your area.

ISBN-13: 978-1-335-44950-4

The Watchdog

Hanover Square Press
22 Adelaide St. West, 41st Floor
Toronto, Ontario M5H 4E3, Canada
HanoverSqPress.com
BookClubbish.com

Printed in U.S.A.

For Lucy

THE
WATCHDOG

INTRODUCTION

Portland, Oregon, January 16, 1943

Saturday night was quieter than usual in war-booming Portland. A cold snap on Friday had killed two people in a storm that brought high winds and left a thin blanket of snow across the city. Temperatures were expected to sink into the low twenties.

At the Swan Island Shipyard in the northern part of the city, the brand-new tanker ship SS *Schenectady* floated gently in calm water, tied up at the fitting-out pier. The 16,500–ton vessel was a source of pride and wonder for the new shipyard, and for the whole city. At 523 feet long and 68 feet wide, it was the largest cargo ship ever built on the Pacific Coast, and the first of 147 tankers that would head down the Willamette River and off to war.

Fully loaded, the ship could carry six million gallons of fuel, and by prewar standards it had been built in no time. The keel was laid on July 1, and the hull launched on October 24. Twenty thousand workers watched that day as it slid down the rails and into the river, "her bow still dripping champagne."[1] *Schenectady* was declared finished on New Year's Eve—two and a half months ahead of schedule. The ship, and the shipyard that built it, were just two examples of the miracles of war production taking place across the United States, achievements that would soon help turn the tide on battlefields around the world.

Outside Detroit, Henry Ford had built a giant airplane factory with an assembly line a mile long. The plant would eventually produce thousands of massive four-engine bombers; at its peak, a finished B-24 Liberator rolled off the line at the incredible rate of one every sixty-three minutes. Liberty ships—the cargo vessels that along with fuel tankers like the *Schenectady* would move the guns and food and planes and millions of tons of equipment across the oceans to the front lines—were being produced in ever greater numbers in shorter amounts of time. Driven by the innovations of shipbuilder Henry J. Kaiser, the first of them took 230 days to build; eventually the average would drop to just over a month.

To build these cargo ships and tankers, new shipyards were needed, and they began appearing in coastal cities seemingly overnight: Seattle, Los Angeles, Vancouver, Jacksonville. In little more than a year, Kaiser had transformed Swan Island, once home to Portland's municipal airport, into a sprawling construction operation with thousands of men and women working shifts around the clock.

One big challenge was getting all those workers to and from their jobs, and finding housing for them when they weren't working. The first dormitories at the shipyard had opened in November, and nine hundred workers moved into what would eventually be enough space for five thousand.[2] A new ferry system was nearly completed that would shuttle workers to and from the yards.

The *Schenectady* was the first ship laid down at the new facility, and it was a new kind of ship—instead of being riveted together, the thick steel plates of these oil tankers (as with the cargo-carrying Liberty ships) were welded—a process that was faster, was less expensive and needed fewer highly skilled workers.

These new techniques were paying off—the *Schenectady* in late December had finished its sea trials and was declared fit for duty. On January 10 the shipyard had turned it over to the US Maritime Commission, and at 3:30 p.m. on the 16th, the ship's new captain, V.P. Marshall, had officially taken charge.[3] He was not on board that evening, though about thirty crewmen were as the ship was being loaded and prepared for her first voyage.

The sound, when it came, at 10:25 p.m., was heard as far as a mile away. Guards at the shipyard felt the ground shake. It sounded like an explosion and, this being wartime, the initial thoughts were of sabotage. An emergency radio call went out that a ship had blown up,[4] and firefighters and police sped to the scene.

What they saw when they got there was the *Schenectady*, split almost completely down the middle. A ten-foot-wide crack ran across the deck and down the port and starboard sides just behind the deckhouse, as if giant hands had picked up the ship and snapped it in two. The keel had fractured through the bottom plates, but did not break, as the center of the ship jackknifed up out of the water. A faded photo shows *Schenectady*'s bow and stern settled to the bottom, the center portion up above the waterline with the dark, jagged fissure reflected in the water below.[5]

Though it happened late, *The Sunday Oregonian* got the news onto the front page the next day, with a banner headline above the masthead: "New Tanker Breaks Apart, Sinks At Swan Island Dock." No one was injured, the paper said, though later it would emerge that a seaman had broken his ankle in the rush to get off the ship.

By Monday, a few new details emerged, though already a veil of secrecy had dropped over the investigation. Armed coast

guardsmen had sealed off the dock, FBI agents had begun in-
terviewing the crewmen who were aboard, and everyone had
been told to keep their mouths shut. Already though, an explosion had been ruled out, reported *The Oregonian*: definitely not,
said the manager of the shipyard—if so, the edges of the giant
crack would have blown outward.[6]

The SS Schenectady, *broken in two at its mooring, Portland, Oregon, January 1943.*

But then, if not an explosion, what? There was some speculation initially that a hogback of sand or gravel on the river bottom had built up and forced the ship to split apart. But that was
soon ruled out, too. With little new information coming in the
following days, the story moved to the inside pages. On Tuesday came news that the FBI, having ruled out sabotage, had
withdrawn, and the paper noted dutifully that morale among
the shipyard's employees, now back to work on the many other
ships under construction, had not suffered.[7]

Gradually—incredibly—it became clear that this brand-new,
$3 million, 523-foot-long steel ship, cleared for sea duty and
resting at its mooring in calm waters, had simply, mysteriously,
broken in two.

Solving that mystery carried an urgency and importance far greater than a sailor's broken ankle or the damage to this single ship. Because the Liberty ships and tankers like *Schenectady* were a vital element of Allied strategy in one of the most desperate and deadly fronts of the war. With Adolf Hitler in control of much of Europe, Great Britain and the Soviet Union depended for their survival on supplies that came by ship from across the Atlantic. And by early 1943, those ships also carried to Britain the troops, weapons, food and supplies that would, eventually, build up armies large and strong enough for the invasion of Europe. Challenging this massive supply effort were the German U-boats—the deadly submarines that throughout the war sent thousands of ships to the bottom of the Atlantic and prevented millions of tons of those goods from reaching their destinations. Both sides were in a race: the Allies to build more merchant ships and develop weapons and strategies to protect them from attack, the Germans to evade those defenses and sink more ships than the Allies could build. The stakes were deadly—during the war, the Battle of the Atlantic claimed more than one hundred thousand lives.

If the Liberty ships and tankers were flawed—if something was wrong with the design or the materials or the new techniques being used to build and launch them in numbers that before the war would have seemed impossible—the ramifications for the battle and for the outcome of the war were huge. Within days of the *Schenectady*'s breakup, a full investigation was underway, and Rear Admiral Howard Vickery, vice chairman of the US Maritime Commission, had arrived in Portland to take charge. But it would be weeks before the mystery was solved, and the answers would come not from the shipyard in Oregon, but from a congressional hearing room thousands of miles away in Washington, DC, and from a man in Pennsylvania who wrote a letter.

1

THE WALK

Early one wintry morning in January 1941, a middle-aged man walked out of a brick apartment building on Connecticut Avenue in northwest Washington, DC. A passerby—out walking the dog, perhaps, very early—might barely have noticed. Just a small, well-dressed man in a felt hat. A more perceptive watcher could have picked up a bit more. The man was meticulous in his appearance, even dapper: his tie impeccably knotted, the shoes freshly shined. A sharp crease ran down the trousers of his double-breasted suit, and a crisp handkerchief peeked from the breast pocket. Perhaps this was a man who'd seen hard times and now took pains to put those days behind him. Or maybe he was someone who'd worked in men's furnishings. Or, in this case, both.

Thick wire-framed glasses gave him a studious air—goggle-eyed, almost. A bookworm? An accountant? Yet his step was brisk, what he liked to count at 120 paces a minute.[1] A former soldier, maybe, whose trim build suggested he was no stranger to physical labor.

Whatever the case, the man was quickly gone. He slid into a Chrysler coupe and drove away, leaving an overall impression, however brief, of a successful and confident man, but an unremarkable one.[2]

At age fifty-six, Harry S. Truman was all of those things, and more. He'd spent six years in the United States Senate, a time in which he'd done virtually nothing of note. He'd just won a very close re-election battle that most people, including the President of the United States, thought he would lose.[3] Now, it seemed likely that he would spend another six years marking time as a reliable but unremarkable foot soldier for the New Deal.

And yet, this was 1941. History was calling, and this short walk—its significance unnoticed by anyone at the time, including Truman—marked his first steps toward answering that call. Both literally and symbolically, he began a journey that morning which would take him in three short years to the vice presidency and the brink of world power in the midst of the deadliest conflict in history.

Four years later, in the unsettling weeks after Truman became president, two journalists who covered him set out to explain how it was, exactly, that he had gotten there. Americans that spring of 1945 had gone to bed on a Wednesday night, secure in the knowledge that Franklin Roosevelt was their president and firmly in control. Then came the shocking news on Thursday, April 12, in flash bulletins over the radio and huge black headlines across "extra" editions of the newspapers, that Roosevelt was dead and someone named Harry Truman was president. As they do now, Americans back then paid little attention to who was vice president. Probably less, given how Roosevelt's supersize personality had come to dominate—almost personify—national leadership like no one since George Washington. Frank-

lin Roosevelt had led them through years of hard times and
Depression, through the ominous rise of Hitler and then the
blitzkrieg, through the infamy of Pearl Harbor, and then three
years of war that touched the lives of virtually everyone in the
country. Roosevelt had lived in the White House for twelve
years, longer than anyone else, and like him or not, most people
expected that he might still be living there through 1948 and
perhaps even beyond. His declining health—obvious to those
around him—had been a guarded secret, whispered about in
Washington but for the most part kept out of the papers. Now,
suddenly, Americans had a new leader, a man they barely knew.
Certainly Truman had since 1941 made a name for himself in
the Senate with his investigating committee, and had won the
nomination and election as vice president the previous year, but
many people knew that about him, and not a whole lot more.

"With all due allowance for the accidents of mortality and
politics, it is clear that Harry S. Truman was lifted into the
White House by his performance as an investigator." So wrote
Wesley McCune and John R. Beal, the two veteran Washington reporters, in the June 1945 issue of *Harper's Magazine*. "In
1941 he was just another obscure Junior Senator with no visible
political future."[4]

In three years, Truman had taken a minuscule appropriation
from the Senate, hired a couple of Capitol Hill bureaucrats, a
former FBI man, a thirty-six-year-old prosecutor, and a bunch
of young men and women right out of college, then shaped them
into the most powerful and feared congressional investigating
arm the country had ever seen. It is one of the most remarkable,
and unlikely, political success stories in American history, and
it begins outside that Connecticut Avenue apartment building
on that cold morning in 1941.

As Senator Truman headed west in his car, war had been
raging in Europe for sixteen months. Hitler's armies had swept
across much of the continent, leaving millions of people dead

and uprooted, with only Great Britain standing against him. In Asia, Japanese armies had conquered huge chunks of China, and its military government was beginning to look south, and west. Some people feared there could be a threat to US interests in the Pacific, in places like the Philippines. Or even Hawaii.

It was becoming alarmingly clear to many in Washington, including the president, that the United States would sooner or later have to fight. Just before the new year, on December 29, 1940, Franklin Roosevelt went on the radio with one of his fireside chats: "Never before since Jamestown and Plymouth Rock," he warned, "has our American civilization been in such danger as now." Roosevelt knew the challenges and hardships that lay ahead, and he knew that in so many ways, the country was shockingly unprepared to face them. When Hitler invaded Poland in September 1939, the United States Army ranked seventeenth in the world in size, behind Romania.[5]

Still, many Americans refused to see the threat as real. The coming war, Roosevelt knew, would be fought and won not only on the battlefield but on the production line as well. And so he set out to convince reluctant Americans exhausted by a decade of Depression that even more, and greater, sacrifices lay ahead: "I want to make it clear that it is the purpose of the nation to build now with all possible speed every machine, every arsenal, every factory that we need."

Looking back, it's hard to grasp the magnitude of this challenge: to convert the entire US economy—farms, factories, shipyards, railroads and in some ways every single household—to one that would make bullets and tanks and planes and ships in greater numbers than anyone ever imagined. Enough to equip not only millions of US soldiers and sailors, but those of its allies, too. "We must," Roosevelt said in one of his most famous phrases, "be the great arsenal of democracy."

The president wasn't the only one to see the threat. In Detroit, the labor leader Walter Reuther, of the United Automobile

Workers union, was calling for the US to build five hundred airplanes every day. "In London they are huddled in the subways praying for aid from America," Reuther said in a national radio speech the day before Roosevelt's fireside chat. "Britain's need is planes and that need is fierce and urgent. We must supply them, and Hitler will not wait while we pursue the normal leisurely methods of production. England's battles, it used to be said, were won on the playing fields of Eton. America's can be won on the assembly lines of Detroit."[6]

It wasn't just planes and tanks and guns that the US military so badly needed. It was literally millions of other things big and small, from food for army and navy recruits to plates to serve it on; tables for those recruits to sit at and mess tents for them to eat in. Trucks and drivers were needed to deliver the food, and stoves and pots and kettles to cook it. The soldiers and sailors would need blankets and cots to sleep in, and socks and shoes and boots and underwear and uniforms to wear, and backpacks to carry their gear, and helmets to protect their heads and rifles to shoot the enemy with. Or, to give a different example, take the Consolidated B-24 Liberator: a giant four-engine airplane that would become the workhorse of the army's heavy bomber fleet.[7] It was considered a miracle of mass production, and by war's end, more than 18,000 of them would be built. But each B-24 was made of more than *450,000 individual parts*, plus some 360,000 rivets in hundreds of different sizes.[8] And the Liberator was just one of dozens of planes designed, built, tested, purchased, and flown throughout the war, and it was not even the largest or most complicated.

All of this change, what was called defense mobilization, had to be managed by the government, working with private industry in ways that had never been done before. Just getting the priorities straight was an incredible challenge. Who should get first dibs on steel? A factory building tanks for the army in Detroit? The gunmaker Remington Arms in Ilion, New York?

The shipyards building the Liberty ships that could carry those tanks and rifles and planes and food across the ocean? Or the shipyards racing to build battleships and submarines and destroyers and aircraft carriers to upgrade the navy's fleet?

It was an unprecedented degree of centralized control over the economy. Rubber, aluminum, gasoline, and thousands of other products faced critical shortages and needed careful consideration—which of course meant countless decisions made by bureaucrats in Washington, decisions that could line the pockets of politicians and procurement officers and expand the fortunes of corporations and contractors. The potential for fraud and corruption, as well as incompetence and inefficiency, was limitless. All this was happening in the midst of a vast, complex, and completely new kind of war. Hitler and the Japanese were racking up victories and gobbling up territory against opponents who were in many cases fighting with obsolete equipment and weapons left over from the last war, and not enough of them at that.

In the arms race to catch up, each branch of the service wanted everything, and they wanted it right now. Bigger, faster, more powerful, no matter how much it cost. "No military man knows anything at all about money," Truman put it years later. "All they know how to do is to spend it. And they don't give a damn whether they're getting their money's worth or not."[9]

With all this money sloshing around, Washington was no longer the sleepy city on the Potomac it had been since the early days of the Republic. The city was growing by about five thousand people a month,[10] and seemingly overnight the dollar-a-year men had taken over. These were corporate leaders—captains of industry—who had left their high-paying jobs in Detroit or New York or Pittsburgh on a Friday and sat down to work for little or no pay in a government office in Washington on Monday. This was all done in the name of patriotism and public service, and these men brought valuable experience and knowledge to the government, but they sometimes found themselves cutting deals on the taxpayers' behalf with the very corporations they had just left.

The most powerful of them was William Knudsen, until recently the president of General Motors and now one of the men leading Roosevelt's defense buildup. From his desk in Washington, Knudsen could pick up the phone and call the head of the Chrysler Corporation, and set up a meeting for the very next day to sketch out a plan—eventually worth some $20 million— to build five hundred tanks a month.[11]

On the heels of the dollar-a-year men came power brokers, lobbyists, and contractors, and behind them came job-seekers by the thousands, along with secretaries and office workers and accountants and bureaucrats. "Until the defense program roared into Washington, it had been a pleasant and comfortable city," one journalist complained. But now, "the cocktail lounges of the city's crowded hotels buzzed with gossip of big contracts got through the influence of brokers," most of whom "hadn't been brokers at all the week before."[12]

It was one slice of that defense program that led Senator Truman west in his car that morning. For a couple of months, he'd been getting letters from some of his constituents about a new army camp under construction in the Missouri Ozarks, called Fort Leonard Wood. Something, the letter writers said, wasn't right.

And so, quietly, Truman set off to see for himself. When he arrived at Fort Leonard Wood, what he saw there was shocking: "There were buildings being built, barracks, mess halls, all kinds of buildings, and they were costing three to four times what they should have. Material of all kind that was out in the snow and rain, getting ruined, things that could never be used, would never be used." Right before his eyes, he saw millions of dollars—tax dollars paid by hardworking Americans—being squandered. "There were men, hundreds of men, just standing around collecting their pay and doing nothing."[13]

From there he kept going, a road trip that would take him to several states and cover several thousand miles: Florida, Maryland, Michigan, Oklahoma, Nebraska, Texas, Wisconsin.[14] He did all this quietly, without a lot of senatorial fanfare, just a small man in a nice suit and a crisp fedora, wandering around and taking notes.[15] At one site after another, the story was the same: waste, inefficiency, incompetence, profiteering. For Truman—a farmer, a war veteran, a businessman who'd struggled and failed, and a public servant with a deep regard for history—this was unacceptable.[16]

If the government was going to spend billions of dollars, tens of billions, even, to get ready for a war, then somebody needed to keep an eye on that spending. Truman returned to Washington "mad clear through,"[17] and began talking with friends and colleagues about what to do about all this. At a fifteen-minute meeting at the White House on February 3, he spoke with Roosevelt about the problems he was seeing.[18] The president, who less than two weeks earlier had been sworn in for his third term, laid on the Roosevelt charm, calling him "Harry" and using his famous knack for *seeming* to agree with everything the person talking to him was saying, without actually committing to anything. Truman was gearing up to make a speech about all this waste in the Senate when a newspaperman, Bill Helm, suggested he take it a step further: Why not propose an investigating committee, with Truman as chairman, to look into all this?[19]

On February 10, Truman stood up on the Senate floor and did just that. It wasn't a great speech—his "Give 'Em Hell" days were still some years off. It was long and overly detailed and delivered in his flat, nasal-sounding voice. And it was full of details and lengthy descriptions of contracts and the methods by which they were awarded, and senators at several points interrupted to ask for clarification on what he was saying.

But there was substance there, too. Truman talked about the waste he'd seen, and about how the owners of small businesses were being shut out of the defense program, and how some contractors and big corporations were getting rich at the taxpayers' expense. It wasn't just corruption and waste, he said. In the rush to catch up, contracts were being put out quickly, with little oversight. "I have had considerable experience," he said, "in letting public contracts, and I have never yet found a contractor who, if not watched, would not leave the Government holding the bag. We are not doing him a favor if we are not watching him."[20]

He noted that, instead of the traditional way of doing things, where the government solicited bids and awarded the job to the lowest bidder, in the urgency of the moment contracts were being made on a cost-plus-fixed-fee basis. In other words, a contractor estimated the costs of doing the job, and then the government wrote up the contract with that amount plus a predetermined fee added on top as profit. It was much faster, but Truman was deeply skeptical of this approach. In addition, he said in his speech, those contracts were too often going to just a few big corporations. Corporations that were concentrated in just few states, usually the industrial states of the Northeast. To a Midwesterner who for much of his life had been a small businessman and often a struggling one, this was deeply unfair. "The little manufacturer, the little contractor, and the little machine shop have been left entirely out in the cold. The policy seems to make the big man bigger and to put the little man completely out of business."[21]

No one, including the president, was very excited about his proposal: a little-known senator with broad investigating powers poking his nose into the administration's business. But it soon became clear that if a Democratic-led committee didn't do it, then Republicans would. And so Truman got his wish—on March 1,[22] the Senate approved his committee. But there was a catch. Truman had asked for $25,000. To keep him from getting in too much trouble, the Senate gave him only $15,000, scarcely enough to hire a staff.

★ ★ ★

Not only was Truman in early 1941 virtually unknown outside of Missouri, but many people who did know of the state's
junior senator considered him a corrupt one, or at least tainted
by corruption. "The Senator from Pendergast" was the nickname that had stuck after he'd arrived in Washington in 1935,
and throughout his first term, when Truman did get mentioned
in the press, it was often in that context. Pendergast was Tom
Pendergast, the longtime boss of the Kansas City political machine and for years a friend of Truman's. Pendergast had gone to
jail in 1939 for tax evasion, and his shadow hung over Truman's
re-election campaign. Truman steadfastly denied any connection with corruption himself, though he kept a picture of his
"good friend" hanging on the wall of his Senate office throughout his years there, and when Pendergast died in 1945, Truman
attended the funeral.

And yet it took more than the support of the Kansas City
boss to win a statewide election, and there was more that voters saw in Truman than the press and the Washington power
brokers gave him credit for. When you looked a little deeper,
the caricature of a crooked, big-city politician just didn't stick.

War hero, farmer, "failed haberdasher," county judge, devoted
husband to Bess and loving father to Margaret—those elements
of his story make up the highlight reel of his early years that
later generations would come to know well; all of them played
a role in his success as a politician.

2

BEGINNINGS

He grew up in Independence, one of those solid Midwestern towns of the late nineteenth century that prided itself on values of hard work, deep religious faith, stable families, devotion to the land. Where, if you were white, you enjoyed much of what seemed to define American prosperity. In the popular culture of the day—and long afterwards—it was a time of church socials, Fourth of July parades, front porch swings, straw hats and parasols, big Sunday meals, and buggy rides in the country. Less idyllic elements in that picture were, of course, the deep-seated racism and segregation of a former slave state. Where the bright promise and the steady march of progress that everyone expected in the new century, it was clear, were for certain people only. Where virtually all of the Black people over a certain age had been born into slavery. Where lynchings were real and talked about openly and enthusiastically in the press[1] and where *nigger* was, regardless of class or income, the word that white people used.

This was the world Truman had entered in 1884 and grown up in; descended from pioneers who'd come west—with the people they enslaved—in the 1840s. An eager, bright boy with loving parents, good teachers and a piano in the parlor, who had, he said later, "the happiest childhood that could ever be imagined."[2] He was also a boy with poor eyesight; wearing glasses from an early age—a rarity for that time and place—shaped his life in serious ways, notably in excluding him from the rough-and-tumble world of sports that made up the social life of boys. He spent much of his time in the town's library, where he and a friend read most—or maybe even all, as some stories have it—of its three thousand books. His favorites were the history books. "When I was about ten, my mother gave me a little blackboard, on the back of which was a column of about four or five paragraphs on every President up to that time, which included Grover Cleveland. And that's how I started getting interested in the Presidency and in the history of this country."[3] His heroes, as with many boys of his time—especially Southern boys—were Andrew Jackson and Robert E. Lee.

He became seriously good at playing that piano, and endured the ridicule that came with it. He practiced every morning at 5:00 a.m., took lessons from the best piano instructor in Kansas City, and at some point in his teens considered becoming a concert pianist. And there was a girl in school, Bessie Wallace, who was good at sports and popular, and she lived on the finest street in Independence. Thanks to the alphabet, she nearly always sat behind him in class.[4]

In high school, Harry was a good student, though not top of his class. He graduated in 1901, looking forward to a good life in a confident age—privileged, shielded, full of the promise and prosperity that everyone expected from the twentieth century.

And then, over the next two years, that prosperity crumbled, and the once-bright future turned dark. Truman's father was caring with his children, and a hot-tempered man outside the home. He loved politics, and shared that passion with his eldest son. A highlight of John Truman's life was a trip to the Democratic National Convention in Kansas City in 1900—he took Harry along with him to watch as William Jennings Bryan accepted the nomination to run for president for a second time. John Truman was a successful farmer and a fiercely aggressive businessman. In keeping with the optimism of the times, he was investing—speculating—in grain futures. At first these paid off, but after 1901 those investments began to go south. He doubled down, borrowing more to cover the losses and conceal the debt, putting up the family savings and land as collateral.

By the summer after Harry's graduation, John Truman had lost just about everything. The family was forced to sell off their home and much of their property and leave Independence. His father "got the notion he could get rich," Truman recalled years later. "Instead he lost everything at one fell swoop and went completely broke."[5]

The Trumans moved to Kansas City, and John Truman took a job as a watchman.

In the days after high school, while things had still looked bright, Truman had thought about college, even traveled a bit. He applied to West Point but got rejected because of his poor eyesight. Soon it became clear he would have to go to work. He cycled through several jobs, notably a stint as a construction timekeeper on a railroad project, where he got to know the rough workers living in tent camps along the railroad. They taught him a skill that would later serve him well in France: a fluency with, and deep appreciation for, profanity that would stay with him for the rest of his life. He said later that on that job he learned "all the cuss words in the English language—not by ear but by note."[6]

He worked in a Kansas City bank, hiring on as a clerk at $20 a month. Here, as with school and the railroad job, he was efficient, hardworking, and well-liked. He was eventually promoted and soon was earning more than his father. The family was getting by, but given the pressures of work and home life, it was during this time that Truman gave up the piano.[7]

In June 1905, soon after his twenty-first birthday, Truman took another of those steps that would shape his life: he joined the national guard, which accepted him despite his poor eyes, and began training with an artillery unit. Here, too, he showed initiative and leadership, and the next year was made a corporal.[8]

John Truman, however, was still struggling, and that same year he left Kansas City and rented a farm about seventy miles away. Harry stayed in the city, where his banking career continued to thrive; he took a job at a different bank and soon was earning $100 a month. Things were again looking bright when his father's financial troubles intervened once more. After a corn crop failed, John Truman and his wife agreed to move in with his wife's mother on the six-hundred-acre family farm in Grandview. Here, things went well for a while, too, but in 1906, as John Truman found the farm work too much, Truman quit his job and moved back with the rest of the family to become a full-time farmer.[9]

And there he would stay for the next nine years. Years of hard work very different from life in a bank office in Kansas City; work that began before the sun came up and ended after it went down. He milked cows and mended fences and tended hogs and sat behind plow horses up and down the long rows for hour after hour. He and his family made the farm a success, and the once-bookish Truman filled out with the routine of physical labor every day. He also developed a deeper relationship with his father than they had known before as, gradually, Harry took on more and more of the running of the farm. His father eventually made him a full partner. They were making good money and the farm prospered, though there was always the shadow of the debts John Truman had run up years before and would take many years yet to pay off.

The work was so hard that Truman had little time for events outside the farm. One thing on his mind, though, was his childhood friend Bessie Wallace. In the years since high school, she too had seen her world turned upside down. In 1903, her father—a popular and well-liked man but a drinker—shot and killed himself.

While he had lived in Kansas City and then in those first years on the farm, Harry and Bess had for the most part grown apart, but he had not forgotten the clever, popular and athletic girl who sat behind him in class. On a visit to Independence in 1910, he spent some time with her again, and from that point on he was in love. After that visit, whenever he could, he made the hours-long journey by horse and buggy, or by walking into nearby Grandview to catch a train to Kansas City and then another train to Independence. Now, too, began the lifelong correspondence between the two—correspondence that would grow into more than 1,300 letters he wrote her over the next half century. He talked about religion, and politics, books and his favorite writers and his love of history—and the day-to-day details of running the farm.

Grandview, Mo.
May 9, 1911

Dear Bessie:
You may be very, very sure that your letters cannot possibly come too often or too regular for me. They are the most pleasant and agreeable (to me at least) of all the correspondence or reading I do. So there, if it pleases you any to have me say it. I am glad you have laid in a good stock of stationery and hope you'll continue to use some of it on me.

Speaking of that calf. It had the impudence to come up and look at me through the window a day or two ago and then kick up and bawl, as much as to say, "See what he got for monkeying with the bandwagon." He had three or four more calves of his own age with him. I have the sincere satisfaction of knowing that he will someday grace a platter—perhaps my very own.

My opinion of Dickens is not so rosy as it was. I read David Copperfield *with delight and not a stop. I was so pleased I started immediately on* Dombey & Sons, *read a hundred pages and have read the* Manxman, *the* Pursuit of the Houseboat on the Styx, *and* Lorna Doone *and still have 500 or 600 pages of* Dombey *to read.* Oliver Twist *must have done you the same way.*

Keep on writing oftener and more regularly and please me more and more.

Sincerely, Harry.[10]

In June 1911, he asked her to marry him.

Speaking of diamonds, would you wear a solitaire on your left hand should I get it? Now that is a rather personal or pointed question provided you take it for all it means. You know, were I an Italian or a poet I would commence and use all the luscious language of two continents. I am not either but only a kind of good-for-nothing American farmer. I always had a sneaking notion that some day maybe I'd amount to something. I doubt it now though like everything. You may not have guessed it but I've been crazy about you ever since we went to Sunday school together. But I never had the nerve to think you'd even look at me. I don't think so now but I can't keep from telling you what I think of you.[11]

Many of Bess's letters to Harry, including the response to this one, do not survive, but it's clear from his follow-ups that she turned him down.

Grandview, Mo.
July 12, 1911

Dear Bessie:
You know that you turned me down so easy that I am almost

happy anyway. I never was fool enough to think that a girl like you could ever care for a fellow like me but I couldn't help telling you how I felt. I have always wanted you to have some fine, rich, good-looking man, but I knew that if ever I got the chance I'd tell you how I felt even if I didn't even get to say another word to you. What makes me feel real good is that you were good enough to answer me seriously and not make fun of me anyway.

You may think I'll get over it as all boys do. I guess I am something of a freak myself. I really never had any desire to make love to a girl just for the fun of it, and you have always been the reason. I have never met a girl in my life that you were not the first to be compared with her, to see wherein she was lacking and she always was.

Very sincerely, Harry[12]

Truman was now twenty-seven. A successful farmer, yes, but constantly worried about money and his father's debts since, now that he was a partner in the farm, they were Harry's debts, too. And though she'd turned him down, Truman kept up his courtship. Bess was a popular girl, and there were other men interested, but the two remained close, and Truman made the journey to Independence to visit whenever he could get away from the farm. And, of course, he kept writing letters.

When war broke out in Europe in July 1914, Truman barely seems to have noticed. He had bought an automobile, a 1911 Stafford, which allowed him to visit Bess in Independence much more often, in their status as just-good-friends, and take her and their group out for drives in the country. It also allowed him to take his father, whose health was failing, to medical appointments in Kansas City. With his father ill, Harry's responsibilities on the farm increased. On November 2, 1914, John Truman died. "I was with him when he died," Truman recalled years later. "I dozed off, and when I woke up, he was gone."[13]

After several years of hard labor on the farm, so far from Bess in Independence, Truman had come to believe that there was something more out there for him than farming. He tried several business ventures, with little success, and then, when Woodrow Wilson asked Congress in April 1917 for a declaration of war and five hundred thousand men, Truman answered the call.

He was thirty-three years old—he had been out of the national guard for several years, but he rejoined (faking his way through the eye exams), leaving the farm with his sister to run it. When the Missouri National Guard expanded its artillery unit into a regiment, the men voted to determine who their officers would be (a remnant of an earlier military era), and Truman was elected first lieutenant. He was surprised by the support, hoping that he might be chosen as a sergeant but never expecting an officer's commission.[14]

The men began training, purchased their uniforms, and practiced drilling. Slowly, Bess and Harry had been drawing closer, and they were in the early stages of discussing an engagement when the war broke out.[15] But now that he was leaving, it was Harry who said they should wait until it was over. "Bess, I'm dead crazy to ask you to marry me before I leave," he wrote, "but I'm not going to because I don't think it would be right for me to ask you to tie yourself to a prospective cripple—or a sentiment."[16]

In September, Truman's guard unit, now federalized into the US Army, headed for Camp Doniphan in Oklahoma, near Fort Sill, for weeks of training in preparation for France. For a new officer, there was so much to learn in addition to the drills and training he was putting his men through. On top of his other responsibilities, he was put in charge of the camp canteen—a little shop that operated like a co-operative, where the men could buy tobacco and snacks and small items. In this project, he teamed up with a sergeant, Eddie Jacobson, he had known previously from Kansas City. "I have a Jew in charge of the canteen and he is a crackerjack," he wrote Bess, adopting one of the many racial and ethnic stereotypes that peppered his letters to her, and which were common in the camp. He and Jacobson made the canteen a success, the envy of other units, paying dividends back to the men in the regiment for their original two-dollar investment. In the process, the two men formed a friendship and working relationship that would outlast the war. Truman made another friendship, too, that would have long-term implications for his future: James Pendergast, the nephew of a powerful Kansas City politician, Tom Pendergast.

Through the weeks of training and hard work, Lieutenant Truman and his men found that he was good at being an officer. He was fair and firm, and he genuinely liked the men and they liked him. He sat for promotion to captain and initially thought he had failed it, though later he heard unofficially that he had passed. And he learned that he had been chosen as part of a select group of officers and men who would go to France early, weeks ahead of everyone else, for special training. In the early morning hours of March 20, 1918, Harry Truman left Oklahoma with the Special Overseas Detail, headed for war.[17] After a few days in New York City (he wasn't impressed), they sailed for France on March 29.

By 1918, the slaughter along the Western Front, stretching some four hundred miles from Belgium to the Swiss border, had continued for more than three years, with little for either side to show for it except millions of dead and wounded. It was widely hoped (and feared, by the Germans) that the arrival of more than a million Americans would finally break the stalemate. The American commander, General John "Black Jack" Pershing, had resisted throwing his troops piecemeal into the trenches to plug this or that gap, preferring to build up a force big enough and strong enough to strike a decisive blow.

Truman spent several weeks in a special artillery school learning to master the French model 1897 cannon, a light, 75-mm artillery weapon famous for its speed and accuracy. The compli-

cated, college-level math involved in artillery warfare he found
extremely challenging. "I've studied more and worked harder
in the last three weeks than I ever did before in my life. It's just
like a university only more so; right out of one class into another
and then examinations and thunder if you don't pass," he wrote
Bess on May 26. A few days later he told her: "I've learned more
in the last four weeks than I did in all my time in high school."[18]

After five weeks of this, he returned to his unit and learned,
officially, of his promotion to captain. He had seen a lot of France
by now and admired the scenery and the people but was still
far away from the front lines. Captain Truman was given command of Battery D—four guns and 194 men, many of them Irish
Catholics from Kansas City known for their rowdy behavior—
and he set about making it the best unit in the 129th Field Artillery regiment.

After more weeks of drilling and training and practice firing,
in which Battery D did become a standout, the regiment left
for the front on August 17. The Germans, after the withdrawal
of Russia from the war in December 1917, had been able to
shift troops to the Western Front and by mid-1918 had gained
a numerical superiority and were on the offensive. In the emergency, Pershing had been forced to commit about 250,000 of
his American troops earlier than he had wished.[19]

Truman and his men were sent to a quiet sector of the front
in the Vosges Mountains, near the Swiss border; it was considered a good place for inexperienced national guard troops
to gain some experience. After several days getting set up, on
the night of August 29, the battery fired its first shells at the
Germans—five hundred rounds of poison gas, widely used by
both sides in the war. After their barrage, the woods fell silent as
the men waited for the horses that would move them to a new
position before the Germans could retaliate. When they failed
to appear, Truman climbed on a horse to investigate, and as
the other horses arrived at last, the Germans opened up. Shells

began exploding among Battery D; many of the animals panicked and ran. Truman's own horse slipped and fell in a shell hole, pinning him underneath. While a lieutenant helped free him, and some of the men worked to dig out two guns that sank into the mud, a frightened sergeant yelled for everyone to run. As some of the men fled, Captain Truman let loose with a barrage of his own, peppered with profanity: "I got up and called them everything I knew." He stood his ground, and that steadiness along with his tirade of abuse prevented a total panic. Two horses were dead and two more had to be shot, but the men who ran came "sneaking back," as Truman got the horses gathered up and everyone back to work.[20] Leaving the two stuck guns behind, he got the men back to safety about 4:00 a.m. for a hot meal and some much-needed rest. He asked for volunteers the next night to go back and retrieve the two guns, and every man offered to go.[21]

In later years, the men of Battery D would laugh about that night, calling it the Battle of Who Run, but they had been terrified, and their captain had led them through it. "The men think I am not much afraid of shells but they don't know," he told Bess. "I was too scared to run and that is pretty scared."[22] Since no one had been hurt, Truman gained a reputation as a lucky commander. He feared he'd be called to account for the performance, but his commander reassured him it was common for men to behave like that their first time in combat. Truman was told to court-martial the sergeant who'd panicked, but he busted the man to private instead and transferred him to another unit.

Soon, he and his men were shifted north to the center of the action, and from then on, Battery D would participate in many of the battles of the closing weeks of the war. On November 11, the unit fired its final rounds in anger as the guns fell silent up and down both sides of the trenches at exactly 11:00 a.m.—the eleventh hour of the eleventh day of the eleventh month. Truman and the men listened in awe as the firing stopped; "the silence that followed almost made one's head ache," he wrote. Four long years of war had come to an end, and Truman and Battery D had fired "something over ten thousand rounds," with only one man killed in action. For the rest of their lives, many of the men would credit their captain for returning them home safely.[23]

It was several months before he was able to return home. He missed Missouri, and most of all Bess. He arrived in New York City on April 20, 1919, and from there he traveled to Kansas, where he was discharged on May 6. Truman was eager to get on with his marriage and the rest of his life. Just what that life would be, however, remained a big question. He knew he would not go back to the farm. He had some business ideas, was well connected in Independence and Kansas City, shared his father's love of politics, and knew that his time in the army could open a path to that. But all that was some ways off—right now he and Bess had a wedding to plan.

They were married on June 28, 1919, in the Trinity Episcopal Church in Independence. Truman wore a sharp gray suit, and Bess an elegant white dress with a matching wide hat. Many of the veterans of Battery D were there, along with Bess's family and Harry's. After the ceremony, the newlyweds left for their honeymoon in Chicago, Detroit, and Port Huron, Michigan.

Back in Missouri, the couple moved into Bess's mother's house in Independence, and Truman and his army friend Eddie Jacobson made good on their plans to go into business. Many years later it became such a part of Truman's backstory that, Margaret Truman wrote, "everyone over the age of thirty has heard ad nauseam about my father's next adventure, his failure as the co-owner of a men's clothing store in Kansas City."[24] Truman called it the "shirt store," but it has come down through history as a "haberdashery," and Truman, in the newspaper shorthand of the 1940s and '50s, a "failed haberdasher." At first things went well at Truman and Jacobson. They chose a good location and with money that Truman had from selling the farm (more than his share, some members of the family thought), they stocked it with the best shirts, hats and furnishings. Of course, many of the war veterans in Kansas City were regulars, and would stop by to chat with their former captain and maybe spend some money.

Harry remained in the army reserve, joined the American Legion, and was active in other social networks, notably the Freemasons—one of the oldest and most popular fraternal organizations in the country. In North America, Freemasonry dates back to colonial times—George Washington was a Grand Master of the Virginia Lodge.[25] There were Masonic Lodges all over the United States, and Truman had helped organize the Grandview Lodge in his farming years. He loved the ceremony and rituals, the charitable work and the call to lead a moral and a useful life, and the social gatherings and the connections it brought him. "He took his Masonry seriously," wrote Jonathan Daniels, "and it played an important part in his political life."[26]

His many connections helped with the business, but in 1920, the economy soured. The postwar boom faded, and expensive shirts fell off the list of things that men needed. The army veterans would come in, but now, as often as not, they were not buying anything. Sometimes they came to borrow a few dollars from Captain Harry. Truman and Jacobson doubled down, going into debt.

And then, one day in late 1921 or early 1922, as it was becoming clear that the store would fail, politics and his army connections came to the rescue. "I was in the store one day just when we were going broke," Truman recalled. He had a couple of job offers, but nothing that really interested him. "I was standing behind the counter feeling fairly blue when Mike Pendergast came in."[27] Mike was the father of Truman's army friend Jim Pendergast, and he was also the brother of Tom Pendergast, the head of Kansas City's most powerful Democratic organization. In the parlance of the time, Tom Pendergast was boss of the Kansas City machine.

Mike Pendergast came with an offer: Would Truman like to run for county judge? In Jackson County, this wasn't a judicial position presiding over courtroom trials and lawyers, but more like a county commissioner, controlling contracts, roads and government service, managing the budget and hundreds of employees. There were three county judges, and in Democratic Jackson County, control swung between factions in the party. Pendergast's organization was known as the "goats," and a rival group was known as the "rabbits." Mike Pendergast had responsibility for the eastern, rural areas of the county, which included Independence, and his invitation to Truman, of course, came with his brother's blessing.

Was Tom Pendergast crooked? The answer, of course, is yes. Boss Pendergast manipulated elections and bullied opponents and made sure that Democrats—his Democrats—got the best government jobs, and that county contracts went to his companies or those of his choosing. For Pendergast, politics was business and business was politics, and both were played rough and dirty. He worked from a small office where he ran the family's liquor and saloon businesses, and other enterprises that were closely intertwined with county politics—a road paving company, a concrete mixing company, an oil company and several others. Though he had once served as a city councilman, he preferred now to pull the strings from behind the scenes. He ran kind of a shadow organization outside the government, and was known for his generosity and humor, and for his sharp understanding of politics and human nature. Like many political bosses, Pendergast and his organization "did favors" for people as well as community outreach—coal and warm clothing for poor families in winter, free meals for the hungry, a county job for an out-of-work father; all with the expectation that such benevolence would be returned at the polls come election time, possibly by voting more than once. For the Pendergasts, Truman as a candidate would bring a lot to the table: veterans—many of them Irish Catholic voters in Kansas City—looked up to him as their "Captain Harry." Farmers in eastern Jackson County knew he was one of them—not just a farmer but a good one—who spoke their language and who knew what it was to wake up before sunrise and work hard all day, rain or shine, year in, year out. He genuinely liked people, had extensive connections in the Masons and the business community, and was widely known as an honest and honorable man. Truman would bring the Pendergast organization some much-needed brand polishing. Or, in the words of one of Harry's old friends, Harry Vaughan, "window dressing."[28]

For Truman, the offer couldn't have come at a better time. The job of county judge paid $3,465 at a time when he had a wife to support and no clear career path, and debts from the collapse of his business that would take him years to pay off. He was thirty-seven and had no interest in going back to the farm. Beyond that, he had the love of politics he'd shared with his father, and he had tasted leadership in France and found that he liked it and was good at it. He jumped at the offer.

As with farming, or running a business or commanding an artillery battery, candidate Truman had a lot to learn, and he had to learn fast. The support of the Pendergast machine was of course a big boost, but the election was by no means guaranteed. Truman was a newbie, and there were four other Democrats in the race, including one with the strong support of the "rabbit" organization. Among the many things he had to learn was public speaking. At first he was so nervous he could barely mumble a few words, but as the days went by, he got better at it. His campaign was for better roads in the county and better and more efficient government, and in the details of how he would do this, he found the beginnings of a speaking style—laying out the problem simply and explaining what he would do about it. Since Jackson County was heavily Democratic, the primary on August 1 was the real battle. In the end Truman won, but it was a squeaker: a margin of just 279 votes over the second candidate, out of more than 11,000 votes cast.[29]

Beginning on January 1, 1923, he served a two-year term, and by all accounts it was a surprising and unusual one. He and his newly elected colleagues had inherited, financially speaking, a mess, including a budget deficit of more than $1 million.[30] Truman brought to the job a focus on fiscal responsibility and ethics. Politics, of course, involves compromise, and dealmaking. Truman would forever be tarnished by his association with Pendergast. But it's also true that Harry Truman, or anyone for that matter, could not get elected in Jackson County without such an affiliation. Truman maintained throughout his life that Pendergast never asked him to step over the line, but he would many times find himself right up at the edge of that line. He struggled with this basic contradiction between his devotion to honest, open government and the system of machine politics and patronage that had put him in office. As historian Alonzo Hamby puts it, "through a process that was probably not fully conscious, he juggled idealism and realism awkwardly for the rest of his public life."[31]

Immediately after taking office, Truman and his colleague H.L. McElroy used their majority on the three-judge panel to start cleaning up the books. Beyond the finances, there were pressing needs for county services. Truman's special passion was roads and bridges, and he made it his mission to become an expert on what was wrong, and what was needed, with the roads in Jackson County.[32] In addition, he kept active in the Masons and began taking some law courses at a night school in Kansas City. On the home front, the Trumans were hoping for a child. Bess had suffered two miscarriages, but their wish was finally granted on February 17, 1924, when Bess, age thirty-nine, gave birth to a daughter, Margaret.

On the national scene, though, times were tough for Democrats. Calvin Coolidge, a Republican, was elected president in

1924, and his victory went way down the ticket in Missouri. And while Judge Truman won the Democratic primary—and praise from the local newspapers—in his bid for re-election, the rival Democratic organization joined up with local Republicans, along with the Ku Klux Klan, in a drive to unseat him. The Klan was on the rise at this time—its membership grew to several million in the mid-1920s as white people responded to its message that Black people, Jewish people, Catholics and foreigners were stealing jobs and poisoning the pure "American" culture. Truman had been pressured to join at a time when the organization wielded great power over elections and public opinion and at a time when many politicians were gladly signing up. In a moment of weakness, or extremely bad judgment, he came close, but ultimately he did not join. Amid these swirling tensions and the continuing battle over Prohibition, Coolidge won the national election for president, and the Republicans swept state and county elections too. Truman was ousted as county judge.

He was out of work, still in debt and struggling to support his mother, his in-laws, and his wife and baby girl. He fell back on networking and his many connections: from the army, the Masons and his time in county politics. He got a job selling memberships in the Kansas City Automobile Club, making good money. He got involved in a complex, frustrating and ultimately unsuccessful career as a banker. And of course, he kept in touch with the Pendergasts.

In early 1926, they urged him to run again, this time for presiding judge—a much bigger job, covering Kansas City as well as the rural areas he'd represented as eastern judge. He ran in the primary unopposed and breezed to victory in the general election. And here, for the next eight years, Harry Truman would find his calling at last. By all accounts, even the newspapers so hostile to the Pendergast machine, Truman turned around the finances and government of Jackson County. By the time his first term ended, writes Hamby, "he enjoyed bipartisan acclaim as the best occupant of the office in its history."[33]

His first big undertaking was an effort to modernize the roads in Jackson County, and in this, Truman swung for the fences. Not just an increase in the county budget to cover maintenance of the existing dirt roads, but a proposal for an entirely new system of modern, paved roads—224 miles of them[34]—that would link farmers in the country, thanks to their Model T Fords, with businesses and services in Kansas City. He won passage of the $6.5 million bond vote, and the project was a huge success. A big reason was that, as he'd promised, he let the contracts to the lowest bidder—sometimes outsiders from other states—rather than the usual suspects put forth by Tom Pendergast. Similarly, a new county hospital for the elderly came in under budget, providing a much-needed social safety net years before Social Security and decades before Medicare.

He remained, of course, tethered to Pendergast and was in this job a vital part of the machine. In large part that involved the distribution of patronage jobs, something Truman for the most part had no problem with at all. It was part of the "to the victor go the spoils" ethos of politics in that place and time. He even kept Fred Wallace, his "drunken brother-in-law," on the county payroll at taxpayers' expense. Nevertheless, while he had many opportunities to do so, Truman stubbornly resisted the urge to make himself rich from this job—Pendergast at one point apparently called him a "sucker" for refusing to steer contracts to machine cronies.[35]

Above all this, he loved this job. He loved the power, he loved the public service, and he loved being out among the people. He studied hard and became the acknowledged expert on all things involving Jackson County roads. He worked his networks—the Masons, war veterans, and, of course, the powerful Pendergast machine. It was during these years he learned many of the techniques and developed many of the qualities as a politician and administrator that would serve him well years later on the Truman Committee.

But he also struggled with the ethical challenges of representing a traditional political machine with the demands of good government and public service. While he would sometimes push back on Pendergast's demands, at other times he would, reluctantly, hold his nose and do what he was told or turn a blind eye to things—like blatant corruption—he knew were wrong. He agonized over the compromises he was forced to make, sometimes accepting smaller evils in the interest of a greater public good. When the stresses seemed overwhelming, he poured out some of these frustrations in undated longhand notes to himself, written on stationery from a Kansas City hotel. "I wonder if I did right to put a lot of no account sons of bitches on the payroll and pay other sons of bitches more money for supplies than they were worth in order to satisfy the political powers and save $3,500,000," he wrote in one of them. In another he asked, "am I just a crook to compromise in order to get the job done? You judge it, I can't."[36]

The demands—people seeking jobs, people wanting favors—were constant and weighed on him. So too did family worries—his finances, and his daughter's frail health. In another precursor of his years on the Truman Committee, these stresses would at times affect his emotional and physical health. He had headaches and trouble sleeping, and came to hate the sound of the telephone.

Despite the worry and the stress, he easily won re-election in 1930 to another four-year term, though this one would be tougher. The Great Depression had arrived. Like the rest of the country, the financial health of Jackson County tanked, and Truman watched helplessly as thousands of residents lost their jobs. Many of them would hit him up for a place on the county payroll, and Truman found himself stuck with budget cuts and deficits.

Instead of building roads and hospitals, this time around he spent much more time dealing with tax policy and administration.[37]

A highlight of this term was construction of a new courthouse in Kansas City. Truman went on long road trips to check out similar buildings in other places and took a keen interest in the design and architecture. The dedication ceremony in December 1934—his final act as county judge—enabled him to end this troubled second term on a high note.

By this time, Truman had his sights set on bigger things. In 1934, as his political career was once again at a crossroads, Tom Pendergast somewhat reluctantly gave him the nod once again. This time, for the United States Senate.

3

BUILDING THE TEAM

In early 1941, Matthew Connelly was looking for his next job. The thirty-three-year-old Fordham University graduate had, in the early days of the New Deal, been an investigator with the Works Progress Administration. More recently he'd worked several House and Senate investigating panels. In the Washington parlance of the time, which borrowed from private eye novels, he was known as a "committee dick."[1] Tall and athletic, with leading-man looks, Connelly was a "shrewd, witty Irishman," as Margaret Truman described him, who brought to the committee a "tight-lipped discretion, and a thorough knowledge of the shifting, complex web of Washington pressures and power relationships."[2] In March he was working his contacts in hopes of landing a job at the White House. Among them was Senator Lister Hill of Alabama, who summoned Connelly to his office one day with a different idea: his Senate colleague, Harry Truman, was going to be leading an important investigation and needed help. Connelly had never met Truman, and wasn't happy about ditching his plans for working in the White House, but he agreed to take the meeting.

"Come in," Truman said when Connelly arrived the next morning. "I know all about you." The senator got right down to business: the first thing he needed for an investigating committee was investigators, and he wanted Connelly to come work for him. "I do not know what I can pay you, but I will say this to you, if you go along with me, you will never have any reason to regret it."[3]

It was a bit of Truman's famous plain speaking, and it worked. "Senator, I came in here to say no," Connelly replied, "but the way you talk is refreshing in Washington and you've got yourself a deal."

He was the committee's first employee, and was able to help right off with the central question facing Truman: How could he run an investigating committee with so little money? The Senate on March 10 had approved his committee, but they'd cut way back on the amount of money he'd have to run it. He asked Connelly outright, "What are we going to do to build up the staff on $15,000?"

Well-versed in the finer points of how to find, and hide, money on Capitol Hill, Connelly filled Truman in on how these things worked: reach out to the Cabinet members, he said, and park the investigators on their budgets. For starters, Connelly went on the National Housing payroll, part of the Federal Housing Administration.

With Connelly signed on and the money problem solved, for now, Truman started looking around for office space. More importantly, he needed someone to run the staff and set the committee's agenda: a serious, dedicated, aggressive lawyer to serve as chief counsel. That, however, in Washington of the 1940s and later, was not how these things usually worked. The job of running an investigating committee was often a chit used to pay off a political debt, or to reward a party loyalist who needed work.

Or it would go to a prominent, high-powered attorney who, when he could, squeezed the work into his busy, and more lucrative, private practice.

But in his first Senate term, serving on an investigating committee looking into railroad holding companies, Truman had learned from one of the masters of Senate investigations, Burton Wheeler of Montana. He'd sat through countless hours of "some of the dullest hearings ever recorded at the Capitol," but Truman had listened, and learned, and as the investigation went on he'd become more and more involved. One of the takeaways he'd picked up from Wheeler was "that technical staff can make or break a Congressional investigation."[4]

And so, in mid-March, he called Attorney General Robert H. Jackson: "I want the best investigator you have on your payroll."[5] Jackson thought it over, and the name he came up with was his special assistant in New York. Hugh Alfred Fulton, University of Michigan Law School class of '31, had worked in private practice in New York before joining the Justice Department in 1938. Now, at thirty-six, he was a skilled prosecutor who had just won a very high-profile case—one of the largest corporate frauds to that time in American history. On New Year's Eve, a federal jury in New York had convicted Howard Hopson, one of the founders of Associated Gas and Electric, of defrauding Americans out of more than $20 million.[6] The trial and the verdict were front-page news all over the country.

Jackson called Fulton, who agreed to come down to Washington to meet with Truman. They met on a Saturday morning, March 22. For both men, it wasn't exactly love at first sight. Fulton "came in wearing a derby hat," Truman recalled. "A big fat fellow with a squeaky voice. I said to myself, 'Oh shucks!'" After the meeting, Truman told the attorney general, "When I first saw him coming through the door, I thought you were playing a joke on me."[7] This was a reference to Fulton's youthful—and portly—appearance. Media accounts from the time often mentioned his weight (250 pounds), usually followed by some version of "round-faced," "rotund," or "chubby and cherubic."

Fulton, riding high in his current job, had concerns of his own. For one thing, who was this senator? From Washington, he called an old friend from his law firm days in New York, Alexander Hehmeyer, who now worked at the offices of *Time* and *Life* magazines. Could he look through the files and see what they had on Truman? Hehmeyer had an appointment in Washington the next morning, and agreed to meet Fulton at Union Station at 7:00 a.m. to talk over the job offer and hand over whatever he turned up.

Which wasn't much. Hehmeyer strolled over to the *Time* newsroom and asked a few of the editors what they knew. No one had anything to say about Truman, and all they had in the files was a single story—the prewritten obituary that the Associated Press put out on every sitting member of the Senate. That night, he took the sleeper train down to DC, and at their breakfast meeting handed over the short obituary.[8] There were other issues besides Truman's relative obscurity. Fulton wanted $9,000 a year, yet Congress had only set aside $15,000 for the whole committee. And he'd be giving up a high-profile job for an unknown quantity. What if Truman's committee fell flat on its face, or, more likely, fizzled out after a few months like most of these investigations? Finally, a big issue was Fulton's concern about whether politics would interfere with his work. "Are you going to let the chips fall where they may?" he had asked Truman in the interview. "Or is this going to be a whitewash?"[9] It was a valid question. Both men knew how things worked in Washington, and Truman had a ready answer: "I don't want a whitewash and I don't want to smear," he told Fulton. "The chips are going to fall where they may."[10]

The interview with Fulton came during a busy week that saw Truman juggling the growing demands of the committee with his normal Senate work. Bess and Margaret, now in her teens, were away in Independence and, as always, that left him feeling gloomy. "Well, it was a rather lonesome apartment when I returned to it," he wrote Bess on Monday. "Had two glasses of buttermilk and some toast, read my mystery story for a while and was asleep by eleven P.M." He signed the letter "Lonesome Harry."[11]

Tuesday saw him horse-trading with the White House over which senators would round out the committee, and he spent Wednesday tied up in the details of Missouri politics. "I've been going around in circles today. Saved the Jackson County Court from insolvency—damn 'em," he wrote Bess that night. "Also the lovely mayor of St. Louis must have spent five dollars crying on my shoulder over the phone and I helped him." On the other hand, "my investigating committee is getting really hot. Feel better about it now. Looks like I'll get something done."[12]

Friday the 21st found him again working late, and still feeling lonesome. He was worrying about a radio speech he had to give in a few days and clearing his desk for a trip home. Before he left the office that night, he filled Bess in on the details: the radio talk Monday night, then a train to Missouri the next day. A speech to the legislature on Thursday and then a meeting with his Masonic Lodge in Jefferson City later that night. "Then I have to speak in Louisville on Saturday night & will catch the same B&O you & Margaret get in St. Louis on Sunday." They would all return to DC on that train. That reunion was more than a week off, though. "I've got to go home now and spend the rest of the night writing a speech. Be sure and take good care of yourself and write to me. I was never so lonesome in my life. The flat looks like a tomb." There was, however, one bright spot: "I hired a counselor today for the committee. He's a good man and I believe we will go from here all right. Name's Fulton."[13]

Hugh Fulton joined the committee as chief counsel ten days later. It was one of the best decisions either man ever made, and one that would change the course of Truman's life. As one committee staffer put it, "If Truman had appointed a political hack he would never have become President of the United States."[14]

Charles Patrick Clark, Associate Chief Counsel; Hugh Fulton, Chief Counsel; and Senator Truman.

Truman had thought a lot about his committee and what he wanted it to be. He'd learned a lot on that railroad investigation with Wheeler, and he'd seen what had happened after World War I, when Congress had launched 116 separate investigations,[15] many of them politically motivated. Some of them dragged on for years. Instead of waiting until the war was over, Truman felt that an investigating committee that began its work while the defense buildup was still under way "would prevent a lot of waste and maybe even save some lives."[16]

He'd also read his history. During the Civil War, a similar effort led by senators of the president's own party had caused Abe Lincoln no end of grief. The Library of Congress had a copy of the entire hearings of the Joint Committee on the Conduct of the War, and as Truman shaped his own committee, he'd spent a lot of time reading those volumes. He was fond of quoting Robert E. Lee as saying that the committee's meddling was "worth at least two divisions to the Confederate cause." Its chairman, Senator Benjamin Wade of Ohio was, in Truman's words, "a no-good son of a bitch."[17]

So the committee had a chairman, a chief counsel and the makings of a staff. It also needed six senators to round it out, and Truman knew that here, too, the choices he made would determine whether his committee spiraled into politics and press releases or actually got something done. The resolution approving the committee had given it broad powers and had increased the number of senators, from Truman's proposed five to seven.[18] In choosing them, Truman faced pressure from the administration to pack the committee with Roosevelt supporters, and Truman had to negotiate with both Senate Majority Leader Alben Barkley and the vice president, Henry Wallace.[19] By the end of March, though, he had his committee: a senatorial B-list whose distinguishing characteristic was, in the opinion of two journalists who covered them, "a sort of unspectacular competence."[20]

Counting Truman, there were five Democrats and two Republicans. Four were in their first terms as senators, and two— Carl Hatch, a Democrat from New Mexico, and Mon Wallgren, Democrat of Washington—were among Truman's close friends in the Senate. Sixty-five-year-old Tom Connally of Texas was the most senior and powerful member, and the one most closely aligned with Roosevelt. Connally was put on the committee as "an administration chaperone," to keep criticism of the president from getting out of hand.[21] He would also be one of its least active members. Rounding out the Democratic side was the committee's other hard-core New Dealer, James Mead, a railroad man from Buffalo who'd arrived in the Senate in 1938.

On the Republican side, Truman tapped Ralph Owen Brewster of Maine, who often served as the committee's vice-chairman. Brewster was a veteran lawyer and an aggressive cross-examiner who would take the point on some of the committee's high-profile investigations. He was also, Truman would learn, vulnerable to political considerations and the senator most likely to inject them into the committee's work.[22] The other GOP member was Joseph Ball of Minnesota, at thirty-five the youngest member of the Senate and a newspaperman from Minneapolis.

Next, Truman needed to fill out the staff and find space for them to work. Using Connelly's budgeting trick, Fulton hired Harold Robinson, a former FBI agent and the committee's only investigator with real law enforcement experience, and put him on the payroll of the Maritime Commission.[23]

Robinson, or "Robby" as everyone called him, was a big, gregarious man on the surface; "he reminded you of a big puppy dog," said one junior staffer. "He would have made a great standup comic."[24] Yet behind the facade was a sharp mind with a degree in accounting and the cynical eye of a lawman, who could "look at a person he wasn't fond of with the fishiest, coldest stare."

At the FBI, Robinson had been an auditor, but he'd also become known as a specialist in electronic surveillance, and in the last couple of years had played a key role in the government's biggest spy case ever—a sting operation against Nazi agents on Long Island. The FBI had infiltrated the ring, and then had its own men, including Robinson, set up a shortwave radio station on Long Island to transmit messages back to Germany. "I got fifty dollars a month from the Gestapo for serving as a sort of double agent," Robinson said.[25]

When the government swooped in and made arrests in 1941, thirty-three spies were rounded up and convicted, and sentenced to a total of more than three hundred years in prison.[26] That case for the most part put an end to successful Nazi espionage in the United States. But Robinson, at 220 pounds, had grown tired of shimmying up telephone poles, and had come to feel that his skills as an accountant were being wasted by the bureau. He thought his undercover work was both underpaid and underappreciated. "So I quit."[27]

He was in Washington that March for a job interview in naval intelligence, and while in town, he stopped by the Justice Department on Constitution Avenue. As he walked into the building, Hugh Fulton stepped off an elevator: "Robby, you're just the guy I'm looking for." The two men knew each other from working cases out of New York, with Fulton as prosecutor. "I hear you quit the bureau?"

Fulton said he had just been upstairs to see the attorney general, "and I've got to go over to Capitol Hill and see some junior senator from Missouri."[28] Robinson was Fulton's first hire on the committee and would work on many of its biggest investigations. He was also the office practical joker, and often it would be Shirley Key, a receptionist and secretary hired in May, who found herself on the other end of his humor. Key was twenty-two, learning on the job, and already having the adventure of a lifetime. Born in Louisville, Kentucky, which gave her a rich Southern accent, Key had lived in Washington from the time she was twelve and loved the city and its place at the center of things.[29]

She was the seventh person hired on the committee, with a starting salary of $1,800 a year. Though she was a graduate of George Washington University, with follow-up at Temple Business School, the male-dominated culture of Washington in those times still fenced her into secretarial work. She heard about the Senate investigating committee from a high school friend, and went down and talked to Charles Patrick Clark, a lawyer and investigator Truman had hired as associate chief counsel soon after Connelly came on board. Clark brought her on to be his receptionist in Room 317, where, in addition to typing correspondence and taking dictation, it was Key's job to greet people when they came in and show them around the Senate building, or take them up to see Truman or Fulton.

The work was hard, the hours were long, but right from the start she loved it. Well, most of it. Clark, her immediate boss, was prickly, and some of the staff found him difficult.[30] Nevertheless, she quickly made friends among the growing staff, and every day brought something new.

Shirley Key in Washington, April 1943.

In those early weeks, while she was still learning some of the secretarial skills, Robinson called her over to his desk one day to take dictation. He was writing a report on an army installation being built in California, Camp San Luis Obispo, and the need for a dam to supply water from the Salinas River. Key transcribed his words as he talked, three or four pages' worth, and by six o'clock she had finished typing it up and was ready to call it a day. She handed Robinson the finished pages and was preparing to head home when he called her back. "Miss Key, you'll have to stay."

"Why?"

"How do you spell dam?"

"D-a-m-n," she responded.

Robinson gently gave her the news: "We'll have to run this through again." Neither ever forgot the incident (each told a version of it in their oral history interviews decades later with the Truman Presidential Library).[31]

Key was a fast learner, though, and as the steno pool grew down in Room 160, she was soon put in charge of it, in addition to handling the people who came in to see Truman or Fulton. This was a thrill: the chance to meet powerful people, whose names she read in the newspaper every day, even United States senators, and show them around.

One of the guests who showed up at her desk in those first weeks on the job was a thin young newspaperman named Walter Hehmeyer. Fulton needed someone to handle the press for the committee, and his New York friend, Alexander Hehmeyer, suggested his brother, who was then working for *Cue* magazine, a weekly that covered theater and the arts in the city.[32]

With the war heating up in Europe, the younger Hehmeyer was getting antsy in his current job and looking for a change, something that would be productive and more of a challenge. So when Fulton sent him a telegram in mid-May, asking him to come down to Washington, he jumped at the chance. Hehmeyer arrived on a beautiful spring day, the kind the city is known for, with azaleas in full bloom and the explosion of cherry blossoms around the tidal basin. Before his interview, Hehmeyer took a stroll through the city, taking in the sights around the Capitol.

He arrived early for his appointment, and Fulton was too busy to see him right away, said the pretty young receptionist. "Could you please take a walk around the Capitol and do some sightseeing and come back?"[33]

Hehmeyer smiled. He'd already done that, he told Miss Key, but he'd be happy to walk a little more. With her, he'd made a strong first impression, and he did so again later that day in his meeting with Truman and Fulton. Hehmeyer had never met a United States senator before, and he liked the way this one talked—simple and straightforward. "Well, we are going to have a lot of national press attention," Truman told him, "and we want to be careful that this doesn't become the kind of committee that's looking for headlines." If he was hired, Hehmeyer would join the staff as an investigator, though his primary duties would be to "handle the public relations for the Committee and at the same time make sure that the press gets all the information that we are able to release."[34]

It was a short interview, and it ended with no firm offer. Fulton and Truman were headed to Florida to check out some army camps. They'd be in touch. A few days later, Hehmeyer got a telegram from Fulton: "Come to work Monday morning."[35]

4

DOWN TO WORK

Truman had intended to start off the committee's work with an overall investigation of the defense buildup, but the letters from Fort Leonard Wood and other places continued to trickle in. Investigating the construction of army camps seemed both urgent, and, since Truman at this point was eager to establish the committee's reputation, an easy victory.[1]

Hugh Fulton had started work on March 31, and within days he was at his desk, sending out letters of inquiry on several tracks:

Whittenberg Construction Company
Louisville, Kentucky

Dear Sir:
I am informed by the Department of War that it has entered into a contract with you on a cost plus fixed fee basis. The Committee is gathering information with respect to all such contracts, including yours, and would appreciate it if you would furnish the Com-

mittee over the signature of a responsible official, as soon as you
reasonably can, the information requested.
Very truly yours,
HUGH A. FULTON
Chief Counsel

These were the first of thousands of such letters he and his
staff would send during the next three years. At the same time,
the committee was gearing up for public hearings, the first of
which was scheduled for April 15.

Two days before, though, at four o'clock on a Sunday morning, Truman woke up in agony, with pains "shooting through
his abdomen and up into his chest." Bess was sure it was a heart
attack, but the doctor who was summoned diagnosed a gall
bladder attack. "It was a very common Washington disease,"
Margaret wrote, "brought on by too many lavish banquets."
Truman was put on a strict diet, rested up a bit, and went back
to work. A freak heat wave had arrived on Monday the 14th,
bringing a record temperature of eighty-eight degrees, and
on Tuesday it was even hotter as Truman—still recovering—
gaveled the Senate Special Committee to Investigate the National Defense Program to order.

Around the United States and the world that day, the news was
bleak as Secretary of War Henry Stimson shuffled his papers and
prepared to deliver his opening statement. In Libya, the British
were struggling to defend the port city of Tobruk against German
attacks. In Greece, British and Greek forces were reported to be
in full retreat and fearing a complete defeat as Nazi forces, sent in
by Hitler to bail out the faltering Italian army, pushed south. At
the White House, President Roosevelt told reporters his administration was considering lowering the draft age from twenty-one
to eighteen, and in a room not far away, Navy Secretary Frank
Knox was telling a House committee that the United States was
facing grave danger on all sides. "I see my country being, gradu-

ally, encircled and isolated," Knox said. "Look where you will, you see abundant reason for the gravest concern."[2]

Stimson began his remarks before the new Senate committee with a similar warning: "Our forces must be prepared for the possibilities of war in many and varied terrains."[3] Turning to the subject of the day, Stimson acknowledged some mistakes and inefficiencies in the defense spending effort, but predicted that, compared with the progress made, those mistakes "will appear quite insignificant when set against the value of the time saved and the size of the task performed."[4]

He touched on a subject that was already sharpening into a key early focus for the committee: the four-headed leadership team Roosevelt had tapped to manage the defense buildup: the Office of Production Management, or OPM. It was run by Stimson, Knox, and two civilians: William S. Knudsen, the former president of General Motors who had left the company to join the defense buildup, and Sidney Hillman, a key figure in the labor movement and a founding leader of the Congress of Industrial Organizations, or CIO.* Questions were bubbling up around Washington over the effectiveness of OPM and its seemingly cumbersome leadership structure, but Stimson defended it as "satisfactory for the present situation."[5]

He also addressed the committee's other main line of inquiry: army camps. The army was racing to grow, from a force of about 550,000 regular soldiers and national guardsmen in July 1940, to about 1.4 million. And those soldiers would need training camps and housing cantonments all over the country. "Today, only a little more than six months after our appropriations were passed in September, 147 new housing projects are either completed or are very closely nearing completion," Stimson said. These were not just temporary training camps of the kind built during the Great War, he noted, but more akin to small cities, with "rec-

---

* The Navy Department and the War Department were later merged, along with the newly created Department of the Air Force, into a new department under a Secretary of Defense, in 1947.

reation buildings, theaters, service clubs, chapels, athletic areas, hospitals, bakeries, laundries, cold storage, plants, etc."[6]

After Stimson's opening remarks, he and Undersecretary of War Robert Patterson took questions from the senators and Fulton until about 4:00 p.m. Two days later (amid cooler temperatures), the navy's Knox appeared. Like Stimson, he began his remarks with praise and supposed enthusiasm for this collaboration between the military and its congressional overseers: "An investigation at this time is bound to be fair, since it will be conducted in the same environment and under the same conditions as we are working."[7]

Later that day, it was the turn of Knudsen, one of the four heads of OPM. His labor counterpart, Hillman, testified the next day, and on Tuesday, April 22, came General George C. Marshall, the army chief of staff. On Wednesday, the committee headed out into the field for the first time, to one of those 147 housing projects Stimson had told them about: Fort George G. Meade, about halfway between Washington and Baltimore. The site, named for the victorious Union commander at Gettysburg, was a World War I camp now being renovated and expanded into a massive training facility.

There, Fulton peppered the head of a construction company with questions about the details of his contract and about the rising cost estimates for the project. Senator Brewster asked about the wages paid to employees and whether those had changed when the workers went on a government contract, and then the committee members took an automobile tour around the site, stopping along the way to taste the soup—and pose for a picture—in the camp's mess hall.[8]

These first days of hearings, of which many, many more were to follow, were largely polite and civil as the committee and its staff found their footing. The gentle back-and-forth between the senators and Fulton on the one hand, and military brass and high-ranking administration officials on the other, would not last.

★ ★ ★

As April turned to May, the committee's plate was filling up: in addition to looking into army camps and the OPM leadership, an aluminum shortage was causing delays across many industries, especially the crucial area of aviation, and there were concerns about shipbuilding and small businesses. Fulton, Connelly, and Clark were juggling these early investigations at the same time they were trying to hire enough investigators and staff to take on the work.

William Abell, a twenty-seven-year-old graduate of Harvard and Georgetown, joined as an investigator on April 15, but resigned six weeks later to accept a commission in the navy. Shirley Key reported for work on May 5. Herbert Maletz, Harvard Law class of '39, started a week later. That same day, May 12, another lawyer joined the committee: twenty-four-year-old Marion Toomey. Born and raised in Washington, DC, to parents of Irish descent, Toomey's father was an attorney who taught law at Georgetown University.[9] But when Marion graduated from high school and asked her parents about college, they told her there was no money for her. They were saving up to send her younger brother instead.

So Toomey began learning stenography. At some point she also entered a writing contest, winning a prize that would cover two years' tuition at night school.[10] Despite having only a high school diploma, she chose Columbus University of Law, where she graduated in 1936 at age twenty, becoming one of the youngest female attorneys in the District. The event—and her picture—made the local papers: "SHE'S LAWYER AT 20; Pretty Miss to Graduate."[11]

As with Shirley Key, Toomey's impressive résumé meant little in the male-dominated workplace, as Fulton put her on the staff as a stenographer. Yet quickly her initiative and her writing and legal skills stood out. She became Fulton's personal assistant, taking shorthand for his seemingly endless output of letters and memos. She worked with him on drafting and editing the committee's reports, traveling on many of the investigative forays into the field. When needed, she followed up with investigative work. Eventually, Fulton would promote her to investigator.

Toomey worked in Fulton's office, Room 449 of the Senate Office Building, the massive marble and granite structure across from the Capitol. This was fast becoming the committee's nerve center, while the other staff—investigators, clerks, and stenographers—worked in a larger space down in the basement, Room 160.

While the public-facing business of the committee was done out of Fulton's office, the chairman and the other senators held their private meetings in "the Doghouse." Truman had a four-room suite in the building, Room 240: visitors entered the reception area at the center, there was a small office off to the right, and to the left was Truman's personal office. Beyond that was a small, cozy room, known as the Doghouse, with high ceilings, small writing desks, a leather couch and black leather chairs. On one wall hung autographed pictures of famous people Truman had met, another featured newspaper cartoons sent to him by the artists, and a third was covered with artillery maps from his World War I service. Essential features of the Doghouse were its refrigerator and a regular supply of liquor: "a fifth of bourbon, a bottle of Scotch and often a quart of Southern Comfort."[12] Truman liked his bourbon with ginger ale, or plain "branch water," as he called it. He would sneak back there for naps sometimes, and it was also the place where he met for drinks with his Senate pals and, throughout the war, held regular meetings with the senators on the committee, as well as off-the-record talks with generals and admirals or high-ranking administration officials.[13]

Already, the outlines of the daily workflow were taking shape—a workflow that often began before sunrise since both Truman and Fulton kept farmers hours; up before dawn and in the office before anyone else.

BETTMANN/GETTY IMAGES.

Truman with senators in the Doghouse, 1944. From left to right: Homer Ferguson, Harold Burton, Harry Truman, Tom Connally and Owen Brewster.

Truman loved to walk, and did so almost every day. In January, he and Bess and Margaret had moved into a two-bedroom apartment at 4701 Connecticut Avenue, and when the weather was nice, the senator would set out around 5:00 a.m. and walk down Connecticut Avenue, meeting along the way his assistant, Ed Faris, for breakfast. Faris would then drive him rest of the way to the Senate Office Building,[14] where he met with Fulton every morning at seven, going through the mail, setting priorities, and determining which of the many complaints and requests warranted an investigation. Most of the staff arrived later, sometimes much later, which periodically annoyed the chief counsel:

MEMORANDUM TO THE COMMITTEE STAFF

The regular office hours of the committee are 9:00 a.m. to 5:30 p.m., and it is important that except for unusual circumstances everyone should be here promptly at 9:00 o'clock.

It should rarely be necessary for anyone to take breakfast in the Senate dining room after 9:00 o'clock.

It looks bad when other offices call people in the Committee and find them not in at 9:00 o'clock or find them having breakfast at 9:30 or 10:00 in the Senate dining-room.

HUGH A. FULTON
Chief Counsel[15]

He was also concerned about media coverage. After the first public hearings the committee was beginning to get some press, and on May 14 Fulton sent out a twelve-point memo to the staff: no communications with government agencies without prior approval from Charles Clark. No loose talk. "Under no circumstances should any member of the staff converse with any newspaper man or visitor to the office concerning the Committee's work." No gossip. "Members of the staff are particularly urged to refrain from any discussion bearing on inter-office Personnel." And finally, point twelve: "We should be conscious, at all times, that we are serving the *Public Interest*, and with that in mind *be most courteous* in our relations with the visitors to the Office as well as officials and employees of other Governmental Agencies."[16]

During this time, Truman established the essential working principles of the committee. It was not to grab headlines but to fix problems. "If something is wrong, let's get it corrected and not make a big to-do about it," he told Walter Hehmeyer. The press would get all the help they needed, but Hehmeyer was to play no favorites: when information was released, it would go to the entire press gallery. Nor was he to spin the findings or play up aspects of investigations that could embarrass the military or the administration. In fact, if problems could be solved with a simple phone call or a written inquiry, so much the better. Otherwise, he told Hehmeyer, if the committee made a big deal about everything, with hearings and headlines, "we'd just become known as a common scold."[17] Fulton had raised concerns in the other direction: whether embarrassing or unpleasant findings would get swept under the rug. "All you have to do is get the facts and nothing else," Truman told him. "We haven't got any sacred cows around here."[18]

From more than two hundred camp and cantonment construction projects underway, Fulton and Truman had narrowed the scope of their investigation to just nine: Fort Leonard Wood in Missouri, Fort Meade in Maryland, Indiantown Gap in Pennsylvania, Camp Blanding in Florida, Camp Stewart in Georgia, Camp Hulen and Camp Wallace in Texas, Camp Davis in North Carolina, and Camp San Luis Obispo in California.

The responses to questionnaires Fulton had sent out in April and May were beginning to come in, and one by one the committee members began traveling to the individual sites to hold hearings. These nine locations were chosen not at random but because they best illustrated some of the problems that, it was becoming clear, were bigger than anyone thought. Together they represented about $154 million in federal spending, about a sixth of the money Congress had allocated for camp construction.[19] And all nine were built on a cost-plus-fixed-fee basis.

Soon, stacks of data and information were piled high on the desks and file cabinets in Rooms 160 and 449. On top of army camps and the overall defense effort, the committee pivoted in late spring to investigate a sudden, desperate shortage of aluminum.

"We held the hearing on aluminum with all the big shots," Truman wrote Bess on June 17.[20] Never a fan of Washington, she'd taken seventeen-year-old Margaret back home to Independence for the summer. That night, her husband was invited to dinner with Hugh Fulton and his wife, Jessie, in their apartment at 2120 16th Street Northwest. It was a nice break from the work. "I have been so busy I have no time to turn around," he wrote Bess the next day. "Had three committee meetings today—made two of 'em and a speech to a bunch of editors."[21]

That evening, he stayed out until midnight playing poker with Fulton and some of the other lawyers on the committee, "winning the tremendous sum of $6.50." The next day, June 19, was a blur. By the time he arrived at the office, there was a line of people waiting to see him: "Aluminum pipeline people, my subcommittee on Interstate Commerce, Frank Monroe, two committees on Military Affairs and one on Appropriations," he wrote Bess from his desk during a break in the afternoon. "So you see I've had a busy day and I hope I can go to bed early tonight. But I can't, just got called out of the Senate to see Neal Helm, Orville Zimmerman, and some oilmen. Have to go to dinner with 'em." Despite the pressures, he was enjoying himself. "My standing in the Senate and down the street [the White House] gets better and better. Hope I make no mistakes. If I weren't working from daylight until dark, I don't know what I'd do."[22]

Even for a fit and healthy fifty-six-year-old, the pace he'd set was unsustainable. And the pace of events around the country and around the world was accelerating. On June 22 came the stunning news that, overnight, Hitler had turned on his temporary ally Joseph Stalin and invaded the Soviet Union with more than three million men. German tanks and planes had overwhelmed the Soviet defenses and were pushing deep into Eastern Europe.

Truman was working nights and weekends and, as always when Bess and Margaret were away, he was lonely. Even the weather offered no respite—pre-air-conditioned Washington was hot and humid, with temperatures into the nineties. By late June he was exhausted, and his stomach was acting up again. He was having frequent attacks of nausea and sometimes vomiting. On the 24th, he cleared his schedule for ten days and boarded a train south, first to Mississippi for the funeral of Senator Patrick Harrison, then to Hot Springs, Arkansas, where he checked himself in for a much-needed rest and checkup at the military hospital there. This was one of several times during the war that the hearings and the paperwork and the speeches and the dinners and the stress would catch up to him.

His initial screening noted that "patient has symptoms of a gastrointestinal disorder of obscure origin. Fatigue and mental worry are perhaps large factors in the formation of some of his symptoms." The doctors noted that his attacks "usually were associated with a particularly strenuous day of work." It seems likely the rest and the break from the constant demands did him more good than whatever treatment he was given, and in fact seems to have been the main point of Truman's stay there: "He has come to this hospital for the purpose of a general survey of his physical credentials and for the purpose of rest."[23]

"Dear Bess," he wrote on June 30 after a couple of days of poking and prodding, "they let me have lunch, a couple of lamb chops, spinach, mashed potatoes, and a cup of coffee." He'd been x-rayed, measured, weighed and examined. His gall bladder showed normal, his teeth were good, and he'd been put on a low-fat diet. "Had all my teeth photographed and my heart tested in between times. I have done nothing but sleep almost night and day, and Fred [Canfil, a Kansas City political associate and friend, now on his Senate payroll as an assistant secretary] says I look much better than when I came in, in spite of the mauling I've taken. They are giving me everything in the book."[24]

By July 3 he was feeling better: "I am finished up with examinations & x-rays and started in on a special course of baths this morning. They are very anxious for me to stay next week and take at least seven of them. I haven't made up my mind yet about it. I feel so much better and have nearly caught up on sleep so I won't know whether to let my Special Committee dangle another week and get into fighting trim or just go back to work by way of home Saturday. I am sorely tempted to stay, but I'm afraid that the time for action on the Committee may go by too."[25]

Throughout his stay most of the tests came back negative, confirming that he was likely suffering from nothing more than stress and exhaustion. He was still fretting about the committee's appropriation—he was burning through that initial $15,000 pretty fast—but in the end he decided to stay and rest up for another week, and was discharged on July 11. The patient, his doctors noted, "has made marked improvement and should be able to resume his duties in the U.S. Senate."[26]

While he was away, the committee had issued its first report, on aluminum. For years, everyone had known that a big part of the next war would be fought in the air, and modern airplanes were made of aluminum. In the First World War, despite a nationwide industrial mobilization, few US-built combat airplanes ever made it overseas. Most of the planes flown by American pilots were made by France. For a nation famed for its mass-production abilities, this was a spectacular failure, and a key focus of several postwar congressional investigations.

Now, two decades later, it looked like the country was headed for a similar crisis.

"As recently as December 1940 news releases had been issued calling attention to the adequacy of supply for all military needs" read the committee's report, which like most of those to come was largely written by Fulton. "In February 1941 there began to crystallize opinion that serious miscalculations had been made." The Office of Production Management, under Knudsen and Hillman, had tried to fix things by issuing emergency regulations, but the report noted that despite the looming crisis, significant amounts of aluminum were still being allocated to Detroit for making cars.[27]

Bottom line, miscalculations by the industry and the government had led to a serious shortage. "It is estimated by the services that the peak of their aluminum requirements for aircraft and other direct military needs of 100,000,000 pounds per month will be reached in March 1942. Based upon completed plans now underway the production capacity will be 75,000,000 pounds per month."[28] In other words, the United States at that time would be short 12,500 tons of aluminum, every month. Just for the military. And of course no one in June 1941 knew that by 1942, events would make even that eye-popping figure seem small. It wasn't just the mining of ore; aluminum plants required massive amounts of electricity, and the report cited the need for additional power-generating capacity to run new and existing plants, and for additional railroads to get ore, and aluminum, where they needed to go.

This first report was fairly muted: seven single-spaced pages in the just-the-facts approach Fulton used in his legal briefs. Blame for the shortage was spread between the Aluminum Company of America (Alcoa), which at the time produced nearly all of the aluminum in the US, and the OPM. Here and there, though, Fulton sharpened his prosecutorial knife: "It is reasonable to conclude that Alcoa had convinced the Office of Production Management of the adequacy of supply in order to avoid the possibility that anyone else would go into a field which for so many years they had successfully monopolized."[29]

The only bright spot on the horizon was that a new company, Reynolds Metals, had recognized the looming crisis as early as 1940 and, without encouragement from OPM, was jumping into aluminum production in a big way.

The New York Times covered the story on page 10: "Lack of Aluminum Menaces Defense." *The Washington Post* ran it on the front page, and around the country, the report received scattered attention. In St. Louis and other places, there was other aluminum news that day—the efforts just beginning in many communities to collect scrap metal for the defense effort. "Aluminum articles such as saucepans, golf club heads and jar tops are to be collected to help meet a shortage" read the *Post-Dispatch*.[30]

It was a solid first inning, but this report had been a bit of a diversion prompted by sudden concerns about the shortage. With aluminum out of the way, and Truman back in Washington rested and recovered, the committee turned back to the two bigger investigations: army camps, and the overall defense effort as it was being run by the administration and OPM.

A big chunk of this latter inquiry, for the chairman, would be a look at small businesses. In his life so far—farmer, businessman, Midwesterner—Truman had had very little contact with the giant financial and industrial powers that had shaped the nation over the past few decades. Like many men of his background, he had a deep suspicion of powerful Eastern banks and massive industrial corporations. It was both a strength and a weakness. His advocacy for the "little man" and his determination to prevent small businesses from being shut out of the defense spending had been key factors in creating the committee in the first place. But at times it left him blind to what those corporations could do, and to the fact that men like Knudsen were capable of mobilizing factories and industries and millions of workers in ways that would, as much as the soldiers and generals on the battlefield, make Allied victory possible.

If a big hunk of the work did have to go to those big corporations, Truman was determined to see that the smaller businesses got their share. "If you saw my correspondence," he told Edward Stettinius, the OPM priorities chief, during a hearing, "you'd think that every little business in the country is going out of business."[31]

From the beginning, Truman had asked Americans to let him know when they saw something in their town, their factory, their shipyard that wasn't right. Back in March, he'd urged in a radio speech that "any citizen who has information or irregu-

larities based on facts" should write in. "The Committee's address is the Senate Office Building, Washington, DC."[32]

On July 22, Truman and Fulton went on CBS Radio for a
program called *The Congressional Mailbag* and asked for help again.
"Each day the mail bags bring letters from all over the country
to me and to my defense committee," Truman said. "We not
only welcome these letters, we need them. It gives us a feel of the
pulse of America."[33] He noted that a lot of the mail he was getting was about army camps. "I have received a surprising number of communications from persons who are shocked at some
of the waste and negligence they have seen. Also, I have personally inspected some of the camps and talked to the soldiers
themselves. And you and I are going to have to pay for the cost,
the waste and the inefficiency in the form of increased taxation
for years to come."[34]

This was powerful stuff, and Truman was now speaking to a
huge audience. The flow of mail coming in to Room 160 every
day grew from a trickle to a stream.

The defense program was reshaping the lives of communities
and individuals all over the country. On the West Coast, a new
shipyard at Richmond, California, offered thousands of jobs
for Depression-weary workers. At the Douglas aircraft plant in
Santa Monica, employees cheered in late June as the prototype
of a giant new bomber, the B-19, took to the skies for the first
time.[35] In Detroit, the automobile companies were retooling
as they shifted work and workers from building cars to making guns, tanks, bullets, trucks, ships, and airplanes. The Ford
Motor Company was setting up a school for aircraft apprentice-
ships, while Packard had a huge contract to build Rolls-Royce
engines for fighter planes.[36]

In communities large and small, the United Servicemen's
Organization was raising money to help build recreational centers at the new army camps. In Greenwood, Mississippi, the

local USO had met its quota of $700; leaders in Hammond, Indiana, announced $125 in donations from local labor unions, while in Sayre, Oklahoma, the local campaign was struggling to meet its goal of $1,000. Thousands of men were joining the army and the navy, and local draft boards were gearing up to register every young man twenty-one and older.[37]

In Missouri, that summer, Wilbur Sparks was one of those young men. At twenty-two, he had just graduated from law school at the University of Missouri. He knew he faced the prospect of military service, but the newspapers were saying that draftees would serve for only a year. His immediate plans were to pass the bar exam and then start work in his father's law firm in Savannah, Missouri, north of Kansas City.

But fate had other plans for Wilbur Sparks. As so often happens, his future turned on a chance encounter. His dad, Grover Cleveland Sparks, was a former prosecutor who had long been active in statewide politics and, like many prominent men of his time and place, was a member of the Masons. Wilbur had joined a year earlier, and that summer, father and son traveled to St. Louis for a meeting of Missouri's Grand Lodge. There, the two men were walking down the street when the elder Sparks ran into an old acquaintance: the Grand Master for the Grand Lodge of Missouri—Harry S. Truman.

They stopped to chat, and the proud father introduced the senator to his son. "Well," Truman asked the young man, "What are you going to do?" Sparks said it seemed likely he'd be drafted, "probably in the fall or winter, and after I get out of the Army I'll be back practicing law with my dad again."[38]

"Between now and the time you go into the Army, what's going to happen?"

Sparks said he'd probably help out with his father's legal work in Savannah, but Truman had another idea: How about coming to Washington? The Senate, he said, had just created an investigating committee, "and I am the chairman of this investigating committee. And I think it would be good experience for you if you'd come back there and work for the committee for a few months. You may never get to Washington again in your life."

Sparks jumped at the offer: "Yes, I'd like to do this."

"I'll let you know when you should come." A few weeks later, a letter came from Charles Clark, with instructions on where to report.[39] Wilbur shoved everything he owned into his car and headed east, leaving his hometown girlfriend, Elizabeth Ibbi-anne Hartley, behind for the time being. They'd been dating since their sophomore year at Missouri, where both had been in the marching band, and were talking about getting married.[40] On October 10, a week after his twenty-third birthday, he reported to work in the Senate Office Building.

COURTESY OF CHRISTOPHER HEHMEYER.

Wilbur Sparks in 1942.

When it came to choosing the staff, Sparks was an exception; Fulton did most of the hiring. Another young attorney, Morris Lasker, joined the committee on July 1. Lasker was a New York native, twenty-three years old, fresh out of Yale Law School. Fulton put him to work on a query about the purchase of basketball equipment by the Army's Quartermaster Corps, and Charles Clark assigned him to look into concerns about the War Department's purchases of a new, lightweight truck for the army. They were known as "bantam" trucks, or increasingly by another nickname, "jeeps."

Fulton was by mid-July deep in the drafting of the army camp report. In this and subsequent reports, Fulton was at the center of a network of writing, rewriting, proofreading, and fact-checking as drafts and revisions were circulated, with a lot of juggling to work around travel schedules of the investigative staff and seven busy United States senators. In mid-July, for example, Charles Clark was on a West Coast swing with Mon Wallgren to California and the senator's home state of Washington. Along the way, they were finishing up the committee's investigation into one of the nine camps, San Luis Obispo. On July 19, Clark sent Fulton a long handwritten list of suggested changes. A big part of Fulton's—and Truman's—work in compiling these reports was to build consensus, and if possible, unanimity. In this case, "Wallgren is going to study the report further and may make further suggestions," Clark wrote. "He asked me to tell you however that he is *100 percent* with the Chairman with regard to anything the latter may do concerning the report."[41] The back-and-forth went on for weeks, and on big reports like this one, everyone from Shirley Key and the stenographers to the investigators and lawyers all the way up to Fulton were pulling long hours and working weekends. No one put in more time than Fulton himself, a workaholic who was often at his desk by 5:00 a.m. and still there long after everyone else had gone home.[42] Investigators would arrive in the morning to find on their desks sections he'd written or rewritten, with empty spaces for dates or specific numbers or information and instructions from the chief counsel to phone around or do the research to fill in the blanks.[43]

As everyone worked through these drafts and revisions, with

accompanying stacks of mimeographs and carbon copies, the final report gradually took shape. While the aluminum report had made some gentle critiques of the government and the industry, its criticisms, while stern, were pretty obvious: more aluminum was needed. This time, things would be much different. At the nine camps, the investigators had found all the problems that Truman had seen on his January road trips, and much more. Whenever there was a fresh draft, Truman would invite the committee senators to meet in the Doghouse, where they would review the pages and air out differences and disagreements.[44] Here, Fulton's plain, fact-based writing style—avoiding opinions, speculation or sensationalizing—melded with Truman's political skills for building consensus: while one senator or another might disagree on a particular point, or whether the findings were too mild, or too severe, at these meetings Truman would work out a compromise, with changes marked on a master draft to be sent back to Fulton and the staff.

On August 1, Fulton sent near-final versions to Truman and to Senator Mead. Walter Hehmeyer began drafting a ten-page press release for reporters, with key findings and some of the best quotes. And Truman began writing the speech he'd give when delivering it to the Senate.

The Senate opened on Thursday, August 14, with a prayer from its chaplain, the Reverend ZeBarney Phillips, and a lengthy report from the House of Representatives on, among other things, a plan to extend the periods of service for draftees. There was a resolution from Kansas wheat farmers, a telegram from a Minneapolis labor union criticizing a recent tax bill, and odds and ends of other business.

Then, the presiding officer called on Truman: "Mr. President, one of the first tasks which the Special Committee to Investigate the National Defense Program, of which I am chairman, undertook was that of examining into the efficiency with which the camp construction program was carried out." In his flat monotone, he noted that a billion dollars had been spent on camp construction—"a large amount even in these days of astronomical figures"—and that planning for more camps was in the works. "Copies of the report are now on the desks of Senators, and I earnestly urge that they look them over carefully."[45]

After that dry preamble, Truman the former artillery man opened up with his full battery: "I am sorry to say that I do not think that the Army has done a good job on camp construction. There has been a lack of foresight and planning and a large amount of inefficiency, as a result of which I believe that several hundreds of millions of dollars have been wasted." Reporters in the press gallery, scanning their own copies of the report and Hehmeyer's summary, struggled to keep up. "As an Army officer, I had always assumed that the War Department had paid some attention to the bitter lessons with respect to camp construction which were learned during the last war." Alas, that was not the case. "I was utterly astounded to find that although a post-war study had been made of camp construction problems encountered in the World War, all the copies thereof had been lost by the War Department; that the general in charge of the Construction Division of the Quartermaster Corps was proceeding under the assumption that there would never be another war, and that the generals in charge of planning did not even conceive of the possibility that we would ever again have a mobilization such as that in 1917."

Several times during the speech, senators broke in to ask questions, and it was Arthur Vandenberg, Republican of Michigan, who got right to the big one: Who was to blame for all this?

"From the Senator's observations, can he tell me where the final authority rests" in terms of setting priorities for defense spending? "If I could answer that question," Truman said, "it would not be necessary for the committee to continue any further."

Not satisfied with that, Vandenberg followed up: "In other words, the Senator is now saying that the chief bottleneck which the defense program confronts is the lack of adequate organization and coordination of the administration of defense?"

"That is exactly what the hearings before our committee will prove."

"Who is responsible for that situation?"

"There is only one place where the responsibility can be put."

"Where is that—the White House?"

"Yes, sir."[46]

For the reporters in the gallery scribbling notes, this was pure gold, and the twenty-thousand-word report was packed with much, much more. In 1940, the army had begun acquiring land about forty miles southwest of Savannah, Georgia, for a new artillery training facility to be named Camp Stewart, after a Revolutionary War hero from those parts. (Today, it is Fort Stewart, the largest army base east of the Mississippi, home to the Third Infantry Division.) Three small towns were abandoned, and several hundred farmers displaced, as carpenters began framing the barracks and workers cleared land and built roads. The area was mostly pine woods and small towns of a few hundred people. And, the committee report revealed, there was one other feature about the location the army had chosen: "The worst malaria area in the Southeastern United States is located 16 miles from the camp site."[47]

At Fort Leonard Wood, the whole project "illustrates the effect of the failure to do simple, common sense, preliminary work." The land was bought and construction begun despite the fact that any hydrographic engineer could have seen that "no water could be made available at any time except by building a huge artificial reservoir and installing heavy pumping machinery and pipe lines." Cost for those additions? $1.25 million. A railroad had been built for $3.5 million "which was not and could not be completed in time to assist the construction of the camp."[48]

At Camp Davis, in North Carolina, "the site selected was swampy area and in effect a peat bog. The spongy nature of the

terrain necessitated the building of concrete parking strips for
the mechanized equipment which would sink if left standing
for any period of time on the ground itself."[49]

The report detailed many instances of contractors and engineers soaking the government for millions. "One architect-
engineer will earn as much as 1,478 percent of his average annual
profits, and one contractor will earn as much as 1,699 of a year's
profits." At Indiantown Gap in Pennsylvania, the cost of utili-
ties, initially estimated at $125,000, topped $1.7 million. At
Camp Blanding in Florida, the government rented hundreds
of new Ford pickup trucks for $885 apiece, when it could have
bought them outright for $628. And across the nine sites, when
the work was done, there were mountains of extra materials
left over, the result of government purchasers overbuying. "At
Camp Blanding there are presently $3,000,000 of excess mate-
rials alleged to be at the camp."[50]

In many cases, contractors didn't even need to cheat or defraud
the government, Truman noted in his speech: "Huge fixed fees
were offered to them by the Government in much the same way
that Santa Claus passes out gifts at a church Christmas party."[51]

The committee took pains to note the accomplishments of
the War Department as it raced to build hundreds of new camps
and training sites in the midst of a national emergency: "By
making such criticism the committee does not wish to detract
in any way from the very important fact that housing, training,
and recreational facilities for 1,216,459 men were provided in
the space of a few short months and in most instances were finished and ready for occupancy before the troops arrived." All
this despite some of the "greatest problems ever encountered by
any construction agency in this country."[52]

Nevertheless, the committee noted and Truman emphasized
in his speech, the army had had twenty years to prepare and
plan and learn from the failures of the First World War, and had,
spectacularly, failed to do so.

★ ★ ★

"$100,000,000 LOSS CHARGED IN ARMY" read *The New York Times* the next day: "Truman Lays Camp Erection 'Waste' to 'Armchair Generals' and President's Policy." More than two hundred newspapers carried the story, and many of them, including the *Times*, the *Chicago Tribune, The Philadelphia Inquirer,* the *St. Louis Post-Dispatch,* and *The Honolulu Advertiser,* featured the report's best sound bite: in planning for the camps, the army had in many cases not even considered the need for heavy roads or parking spaces for motorized equipment, or for adequate storage of gasoline: "The generals were running the Army along Civil War lines and had not properly worked out the requirements of a mechanized Army."[53] All this as Hitler's tanks and motorized divisions were driving over, through and around the armies of Western Europe and now the Soviet Union.

Most of these stories noted that the report was issued by the Special Senate Defense Committee, or the Senate defense investigating committee. But from now on, most reporters and everyone else just called it the Truman Committee.

5

OUT WEST

After weeks of long hours and late nights getting the camp report out, there was to be no letup in the workload. The next day, Truman saw Bess off at Union Station as she headed back to Independence, while he prepared to leave the following morning with Fulton and Mead on a long West Coast swing. In Los Angeles, they would meet up with Charles Clark, as well as Senators Brewster, Hatch and Wallgren.[1]

On top of the hearings, inspection tours, chicken dinners, phone calls and meetings, travel in the propeller age was exhausting in itself. Truman was up at 4:30 the next morning and out the door in time to stop by 16th Street to pick up Fulton for their six o'clock flight. "I'll wire you from Amarillo, or Albuquerque or some other S.W. Airport," he wrote Bess.[2]

The army transport left Bolling Field in Anacostia twenty-five minutes late, for a "bucking bronco ride to Knoxville";[3] from there they flew to Memphis, where Mead bought some magazines for a flight to Dallas. There they spent the night at the Adolphus Hotel, then boarded another army flight for California the next morning.

Air travel was still a novelty, and Truman was enjoying himself. "We've just come through the pass east of Los A at 10,000 feet," he wrote Bess from the plane on the 17th. "It has been a pleasant day except that we've done some rocking around on account of air currents off the desert. Had lunch at Tucson, gave Phoenix the go by and will soon land in Los Angeles."[4]

Gone were the days when Truman could get in his car and show up unannounced and unnoticed at a construction site or military base. A reporter and photographer from the *Los Angeles Times* were at the airport when his plane landed, and a picture of Truman and Mead was on the front page the next day.

The story made clear that Truman, with the ink barely dry on the camp report, was looking ahead to questions about the Office of Production Management and the cumbersome two-headed structure Roosevelt had burdened it with: the biggest problem with the defense program right now, Truman told the reporter, "is for a single directing head who can handle all the interdepartmental disputes and keep things moving along steadily."

His comments also gave a look into his thinking at the six-month mark of the committee's work: "We are doing what we can to make the program successful. It is better to kick now than let the whole program go to pot and have a big investigation afterward as in the case of the last war."[5]

The Biltmore put him up in the presidential suite ("How do you like living in such a swanky hotel?" Bess asked), and already there were phone messages, dinner invitations and an offer from a businessman of two Packard cars for his personal use, which he declined. "I've had a hundred phone calls—and I'm being conservative," he told Bess, "since the paper spread our picture all over the front page."[6]

After six years in the Senate in which he had either been ignored by the press, or treated with open hostility—the *St. Louis*

Post-Dispatch,[7] especially—Truman was bemused, and clearly thrilled, by the attention he and the committee now got everywhere they went. "Must have walked five or six miles and had our pictures taken a dozen times in each plant," he told Bess after a tour of Los Angeles airplane factories. "A photographer for *Time* and *Life* dogs our steps all day long as do the local boys."[8]

While Truman and the senators, or occasionally Fulton, got most of the press attention, at a news conference at the Biltmore it was associate chief counsel Charles Clark who caused an odd stir. Before the senators arrived, he asked the names of the six newspaper reporters present "but forgot to ask their papers." Without having them repeating their names, he asked them what papers they were from. Minutes later, when the senators arrived, he introduced the six reporters and correctly matched them with their newspapers. "Lawyer's Memory Astounds Legislators," said the *Los Angeles Times,* which went on to detail other feats of Clark's memory and recall, calling him the "wonder boy of Washington so far as memory goes."

"Don't ask me how I do it," Clark told the reporter. "I never try. I guess I'm just a freak."[9]

On Wednesday they flew on a navy transport plane down to San Diego for a five-hour tour of airplane factories, naval establishments, and defense housing projects. For lunch with the recruits at the new marine barracks, Truman was assigned a "Missouri boy from St. Louis" to wait on him, while "one from New York took care of Mead, and one from Washington, Wallgren."[10]

On a tour of a large Consolidated aviation plant, Truman was not impressed. "The managers are all such liars you can't tell anything about the facts," he told Bess. But by questioning some of them privately, he heard one of the central problems that would come up again and again in the committee's investigations: that aircraft manufacturers were falling behind on production because of constant design changes requested by the military—demanding modifications that required new parts,

new tools, and new manufacturing methods even while the
planes were on the assembly lines. "We are turning out a very
large number of planes and could turn out more if the navy and
army boys could make up their minds just what they want."[11]

By now, the trip was setting the tone for many to follow: the
Truman Committee as traveling road show, with the substantive hearings and inspections mixed in with photo opportunities and press conferences, welcoming ceremonies with windy
speeches and lunches and dinners that pushed the long workdays
into the evenings. In between all this were constant demands for
face time from businessmen, inventors, reporters, local celebri-
ties, and all kinds of people wanting a word with the chairman.
"Have about fifty phone calls a day," Truman complained, "and
all the crackpots in California have tried to see me."[12]

After two more days of hearings, the group headed to San
Francisco for the weekend, where Truman got a bit of a breather,
carving out time for a couple of long walks and a visit to China-
town to buy souvenirs for Margaret and Bess. As always, the
excitement of his road trips mixed with his loneliness whenever he was away from his family, and the frustrations with the
mail when there was no letter. Margaret had switched over from
piano lessons to singing lessons, and many of Bess's letters to him
on this trip were written while she sat in the car outside Mrs.
Strickler's house while Margaret sang. "Am anxious to have you
hear Marg after all these lessons this summer. Hope you see the
same amount of improvement I do."[13] Truman, when he saw this
a few days later, responded cautiously, "I am sure Margie has a
voice and I know there has been improvement but I'm preju-
diced. It would be perfect to me no matter how it is to other
people—so we must have unbiased advice which may make us
mad—but I'm very sure we won't get that kind."[14]

Truman and his party left Sunday on a navy plane for Seattle,
with views of Mount Shasta and Mount Rainier. "Went up to
12,700 feet when we passed Mt. Shasta and it was cold as winter-

time. They turned on the heat."[15] On Monday, it was back to work as he chaired hearings in Seattle, before Mead and Brewster and Fulton headed off to Alaska for a tour of facilities there. The topic was once again aluminum, and the committee heard testimony about continuing delays and stonewalling by Alcoa and OPM in getting new factories in the Pacific Northwest up and running—an issue even more pressing in a part of the country that was home to Boeing, maker of the army's flagship bomber, the B-17 Flying Fortress. "The committee has made every effort to increase production," Truman said, but from the evidence they'd heard it seemed that "Alcoa is more interested in remaining a monopoly than in saving the country's National Defense Program."[16]

And this from Mead: "In the absence of rebuttal arguments, it appears that the OPM is entirely at fault and responsible for the delay in the aluminum production here in this area."[17] On the West Coast, home to so many aircraft manufacturers, this was big news; Truman's and Mead's comments were widely reported in the Oregon, Washington and California papers.

In addition to writing Bess nearly every day when they were apart, Truman was now corresponding regularly with his daughter, who was now seventeen and starting her senior year of high school at Washington's Gunston Hall, a private school for girls. In these letters he talked of history, or music and theater and, often in a playful sense, what it was like to be a senator. The expectation, of course, was "that I had to write letters to him, too," she said. "Or else."[18]

On the 27th, he toured the Boeing plant and the Seattle-area naval facilities. Back at the Olympic hotel, full of excitement, he sat down to tell Margaret all about it:

I inspected a British Battleship today that was being repaired at our navy yard. Lord Somebody or other met me at the gangplank with bugles, pipes, salutes etc and then a nice tall Englishman, a

Lt. Commander in His Majesty's Royal Navy showed me the hole a Nazi bomb made at the battle of Crete. He said it killed fifty men and knocked four guns into the sea. Another bomb exploded alongside and made a big dent in the hull. He said the Stuka Bombers came over in waves every half hour and just kept dropping bombs; that they shot down some seventeen of them and some of them fell into the sea before they could come out of the dive. He said one battleship was sunk as were several destroyers, that many more of them were hit just as he was. They were under terrific fire for four days.[19]

The next day it was on to Spokane by car for more hearings, and from there a long flight to Salt Lake City, where he planned to meet up with Fulton, Mead, and Brewster on their way back from their Alaska trip, for yet more hearings. But with an important vote looming on a $3.6 billion tax bill, and piqued that a House investigating committee had recently covered much of the same ground in Utah, Truman canceled those hearings and left by train for Kansas City, where he met up with Bess and Margaret for the journey east.[20]

He had been away more than two weeks, and had traveled by plane, train, and automobile more than seven thousand miles.

The committee's original $15,000 appropriation had run out pretty quickly, and in August, he'd gone back for more. The success of the camps report had helped, and on August 11, the Senate gave him another $25,000 (though he had asked for $50,000).[21]

Throughout the war, Truman's wasn't the only investigating committee looking into economic mobilization and defense contracts. Truman himself sat on the Senate Military Affairs Committee, which was concerned with some of the same issues. Representative John Tolan, a California Democrat, ran the "House equivalent of the Truman Committee."[22] Its formal name was the House Select Committee Investigating National

Defense Migration, and it had initially looked at the refugee crisis created by the Dust Bowl drought, and then later at how workers were migrating to areas where defense jobs were opening up. But it was eventually overshadowed by the Truman Committee and ceased operation in 1943.[23] The House Military Affairs committee also covered some of the same ground, and occasionally when the competing investigations stepped on each other, there would be calls for consolidating them. "Certainly in the crisis that now confronts the United States these committees should be combined," *The Washington Post* editorialized in early 1942.[24] But these suggestions never went anywhere.

For now, with the money question settled at least in the short term, Truman and Fulton turned back to the investigation they'd set out to do from the very start: "to make a full and complete study" of the national defense program. Among the areas it would touch on were the types and terms of defense contracts awarded; the methods by which those contracts were awarded; the role and degree of participation of small businesses; shortages of key materials and the process for allocating them; and the location—and concentration—of plants and facilities. Truman the Midwesterner had noted in his February 10 speech on the Senate floor that "I am reliably informed that from 70 to 90 percent of the contracts let have been concentrated in an area smaller than New England."[25]

One thing the Truman Committee was not investigating was widespread and systemic racial discrimination in defense plants and in the military. Soon after the committee was formed, Rayford W. Logan, a Howard University historian and adviser to President Roosevelt on race issues, met with Hugh Fulton and Charles Clark to ask for just such an investigation, which seemed to fall clearly within the committee's scope. It was agreed the committee would hold hearings, and Fulton and Clark began sending out letters to key organizations asking them who should testify and what issues should be covered. The committee was

sent a list of prospective speakers, including Logan, NAACP lawyer Charles Houston, Lester Granger of the Urban League, and
other Black leaders. A preliminary hearing was held on June 25
in the Senate Office Building, with Logan and others meeting
with Clark and Fulton,[26] and three days of hearings were scheduled to begin on June 30. Logan's efforts were part of several
campaigns underway designed to prod Roosevelt and Congress
to do something about the rampant discrimination and racism,
and in 1941 they were getting the familiar runaround. A. Philip
Randolph, the head of the Brotherhood of Sleeping Car Por-
ters union, had in January called for a march on Washington in
July to put pressure on Roosevelt and to draw national attention to the issue, and in February a bipartisan group of senators
had introduced a bill, SR75, to create a separate, eight-member
investigating committee to "make a full and complete investigation into the participation of negro citizens in all industrial
and other phases of the national defense program, including all
educational courses and apprentice training."[27]

James Byrnes of South Carolina, the Senate majority leader
and a segregationist known for his opposition to anti-lynching
bills, had the proposal transferred from the Military Affairs committee to the Education and Labor Committee, where it could
be tabled or otherwise put off. Nevertheless, letters poured into
that committee from all around the country, urging a full investigation of Jim Crow racism in defense plants and the armed
forces. In April, the education committee met and decided that,
since Truman already had broad powers to look into defense
contracting, his committee should look into the issue. Truman
replied that he would be glad to, "as soon as possible and as soon
as funds were available." Truman told the NAACP leadership
that his committee was "swamped with work" and could not
possibly get to the issue until midsummer or later, "and that even
then his committee could hear only two or three witnesses."[28]

Some of this was possibly true, much of it probably wasn't, and most of it was likely politics. Truman had said early on that he chose camp construction because it was a safe and easy win, and that he wanted to establish the committee on a solid footing with such low-hanging fruit before taking on tougher issues.[29] Byrnes was, essentially, his boss in the Senate.[30] He had power over the committee's funding, and he had Franklin Roosevelt's ear. It had been hard enough getting Byrnes to sign off on the initial appropriation, which he had cut from $25,000 to $15,000. Knowing that, Truman almost certainly had little stomach for taking on this potentially explosive topic, at least this early in the committee's existence. He was abruptly saved from having to do so when an internal fight broke out among the civil rights organizations asking for an investigation: the scheduled hearings were canceled at the request of the NAACP and its leader, Walter White.[31]

Rayford Logan had come to Fulton as chairman of the Committee on Participation of Negroes in the National Defense Program, a group created by the *Pittsburgh Courier,* an influential Black newspaper. Though Charles Clark had written to White about the proposed hearings on June 17, the preliminary meeting with Fulton and Clark had not included White and the NAACP. Afterwards, one of the attendees, Mary McLeod Bethune, phoned White in Houston, where the NAACP was holding its annual convention. He told her he opposed the Truman Committee hearings, believing they would include only "handpicked" Black representatives. With so few witnesses, White believed the hearings would be "but a token investigation and superficial inquiry" of the kind Black leaders were very familiar with in Washington. And, he believed, such hearings would be an attempt to divert the momentum from Randolph's proposed march.[32] White favored a full-blown investigation along the lines of SR75.

On July 3, Logan denounced White in a story on page one of the *Pittsburgh Courier,* saying the cancellation of the Truman Committee hearings was a power play by White. Two days later, the newspaper followed up with a page one story under the banner headline, "LEADERS FLAY WALTER WHITE." In a letter to Truman on July 8, White outlined his fears that a full investigation along the lines of SR75 was the only way for serious inquiry into the matter, "since the time and funds of the Truman Investigating Committee authorized by Senate Resolution 71 make it impossible for your committee to go as thoroughly into the issue." On July 12, the *Courier* accused White of sticking "a dagger in the back of the long-sought immediately and urgently desired senate investigation of national defense discrimination against millions of Negroes everywhere." Edgar Brown of the National Negro Council agreed: "The NAACP has muffed a grand opportunity to be of service merely because its officials could not be present because their national convention was in Houston."[33]

White fired back the same day, calling the Courier's editorial a "'frenzied attempt' to dodge a real investigation into discrimination against the Negro in national defense."[34] He was probably pretty close to the mark there, and he and other Black leaders would be watching the Truman Committee closely to see if it found time for hearings when he was less "swamped."

Truman's views on race at this point in his life were, at best, evolving. Those views were shaped by the time and place he grew up—a place of bitter and often violent racism—and Truman's thoughts and statements, especially as a young man, reflect that. His letters to Bess are sprinkled with references to "niggers," "Chinks," and "Hebrews." As young men do, Truman matured, and adult life brought him into contact with actual Black and Jewish people—notably his army friend and later business partner, Eddie Jacobson. As a Missouri politician, he had run for office opposed by the Ku Klux Klan. In his Senate re-election campaign in 1940, against the deeply segregationist Lloyd Stark, Truman had enjoyed the support of many of Missouri's Black leaders, and Black newspapers including Kansas City's *The Call*.[35]

He had reached out specifically in his speeches to the state's

245,000 Black citizens, showing at least empathy, if not offering much in the way of concrete solutions: "In the years past, lynching and mob violence, lack of schools and countless other unfair conditions hastened the progress of the Negro from the country to the city. Negroes have been preyed upon by all types of exploiters. The majority of our Negro people find but cold comfort in shanties and tenements."[36]

He had developed by this time a measured approach to race relations: he did not favor social equality, but his sense of fairness had brought him to a strong belief in equal opportunity: "I believe in not merely the brotherhood of white men but the brotherhood of all men before the law." While such statements sound tame by twenty-first century standards, as historian Alonzo Hamby notes, "in the Missouri of 1940, this was fairly strong stuff."[37]

By the time of the Truman Committee, the slurs in his personal letters appeared less frequently, and he had begun to use the word "Negro," but they did not disappear entirely. Here he is in a September 1941 letter to Bess: "I came back over here, picked up my nigger preacher suit and went out to mamma's,"[38] and in December: "Harry Newman has asked me to dinner this afternoon at five. I'm going home and sleep some and then go. Had a fine time at Baltimore, and those Jews took me in the little poker game."[39]

As president, of course, he would become a strong supporter of civil rights, and would force the US military and the federal workforce to integrate. The Truman Committee finds him not that far along. As a liberal and progressive senator, he had taken his first steps toward embracing civil rights, but he was not yet, in the summer of 1941, ready to stake the reputation and the future of his committee on it.

Since those first public hearings in April, the committee had now interviewed more than two hundred witnesses—the transcript of the public hearings alone stacked up to more than three thousand pages, and on top of that were thousands of contracts, documents and supporting paperwork. Fulton and Truman, in their morning meetings, began to work out an outline for this big report.

The process was long, in part because of the Truman Committee's policy—a new approach for congressional investigations—that representatives from the government or private sector be given a chance to review and comment on early drafts. And Truman's goal of unanimous support meant a lot of time with the other senators in the Doghouse, hashing out details and working through objections.

While they were shaping this comprehensive report, a flurry of other issues—the committee, his home life, senatorial duties, even his Masonic commitments—meant that no sooner was Truman back from the West Coast than he found himself at the breakneck pace he'd been going at all year.

There were questions and follow-up reporting on army camps. Morris Lasker and Matt Connelly were continuing to investigate contracts for jeeps. Truman wrote to Senator Harry Byrd to see about getting the committee's office redecorated. And he was back on the road. In mid-September he left Washington by car for another road trip: an overnight stop in Fort Wayne, Indiana, then Chicago, Milwaukee, and finally Missouri for ten days to wrap up his year as Grand Master of the Missouri Masons. He'd scheduled a series of ceremonial Masonic visits, mixed in with his usual commitments: constituent duties, state and local Democratic politics, and work for the committee. He'd enjoyed his time as the Grand Master, but his world had changed dramatically since he'd taken on the role in 1940. "I'll be happy when my Masonic career ends and I can work altogether on the Senate Committee, go where I please, say what I want to, and maybe do the country some good," he wrote Bess from St. Louis. Apart from the usual small annoyances, he loved being out on the road and back in the Midwest. "By the way I feel better than I have for a month. Been reading Chicago, Milwaukee and St. Louis papers and talking to people who are not influenced by that crazy Washington complex."[40]

On the 18th and 19th, he was in Kansas City. His arrival anywhere in Missouri these days was news, and he told reporters he was holding an open house at the Muehlebach Hotel for "anybody that wants to see me." Hundreds took him up on the offer. "You should have seen the mob," he told Bess. "There were four rooms and phones in all of 'em and they went constantly all day. Vic [Messall, an aide] said I must have talked to three or four hundred people. I don't know how many but I saw 'em in batches and singly from 9 A.M. until 9 P.M." He took a break at lunchtime to speak to a gathering of mayors and officials, touching on a favorite theme: "As far as the OPM is concerned, the little manufacturer has been left out in the cold. Over 75 percent of the defense contracts have been awarded to 50 or 60 firms."[41]

For a man who often professed not to care about press coverage, he of course was paying close attention to his press coverage. "The *Star* gave me a very nice write up in the noon edition which doesn't go out of town but cut me out of the main edition entirely." All this attention, for a man who had for years been all but ignored by the media, even in his home state: "My, what a difference from last year this time and what a kick there is in it."[42]

Somewhere in all of this, he found time to visit Independence, where he dropped in on his mother and sister, met with some old friends, and spent $16 on a tune-up for his car. Then it was back across the state again, with several stops to visit Masonic Lodges. He was up most mornings by 6:30, and writing to Bess after midnight, and his letters are peppered with references to the workload and details of where, and how, he'd managed to sneak in a nap.

On the 30th he was in St. Louis for the annual convention of the Grand Lodge of the Missouri Freemasons, where he made a farewell speech to more than one thousand delegates. "Well my tour of duty as Grand Master ended up in a blaze of glory," Truman wrote Bess afterwards. "My good friends were the happiest men you ever saw and I felt like it was worth all the effort and time."[43]

He'd been on the road, though, for much of the past few months, and the strain was wearing on both of them. Bess had never enjoyed Washington very much, and with Truman away she was unhappy and let him know it. As it was, there was plenty of work waiting for him in Washington, and in the first week of October, Truman headed back to DC.

There, the committee soon got caught up in a battle raging in Detroit between two big labor unions over a contract to build homes for defense workers. The Currier Lumber Company had submitted a bid for a federal contract to build three hundred houses for defense workers in the western suburb of Wayne, but the company's agreement to use labor provided by the CIO and not those represented by the AFL had led to conflict, and even violence. At one point the AFL and the Teamsters had threatened a citywide housing strike.[44]

The company's bid, initially granted by the Federal Works Agency, was held up at the request of Sidney Hillman, one of Roosevelt's OPM heads. Called to testify before the Committee on October 22, Hillman said he'd done so because he feared the dispute could escalate into open warfare between the unions. Letting Currier have the contract, he said, would be "putting a match to a place where there is plenty of powder." Truman felt this was irresponsible meddling by a high-ranking member of the administration: "If we can't let a contract to a responsible bidder, the low bidder, without a strike, then what is the country coming to?" On October 29, he spoke about the issue on the Senate floor: "I cannot condemn Mr. Hillman's position too strongly." He noted that the United States government, as well as the governor of Michigan and the mayor of Detroit, were more than capable of handling any threats of violence.[45]

Senator Mead, however, countered that the committee had also heard testimony that the company awarded the contract was strongly anti-union, "a notorious wage-cutting organization in the past," and that "I believe Mr. Hillman is acting in good faith."

"We stand to save $216,000 by letting this contract to the low bidder," Truman shot back. "I do not think it is our interest whether the AF of L and the CIO engage in a dispute as to who shall do the work."[46] The government's rejection of the contract stood. Two months later, though, on December 3, Hillman's predictions of violence came true when a bomb exploded in the Detroit home of P.J. Currier, the building company's president. Though several people were in the house at the time, no one was injured.

Meanwhile, Fulton was continuing to fill out the staff, nearing its full complement of about a dozen investigators and twenty or so stenographers and secretaries. Wilbur Sparks arrived from Missouri and started on October 10. Franklin Parks, a Washington, DC, native out of Georgetown Law and a stint at the General Accounting Office, started a few days later.[47] It was a young staff, the work was exciting, and people formed quick friendships; after the long days, everyone headed out to unwind. Walter Hehmeyer, who made a mean martini, was dating Shirley Key by this time, who had become close friends with Marion Toomey, who was going out with Morris Lasker.[48] Sparks, once he settled in, became known for being very serious about his work, and was the subject of some good-natured teasing for it.

Hugh and Jessie Fulton enjoyed entertaining at their apartment on 16th Street, and they liked having the young staff over. Jessie was somewhat shy, but Shirley Key enjoyed the evenings there and the flair with which Jessie had decorated their apartment. Fulton had a farm in New Jersey where the couple often spent weekends, and there was talk of inviting the staff to come up.

As the weather turned colder, most everyone was put to work on the big report on the defense program, though other investigations were percolating. In late November, Fulton and Clark sent out questionnaires regarding a growing scandal in Washington—former New Dealers and administration officials who were alleged to be putting their inside knowledge to use to win defense contracts.[49] This investigation was linked to the broader question of the dollar-a-year men, a class for whom Truman's suspicions had only deepened since the committee began its work.

When it came to holding hearings, the other senators were so busy at times that Truman was sometimes having trouble getting more than a couple of them in a room. Tom Connally had been named chairman of the foreign affairs committee, and other members had taken on new duties as well. Mead suggested that Truman ask the Senate for help in the form of three more members. After some back-and-forth, the request was granted, and Styles Bridges, Republican of New Hampshire; Clyde Herring, an Iowa Democrat; and Democrat Harley Kilgore of West Virginia joined the committee on November 27.

Truman himself was also serving on Appropriations, Military Affairs, and several smaller committees, and once again, as in June when he'd gone to Arkansas, the work and the travel and the dinners and meetings were wearing him down.[50] In mid-November he traveled to Memphis with Hugh Fulton and some of the senators to inspect a huge ordnance plant nearby, where there were complaints about contractors overbilling the government.

Harold Robinson went along, too, and it was his job to make sure the witnesses—army employees in this case—were present and on time for the hearing: "It's embarrassing as hell when you try to call a witness and he isn't there. He's 'checked out' or something." Robby's approach was to check them into the hotel and treat them to a nice meal the night before, and then invite them for drinks in his room—which, on this night, turned into more than a few. About ten o'clock, Senators Truman and Brewster returned from dinner just as the party was getting "a bit boisterous in my room."

Brewster was a teetotaler—"he doesn't even drink coffee," Robinson said—and as they walked down the hall and heard the laughter and ruckus, Brewster turned to Truman. "Isn't that Robby's room?"

"No, I think he's two doors down the hall," replied Truman.

"He knew it was my room," Robinson said, telling the story many years later. "How can you hate a guy like that?"[51]

On this trip, Truman was able to swallow his dislike of Washington newspaper columns, especially Drew Pearson's widely syndicated "Washington Merry-Go-Round," for a moment to send Bess a clipping. Pearson and coauthor Robert Allen had previewed the Memphis trip with a glowing column on the committee's work and Truman's surprising rise from "henchman of the Pendergast machine" and political nobody: "So far as the man in the street was concerned, there was only one senator from Missouri—Bennett Clark." The piece retold the story of Truman's surprising re-election win in 1940 and sketched him as a modest, hardworking and principled public servant. Truman clipped it from the Memphis paper and sent it to Bess that night. "Here's a Merry Go Round piece that has been published all over the country. Not so bad for those untruthful birds to put out, I'd say." He mentioned it in a letter to his daughter as well: "Your dad won the brass ring in the Washington Merry Go Round day before yesterday. Why? Because the two liars who write it said that publicity means not so much to him. It doesn't," he wrote, apparently unaware of the contradiction in those words, "but they don't believe it."[52]

Bess was by this time urging her husband to take a break. Back in Washington, he was scheduling meetings and hearings for the next few weeks when the sudden death of Colorado Senator

Alva Adams on December 1 offered Truman, oddly, a chance to step away from the grind. He would be part of the congressional delegation to attend the funeral—a leisurely train ride west with some of his colleagues, and a stop in Independence on the way back to visit his mother.

For the following weekend, he quietly booked a room for himself at the Pennant Hotel in Columbia, Missouri, where he planned to relax for the day and catch up on his sleep.[53] On Sunday morning, December 7, he chatted on the phone with Bess back in Washington, where the weather was cold and gloomy and Margaret was suffering from a cold. Then he went to breakfast and, back in his room, wrote Bess a letter, marveling once again at how far he'd come in such a short time: "It's funny how things change around in thirteen months. I'm on the front pages of the *Kansas City Star, St. Louis Star-Times,* and *Kansas City Journal* for yesterday and am on the front page of the *Post-Dispatch* editorial section for today and mentioned in about three or four other places in the other parts of the paper and the *Globe.*"[54]

He signed the letter, "Love to you, Harry," and went back to bed, with no idea how much more their lives were about to change. Around three o'clock in the afternoon, the phone rang. It was the man who had driven him to the hotel, calling to say he'd heard on the radio that the Japanese had bombed Honolulu.

In Washington that morning, Bess told her daughter to stay in for the day with her cold, and Margaret turned on the radio to listen to the New York Philharmonic. Suddenly, a voice came on, interrupting the music, announcing that the Japanese had bombed a place called Pearl Harbor. Bess wandered by, and Margaret wondered aloud why the newscasters were interrupting with news of a Japanese attack on some far-off place.

"What was the name of the place you said they were attacking?" her mother asked.

"Pearl Harbor."[55]

The phone rang—it was the secretary of the Senate calling to say there would be a special joint session of Congress the next day and that her husband should be there. Bess put in a call to Truman, who was packing his clothes and trying to figure out how he was going to get back in time. "I had no car and no driver," he told his close friend Ethel Noland a few days later, "so I called the little airport at Columbia, which was right across the road from the hotel, and the manager said he had a plane and would take me to St. Louis."[56]

The flight took just forty minutes, and he was on the ground there by 5:35 p.m. "Then, my troubles began." A flight to Chicago was full, and so was one to Memphis. After several hours of waiting, "finally, I think TWA dumped some body off and I got on the 11 p.m. plane to Pittsburgh." Landing there about 3:30 in the morning, he met up with several of his Senate colleagues also racing to get back. One of them was Charles "Curly" Brooks, "the great Republican isolationist from Chicago." Brooks, no friend of the administration, was aligned with the movement that sought to keep the US out of the war at all costs. "He looked as if he'd swallowed a hot stove," Truman said, "and that's the way all those anti-preparedness boys looked the next day."[57]

Truman arrived in Washington about 5:30 a.m., where his secretary, Harry Vaughan, was waiting with a car. When he got home, Bess was up, fixing breakfast. He crawled into bed for a few hours' sleep and then went in to the Senate. Margaret convinced her mother that her fever had gone, and Bess allowed her to join her father on Capitol Hill. "I was not going to let a cold keep me from seeing history made." Bess gave her a pass for the special session, and by the time she got to the packed House chamber, the only place she was able to get a seat was in the photographer's gallery.[58]

Both father and daughter were there listening as Franklin Roosevelt spoke the words that defined an era: "Yesterday, December seventh, 1941, a date which will live in infamy, the United States of America was suddenly and deliberately attacked by naval and air forces of the Empire of Japan." The speech lasted just six minutes. "We will not only defend ourselves to the uttermost but will make it very certain that this form of treachery shall never again endanger us. Hostilities exist. There is no blinking at the fact that our people, our territory, and our interests are in grave danger. With confidence in our armed forces, with the unbounding determination of our people, we will gain the inevitable triumph so help us God."

Roosevelt ended his short, somber remarks with the request that everyone expected: "I ask that the Congress declare that since the unprovoked and dastardly attack by Japan on Sunday, December seventh, 1941, a state of war has existed between the United States and the Japanese Empire." Margaret followed the senators back to the Senate side of the Capitol, where she watched as her father voted to go to war.

Four days later, Adolf Hitler declared war on the United States.

6

WARTIME

Sixty million people heard Roosevelt's speech, "the largest audience in the history of radio."[1] While he had told Americans the news was bad—"The attack yesterday on the Hawaiian Islands has caused severe damage to American naval and military forces. I regret to tell you that very many American lives have been lost"—it would be months before people outside the government knew just how badly the US had been caught sleeping.

The Sunday morning attack, launched from aircraft carriers north of Hawaii, was a spectacular success. Pearl Harbor was the main US naval base in the Pacific Ocean, and when Japanese planes appeared overhead at 7:48 that morning, many of the ships in the fleet—including eight battleships, still considered the most fearsome weapons afloat—were lined up at their moorings: the sailors eating breakfast or enjoying a quiet morning. By the time the second wave of attackers headed back to their carriers ninety minutes later, twenty-one ships had been lost or damaged. Four of the battleships were sunk, the other four damaged. *Arizona* and *Oklahoma* were completely destroyed, and the others were out of commission for months if not longer; *California* and *West Virginia* would not return to active service until 1944. When *Arizona* exploded and sank, 1,177 men perished—nearly half of the US servicemen killed that day. The army and navy air forces had been caught off guard as well. The attack destroyed more than 150 airplanes and damaged many more; only a few got off the ground to offer any resistance to the Japanese fighters, bombers, and torpedo planes. All told, 2,403 Americans died, and more than one thousand were wounded.[2]

US military power in the Pacific Ocean was all but crippled, with one key exception: the Pacific Fleet's aircraft carriers had not been at Pearl Harbor that day, one piece of luck in what otherwise was one of the worst defeats in American history. Roosevelt obviously feared political damage if it was known just how bad things were, but military leaders—at that time preparing for possible attacks on the West Coast or an amphibious assault on Hawaii—also feared letting the Japanese know how well their attack had succeeded.

Overnight, Washington was a different city. Military officers the next day received orders to report for work in uniform; suddenly khaki, olive green, and blue were everywhere. Shirley Key and Walter Hehmeyer were among the many residents of the city who drove over to Massachusetts Avenue to see the bonfires and smoke on the lawn outside the Japanese embassy, as the diplomats and staff burned documents. The newspapers reported that on the West Coast, there were fears and rumors of sabotage and attacks; "strange planes" had been sighted, as word came too of additional Japanese attacks on the Philippine Islands and Guam. Authorities in the nation's capital announced air-raid drills. The DC police took steps to guard against sabotage and issued guns to auxiliary officers. The streetlights were dimmed in preparation for blackouts that would protect the city from nighttime bombardment. "On the roofs of buildings," wrote Donald Nelson, an executive in the Office of Production Management, there were soon "more antiaircraft guns and gun crews than there had been in the entire country only a few years before." Everyone was jittery—in the days that followed, there were false alarms of air raids up and down the East Coast.[3]

Housing, already scarce, became scarcer as the city's population boom shifted into overdrive. *The Washington Post* urged homeowners to consider converting their front porches into bedrooms[4] that could be rented out. For months, the requirements of the defense program had caused shortages: gasoline, wool, office paper, anything made of brass or copper, silk stockings, electric motors, lighting fixtures. Now even basic food items disappeared from store shelves as everyone hoarded necessities. Across the country, some recruiting stations were forced to stay open twenty-four hours a day, as hundreds of thousands enlisted in the military.

Truman himself got caught up in the war fever. He was still a colonel in the field artillery reserve, and the previous year he had gone to see the Chief of Staff of the Army, General George Marshall, to ask about returning to active service. Marshall told him to forget about it—he was too old, and more use in the Senate. In the days after Pearl Harbor, it was on his mind again. "I wish I was 30 and in command of a Battery," he wrote Ethel Noland on December 14. "It would be a lot easier. They may let me run a regiment yet although they say not." Wishful thinking, of course, for a fifty-seven-year-old United States senator.[5]

On December 8, the government announced an end to the "defense" buildup and replaced it with a "victory program" that was twice as big—a "gigantic production effort that is said to contemplate a total expenditure of 150 billion dollars."[6]

The work of the Truman Committee, too, had changed—from a peacetime investigation of defense spending into an examination of an ongoing war effort, and critics were quick to suggest that this was inappropriate and unpatriotic. Undersecretary of War Robert Patterson wrote to Roosevelt, asking him to abolish the committee: "It will impair our activities if we have to take time out to supply the Truman Committee with all the information it desires."[7] Truman moved quickly to pull the senators together and discuss whether their work should continue. They agreed it should—if anything, their work was now even more important.

On December 10, they issued a one-page statement clearly aimed at putting the White House at ease: "The committee never have investigated, and they still believe that they should not investigate, military and naval strategy or tactics. Such matters should be handled strictly by the Military and Naval Affairs Committees of the Congress." It laid out the high points of the committee's investigations to date and made the case for continuing that work: "During the eight months in which the special committee have operated, they have noted and called attention to many things which have adversely affected production"—notably, shortages of strategic materials and a too-heavy focus on big manufacturers. "The committee are determined the war should not continue weeks or months longer because of the failure to get the production which we need as soon as possible."[8]

The national crisis placed new demands on the investigators and staff in Room 160. "The heavy increase in the workload of the Committee," Fulton wrote in a memo to everyone, meant that investigators should get things done "with a minimum of supervision and a maximum of initiative." With so many requests to check into this or that topic, no two investigators could be spared to work on the same problem. They were free, he said, to explore topics that might be worth a full investigation and should submit written proposals to Clark or Fulton himself for approval. "Emphasis should be given to the slogan 'get it organized and get it down on paper.'" Since everyone would be working long hours, "there is a liberal policy of time off for reasonable personal reasons, as an offset to overtime work frequently rendered necessary by circumstances not capable of control."[9] In the coming weeks and months, there would be plenty of those circumstances.

On December 18, Bess and Margaret headed home for a somber and quiet Christmas holiday, while Truman stayed behind in Washington. He was working hard and still enjoying his new eminence on Capitol Hill: "I had quite a fight in the Senate yesterday but got the job done," he told Bess. "It seems that the majority on both sides of the aisle have some confidence in your old man. That's worth more than all the money in the world."[10]

As always when Bess was away, Harry was lonely and a little irritable. He was trying to clear his schedule enough to get back home for Christmas, fretting about attacks on the committee and worrying about Roosevelt's approval now that the nation was at war. On the 21st, he vented his frustrations in a letter to Bess: "The President is supposed to call me about my committee but I don't suppose he will, and I'll probably have to rush right back for the purpose of seeing him. It must be done or I'd tell him to go to hell. He's so damn afraid that he won't have all the power and glory that he won't let his friends help as it should be done."

Truman and Roosevelt had never been close, and his growing stature in the Senate had, so far, done nothing to change that. In the year since Truman's re-election, he had met with the president only once.[11] Truman admired Roosevelt and had been a loyal supporter of the New Deal, but at times he felt that loyalty was taken for granted. At one point in 1937, when he opposed Roosevelt in a debate over who would be the next majority leader, someone in the White House had reached out to Tom Pendergast, asking the Kansas City boss to try to change Truman's mind. Truman was furious. "I'm tired of being pushed around," he said, "tired of having the President treat me like an office boy."[12] In the years since, the junior senator from Missouri had remained very far down the list of Roosevelt's priorities.

In February, Truman had gone to the White House and re-

ceived Roosevelt's initial blessing for his committee, but they
had not spoken since. Now he was nervous about the questions
being raised about his committee's future. Still, his rant to Bess
was just that, a private complaint written at a low moment
when he was tired and frustrated. He did get away to Missouri
for Christmas but was back in Washington by the 29th. Two
days later, he closed out the year with a letter to Bess. During a blackout drill the night before, "I moved your blue chair
into the little hall between the bedrooms, took Margie's radio
and *Adventure* [magazine], opened the coat-closet door, and really had a very pleasant fifteen minutes."[13] He had a quiet New
Year's Eve dinner with friends, and was home by 12:30. As 1942
began, a gray, gloomy day in more ways than one, he was at his
desk early, working his way through a thick stack of paperwork.

Many newspapers around the country carried a feature, distributed by the International News Service, called "The President's Day," which described Franklin Roosevelt's meetings and
social events in bright, chatty prose. Readers following the com-
ings and goings from 1600 Pennsylvania Avenue learned that on
Monday, January 12, the president had just finished his morning
coffee when a group of top congressional leaders "pounded up
the front stairs." While they talked price controls and defense
bills, an "impressive cavalcade" of British and American generals and admirals began arriving for high-level strategy meetings.
The third item down revealed that Roosevelt's next appointment was with the junior senator from Missouri. "Slated for
an 11:30 date with Mr. Big, Senator Truman got the come on
finally around noon. Some 20 minutes later Senator Truman
exited smiling." He had received "a big slap on the back and
the Presidential go-sign on his committee's investigation of national defense."[14]

That wasn't the only thing they talked about that day. Truman was about to drop a bomb in the Senate, and he was giving

Roosevelt a three-day head start on the news. Fulton and the staff were putting the finishing touches on what was now called the committee's First Annual Report, and Truman had gone to the White House to give Roosevelt a heads-up on what it contained. While the army camp report had come in at just thirty-five pages, this document ran to 180 pages of single-spaced condemnation of everything that was wrong with the sprawling, lumbering effort to convert the US to a wartime economy. Most importantly for Roosevelt was its criticism of the OPM and his administration's leadership of the production effort.

Three days later, Vice President Henry Wallace was presiding, and many of the desks were empty, as Truman rose early in the Senate. "Mr. President," he said, speaking softly, "I should like to submit a report from the Special Committee to Investigate the National Defense Program." Perhaps out of nervousness, he had risen a little *too* early. Charles McNary, Republican of Oklahoma, reminded him that the Senate first had to get through its usual preliminaries: "I could not very well hear the statement of the senator, but if he desires to address the Senate on a very important subject—I understand it is important—I should object during the consideration of the routine morning business."

Kentucky's Alben Barkley gently agreed. "May I suggest to the senator that he withhold his remarks until the conclusion of morning business, for under the morning business he would be limited to five minutes anyway."

"Very well," Truman replied and sat back down to wait his turn.[15]

You can almost hear his foot tapping with impatience as he listened to the introduction of a bill that would give servicemen and women on active duty free use of the postal services, and a resolution that would exempt members of the clergy from new restrictions on purchases of rubber tires. Then followed a lengthy discussion about a bill to encourage the planting of guayule, a desert shrub common in Mexico and the Southwest that, it was hoped, would become a domestic source of rubber.

At last, Truman got his turn: "Standing up straight behind his desk in the back row, he adjusted his spectacles and occasionally tugged at a button on the coat of his gray suit."[16] He began speaking, rapidly and so softly that some of the senators strained to hear him. He opened with a restatement of the committee's purposes and a description of the massive challenges the government faced in deciding "what is to be produced, the quantities and the materials to be used, and even the exact methods by which the articles are produced."

Then he got down to business: "The committee, in the investigations which it has already conducted, has found numerous instances of gross inefficiency, and still more instances in which the private interests of those concerned have hindered and delayed the defense program. A considerable quantity of supplies and material which we should have today has not been produced, and as a result the war effort has been seriously handicapped."

One by one he went through the problems, beginning with a scathing critique of the OPM and the administration's leadership. "Its record has not been impressive; its mistakes of commission have been legion, and its mistakes of omission have been even greater." His committee's report dismissed—perhaps too quickly—the arguments that Roosevelt had created OPM but failed to give it real authority or decision-making power. Instead, Truman said, "in the instances where it has failed, the failure has not been due so much to the lack of power as to the ineptness of the officials of the Office of Production Management." He harshly criticized the "dollar-a-year" and "w.o.c." (without compensation) men who, whether intentionally or not, were awarding far too many contracts to big companies and cutting small businesses out. To clean up this mess, he said, the committee was calling for a new agency, with a single, powerful leader, to oversee the entire production program.[17]

From there he went on, summarizing the high points, or rather the low points, of the committee's findings. Delays, overruns, and shortfalls in shipbuilding and airplanes. Shortages and lagging production of steel, rubber, copper, lead, zinc. Why were the automobile companies still making cars? Why were so many of the airplanes being sold to the government inferior to those flown by German and Japanese pilots? Why were some naval contractors making twenty, thirty, forty times their normal profits?

As he spoke, small groups of senators gradually made their way over to his desk, and now they stood around him. As he neared the end of his summary, they began interrupting with questions.[18] Were the companies and individuals who were cheating the government or making huge profits being prosecuted? Who was going to jail? "What happens to the men in procurement," Arthur Vandenberg, Republican of Michigan, wanted to know, "responsible for this scandal?"

"They usually are promoted," Truman said.

And what about the White House? "Would not the Commander in Chief, as well as the Congress, be interested in the committee's report?"

"I sent him a copy," Truman said.[19]

Roosevelt had made good use of his early warning. The night before Truman's speech in the Senate, the president announced a complete shakeup in the war production leadership. He abolished the OPM and created a new War Production Board under the leadership of one man, Donald M. Nelson, a former executive at Sears, Roebuck & Company. Roosevelt was impressed by Nelson's abilities managing production and distribution of tens of thousands of items for Sears, and his deep knowledge of American industry. FDR had brought him into the government in 1941 as a dollar-a-year man to set priorities at OPM, and then put him in charge of a new Supply Priorities and Allocation Board.

While Sidney Hillman would remain as the head of the new

agency's labor division, William Knudsen was being nudged aside, at least for the time being. The former General Motors president, "generally considered to be the country's top production genius," said *The Washington Post,* would be given a new role as "inspector general of the process of turning out munitions of war." Knudsen was reported to be okay with the decision, feeling that "he is more competent and more at home with a blueprint or in a factory than as administrative head of a non-production job." Whether that was spin or not, Knudsen was out. In his new position, with the rank of lieutenant general, he would indeed put his brilliance to good use.

With Nelson's appointment, Roosevelt ended the clamor for a "production czar" and centralized control that had been building in Washington for months. The advance notice of the impending report urging him to act had provided political cover for the shakeup. Truman was walking a tightrope between the public interest and protecting his party and the administration, and his deft handling of this issue allowed Roosevelt to get the credit. "That was all right with me," Truman wrote later. "I wanted action more than credit."[20]

While the OPM section was the most politically explosive, there were plenty of other revelations in the report. Truman cited the excess—sometimes astronomical—profits contractors in many industries were making at government expense. In the case of shipbuilding, he said, once his committee began to investigate, some companies had "voluntarily" offered to give some of the money back and reduce their future payments. "This ridiculous situation never should have been permitted to exist in the first place, and necessarily has greatly increased the cost of the shipbuilding program."

Ellison Smith of South Carolina followed up on that. "Mr. President, did the senator from Missouri, who is making the report, say that one company asked the Navy Department to reduce its profits?"

"Not one, but several did so."

"They asked that their profits be reduced?"

"They paid back to the Navy Department at least four million dollars," Truman responded. "That is a matter of record."

Are those companies, Smith wanted to know, "to be put in the Smithsonian Institution?"

As laughter rippled through the Senate chamber, Truman replied, "They should be."[21]

Several senators asked for additional copies of the report and urged that Truman distribute it widely. As he finished his remarks, he submitted a resolution asking that three thousand more copies be printed. And while he was on a roll, he asked the Senate for more money—another $100,000 in continued operating funds (on January 23, the Senate approved his request, but lowered it to $60,000).

While it touched on many of the current questions and debates—OPM, camp construction, the conversion of the auto industry—the most surprising comments in the report, at least to the Washington press corps and to millions of Americans reading the newspaper the next day, came in the section on aviation. Here, the committee hit the facts hard: "Information developed by the committee indicates that at the outbreak of war on Dec. 7, 1941, our production of aircraft was such that the armed forces possessed only enough airplanes to furnish skeleton forces with equipment, a great deal of which was of inferior quality."[22]

The army's bombers—notably the four-engine B-17 Flying Fortress and B-24 Liberator—were among the best in the world, but the smaller, faster, pursuit (fighter) planes flown by American pilots were in many cases slow, underpowered and vulnerable. The report quoted a speech in October by Henry H. Arnold, the top general in the army air forces, in which he said that development of pursuit planes had been allowed to "drift in the doldrums." Specifically, when it came to the army's main fighter plane, "We no longer rate the [name deleted] as better than a good pursuit trainer because of its limitations of speed, ceiling and fire power."

While for security reasons the committee did not name the airplane, Arnold was speaking of the Curtiss P-40 Warhawk.[23] While newer, faster, better planes were in the works, they were not yet proven in combat. On the drawing boards were many high-performing planes, the committee report said, "but in January 1942 very few will be produced which can be considered better than mediocre." Ditto for the navy: a plane was being developed that was "considered to be the fastest naval fighter in the world, but it will not be in quantity production for many months to come."[24]

Who was to blame for all this? The committee had plenty to say about that. Fulton and the investigators identified several key factors, some of which would hamper US aircraft production for months and years to come. Among the biggest problems was the military's constant demands for revisions to the designs and specifications of airplanes that were already in production. While it was important to make improvements based on feedback from combat pilots, these modifications often involved delays while the manufacturers drew up new plans, created new tools and machines, and retrained their workers. Next on the list were the shortages and bottlenecks in supply: of engines and propellers, of machine tools, of strategic materials like magnesium and aluminum. Other problems, the report said, included the failure to make use of dozens of small airplane manufacturers, "outmoded concepts of aircraft production," and, finally, labor disputes and strikes.[25]

Truman and his Democratic majority on the committee were of course strongly pro-labor and pro-union, but they had not let organized labor off the hook. The report quoted government figures showing that, across all defense industries, 26 million "man days" were lost from June 1940 through October 1941. (Of course, there were tens of thousands of women workers in defense industries, a number that would grow into the millions.) "There is no question but that the defense program has been very seriously handicapped" by strikes and threatened strikes, and many of those strikes, the report said, "ought not to have taken place." Walking a careful line, the report noted that both "labor and industry have been too much concerned with their own interests and too little concerned with the national interests." And many of the strikes "were inspired by noting the tremendous profits being reported by companies having defense contracts."[26]

"Defense Bungling Charged By Senate's Investigators," read the page one headline in *The New York Times*. The story detailed the "waste, inefficiency, self-interest and failures" cited in the report, describing the findings as so extensive that "calls came from the Senate floor for a fixing of 'criminal' responsibility."[27]

The Washington Post also had the story on the front page, as did *The Arizona Republic;* the *Sentinel* in Carlisle, Pennsylvania; the Havre, Montana, *Daily News;* the Shreveport, Louisiana, *Times*; and more than fifty other papers around the country. Dozens more carried it inside: yet another bleak story in one of the darkest months of the twentieth century.

On January 6, while salvage workers were still finding bodies in the wreckage of ships in Pearl Harbor, Roosevelt had given his annual State of the Union message. To a nation weary from a decade of economic sacrifice and hardship, he told them frankly that more of both were coming: "This production of ours in the United States must be raised far above present levels, even though it will mean the dislocation of the lives and occupations of millions of our own people. We must raise our sights all along the production line. Let no man say it cannot be done. It must be done—and we have undertaken to do it."

American workers and American industry would rise to his challenge, and how that happened is one of the most inspiring stories of World War II.

In the meantime, life went on. "Dear Margie," Truman wrote his daughter that first week in January, "Abbott & Costello have not been here in 'Keep Em Flying.' Hope I get to see it." He hadn't been to the movies, but he had gone out to dinner at the Shoreham Hotel with Hugh and Jessie Fulton:

> *They had a right good floor show—some girl tumblers and some South American dancers. The orchestra played Vienna Woods and the Emperor Waltzes, and the pianist played a Chopin Nocturne and a couple of other classics which I didn't recognize in the intermission. I got home at 11:30 and was down here at seven this morning. Be a good girl and I'll see you Tuesday. Kiss mamma & tell your grandmas hello.*
> *Lots of love*
> *Dad*
> *XXXXXXXXXX*
> *OOOOOO*[28]

7

STEEL MAN

Pittsburgh, Pennsylvania, February 2, 1942

Groundhog Day. George Dye pulled his coat tight as he eased his car out of the parking lot at the Irvin Works and headed northwest for the fifteen-minute drive home. The temperature was down in the teens when he'd left for work that morning, and the paper said it would be even colder tonight. Punxsutawney Phil had called it for sure: six more weeks of winter.[1]

It was Monday, and already shaping up to be a long week. But first, Dye had a long night ahead of him. Alice would have dinner ready and hopefully Robert would have his homework done by the time he got home. Because tonight, he would write the letter. It wasn't an easy decision, and he'd been thinking about it for days. If he wasn't careful, writing it could cost him his job. With a war on, and his son headed to college next year, this was no time to be out of work, especially in a job like his, where his expertise could make the difference between a ship that carried its men and cargo safely across the oceans, and one that didn't.

In the dark weeks after the Japanese attack on December 7, George Dye was eager and determined to do his part. While the papers were trying their best to put a shine on the news, things looked bad all over. In the Philippines, General MacArthur and his army were barely hanging on at a place called Bataan. In North Africa, the German General Erwin Rommel was on the march, pushing back the British. The headlines talked of Allied "blows" and counterpunches, but if you read a little deeper into the story, you saw more about "withdrawals" and "strong enemy thrusts." Which was all the more reason why Dye couldn't just sit by and watch as his bosses at the Carnegie-Illinois Steel Corporation took advantage of the crisis. He'd been working in steel mills for more than twenty years, and what he'd seen happening over the last few months—what he saw just about every day— made him sick. In the past few days, a couple of stories in the newspaper had given him an idea of what he could do about it.

First was the news that Congress was taking up a huge naval spending bill. If the government had been on a spending spree before Pearl Harbor, that was nothing compared with now. At $17.7 billion, the paper said,[2] this was the largest appropriations bill in US history: 950,000 tons of new warships, 500 small craft, 1,709 miscellaneous vessels and thousands of new airplanes. The dollar amount worked out to $133 for every man, woman, and child in the nation. Eventually, all those ships and planes would make the US Navy the most powerful in the world. The top Admiral, Ernest J. King, cautioned, though, that it would take time for all these ships and planes to have an effect. The US could only "hold its own" in 1942 before slowly turning the tide in 1943 and 1944. His comments made it painfully clear that victory was years away. Reading this, George Dye knew that many of those ships would be built with the steel he inspected as it moved down the line, headed for shipyards all around the country.

And then, there was the story from last Tuesday, about the senator who was shaking things up in Washington. This Harry

Truman seemed to be saying exactly what Dye saw happening at the Irvin Works: that the navy didn't really care how much it was spending on ships. This line almost jumped off the page: "He charged that Naval observers stationed at shipyards had shown little interest in saving money for the Government."[3] And some contractors, Senator Truman added, didn't really care about the quality of the work, focusing instead on huge profits at a time when they should be trying to cut costs and increase production. Amen to that. Dye could tell the senator a thing or two about companies making huge profits on navy contracts, and cutting corners on quality and safety to do it. And so he sat down on that cold February night with a clean sheet of paper, in his house at 2902 Brownsville Road, and uncapped his fountain pen.

"Dear Sir," he wrote, "I am sorry I must submit this information without typing but for obvious reasons I didn't want it scrutinized by a typist." His letter unloaded many of the things he'd seen in recent weeks. Five pages written very much in the style of a high school composition, with an introduction followed by a concise thesis statement: "While the 17 billion dollar naval appropriation bill is being considered is a splendid time for our representatives in Congress to take inventory of our shipbuilding performance over the past few months and to correct any irregularities that may be responsible for inefficiency in the ship yards.

"One matter that should be given very careful consideration is the method of placing orders for common or stock sizes of plates and sheets."

In closing, he told the senator, "I admire the courage and sincerity displayed in your recent investigations, and am offering the above information in the hope that it will be helpful in your efforts to promote better conduct in the navy dept." He ended with a plea to keep the information confidential, as "this communication is written without the knowledge or consent of my employer."[4]

With a touch of pride, George Dye bundled together the papers, placed them into a large envelope, and sent it off the next day to Washington.

★ ★ ★

The incoming mail was opened each morning by a file clerk in Room 160, who stamped each letter as "received" and then routed it to the chief investigator, who in turn assigned an investigator to check things out and respond. After the widespread coverage of the annual report, the heavy volume of mail grew heavier—eventually reaching more than a hundred letters a day.[5] There were suggestions for how to build better ships or save lumber or conserve fuel or increase farm output. There were many thoughts on how to improve the production of airplanes, or landing boats or oil and gas—eventually thousands of letters during the course of the war.

"Dear Senator," wrote Aaron Sadoff of Marquette Michigan. He'd read Truman's comments about the steel shortage, and he had an idea. There was lots of steel, he said, just laying around railroad yards all over the county, discarded rails and other unused scrap. "Why not make the railroads bring in their old rails to relieve our steel shortage?" he asked. "I would also suggest that old light bulbs be saved."[6]

In early 1942, Wilbur Sparks was spending a lot of time responding to these letters: "The more we had hearings, the more national publicity we got. The more letters we got, the more we had hearings."[7] The responses usually went out under Fulton's signature or one of his deputies. Every letter was acknowledged, if only with a short paragraph or two saying the idea would be "carefully considered."

Mr. Aaron W. Sadoff
Sadoff Clothing Store
Marquette, Michigan

Dear Mr. Sadoff,
Senator Truman has asked me to thank you for your recent letter in which you suggest that we require the railroads to bring in their

old rails. The Committee is carefully studying the steel situation
and appreciates your suggestion in respect to this matter. We also
agree with you that now is the time for toughness.
Respectfully,
Rudolph Halley
Executive Assistant to the Chief Counsel[8]

In his first days in Room 160, Sparks got the lecture from
Charles Clark about how to handle this correspondence: "We're
working for the public and if they write us, they are at least entitled to an acknowledgement from the committee that the letter
has been received." On the other hand, Clark warned, "Don't
promise them anything except that we'll look it over carefully."[9]

Because, inevitably, many of these letters were from "crackpots." "We got all kinds of crazy mail," said Robert Irvin. In
February 1942, Irvin was twenty-four years old, fresh out of law
school at the University of Michigan. He'd come to Washington
after his graduation, thinking he had a line on a job with the
Federal Communications Commission. When that didn't pan
out, he applied at the Justice Department, where someone told
him there was an opening on the Truman investigating committee. Not really knowing anything about it, he went over to
the Senate Office Building and put in an application. He got
an interview with Hugh Fulton, a fellow Michigan Law alum,
who sent him downstairs to talk to Charles Clark, who referred
him to Matt Connelly. In all these conversations, one thing that
Irvin, who voted Republican, noticed was that no one asked him
about his party affiliation, or seemed to care. A few days later, he
got a call, offering him a job as an investigator at $2,000 a year.
On Monday, February 9, he went into Clark's office to sign the
papers. Still not knowing exactly what his new job was, he asked
what kind of duties he'd be assigned.

"Robert, you're free to travel, aren't you?"

"Well, hell yes," Irvin said.

"Well, all right."[10]

Clark sent him back to Connelly, who assigned him a desk in Room 160 and gave him a little more detail, telling Irvin to read up on the committee's reports and hearing transcripts, and from there he could get started on a couple of the ongoing investigations. One of them was shipbuilding, specifically the desperate need to build cargo ships at a time when so many were being sunk by German submarines. And, of course, there was the mail.

Robert Irvin on E. Capitol St. in Washington, 1942.

On the same Monday that Irvin started, Charlie Clark was responding, among other things, to a letter and packet of literature sent to the committee about an invention "so perfect and unbelievable" it was certain to help win the war: the "Christmas Battle Plane." On paper, and in the imagination of its inventor, this was a giant bomber with six engines, eighty-eight machine guns and cannons, and a crew of twenty-six men.[11]

It was designed by William Whitney Christmas, a self-styled "outstanding authority in aeronautics," who had been proposing far-fetched airplane designs for decades. The information, Clark wrote, "will be given the attention of the Committee."[12]

Two days later, a letter went out to George Dye, the steel man in Pittsburgh, with the formulaic "careful consideration" brushoff:

Dear Mr. Dye,

Senator Truman has asked me to thank you for your letter of February 2 with the attached data concerning "centralized planned purchasing of ship building materials."

Please be assured that the contents will be given careful consideration.

Respectfully,

Charles P. Clark,

Associate Chief Counsel[13]

George Dye refused to take the hint. He wrote another letter a week later, correcting an error he'd made in his first one: "I believe I stated that secondary shipments by all sheet and plate producers amounts to approximately 30,000 tons per *year. This should read 30,000 tons per month.*" From there, the six-page letter described, in great technical detail, the practices used at the Irvin Works in manufacturing and shipping steel plates. To Thomas Flynn, the investigator in Room 160 reading Dye's letter, the extremely specific technical information must have seemed overwhelming: "If the product does not require a critical inspection and the size and class product is favorable the yield may amount to 95% and 5% or 10% may be placed in X stock."[14]

Dye ended with some of his broader concerns about inefficiency and waste: "The management has plans for converting to all-out defense production but in a large corporation changes are brought about slowly and even small changes usually require several months." He seemed uncertain about whether any of this

was helpful—"I shall not burden you with any more communications"—and closed with yet another request for confidentiality:
"If you consider the above information of any value and decide
to submit it to someone else, please remove my signature."[15]
    This letter got an even shorter response, written by Flynn:

Dear Mr. Dye,
Thank you for your letter of February 17, concerning secondary
steel.
    Your comments have been noted with interest.
Respectfully,
Charles P. Clark
Associate Chief Counsel

The committee, however, had not heard the last of George
Dye. He wrote to Truman again in March, and several times
more in May. In these first letters, he set the tone that he would
follow in some three dozen letters over the next year: sometimes
cryptic, often conspiratorial, occasionally a little petulant, and at
other times boyishly patriotic. "Although I feel I am rendering
my company as well as my country a service by bringing these
matters to your attention, I am confident that the general superintendent of the plant would disagree with me and as I have a son
entering medical school next year I can't afford to be discharged."[16]
    Always, the points he was trying to make were smothered
in a thick layer of the impenetrable jargon of his work: "At an
order meeting April 22nd the general foreman of the Hot Strip
Finishing dept admitted that nearly 30% of his plate production
was being put in 'X' because of improper slab sizes." It's easy to
see why Flynn, Herbert Maletz, Bob Irvin, and the other investigators didn't take them seriously. And so Dye continued to
get the brushoff—"Thank you for your letters of May 13, 14,
15 and 16, in further reference to alleged improper shipments
of steel plate from the plant at which you are employed"—as

his letters went into the file with the other "crackpots." In the early months of 1942, the Truman Committee, and the United States, had far bigger things to worry about.[17]

On March 3 came news that a World War I-era destroyer had sunk off Cape May, New Jersey, torpedoed by a German submarine. On March 5, the Nazis announced by radio that in the first five days of March, they had sunk thirteen ships in the Atlantic Ocean. That same day, the first survivors from a cargo ship sunk in the North Atlantic back in February made it home to Boston. On March 8 came the confirmation of five more merchant ships sunk in the western Atlantic in the past week. Three days later, the Nazis announced they had sunk eleven Allied freighters in the past twenty-four hours. And so it went through March, the worst month yet in the battle in the Atlantic Ocean that had been raging for more than two years. In 1942 the amount of goods and materials reaching Great Britain fell to alarming lows. The first U-boats had arrived off the coast of the United States in January. While the US Navy had been fighting them unofficially for months, and now openly after Pearl Harbor, at this phase of the battle the Germans had the upper hand. Since the United States had not even imposed a blackout along the coastline, the submarines could lurk offshore and watch the lights twinkling, alerting them to targets. Radar, longer-range aircraft patrols, cracking the radio codes the U-boats used, and other innovations by the US and Britain would eventually have an impact, but in early 1942, the Battle of the Atlantic was close to being lost. In March, the total Allied and neutral losses in the Atlantic were ninety-eight ships and 547,000 tons of shipping.[18] German submarines, airplanes and mines were sinking more than three ships a day—ships carrying the fuel and food and guns and planes that the British and the Soviet Union so desperately needed.

Building cargo ships by the hundreds, thousands even, was just one of the incredibly ambitious goals Franklin Roosevelt had set in his State of the Union speech in January. A country that in 1941 had produced 1.1 million tons of merchant shipping, he said, would aim for 6 million tons in 1942 and 10 million tons in 1943. Airplanes, 60,000; tanks, 45,000; antiaircraft guns, 20,000. All these priorities would be competing for the same scarce materials—steel, aluminum, copper, magnesium and countless other resources. Donald Nelson, Roosevelt's new "production czar," had his work cut out for him. Each of the services—the army, the navy, the merchant marine—wanted huge quantities of these resources, and they were extremely reluctant to let civilians make decisions about allocation that they felt belonged in the realm of strategy—such as determining whether battleships or tanks or cargo vessels should get priority for steel.

Nelson, initially at least, brought political skills and a comfort with high-level policymaking to his new role. Born in 1884 in Hannibal, Missouri, Mark Twain's hometown, he remembered from his childhood the great man's visits: "I used to see him sitting in a straight-backed chair in front of the Kettering Hotel." Nelson, the son of a railroad engineer, did well enough in high school to study chemical engineering at the University of Missouri, where he graduated in 1911.

In 1912, hoping to raise money for graduate school, he took a temporary job at Sears, Roebuck in Chicago, where he ended up staying for twenty-eight years.[19] He learned the textile business from the loom up, and helped organize the company's testing laboratories. In 1921 he was put in charge of boys' clothing, and later of men's furnishings. As he rose through the ranks, he developed a deep understanding of how the more than one hundred thousand articles the company sold and advertised were produced, purchased, and distributed. A man in his position at Sears, he wrote, "buys everything, from the finest thread to the bulkiest heating plant, from drugs to fertilizers, and if there is any 'procurement trouble' in his department he must investigate and decide how to check it."[20] By 1940, when Roosevelt brought him into OPM, he was the company's executive vice president.

In Nelson, Truman and the committee found a man they could work with (the fact that he grew up in Missouri certainly didn't hurt). For his part, Nelson approached congressional invitations with less suspicion and combativeness than others in industry and government—notably the top military officials. "I enjoyed meeting with members of the Committee," he later wrote, "even when it made me perspire a trifle." He became a regular at Truman's informal gatherings in the Doghouse.

At his first public appearance before the committee, on January 28, Truman told Nelson the committee "fought to get you this job, and we'll fight to help you carry it out." But Truman was still on a tear about the dollar-a-year men, and never would fully accept their presence in the government. How, he asked again and again, could they not consciously or unconsciously favor the big corporations they were on leave from, at the expense of his beloved small businesses?[21]

Nelson came to Washington as a dollar-a-year man himself—he had joined the Treasury Department for what was initially supposed to be a two-month leave. He'd been making $70,000 a year at Sears; his current job paid $15,000[22] (Truman earned $10,000 a year as a United States senator). Peppered by Truman and others about these volunteers from industry, Nelson pushed back: the dollar-a-year men were not only valuable to the war program, he said, but also likely "indispensable." He told the senators bluntly that their attacks on the dollar-a-year men had hurt his efforts to bring experienced leaders into the government, saying that some of them were now afraid to come to Washington and face the backlash for their public service. Senator Joseph Ball, the Minnesota Republican, asked Nelson if most of his department heads at the WPB were dollar-a-year men. "Yes sir, they are." Isn't the problem with them, Ball asked, "that their whole psychology is toward maintaining the present industrial setup?"

"Isn't that criticism of all businessmen?" Nelson shot back.

"Wouldn't that be true whether or not they are on a salary basis?"[23]

Truman, surprisingly, backed down: "If you need the dollar-a-year men to win the war," he told Nelson, "this committee feels that you should have the dollar-a-year men."[24] Nelson, for his part, vowed to lay down strict ground rules for hiring these executives, notably barring them from any decisions directly affecting their own companies.

Nelson was fresh and new, and his elevation at such a crucial time—Roosevelt's latest Man of the Hour brought in to save the day—granted him a certain honeymoon period. He used that to his advantage on January 20, when the new WPB finally put a stop to civilian production of automobiles.[25] He was more comfortable in policy discussions—and in Senate hearing rooms—than Knudsen, and this, too, gave him some room for maneuvering. But the WPB had also inherited many of the same problems that had plagued Knudsen and Hillman at OPB, notably Roosevelt's dislike of placing too much power in anyone's hands but his own, the age-old tensions between civilian and military control and between bureaucracies in the government, and the millions of individual decisions that went into converting a sprawling peacetime economy to a centrally controlled wartime footing.

Among the most difficult and pressing of those decisions was how much, if any, of a given material to allot for the civilian market. In early 1942, the place where that tension bubbled up most often was where the rubber hit the road. Days after Pearl Harbor, the OPM had severely limited the sale of rubber tires and tubes, and on February 1 the government had prohibited the use of rubber in all but a few products. Much of the world's rubber supply came from South Asia, and the Japanese victories had cut off 95 percent of the world's supply. The synthetic rubber industry was slowly getting started but, as historian Maury Klein writes, "that program, after long delays, was bogged down in a maze of contradictory stories, rumors, and warnings."[26]

Following up on the success of the First Annual Report, the Truman Committee had several major investigations underway in early 1942, but the most urgent was the rubber situation. The committee held nine public hearings in March and early April as the staff gathered statements and statistics from experts around the country. Fulton began drafting a report that would examine the state of the nation's rubber supply in 1940 and '41, how much was on hand as 1942 began, the immediate prospects for ramping up the production of synthetic rubber, and efforts to conserve and recycle.

At times during the war, it seemed one of the most important roles played by the Truman Committee was bringing Americans bad news they did not want to hear, and when its chairman rose again in the Senate on May 26 to deliver the report on rubber, this was one of those times. "It is perfectly clear," Truman said, "that there will be no new tires for civilians during the next three years." Every day that Americans spent driving their cars, the report said, used up six hundred tons of rubber. "3-YEAR RUBBER BAN IS FACING CIVILIANS, SENATORS DECLARE," read the page-one story in *The New York Times*. "ARMY, NAVY MUST SAVE ON RUBBER, TOO," read a typical headline, this one in the Minneapolis *Star Tribune*.

Truman noted that the military, too, was wasting rubber and would have to cut back: "The armed forces should exercise the same degree of care that is recommended to civilians." But it was the drastic cutbacks coming to everyday life that got most of the attention.[27]

The government was at that time considering gasoline rationing, which would eventually happen, but it was wildly unpopular, and Roosevelt was dragging his feet. Truman noted that for all practical purposes, gasoline rationing was really a question of rubber: "even if drivers could have all the gasoline their motors could burn," he said, "they would still have to reduce driving to a bare minimum in order to conserve rubber."[28]

And while he said at the top of his speech that this was a "fact-finding not a fault-finding" report, there was plenty of fault to go around: the government's slow response to the shortage; control of the industry by British and Dutch concerns; complex and misguided shipping priorities. And while many people in and out of government had been warning of a rubber crisis and potential threats to the world supply, US businesses "indulged in an orgy of consumption, laying in stocks of finished goods at a rate which reached in June of 1941 a new high of over a million tons per year."

The release of a big report involved just about everyone on the committee. Fulton was the nerve center, sending out drafts and assigning sections to be written. Investigators followed up with phone calls and inquiries and fact-checking. Drafts went out to the various agencies and companies named or cited, and their comments were incorporated when appropriate. Marion Toomey helped with the writing and proofreading. Early versions went upstairs to Truman and to the other senators for their discussion and amendments. Then, Walter Hehmeyer edited and revised the drafts and prepared summaries for reporters. Hehmeyer was a friendly, easygoing colleague with a ready smile and a hearty laugh—well suited to his job of handling the press. Already, he was known among reporters for being fair and honest; he did not play favorites or give "scoops," and everyone had access to the same information.

For Shirley Key, the long hours and the deadlines were exciting. The young staff, working long hours in close quarters on challenging and exciting work, became a close-knit group in and out of work. For the final push, everyone came down to Room 160 to help with the collating and stacking, and to take a turn running off copies on the old mimeograph machine. Key, after a few months, had been promoted up to manage the whole secretarial staff, and counted many of the staff—men and women—as good friends. After the long days, they'd head out together to unwind. "It was a partying staff," recalled Bob Irvin, who shared an apartment on East Capitol Street with Hehmeyer, another of the committee's bachelors. There, they had a running joke whenever the phone rang: the one who picked up answered as if he were the butler or servant for the other: "Good evening, Mr. Hehmeyer's residence."[29] Walter's relationship with Shirley Key was now pretty serious, and they had begun talking about marriage. Marion Toomey had been dating Morris Lasker, but he left in March to go into the army.[30]

COURTESY OF CHRISTOPHER HEHMEYER.

Walter Hehmeyer in Washington, 1942.

Fulton's office and Truman's office and even Room 160 were busy places, with a steady stream of callers: the important, the powerful, and sometimes people who just dropped in. The rubber investigation brought more than its share of what everyone called crackpots or cranks. Somehow, maybe because of his size or commanding presence, many of them ended up at Harold

Robinson's desk. Bob Irvin's favorite was the guy who showed up one day to pitch an invention that would solve the rubber crisis "by scraping all the highways in the country, all the rubber that had worn off the tires." Another visitor said he had invented a machine gun that would win the war. As they talked, Robinson asked him, "well, where do you have this weapon?"[31]

"Right here," the man said, patting his pocket.

As Robinson edged away cautiously, the man pulled out a length of pipe, "just ordinary plumbing pipe." You hook an air hose up at one end, he explained, and drop the bullets into a little hole at the top, "and this compressed air just fires through the tube just as fast as you can drop them in the slot." Truman's favorite was the man with an idea to build an individual airplane for every soldier in the army, and then fill each plane with dirt. Then, "at a given signal" all of those thousands of planes would take off "and fly over enemy capitals and completely cover them with United States soil."[32]

8

OF CARGO SHIPS AND NECKTIES

July 1942

This midsummer day, like most days in Shirley Key's new job, was going by so fast it would be over almost before she knew it. Hugh Fulton had called her in to take down a section of yet another long report, and as she sat there with her pen flying across the steno pad, Key worried as always that she wouldn't be able to keep up. And in these first few weeks, anyway, without Marion Toomey's help, she couldn't.

Fulton had come down one day to Room 160, where Key was in charge of the stenographers, and asked her to come upstairs to be his secretary. The promotion was exciting and terrifying at the same time. Fulton was an imposing figure, and while Key could take dictation using shorthand, she wasn't nearly as good as the legal secretary who had just left. And that's where Marion had stepped in. While she did a lot of reporting and writing for Fulton, Toomey also handled a lot of administrative work.

Luckily for Key, Marion could work a stenotype machine—the kind court reporters used to take down word-for-word transcripts of trials and hearings. And so today, while Fulton talked and Key sat in front of his desk, scribbling on her pad, Marion sat on the other side of those bookshelves taking down every word, too. When Fulton was done, Shirley raced around to her own desk, and began typing up what she'd written. As she worked, Toomey brought over her notes to make sure she had everything down right. Fulton would never know.[1]

Meanwhile, there was so much other work to do. As always, people wandered in and out with some kind of business before the committee. While she was typing up the draft for Fulton, a balding, elderly man in a suit and wire-framed glasses walked in and sat down. She looked over and smiled, and told him she'd be with him in a moment.

The work was hectic, but it was exciting and glamorous, too. Key marveled that people she was reading about in the newspapers, some of the most important people in the country, would appear right there in front of her desk. She'd met James Forrestal, the Secretary of the Navy. And Andrew Jackson Higgins, the New Orleans businessman who was making torpedo boats and landing craft for the navy. The senators came in, sometimes, and even Chairman Truman, who was always so polite. With all this going on, no one really complained about the long hours. It was kind of intoxicating, and everyone just got caught up in it. When there was a big report coming out, she'd head back downstairs to Room 160 with everyone else and work late into the night. Matt Connelly, all the investigators, even Hugh Fulton would come down to stuff envelopes.

If she had to admit it, Key was a little scared of her boss. To someone twenty-three years old, in her first real job, he seemed old (in his thirties!), and he was the first person she'd ever met who was totally driven by work. Like most days, when Key and Toomey arrived this morning at 8:30, Fulton was already at his desk, and there was a stack of work to go through. He wasn't as friendly and easygoing as Senator Truman; colder, more businesslike. But she had learned that you could make a mistake with Hugh Fulton and get through it and, slowly, she was getting to know him better. Shirley had met Fulton's wife, too. Jessie Fulton didn't like Washington all that much and spent much of her time on their farm in New Jersey, where Hugh would go up sometimes for the weekends. The Fultons loved having people over to their apartment on 16th Street, and Jessie was a gracious hostess.

Beyond all the excitement, and being a part of history, Key was making great friends too, friends like Marion Toomey and Laura Mayo and Herb Maletz and Robby Robinson, the former FBI man, who joked and poked fun at her. And there was Walter Hehmeyer: they'd hit it off from the first day he had come down from New York.

Lost in her work, Key finished typing the final page, ripped it from the typewriter and began looking it over for errors. She looked up, realizing she'd forgotten about the nice businessman who'd been sitting there so patiently. "Well, I'm sure Mr. Fulton will be ready to see you shortly," she said, handing him a small white card, "but would you put your name on this card? And I'll take it in to him." That way, she could take the card in to Fulton and, if needed, he'd hurry up whatever interview he was doing and move things along.

The man wrote his name down, and as she looked down at it, Key had to swallow a laugh. There, sitting quietly waiting to see her boss, was one of the most powerful and important men in the country. The name written on the card was Henry J. Kaiser.[2]

As often happens in desperate times, a hero had risen to meet the crisis. In this case, the crisis was one of the defining questions of World War II—how to build cargo ships and fuel tankers fast enough to replace the ones that German U-boats were sending to the bottom of the Atlantic at the rate sometimes of two or three a day. Enough ships to keep Great Britain alive and fed and armed; enough ships to carry all the equipment that US forces would need to fight overseas; enough ships to carry millions of tons of supplies and weapons to the Soviet Union. Perhaps nowhere else in the whole production effort were the numbers so cruel, and the stakes so high. "Sinkings outran new construction" is how Donald Nelson put it. "Production got into a life or death race with destruction."[3]

Nelson told the Truman Committee in early 1942 that the nation was on track to meet the ambitious goals Roosevelt had set out after Pearl Harbor. "While we are producing vast amounts of planes and tanks and guns," Truman said in a radio speech in St. Louis in May, "the problem we have now is to move them into the hands of our fighting forces throughout the world. We must have ships and more ships to move this tremendous amount of material. Never before has it been as necessary to build so many ships in so short a space of time."[4]

The hero was—from outside appearances, at least—an unlikely one: a portly, sixty-year-old businessman who at first glance seemed better cast as the kindly grandfather than the cowboy in the white Stetson. And yet, Henry Kaiser makes any list of the handful of people who contributed the most to winning the war on the home front. His early years follow a story arc that mirrors so many of the self-made men who pop up in American history in the late nineteenth and early twentieth centuries. Born of humble origins in upstate New York, he dropped out of school at thirteen and eventually headed west to make his fortune and win the hand of the girl back home.[5] He'd met Bess Fosburgh, the daughter of a wealthy Virginia lumber merchant, while working in a photo studio in Lake Placid, New York. He'd shown an early head for hard work and business and an interest in photography, but by his early twenties had little to show for it. Bess's father, as a condition of the two getting married, urged Kaiser to head west and make something of himself first. In 1906, Kaiser boarded a train for Spokane, Washington.[6]

He found work at a hardware store and quickly made himself indispensable. In less than a year he'd exceeded the demands set by Bess's father, and the two were married and eventually settled down in Spokane. But it was not hardware that would bring him fame and fortune. In Detroit, Henry Ford was turning out Model Ts by the tens of thousands, and selling them at ever-cheaper prices. General Motors and others were catching up, and all these people buying all these cars meant a huge demand for roads to drive them on. Kaiser sensed an opportunity, and in the 1910s he created a successful business paving roads, first to the north in Vancouver and British Columbia, and then, after the outbreak of World War I, in Washington, Oregon, and then California. As his business prospered, Kaiser developed the traits that would be a hallmark of his success in later decades: he embraced technological advances like earth-moving machines and bulldozers—anything that would reduce costs and make the work go faster. He had a driving, workaholic lifestyle and expected his managers to keep up with him. And he developed a knack for scoring government contracts and bringing them in ahead of schedule—all this making him one of the most successful road builders in the United States.[7]

Then came the Great Depression, and the project that would take his work to a much larger—monumental—scale, and spread his fame beyond the West to the whole country. For decades, there had been talk of building a giant dam on the Colorado River that would control the river's flooding, provide irrigation, and generate enough electric power to light up several states. Eventually a site had been selected in Black Canyon, about thirty miles from Las Vegas. The Hoover Dam project would consume 4.3 million cubic yards of concrete, use 45 million pounds of steel, and require several thousand workers, who lived in a city in the desert built just to house them. It was too big even for

Kaiser's ambitions, and eventually he joined a coalition of businesses that became known as the Six Companies. Over the next five years, they and those thousands of workers—more than a hundred of whom would lose their lives in the process—built the massive dam rising up 726 feet out of the desert along the Nevada/Arizona border.

Kaiser's profile had risen, too. He had been the Six Companies' point man in Washington on the project, and there he had developed valuable contacts in Congress and in Franklin Roosevelt's New Deal, contacts that would serve him well as the world crisis deepened and leaders in Washington began to wake up to the threat overseas. In 1940, as the British were desperate for merchant ships, Kaiser and the Six Companies again saw opportunity. The US Maritime Commission worked up a design for a basic cargo ship—extremely basic—about 440 feet long, that could carry about ten thousand tons of cargo. It was a modified version of an older British design. It would be ugly, cheap, simple and quick to build—an "unglamorous 'Model T' so to speak, of the seaways," said Donald Nelson.[8] It would for the most part be made not with rivets, as metal ships had always been made, but with new technologies for welding that could join the metal plates together using much less skilled labor. The ship would use an older, obsolete type of steam engine which was cheaper and easier to build than the newer steam turbines, since those were in great demand elsewhere for other types of ships. Kaiser—who knew nothing about ships or shipbuilding—and his partners came up with a plan for a series of shipyards that would mass-produce these new "Liberty ships."

For starters, he ordered construction to begin on a shipyard in Richmond, California, on the eastern shore of San Francisco Bay, and another one in Portland, Oregon. In a few months, thousands of workers were swarming over the first of the new vessels. Kaiser had developed a passion for finishing projects ahead of schedule, for working out the most efficient ways of bringing workers and materials together, and for identifying talented young managers and "piling work on them." He poured all these traits into the merchant ships and the facilities that built them, and during the war his shipyards produced more than 700 of the more than 2,700 Liberty ships built.[9] Gradually, his obsession with efficiency and competition brought down the amount of time it took to make one from roughly 230 days to, incredibly, about a month.

Henry Kaiser made his first appearance before the Truman Committee on July 31, as the senators explored the question of whether huge airplanes—flying boats—could be mass-produced along the lines of the Liberty ships. The idea never panned out—for one thing, it would divert too much aluminum, too many aircraft engines and other resources from bombers and fighter planes—but it was an example of how Kaiser's stature as an industrial miracle worker had risen to the point where, in the newspapers and popular thinking, it seemed there was nothing he couldn't do if he really put his mind to it. He would be back several times before the committee, answering questions about steel, about shipbuilding, about women in the workforce, and about how to increase productivity and efficiency throughout the economy.

Giant cargo planes were just one of the things competing for the attention of the Truman Committee. In June alone, the committee's files show Fulton and his team pursuing more than twenty active investigations: Herb Maletz was looking into shipbuilding and landing boats; Donald Lathrom was on aviation; Harold Robinson was investigating magnesium, fixed-fee contracts, and ordnance plants; Thomas Flynn was assigned to gas rationing; Wilbur Sparks was poring over plans for antisubmarine boats and examining efforts to salvage and reuse tin and silver; Bob Irvin had landing craft for the navy and housing complaints; Haven Sawyer was examining plans for a low-cost pump that could help cities put out fires in case of bombing attacks, and shortages of copper and zinc; Franklin Parks was looking into helium and a contract for submachine guns. Rudolph Halley, a talented young lawyer from the antitrust division of the Justice Department, joined the Committee on June 16 as executive assistant to Fulton, who assigned him the broad topics of steel, small business, and labor. Peter Ansberry, a graduate of Georgetown University law school who had joined the committee in 1941, was following up on rubber and also beginning an inquiry involving Hollywood, and whether top movie executives had obtained "cellophane commissions"—high-ranking officers' positions despite little or no military training or experience; Marion Toomey was investigating domestic passenger transportation.[10]

Beyond these formal investigations were at any given time dozens of one-offs—inquiries from senators or business leaders or the general public that Fulton and Truman, in their morning meetings, deemed worth a look:

The Eagle Parachute Company
Lancaster
Pennsylvania

Dear Sirs:
Mr. Richard Hart has called the Committee's attention to a parachute which he has developed which he states is considerably better than the standard American parachute Army type, in that it is more steerable. The Committee would appreciate it if you could furnish it with a statement of the opinion of your company as to such parachute.
Very truly yours,
Hugh A. Fulton
General Counsel[11]

Many of these inquiries died out or cleared up after one response; others went away after a phone call to the War Department. Some spun into weeks-long affairs that either turned up real abuse or fraud, or sputtered into nothing after a few initial sparks. At the start, it was impossible to tell. Which is how, in the summer of 1942, the Truman Committee for several weeks found itself tied up, so to speak, in the affairs of Beau Brummell Ties Incorporated of Cincinnati, Ohio, and the "official neck tie" of the US Army Air Forces.

On June 25, the owner of a Kansas City uniform company, Harry Craddock, wrote a personal letter to Truman, enclosing an advertisement "that seems to be about the most unheard of monopoly that it has been the writer's pleasure to see in this good, free America." The advertisement is lost to history, but the letter made clear that the Beau Brummell company was selling an "official Air Forces tie" for the "ridiculous figure of $7.25 per dozen," which would require a retail price of about one dollar, whereas "reasonable profit" would be made if the tie "were wholesaled at $5.00 a dozen and retailed at $9.00 a dozen or 75c each."[12]

This, Mr. Craddock said, was "about the most un-American procedure that I know of," and he urged Truman and Congress to step in and take action. As Truman had apparently met Craddock before, the letter made it all the way to his desk. There, after reading it, the future President of the United States reached for a pen and a pad of bright pink Senate notepaper: "Have Hugh look into this. There is skullduggery some where. HST."[13]

Paper at that time was the lifeblood of Washington, and without its efficient circulation, the city would cease to function. It came in highly evolved shapes and forms and textures, each serving its own, very specific function: letterhead for signed originals, stationery for personal communication, onionskin for file copies, legal pads and steno pads and notepads for, well, notes. The shape or color of a piece of paper alone conveyed vital information regarding its urgency, or importance, or destination. From each desk, each office, each building it flowed, through the veins and arteries of hallways and streets; a rich, nourishing stream of letters, reports, drafts, copies, memos, minutes, and briefs. Some were handwritten, others typed on carbon paper in duplicate or triplicate, or copied on mimeograph, or set in type and printed and bound. Back and forth it went in envelopes and folders and boxes and carts—into inboxes and out through outboxes—gathering along the way stamps and initials and notations and appendages; sometimes coming to rest in the quiet pools of files or drawers, other times reentering the stream, back out into the hallways and up and down floors and outside, to other buildings across the city and back again.

When the system broke down, the consequences could be disastrous, and so there were strict and complex rules that governed the care and handling of paper. "The original correspondence as well as all carbons of answering letters should be attached to outgoing originals," Matt Connelly wrote in one of many such memos to the staff in Room 160. "If an investigator desires to have the correspondence returned it will be routed first to the file clerks who have been instructed to make a charge out slip for the files so that any correspondence may be easily located when inquiries are received by the office."[14]

From Truman's desk, Mr. Craddock's letter entered that stream, flowing back and forth over the next few weeks, gathering more paper as it went along, like a snowball rolling downhill. Its next stop, with Truman's pink note attached with a paper clip, was Hugh Fulton's office in Room 449. There, on July 8, thinking that somehow a Maine company was involved, the chief counsel forwarded a copy to Senator Owen Brewster, with a note: "Evidently your Maine friends are pretty good businessmen. It looks like they have locked up a monopoly of official Air Corps ties." That same day, Shirley Key typed up a reply to Mr. Craddock on Truman Committee letterhead and sent it off to Kansas City, with multiple carbon copies in yellow onion-skin for the files: "Senator Truman was very interested in your letter with respect to the official Air Corps tie, and the Committee has instituted an investigation of the matter. Very truly yours, Hugh A. Fulton, General Counsel." At the same time, Fulton launched another copy downstream to the War Department, where it reached the desk of Julius Amberg, the special assistant to the secretary who'd been designated the army's liaison for congressional relations, and point man on war frauds. Fulton attached a note: "The committee would appreciate being furnished with the facts concerning it." From there, Amberg sent it to an air corps colonel, W.F. Volandt, in the headquarters of the Material Command, who kicked it back the next day, with a response, this time to Lieutenant Colonel Miles Knowles in Amberg's office, who oversaw relations with congressional investigating committees.[15]

The ties, Volandt wrote, "are manufactured from Palm Beach cloth for civilian use only. They are not manufactured under contract to the Army Air Forces." As a matter of fact, he added, "There is no monopoly in the manufacture of this tie and any firm that desires to may obtain permission from the Secretary of War."

This was good enough for Amberg, who forwarded Volandt's note back upstream to Fulton. "I trust this gives you the information you desire."

Fulton, aware that his boss had taken a particular interest in this case, was not quite satisfied. "The memorandum from Colonel Volandt," he wrote back to Amberg on July 17, states that any company that wanted to could make the tie, "but the monopoly as I understand it was based not upon the design of the tie" but the fact that it was made of a certain kind of cloth—"Palm Beach cloth." And so the paper flowed once again, from the Senate Office Building down Constitution Avenue; past the Capitol and down Constitution Avenue to the Munitions Building on the National Mall. Back to Lieutenant Colonel Knowles, whose frustration at having his time wasted is palpable in his response to Fulton on August 15: "In order to answer properly your inquiries I have had to obtain information from several sources which I now pass on to you." The so-called "official tie," it turned out, wasn't really part of the military uniform but rather a simple tan cotton tie with gold-and-blue diagonal stripes for civilian wear. Before the war, Knowles explained, the air corps had decided for morale-building purposes to create an "official" tie that members of the service and their families could wear when they were off duty. "The tie cannot be worn by the Air Corps when in uniform. Neither the tie nor the cloth are manufactured under contract to the Air Corps." The Beau Brummell company had submitted some samples to the procurement office for consideration, and one of those was approved. "No other manufacturer has requested the War Department for similar authority," he noted, and if anyone did, they would probably receive the go-ahead. "If the above information does not cover the entire matter to your satisfaction, would you please advise me?" You can imagine the satisfied grin on Knowles's face, when, after a full two weeks had passed, he received Fulton's one-sentence reply: "Thank you for your letter of August 15 with respect to Beau Brummell Ties, Incorporated. Sincerely yours, Hugh A. Fulton."

The military often resented, and resisted, being called on the carpet by civilians in Congress. Fulton had anticipated this back in January, in one of the most elegant passages of the First Annual Report: "There is a natural tendency on the part of those whose conduct is the subject of scrutiny to suggest that a review of their acts is a waste of time." The committee was aware, he wrote, that "in any war program the ultimate goal is winning the war, and that time taken to prepare information for the committee or to testify before the committee means that there is much less time to devote to other matters." But, "the existence of such a forum during wartime is imperative, and the public as a whole is entitled to know that its money is not being wasted and everyone receives fair and equal treatment."[16] Already, Fulton and Truman could cite examples: $100 million wasted on army camps, for one, or life-threatening delays in acquiring modern combat airplanes for another. They would find many more in the years to come.

Nevertheless, one of the later criticisms of the Truman Committee was that by assigning investigators to chase down every complaint and accusation that arrived in the mail, Fulton and Truman may have "diverted some of the Committee's energies that might better have been devoted to problems of policy and administration."[17] Truman had committed early on, though, to involving the public, and he and Fulton felt the costs were outweighed by the fact that, because of the committee's prying, "public officials constantly have before them the knowledge that their acts or failures to act may be subject to public scrutiny." As the committee's reputation grew, so did the number of times investigators in the early stages of an inquiry found evidence in the files that officials had already taken steps to fix a particular problem out of fear that if they didn't, they could wind up sitting across a table answering questions from United States senators, with newspaper reporters taking notes.[18]

Early on, the investigators had noticed a pattern when dealing with the military: the army was the easiest to pry information from, and the most cooperative in following up. The chief of staff, General George C. Marshall, had a good relationship with Truman, and in mid-1942 assigned a brigadier general, Frank Lowe, to serve full-time with the committee as executive aide, with the aim of cooperating and keeping both sides informed. The navy was the hardest to work with, and the most likely to stonewall. "I always had the belief that the Annapolis grads had a very close-knit club inside the Navy," said Bob Irvin, "and if one made a mistake the others protected him."[19]

Such was the case in mid-1942: while the army brass was rolling its eyes over neckties, but at least responding, Truman and Fulton were fighting toe-to-toe with the navy in an effort to prevent a blunder that could have spelled disaster in some of the most important battles of the war.

9

TANK LIGHTERS

Sooner or later, the Allies were going to have to invade Europe. Which raised another of those central questions of World War II: How could an invasion force of thousands of men, carried across the seas or oceans on large ships along with the vehicles and tanks and artillery and supplies and other equipment they would need to fight with, disembark from those ships and make their way to a beach while under heavy fire from a fortified and well-armed enemy? Much of the Pacific war would hinge on answering this question, and of course the invasion of Hitler's Fortress Europe depended on it, too. A new kind of boat was needed: one that could move over or around reefs and obstacles and through shallow waters to land soldiers and vehicles on, or nearly on, the beach. In the war's early years, all sorts of people in many different Allied countries were working on this problem of landing craft, and here, too, one of those self-made heroes emerged: a flamboyant and hard-driving New Orleans businessman named Andrew Jackson Higgins.

Higgins was born in Nebraska in 1886 and grew up with a love of forestry and boats (from sailing on a lake near his home), and an early talent for entrepreneurship. At age twenty he left Nebraska and moved to Alabama, near Mobile, where he married and went into the lumber business, eventually relocating to New Orleans.[1] As his lumber business grew, it made use of boats for pulling rafts made of logs, and along the way Higgins gradually shifted his main business over to boat building and design. He became an expert in small, specialized boats for work in shallow waters. In the 1930s, he developed a wooden boat for working the swamps and marshes of Louisiana, called the Eureka boat, which became the grandfather of the landing craft that would carry soldiers and equipment ashore on the beaches of Normandy and islands in the Pacific. Higgins was brash, he was loud, he did not suffer fools gladly and, like Henry Kaiser, he had a knack for cutting through production problems to make things faster and cheaper.

While the Eureka boats had been tested and used in the 1930s by the Army Corps of Engineers, the coast guard, and major oil companies in Central and South America, the US Navy had shown little interest in Higgins or his boats. The navy had its own design unit, which had created its own landing craft, and preferred that model despite numerous tests showing it was inferior to the one Higgins had developed. In 1938, he finally secured a trial and shipped a thirty-foot Eureka-based landing craft to Norfolk, Virginia, at his own expense, where it did everything the navy and marine corps asked of it. By 1940, Higgins finally secured a contract for 335 landing boats, as well as a deal to build the fast boats known as "patrol-torpedo," or PT boats, and began expanding into a much larger factory to build them.

The Landing Craft Vehicle Personnel (LCVP), known to the men who went ashore in them simply as "Higgins Boats," would be widely praised by Dwight D. Eisenhower and others as crucial in making the D-Day landings at Normandy a success.[2] Higgins built thousands of them during the war, and yet he had to fight the bureaucracy virtually every step of the way.

And when the navy needed a larger, heavier landing craft, one that could carry a tank ashore, he had to fight that same battle again. This vessel, called a "tank lighter" or LCM (Landing Craft, Mechanized), would have a ramp that could drop down so the tank could drive off onto the beach. Once again, the navy had designed and developed its own tank lighters in the late 1930s and, despite serious flaws, stuck with them. When Higgins learned of the navy's interest, he turned around a prototype in less than three days and showed it to a group of shocked and impressed navy and marine officers in New Orleans.[3] He eventually received a contract to build fifty of them. Soon, though, the navy needed 131 more tank lighters, and then, at an April meeting at the White House, the administration ordered 600 more. Both times Higgins was shut out in favor of the navy's own models. Exasperated and furious, Higgins went to Capitol Hill for help—to Senator Harry Truman. They met in Truman's office, and afterwards, according to Higgins, Truman issued a challenge to the navy: "Produce one of your own boats. Put it in a head-to-head operational test in competition with Higgins' product, and see what happens."[4]

Fulton assigned Bob Irvin and Herbert Maletz to the investigation, and on May 25, both took the train from Washington down to the navy base in Norfolk, Virginia, for the side-by-side comparison between the Higgins design for a fifty-foot tank lighter and one designed and built by the Bureau of Ships. Officials from the navy, the marines, the British Admiralty and the US Army were there to observe, too. Each boat was loaded with a tank weighing thirty tons and set out from Norfolk, headed for the beach at Fort Story a few miles away. In earlier trials, the navy version had been tested only in calm waters. "For the first time since tests were conducted with the Bureau 50' lighter the water was choppy," Maletz reported to Fulton, "wave heights being estimated at 1½ to 2½ feet." For an expert description of what happened next, Maletz relied on a report written by a navy officer, W.E. Howard Jr.:

> Enroute to Fort Story the Bureau tank lighter shipped so much water off Thimble Shoals that it was forced to turn back for fear of foundering. The Higgins tank lighter reached Fort Story successfully and disgorged the 30 ton tank on the beach without difficulty. To put the matter baldly, the Higgins lighter fulfilled its mission under reasonably rough water conditions and the Bureau tank lighter did not.[5]

The navy had backed a design that, in the waters off Normandy on June 6, 1944, would have been disastrous and fatal. Even after this latest test, in closed-door hearings of the Truman Committee on June 8 and 9, navy officials were still insisting their own tank lighters were sound. On hand to testify were a rear admiral who was assistant chief of the Bureau of Ships, two captains in the design division, the chief of the contract design section in the bureau, and several other officials. And there, not for the first or last time during the war, unsuspecting military officers sailed straight into the prosecutorial storm that was the Truman Committee's chief counsel.

"Hugh Fulton just had no fear of high places at all," said Walter Hehmeyer. When questioning a witness, he worked slowly and methodically, building his case step-by-step with a series of small, incremental questions. "If you've got a hostile witness," Fulton explained, "he isn't going to admit to a conclusion unless you've built the conclusion to the point where he *has* to admit it."[6]

"I think he's the greatest on cross-examination of anybody I ever knew," said Harold Robinson, who as an FBI agent had worked with Fulton on cases in New York. "He'll lead you out to the end of a limb and then cut the limb off."[7] In a closed-door, executive hearing on June 8, it was Navy Commander

R.B. Daggett who found himself out on that limb. Fulton questioned him at length about a forty-five-foot model of the Bureau of Ships design that the navy had tested three years earlier and then ordered into production:

Fulton: Did you ever have any report that suggested in any way whatever that the boat was not to the satisfaction of the user?

Daggett: The chief criticism that we have had of that particular model was of the engineering installation. The engines did not seem to stand up in service.

Fulton: From whom was that criticism?

Daggett: Various people in the Forces Afloat that have used them.

Fulton: Do you recall anyone contending that the boat was unstable?

Daggett: I do not recall that.

Fulton: Or that there was danger to equipment or life?

Daggett: I do not recall that.

Fulton: Would you recall that if it had occurred?

Daggett: I think so.

Fulton: Are you the officer who would have knowledge of that?

Daggett: I am.[8]

Among several reports Maletz and Irvin had turned up in their investigation, and which Fulton had in his hands at that moment, was one from September 9, 1941, written by the commanding general of the Marine Corps' Atlantic Amphibious Force. It said the bureau-designed tank lighters "are heavy, slow, difficult to control, difficult to retract from the beach, and equipped with an unpredictable power plant." Another, by a navy officer, said that unless the defects were fixed, the boat had little military value "except on favorable beaches where there was no surf."

And still another, from December 1940, noted that during a test in waters near Culebra, Puerto Rico, one lighter carrying a thirteen-ton tank had capsized. Having carefully set his trap, Fulton lured his prey into it: "As an officer of the Navy, you have made it a matter of record, and in your opinion it is a successful design?"

"It was successful insofar as we went, but the capacity was the thing we were trying to increase."

"It was just a question of how much load it could carry?"

"Yes sir."

"And that is all?"

"Yes sir."[9]

When the hearings resumed the next day, Commander Daggett had a different story to tell. His memory had cleared up overnight, and now he remembered that he *was* aware of the report about the boat that capsized in the Puerto Rico tests. Fulton pounced: you knew of such a report, "and yet you did not refer to it?"

"As you recall, yesterday I arrived rather unexpectedly," the officer explained, "and I did not know what the nature of the meeting was, and I did not have all my thoughts and facts in order, so that I could give a very chronological resumé of their entire development. I knew there was such a report existing."[10]

It wasn't just this hapless officer. Fulton grilled Rear Admiral Claud Ashton Jones, too, asking him a seemingly basic question about a boat the navy had approved for use in combat, and then placed an order for ninety-six of them: "Did you ever put a light tank on that and carry it out to choppy, rough, ocean water?"

"Not to my knowledge."

"Why not?"

"Well, you are getting into the operational end."

"I take it then that you do not even now know the limitations of the 45-foot lighter?"

"No; definitely not."[11]

Fulton drafted a report based on the closed-door hearings and the findings of his investigators, and after conferring with the other senators, Truman sent it to Navy Secretary Frank Knox on August 5. It contained some of the committee's harshest criticism of the military since the army camp investigation: "It is clear that the Bureau of Ships has, for reasons known only to itself, stubbornly persisted for over 5 years in clinging to an un-seaworthy tank lighter design of its own, even after receiving reports from the Armed Forces that the Bureau lighter was of questionable seaworthiness and that the Higgins design was su-perior." This was not only a waste of time, "but has caused the needless expenditure of over $7,000,000 for a total of 225 Bureau lighters which do not meet the needs of the Armed Forces."[12]

Since planning for amphibious landings was a highly guarded military secret, Truman did not make the report public. He of-fered to keep it confidential if, in Knox's judgment, security con-ditions warranted.[13] In his cover letter to Knox, which he did release to reporters, Truman accused officers in the Bureau of Ships of "negligence or willful misconduct," but did not reveal details of the tank lighter itself, or how the unspecified "craft" would be used in combat.

Knox wrote back the next day, taking Truman up on his offer: "I have gone over details in the report and it is my judge-ment that it would not be in the public service at the present time to publish this report and I hope it will be withheld."[14] His request, while conveniently shielding the navy from public embarrassment, also stemmed from genuine security interests: the military was at that time in various stages of planning for several future invasions—in North Africa, in Italy, in France, and in the Pacific—and the information the investigators had gathered about landing boats, their size and number and how they might be used, and their weaknesses and defects, could be valuable to the enemy.

Truman agreed, and Knox ordered his own internal investigation, which—months later—reached many of the same conclusions. It found the Higgins design superior to the bureau lighter, and recommended an overhaul in the management and operational structure of the Bureau of Ships. And it found Higgins had been treated unfairly, though attributing that not to negligence or misconduct, but a "clash of strong personalities and diametrically opposed systems of procedure."[15]

Fulton and Truman viewed that as a whitewash, given the vast amount of evidence they'd gathered detailing what they considered negligent and dangerous conduct. As to "strong personalities," the navy to some degree had a point. Andrew Higgins was the kind of self-made businessman Harry Truman could identify with and admire. He was also the kind of brash, loud self-promoter who rubbed tradition-bound navy bureaucrats the wrong way. Or, as Drew Pearson put it in his "Washington Merry-Go-Round" column on September 22: "Blustering Andy Higgins can be very disagreeable, likes to write insulting letters to admirals, gets on almost everyone's nerves, but is a genius when it comes to small boat design."[16] In describing the controversy, Pearson's column that day went much further—reporting in detail, and quoting directly from, many of the findings in the report Truman had sent Knox. This was one of the rare times during the war that sensitive information gathered in one of the Truman Committee's investigations leaked.

The draft report was kept under lock and key in the committee offices, copies were numbered, and individual senators had to sign them out for review. "And lo and behold it appeared in Drew Pearson's column, and all hell broke loose," said Bob Irvin. "It's kind of a shock for a young guy to be working on something so confidential and pick up the *Washington Post* and there it is."[17] The leak could have come from Room 160, or the Government Printing Office, or one of the senators, or even Knox's office—Irvin never found out.

Truman had mentioned the report in the Senate six days before Pearson's story ran. The tank lighter investigation was one of those times when Truman was willing to let the military sort out its own problems without going public, but when he sensed his committee was being stonewalled, his patience ran out. "Weeks ago the Committee sent a confidential report on tank lighters to the Secretary of Navy," he said. "The committee did expect that in a matter of such importance the Secretary of the Navy would take prompt and effective action. I am sorry to say that so far as the committee can ascertain the Secretary of the Navy has not yet made up his mind what to do.[18] The committee will insist upon action by him." Truman concluded by saying that "the committee will continue its investigations, and so far as possible, will do so privately. It will support every two-fisted fighter who tries to make progress, but it will insist that progress be made."[19]

Whether that insistence came in the form of showing the confidential tank lighter report to an investigative reporter seems unlikely, but Truman's public reference to it may have put Pearson on the trail.

In the end, the investigation into tank lighters was one of the Truman Committee's major contributions to the war. The report itself would not be made public until March 1944, when it was included—with the navy's approval—in the committee's Third Annual Report. Fulton added a new introduction, noting that in the year and a half since Truman sent it to Knox, the mistakes it outlined had been corrected, the Bureau of Ships had been overhauled, and, with the exception of a few already under construction, "no lighters of the Bureau type were manufactured; and that all manufacturers holding contracts for Bureau type lighters were ordered to shift to the Higgins type."

In describing the bureau tank lighter, Marine General Holland Smith, considered the father of modern amphibious warfare in the US, gave it a fitting epitaph: that version, he said, "would have got us nowhere in combat, but killed."[20]

★ ★ ★

It seemed to Margaret Truman that her father "was always on a plane or a train en route to hear testimony at a shipyard or aircraft production plant, an army base or a munitions depot."[21] He was back and forth to Missouri as well, dealing with Senate business and family business and Democratic politics. The long hours on the train offered a welcome bit of down time; a chance to unwind, sit with a book, and watch the miles roll by. On one trip back to Washington in June, with the train chugging east toward Cincinnati, a couple of small children wandered over to his section. One was a yellow-haired girl of about five, and as Truman watched them explore, the girl's mother came by, and struck up a conversation.

"I just heard up in the diner," she said, "that Senator Truman from Missouri is on the train."

"Is that so?" he responded. His enjoyment of the moment lasted only a few minutes, he told Bess in a letter, until "a soldier from Fort Knox came along and called me by name and I felt like a fool."[22]

Truman wasn't the only person surprised and a little bit puzzled by just how quickly he'd become a national celebrity. "A year ago," said *The Washington Post*, "if you'd asked the fellow next door to name the two Senators from Missouri, it's an odds-on bet he'd have said: 'Bennett Clark and some other gent.'" Now the tables were turned, and Harry Truman, "modest affable junior Senator from Missouri" was on top in his home state.[23]

"I'm tired as a dog and having the time of my life," he told a Kansas City reporter.[24] On June 15, he delivered a nationwide speech over the NBC Blue network. "It'll be on KCMO at 8 p.m.," he told Bess. He spoke about the continuing problems of the rubber shortage and the conflict between the needs of the military and the civilian demand for tires. "Your speech was really 'somethin',"" Bess wrote the next day from Independence. "I think it was the best radio speech I have heard you make."

That said, like most of Truman's staff, she was well aware of his shortcomings as a public speaker: "Your radio 'technique' really has improved immensely. In your 'spare time' it really would be a good idea to take a few speech lessons if you are going to be on the radio from now on."[25]

While the tank lighter investigation was playing out, the committee had several other major inquiries in the works. Truman was about to deliver a critical report on the nation's efforts to convert from civilian to wartime production. Once again, the question of dollar-a-year men would come up, this time in connection with one of Donald Nelson's lieutenants at the War Production Board. Donald Reed, on leave from General Electric and his six-figure salary there, had been accused by the committee of moving too slowly on converting to war production. But Nelson refused to get rid of him. And then in late June, the committee scheduled hearings on the massive bomber plant Henry Ford was building at Willow Run, outside Detroit. One of the many big questions looming over the project was where the tens of thousands of people needed to work there would live, and the company's founder, now seventy-eight years old, was resisting efforts to build federally financed housing nearby.

And then, in early July, Truman found himself in the awkward position of having to investigate one of his colleagues in the Senate: Albert Benjamin "Happy" Chandler. The Kentucky Democrat was in a tough re-election battle with a Lexington attorney and former congressman, John Young Brown. In the campaign, the newspapers broke the story that Chandler had a new sixty-foot swimming pool at his home—built for him by a businessman connected with a firm that was supplying building materials to companies that had federal defense contracts.[26]

The issue was all over the Kentucky papers as Chandler squirmed, describing the pool as "a gift" that was built "in the name of friendship and accepted in the same spirit." His opponent charged that the issue was worthy of Senate investigation, and claimed in a letter to Truman that the pool contained four tons of steel, as well as another scarce war material, brass. "No other citizen could have obtained brass," Brown wrote. "Not even the Army can secure it."[27]

Truman wanted nothing to do with this, but since it touched on defense contracts, and there was such a public demand for his committee to investigate, he felt trapped. Fulton told Harold Robinson: "I want you to go to Louisville and investigate Happy Chandler's swimming pool."[28]

Robinson did some quick political calculations and smelled a whitewash: "Senators don't request investigations of other Senators. Democrats don't investigate other Democrats." He looked at Fulton and said, "I don't know what's going on here, Hugh, but there is only one way that I cut this. If I come back from Louisville, you're going to have a report on your desk that tells you all about Happy Chandler's swimming pool. I just want to make sure you want it."

Fulton told Robinson to hold off; he'd get back to him. Over the years, Harry Truman and others have cited the committee's remarkable bipartisanship as evidence that somehow it was immune from, or rose above, politics. But Truman was a politician as much as a civil servant—a veteran of the Pendergast machine and loyal to his party and the administration. And since nobody was "above politics" in Washington, investigating a fellow Senator in the middle of a campaign was a no-win situation.

Fulton called Robinson back the following day: "We're sending Matt Connelly." Connelly was "a much more politically astute type of investigator than I am,"[29] said Robinson. Truman called Connelly himself, laying out the details and saying he'd talked with Kentucky's senior senator, Alben Barkley, who was now the senate majority leader.

"I know that Barkley wants Chandler back in the Senate," Truman said.

Connelly replied, "Oh, one of those."[30]

"Well, you go see Chandler and get his side of it."

On July 7, Connelly left for Kentucky, using the long train ride to come up with a plan. He decided to make his first stop a visit to Chandler's opponent in his law office. Already it was in the papers that Truman was sending an investigator, and when Connelly arrived at Brown's office, there was a full media scrum—reporters and photographers waiting. Brown described his complaint to Connelly, who asked him, "Have you ever seen this swimming pool?" No, Brown said, "but here are pictures of it." They talked for half an hour or so, and finally Connelly asked Brown: "Now, would you sign an affidavit for me?"

Brown said he couldn't—all of his evidence, he said, was hearsay. Which was exactly what Connelly was hoping for: "Thank you very much."

He walked out to the waiting reporters and photographers: "No pictures, no interviews," he said. "I make my report to the committee." He then met with the contractor, Ben Collings, who told him the steel in the pool was "used steel" and not "structural steel." Connelly examined his records, then went out to see the swimming pool, met with Chandler's wife, and "got the whole thing wrapped up."

He returned to Washington and reported to Truman directly. "Well, Barkley is edgy," Truman said. "What are we going to do?" Connelly briefed Truman on his findings and said he could write it up in a report that would clear Chandler. Keeping Truman as far away from the whole business as he could, Connelly suggested that Carl Hatch of New Mexico was just the man to deliver the report on behalf of the committee: "Let me write out a statement for Senator Hatch, the father of the Clean Politics Bill."[31]

Hatch presented the five-page report to the Senate on July 16. It found "no evidence, and Mr. Brown has supplied no evidence, in any way indicating that Senator Chandler interceded with anyone to assist Mr. Collings or his companies to obtain any contracts." Having made that carefully worded statement based on Connelly's selectively managed "investigation," Hatch declared the Truman Committee's role in the matter closed: "All matters affecting elections should properly be referred to the duly constituted committees of the Senate. The jurisdiction of this committee is limited to matters involving the war effort." With that, Barkley rose to thank the committee for "the promptness" and "thoroughness" of its investigation. Chandler easily defeated Brown in the primary, and that, for the most part, was that.[32]

Looking back years later, Connelly summed up his role in the affair: "All it meant was that I put holy water in the swimming pool, but that was what you call politics."[33]

Truman had in many ways shed his "Senator from Pendergast" public image, but in others he was still the same man he'd been as county judge, handing out patronage jobs in the way politics in those days was done. He was also, unlike many of his colleagues in the Senate, not a wealthy man and constantly worried about finances. And so, in July 1941, he had handed out one of those patronage jobs to his wife, putting Bess on his office payroll at $2,400 a year,[34] which was more than some of the staffers on the committee—like Shirley Key—were making. While the practice was not uncommon in Washington, since Truman had set himself up as a fighter of corruption, he worried about publicity.[35] (It would, indeed, come out in the campaign of 1944.)

But they needed the money, and Margaret Truman maintained that her mother actually earned her paycheck: "For all practical purposes, Bess had been working as a member of the staff since 1934." While her father was away on his many trips, she wrote, "Bess stayed in DC, running the office, signing letters, dealing with jobseekers and visiting Missourians." When Truman was planning an inspection trip to Maine in August 1942, Bess wrote to him that "I should be in W[ashington] to help out in the office if possible." In a letter to Bess back in April, however, Truman gives the strong impression that her work was less substantive: "I'm sure glad you went to the office," he wrote. "It's much better for you to go there a few days a week and see what goes on. You don't have to say a word only just drop in and do some signing. It helps all concerned."[36]

On top of the stresses and demands coming from his committee work, there were Truman's other senatorial duties. "Went to three committee meetings," he told Bess, who'd gone back to Independence with Margaret in June. "One of my own on gasoline transportation," another on agriculture, and a third on steel and iron. On top of that he was in a fight over appropriations and had lunch with the undersecretary of the navy. To top it off, when he got back to Connecticut Avenue from his long day as a United States Senator, there was housework to do: "The rug cleaned up fine. Had to iron some tonight—the d—d laundry sent some wet clothes back two pajamas, underwear and some handkerchiefs."

Many of his letters from this time mention how tired he is: "I never was so tired, I don't think," "I was so tired I could hardly sit up." He was considering another trip to the military hospital in Arkansas.[37] The fights in the Senate, the long hours, and coming home late to an empty home were again getting him down. On June 27, he was feeling the blues even worse than usual—tomorrow was his wedding anniversary and his bride was one thousand miles away:

Dear Bess:
Well I doubt if you will remember it but tomorrow is an anniversary of vital importance. Wish I was there to celebrate it. Had expected to be.
    Twenty-three years have been extremely short and for me altogether most happy ones. Thanks to the right kind of a life pardner for me we've come out reasonably well. A failure as a farmer, a miner, an oil promoter, and a merchant but finally hit the groove as a public servant—and that due mostly to you and lady luck. The

lady's best roll of the dice was June 28, 1919. We have the pret-
tiest and sweetest daughter in the world, a reasonably comfortable
living, and the satisfaction of having helped everybody we possibly
could, both in the family and out of it. And my sweetheart is the
same one I've always had—just as good looking and lovable as
when she was sixteen.

Hope the rains quit, it's been coming down in sheets here. Is
there anything I can bring from the apartment that you want,
now's a good time.

Love to you, lots of absentee hugs, Harry.[38]

He sent her roses, and another letter, the next day:

Well this is the day. Lots of water has gone over the dam. There've
been some terrible days and many more nice ones. When my store
went flooy and cost my friends and Frank money, when Margie
came, don't think I ever spent such a day, although the pains were
yours. And to name one more, when we thought Stark had won
and when I lost actually for eastern judge. But the wins have far
outweighed 'em. June 28, 1919, was the happiest day of my life,
for I had been looking forward to it for a lifetime nearly or so it
seemed. When a man gets the right kind of a wife, his career is
made—and I got just that.[39]

Bess wrote back: "Thank you very much for the lovely roses—
all twenty three of them, and for the lovelier letter, which really
arrived when it should have. It always amazes me that you can
write a so-called love letter when you have had so little practice—Anyway it was very nice—especially so coming on one's
twenty-third anniversary. It doesn't seem at all possible it has
been that long but I'm pretty sure it has."[40]

With all the demands in Washington, Truman enjoyed the
chances to get out of town. There were long train trips, often with
time for the small-stakes poker games he loved, good conversation

and, of course, "bourbon and branch water" for refreshment. On one of his swings through St. Louis, he made a strong impression on a young journalist for the *Globe-Democrat*, who was at work one evening when he received an assignment from the city editor: head over to the Jefferson hotel and interview Senator Harry Truman. The reporter walked the few blocks to the hotel, asked the clerk to dial up Truman's room, and was surprised when the senator himself answered the phone and said, come on up.

Truman answered the door in his shirtsleeves, holding a book. He found two glasses, poured some bourbon, and the two men sat down to talk. "We talked, without interruption, for almost an hour. What we talked about, what I later wrote, I have no real recollection of. All I remember is that the book he was reading was Volume III of Douglas Southall Freeman's biography of Robert E. Lee. That the bourbon we drank was Old Crow. That he was completely relaxed and responsible. And that there was no one else around."[41]

10

A CLOSE CALL

Throughout the spring and into the summer of 1942, the letters from the steel man kept coming. "If you ever visit Pittsburgh and have a few spare minutes," George Dye wrote Truman on May 5, "I can convince you that several million dollars can be saved and production increased on several current government contracts."[1]

He wrote eleven times in May alone, and each one brought a polite but noncommittal response back to his mailbox at 2902 Brownsville Road. The frequency of his letters—sometimes one every couple of days—only added to the feeling in Room 160 that they belonged in the crackpot file. That, and the impenetrable jargon: "I overheard Rolf Hammer, general foreman of our shipping dept tell John Elliot, Asst. General Superintendent of Irvin Works, that 400,000# of the rejected Navy plates was loaded 4 to 12 and 12 to 8 turns last night. Mr. Elliot stated the entire 750 tons must be loaded by 8 o'clock Sunday morning. He instructed Hammer to ship 21 turns if necessary, instead of the scheduled 20 turns."[2] Often the letters, filled with language like that, ran on for pages.

Dye was proud of his work and continued to insist that the problems he saw at his job could be fixed. The Irvin Works was one of the biggest, most modern steel mills in the country, and it was playing an important role in the war effort. But more and more he'd seen people there—foremen, bosses, and some of his colleagues—cutting corners on the strength tests on the steel plates they produced.

When Dye tried to argue for changes in the inspection process, his superiors shut him down, telling him, essentially: Nobody has complained, so what's the problem? He'd even written to the president of Carnegie-Illinois Steel, Lester Perry, pointing out problems and offering to help solve them, but that went nowhere, too. By late June, he'd written some fifteen letters to Washington, and at times he sensed that here, too, no one was paying attention. "Hope I have not attached too much importance to this matter and made nuisance of self by frequent communication."[3]

Yet deep down, he knew this really *was* important—how much more steel could be produced, how much better and safer that steel could be, and how much money could be saved. Writing letters, he decided, wasn't enough.

July 2, 1942

Harry S. Truman
Attention Hugh A. Fulton

Dear Sir,
I expect to be in Washington Monday and Tuesday July 6th and 7th.
Will appreciate it if meeting can be arranged on one of those days.
I shall call Mr. Fulton Monday A.M.
George E. Dye[4]

Though Fulton was in the midst of the tank lighter investigation, prepping for hearings on defense housing in Detroit, and a hundred other things, he found time to meet with Dye on Tuesday, July 6. Afterwards, Fulton jotted down his thoughts in a memo to Rudolph Halley: "He showed me a number of orders which indicated that that plant is delivering sheared plate steel on orders with what he termed a very large margin of tolerance with the result [that] the plate before being used would have to be sheared to closer tolerances by the fabricator."[5]

Fulton told Halley he had written to Carnegie-Illinois and to an official at the WPB asking them to look into Dye's claims. "I am also attaching a memorandum which Mr. Dye made for Senator Truman," as well as several letters that were to be returned to Dye in Pittsburgh.

In his letter, Fulton informed Dye's employer that "a complaint has been made to the Committee" about production practices and loose inspection tolerances, and asked the company to look into it.[6] There the matter seems to have died, at least for the time being. It's unclear whether Fulton received a response to this letter or to the one he sent the WPB; if so, there is no indication in the committee's files. Dye sent another long, extremely dense letter to Fulton on July 15, noting that it wasn't just the Irvin Works alone—other steel mills and other companies, he said, were bragging about setting production records that were accomplished by cutting corners on inspections and tolerances. If no one was willing to listen, he was ready to take drastic action: "I believe this can be corrected by quiet criticism but if necessary I shall return to Washington with all the evidence I can gather—and resign before the mill has an opportunity to discharge me."[7]

Around the world, news from the war fronts was not the daily stream of disaster, defeat and surrender that it had been in the first part of 1942. But the United States and its allies remained on the defensive in every theater of the war. In North Africa, the British had retreated east into Egypt, and in July were struggling to hold off a German attack near El Alamein. In the Atlantic Ocean, sinkings by U-boats reached a new high in May and June. In the Soviet Union, the German invasion in 1941 had failed to gain complete victory, but the Nazi armies still held the upper hand and controlled vast chunks of Russia, Ukraine, and Belarus. Hitler planned a summer offensive that would push toward the Soviet city of Stalingrad. In China, disarray, infighting and a chronic shortage of resources hindered Chinese, British, and American efforts to turn back the Japanese. And while in the central Pacific, the US Navy had defeated the Japanese in a major battle near Midway Island in June (a direct result of the Japanese failure to destroy the US aircraft carriers on December 7), the Japanese continued to push forward in the South Pacific. In August, the Allies launched their first attempt to halt that advance when US Marines landed in the Solomon Islands, northeast of Australia. A bloody land and sea battle began that went back and forth for several months, and made a faraway place called Guadalcanal a familiar name back home.

The Senate had been in nearly continuous session since Pearl Harbor, and no one on the committee staff really took vacations.[8] July was consumed with tank lighters, the Beau Brummell affair, steel, hearings on defense housing, and Happy Chandler's swimming pool. Truman was planning a trip to Missouri for a few days over the Fourth of July, but this would be a working trip. "It's like getting out of jail," he told Bess, "but I expect to get into the penitentiary by comparison when I get home. It'll be a change of scenery anyway."[9]

Margaret had graduated from high school and was headed to George Washington University in the fall. Truman absolutely doted on Margie. She sent him recommendations for records to listen to and movies to see; he sent her novels—in one case a couple of detective thrillers he'd just finished: "one of 'em has a murder in every chapter."[10] And, of course, fatherly advice:

You're now a young lady eighteen years old and you are respon-
sible from now on for what Margie does. Your very excellent and
efficient mother has done her duty for eighteen very short and very
happy (to me) years. Your dad has looked on and has been satis-
fied with the result.

You have a good mind, a beautiful physique and a possible suc-
cessful future outlook—but that now is up to you. From a finan-
cial standpoint your father has not been a shining success but he
has tried to leave you something that (as Mr. Shakespeare says)
cannot be stolen—an honorable reputation and a good name. You
must continue that heritage and see that it is not spoiled. You're
all we have and we both count on you.[11]

In late July, Truman's stomach was bothering him again, and so
was the social life in Washington: "Too much society to suit me,"
he complained to Bess after declining a dinner party invitation.
"Maybe I'm nutty but I can't see anything to those people but a
bunch of drunks and parasites, most of whom would be better
off in some institution. And they are not conferring any favor on
me by asking me out as one of the animals for display purposes."[12]

Hugh Fulton invited him to spend a weekend at his farm in
Flemington, New Jersey, in early August, but Truman begged
off—his mother was ailing back in Missouri, and he might need
to go out there at any moment. "I told him I had to stay close
to a phone and a plane." Fulton, too, found relief from the long
hours in domestic life and his marriage, and tried to preserve
the weekends for his wife. Jessie Fulton, like Bess Truman, cared
little for the Washington social scene, and though she'd made
a comfortable home in their apartment on 16th Street, she was
much happier away from the city. The original farmhouse had
burned down in 1937 or '38, and as a present to his wife, Fulton
used the foundation of that house to make a swimming pool.

He and Jessie were enjoying their new home on the seventy-
seven acres there and frequently entertained friends and colleagues from Washington. Shirley Key, Walter Hehmeyer,

Marion Toomey and others went up for a weekend there in August—enjoying the quiet, the countryside, and the fact that Fulton was as talented in the kitchen as he was in the court-room. "Almost his only relaxation is cooking," wrote the jour-nalist Marquis Childs. On weekends at the farm with a houseful of guests, Fulton "has been known to turn out as many as six apple pies in a morning."[13]

Marion Toomey, left, and Shirley Key at the Fultons' farm in Flemington, New Jersey, August 1942.

The important work, the long hours, and the sense of being part of history had forged the young staffers into a close-knit group. A birthday or anniversary was cause enough to close the office in the afternoon for a party. Someone would pick up a case of Coke and a cake with candles to celebrate. Truman liked to wander down for these events; he'd shake hands and say a few words about the honored guest. For the staffers, this was a big deal; most of them admired and liked him and the work they were doing, and he had the knack of using these small moments to make the people working for him feel valued.[14]

Sometimes, though, with all the committee's success, it seemed to Truman like every move he made was being watched. In late July he unloaded these worries in a private letter to Lewis Schwellenbach, a Senate colleague and friend from his first term who was now a federal judge in Washington State: "We are in a much more delicate position now, so far as the reputation of the Committee is concerned. We have created a feeling of confidence, both in the Senate and with the public, that we must make every effort to maintain. One bad tactical error, political or otherwise, can ruin the whole structure more easily now than it could have done when we were first starting." He touched on that same theme with Bess three weeks later: "I am more surprised every day at the respect with which the special committee is regarded by people in high places. If I can just keep from making any real errors we are on the way to help win the war and to make the job more efficient and quicker."[15]

At that moment, the Truman Committee was very close to making just such an error, and the slipup came from the chairman himself. The first hint of it came in a letter to Bess on August 8, when Truman mentioned that *The American* magazine "is preparing an article on me and the committee for publication on October 6th." Truman was interviewed in his office on August 23, and he talked openly and frankly about the waste, mismanagement, corruption, lack of leadership, and military bungling he'd seen in more than a year of investigating the defense effort.

Over time, though, the idea for the piece changed: the reporter would ghostwrite the story, and it would appear in the magazine under Truman's name as author. The problem was that Truman had during the interview come dangerously close to outright criticism of Franklin Roosevelt. As historian Alonzo Hamby put it, the reporter had "caught him in a mood of anger

at the fumbling of the rubber situation and the widespread disarray in defense production."[16]

All of which should not have been a problem, since Fulton
and Walter Hehmeyer had signed off on the idea with the clear
understanding that the article would be thoroughly reviewed
by one or both of them before it ever went to press. But a few
days later, it was Truman who was asked to review the draft,
in the middle of a busy day. Since he was told it contained only
his own words, he signed off on the piece, writing his signature
across the top. Without reading it.

Fulton and Hehmeyer, meanwhile, had seen a draft and
had made extensive revisions, careful to remove anything that
smacked of criticism of Roosevelt. But whether the revised version wasn't the same one Truman approved, or, as Margaret
thought, her father had been the victim of a "literary double
cross," it was not that edited version that appeared in the magazine's galleys in late September, ready for publication. ("We
never did figure out that mix-up," said Hehmeyer.[17])

With crucial midterm elections just a month away, an article
was about to appear under Harry Truman's name, highly critical of the Roosevelt administration's handling of the war effort.[18]
Even though it contained his own words, Truman ordered Fulton
to do anything he could to stop it. "I don't want Hugh to leave
any stone unturned to head off that American Magazine article," he wrote Bess from a St. Louis hotel. "The more I think the
worse it gets from a political angle. I was feeling hostile over the
rubber thing and went off half-prepared—and it doesn't pay."[19]

Fulton and Hehmeyer rushed to New York, where Fulton
sought an injunction in federal court to prohibit the magazine
from publishing. The problem, of course, was that they had no
real justification for doing so. At a court hearing, "the attorney
for the publishers held up the manuscript and it had Senator
Truman's name on it." Fulton, embarrassed for once in court,
realized there was nothing he could do.

And then, Truman caught a break: during an adjournment,

Fulton and Hehmeyer left the courtroom to look over the latest version of the article they'd been given, a final version ready for the presses. Both men were stunned to find that the worst passages—the ones most critical of Roosevelt—were gone. It turned out that the article had been too long, someone at the last minute had made some cuts, and incredibly it was those passages that had been taken out. On the train back to DC, Hehmeyer turned to Fulton and said, "Hugh, this guy Harry Truman has got to be the luckiest human being in the world."[20]

The article appeared on newsstands the first week of October, with the headline "We Can Lose The War In Washington." Though it could have been much worse, it was still a frank and blunt assessment of the production effort, containing many of the points that Truman had been making for months, and details taken right from the committee's reports. "They did cut out the bad paragraphs," Truman told Bess, "and maybe it won't hurt anything."[21]

The piece condemned the "red tape and bureaucratic waste" of the Washington bureaucracy, and the "military old-fogyism" and "fear of new ideas" among admirals and generals. And so on. Truman went off on big business, too, and of course the dollar-a-year men. And then, in one passage, he came pretty close to suggesting that the problems went all the way to the top: "Leadership is what we Americans are crying for. We aren't complacent. We are by no means downcast. We are fighting mad, and ready to tackle any job and to make any sacrifice that will contribute to the defeat of our Axis enemies. All we ask is that we be intelligently and resolutely led."

Hehmeyer believed Truman had dodged a bullet. But Truman and others felt otherwise. Coming so close to the midterm elections that had gone badly for the Democrats, the article left Roosevelt so angry with Truman that "he cut off all relations with him," according to Senator Harley Kilgore. It was several months before Truman felt any warmth coming from the White House.[22]

11

NEWLYWEDS

November 11, 1942

Veterans Day. As George Dye walked his rounds through the long plant—it was warm inside despite the fall chill as the massive, glowing plates of orange-hot steel moved down the line—one of the foremen waved him over. He had some papers in his hand and showed Dye a list of eighteen plates that showed "laminations." This was one of the worst defects a steel plate could have, when imperfections cause layers within the plate to separate, or laminate, as the steel is progressively rolled into thinner and flatter shapes. The foreman told Dye that he'd been instructed to throw out the tests for those plates and substitute "ringers"—good results that were taken from different plates. Thirteen of these laminated plates, he said, were on their way to a shipyard in Los Angeles.[1]

These days, this kind of thing was happening all the time. It wasn't even the only time that week. When Dye himself had rejected several plates for laminations, his boss, D.M. Evans, told him to knock it off. With a weak attempt at humor, Evans said that when making his inspections Dye should "keep one eye closed and the other for reading the comics." Dye had complained so much that Evans began ridiculing him in front of his inspectors, calling him "Lamination Dye."[2]

The Irvin Works is what's called a continuous strip mill. It didn't actually make steel—instead, it got big slabs of steel that were made in the furnaces at other mills. It heated them up again to glowing hot in a giant furnace at one end, and then, as they moved down the long continuous line, giant machines rolled and shaped and sheared them into plates that were, ultimately, the size and thickness needed by their customers. The mill was fairly new—the $60 million facility had opened in December 1938, with the local papers touting it as the finest of its kind in the world and one of the largest—fifty acres under a single roof. US Steel, which owned Carnegie-Illinois Steel, liked to brag that more than 4.4 million cubic yards of earth had been moved to carve the plant out of a hill above the Monongahela River—a feat "second only to the Panama Canal." Special trains brought thousands of visitors to the dedication ceremonies for a tour.[3]

The Irvin Works had been designed for making sheet metal for automobile production, and like other mills of its type had now joined the war effort, switching to the manufacture of heavy steel plates for use in ship construction. This created some challenges, notably in the lack of space for allowing the huge plates to cool off. There was no room for additional stacking space for air-cooling, or to quench and cool the plates by other means.[4] All of which made the various means of testing and inspecting even more important.

Each of the giant slabs was marked and coded when it arrived, and checkers noted down the numbers, testing and measuring as it moved down the line. At the end, small bits known as "coupons" were cut off the plates for strength testing. These six-inch coupons—shaped kind of like a dumbbell—were fed into a tensile testing machine, which, basically, pulled the pieces apart and measured how much strength it took to do that.

But every day, George Dye saw the culture of cheating on these and other inspections getting worse. He heard guys joking about it. At night, he unloaded his worries on Alice, and again and again in his letters to Truman. When he sat down on Saturday, November 14, in the house on Brownsville Road to write another one, the frustrations came pouring out: "If you decide to investigate, I can put the finger on the culprits and direct you to testers and foremen who will give you the information necessary to substantiate my charges."[5]

Things were getting so bad that Dye was thinking of quitting Carnegie-Illinois and finding another job. His boss was no help. The chief metallurgist, W.F. McGarrity, tried to keep things honest, but there was no way he could properly inspect all the steel they were moving—really inspect it—within the current budget and the pressures from above. The mill had been gaining all kinds of attention for setting production records; just a few weeks ago, Dye read with disgust a story in the paper: "More than enough steel plates for 35 new Liberty Ships rolled off the stands last month at the Irvin Works. The August production record exceeded that of any other plant in the industry." He'd written to Truman about it: "It is not my intention to belittle real accomplishment, but all the glittering figures are not 24 carat and I am bringing these facts to your attention so you will not be confused by published claims of record production."[6]

Dye watched his once-robust crew shrink as inspectors were assigned away to clerical duties. Sometimes, plates headed to the navy, or the British, or the Kaiser shipyards on the West Coast were barely inspected at all. Once in a while, one of the navy officials assigned to the plant would spot something. A few months ago, one tester had been transferred when the navy caught him

cheating. But that was an exception. Dye knew there were good
people working here; he was proud of his work and of the mill's
genuine accomplishments thanks to its modern equipment and
good workers. If given the chance, he could help turn this place
around: "In one week we can organize a department that will
prevent shipment of death trap materials."[7]

In addition to his correspondence with Truman, Dye had
also tried going over the heads of his bosses: he'd now written
several times to J. Lester Perry, the president of the company.
But nothing seemed to work. Just a few days ago, he'd complained—again—to McGarrity, who'd told him: okay, go ahead
and reject bad plates. But Dye heard later that in a meeting with
higher-ups, McGarrity had "gotten his ears beat back when he
brought the subject up." Dye was, once again, told to back off.[8]

All this was on his mind Saturday as he put his latest letter
in an envelope and addressed it to Washington. But here, too,
Dye felt a growing sense of unease. His early letters to Truman
had gotten a good response, especially after his meeting with
Hugh Fulton in July, but lately they seemed to disappear down a
well. When he did get a response, it was only a sentence or two.

That same Saturday, November 14, the Pittsburgh papers carried a story from one of Henry Kaiser's shipyards out West.
Workers at his Richmond Number 2 yard had done something
incredible: they had laid down the keel of a 441-foot Liberty ship
on the previous Sunday, and launched the hull into the water
on Thursday the 12th—just *four and a half days* later. Sure, it was
a publicity stunt—the feat would not be repeated throughout
the war, and the ship was hardly finished at that stage—but it
was more than that, too. Kaiser, who at the start of World War
II had no prior experience building ships, had shown that it
could be done faster and in greater quantities than anyone had
ever imagined.[9] It was his hope and intention, and those of the
Roosevelt Administration, that stories about these production
miracles would find their way to Berlin, and Tokyo.

★ ★ ★

As the grim anniversary of Pearl Harbor and the end of 1942 approached, it was a time of transition for the Truman Committee. On October 31, Charles Clark, one of its first employees, resigned to be inducted into the army; Investigator Herbert Maletz left for the army two weeks later. On November 1, Fulton handed out raises and some promotions: Shirley Key got a bump, from $2,000 to $2,200 a year. So did Bob Irvin and Wilbur Sparks, to $2,400.[10]

Walter Hehmeyer's pay went from $3,200 a year to $3,800, as he took on new responsibilities over managing the mail and requests for investigations. More and more, the committee was hearing from inventors, or would-be inventors, who were dissatisfied with their response from the navy or army or the National Inventors' Council and wanted a second or third or fourth opinion. These would now be routed to Hehmeyer: "90% of these complaints represent 'crack pots' and persons with obsession complexes," Fulton told the staff. "However, each complaint is handled in the hope that an invention of good military value will be brought forcibly to the attention of the proper parties." Hehmeyer was also handling an investigation of aircraft gun turrets made by a St. Louis company. And, of course, "contacts with press officials, press releases and the primary jurisdiction of these press matters are under the jurisdiction of Mr. Hehmeyer."

Peter Ansberry, whose raise brought him up to $3,200 a year, had recently begun asking questions about Hollywood and government contracts for the making of training and propaganda films—the beginnings of an investigation that would blow up onto the front pages in 1943. Fulton, probably with Truman's blessing, requested that his own salary increase to $10,000, but learned a few days later that this was not allowed: senators at the time made $10,000, and the highest salary allowed for a congressional investigator was $9,000—what he was already making.[11]

Marion Toomey got a $200 raise—to $2,600—and a promotion: from "stenographer" to "investigator."

Christmas this year would be a somber one, with millions of Americans in uniform and in harm's way. United States soldiers, sailors, marines, and airmen were fighting in North Africa, in Alaska, in the Central and South Pacific, in New Guinea and in China, in the skies over Europe and on the treacherous seas of the North Atlantic. The battle over Guadalcanal in the Solomon Islands was in its fifth month, with heavy losses and no end in sight. Once again there would be no lights on the big Christmas tree on the White House lawn, and in his holiday message, the closest thing to optimism that Franklin Roosevelt could summon was that "the forces of darkness stand against us with less confidence in the success of their evil ways." With so many people away from their homes and loved ones, a song written by a Russian Jewish immigrant, Irving Berlin, and mournfully sung by Bing Crosby, seemed to capture the national mood perfectly. "White Christmas" was well on its way to becoming one of the most popular recordings of all time.

In Room 160, Wilbur Sparks was looking forward to a quick trip home to Missouri, to spend the holiday with his family and his girlfriend, Elizabeth Hartley. It would be his first visit since leaving to join the committee the previous fall. He and Ibbianne, as everyone called her, were talking about getting married, and he'd sent photographs to her of the apartment on E Street in Northwest Washington where he hoped they'd live someday. He arrived in his hometown of Savannah on December 20, and like many Americans caught up in the uncertainty of the times, the couple decided on impulse to get married right away. They took out a marriage license on Christmas Eve, and Sparks sent a telegram back to Hugh Fulton in Washington: "Sorry, but weekend honeymoon now pending makes my being at work before Wednesday morning impossible."[12]

The wedding took place in the home of Ibbianne's parents

at eight o'clock on Christmas night. Among those crowded into the living room were Wilbur's mother, Lillian Sparks, and his father, Grover Cleveland Sparks, who for decades had been a prominent figure in Northwest Missouri legal and political circles. The newlyweds enjoyed a two-day honeymoon before Wilbur boarded a train back to Washington, leaving Ibbianne behind to pack up and settle her affairs in Missouri. He was still on the eastbound train on Tuesday the 29th when a conductor found him with a telegram. Sparks, still wrapped in the warm glow of Christmas with his family, and the unexpected thrill of his wedding and his honeymoon, read the shocking news that his father had died the previous night while attending a meeting. He got off at the next stop and headed back home.[13] Hugh Fulton sent a telegram from Washington: "EVERYONE HERE EXTENDS SINCERE CONDOLENCES AND SYMPATHY AND OF COURSE YOU ARE NOT EXPECTED TO RETURN UNTIL AFTER YOU HAVE DONE WHAT IS NECESSARY."

In the year since Pearl Harbor, the Truman Committee had grown from a shoestring operation into a powerful investigating force with fifteen investigators and fifteen stenographers. Truman had done this with, so far, just $200,000 from Congress, and many of the employees were still on the payrolls of other agencies.

The release of two new reports in December—on gasoline rationing and lumber—brought the total to fourteen.[14] By now, some observers were beginning to notice a curious thing about them. *Business Week* said it outright: the Truman Committee "has never issued a minority report, something unique in the annals of long-standing committees handling controversial war matters."[15] The bipartisanship, along with Truman's efforts to keep politics whenever possible out of the work, was one source of the committee's status with the press and with the public. Another was the extreme effort Hugh Fulton made to get the facts right, and his innovation of allowing affected parties to review the drafts and suggest corrections or changes. All this created the impression that the Truman Committee was largely free of the hype and grandstanding typical of these investigations.[16]

Its reputation had spread, too, throughout government agencies and the defense industries. *Business Week* observed that the committee had now become a deterrent to waste and corruption, just by the fact of its existence: often, "a threat to 'take everything to the Truman Committee' is sufficient to force a cure of abuses." In the vastness of the war production effort, Truman told a reporter, "We can only stick a pin in here and there. But nobody knows where the pin is going to strike, and that keeps everyone on the alert."[17]

Reporters noted, too, that while Truman certainly enjoyed his new stature in the Senate, and being recognized on the train or in a restaurant, he remained in many ways the same plainspoken man who had sat quietly at his desk in his first term. "He was not florid or promiscuous," wrote historian David McCullough. "He made no pretense at being superior in any regard. He did not seem to need the limelight, flattery, or a following. He did not want to be President."[18]

12

TURNING POINT

As 1943 began, there were signs that the tide was beginning to turn, but in Europe, the Atlantic, and the Pacific, the battle had not yet been won, and victory was far from certain. In November, after more than two years of back-and-forth fighting across northern Africa, the British had won a major battle over the Germans in the Egyptian desert at El Alamein. Winston Churchill, in bringing news of the victory to the British people, had in his unique fashion captured the broader outlook as the war entered its fourth year: "Now this is not the end, it is not even the beginning of the end. But it is, perhaps, the end of the beginning."

Franklin Roosevelt, looking west to the fight against the Japanese, struck a similar tone in his State of the Union address in January: "The period of our defensive attrition in the Pacific is drawing to a close. Now the aim is to force the Japanese to fight. Last year we stopped them. This year, we intend to advance." On the home front, the picture was much the same.

The US economy was on its way to becoming the production juggernaut that would eventually prove decisive. But it wasn't there yet, and a lot of very real problems remained. A year earlier, Roosevelt had set what looked like ridiculous goals for the production of airplanes, tanks, ships, and weapons of all kinds. And while many of those goals had not been met, or were revised downward, the accomplishments—by the standards of 1940 or even 1941—were staggering. A nation that in 1940 had produced 3,611 military airplanes, Roosevelt said in his speech, had in 1942 made 48,000: "more than the airplane production of Germany, Italy, and Japan put together. Last month, in December, we produced 5,500 military planes and the rate is rapidly rising." US workers and businesses had made 56,000 combat vehicles, 670,000 machine guns, 181 million artillery shells, and more than 10 billion rounds of small-arms ammunition. "I think the arsenal of democracy is making good."

But there were still problems, and Roosevelt was forced to acknowledge them: "We all know that there have been mistakes." Mistakes which he laid not to his administration's handling of things, but to the "inevitable process of trial and error inherent in doing big things for the first time." Among them were too many questionnaires, too much paperwork, too much bureaucracy, and while he promised to try to keep that to a minimum, "we do not intend to leave things so lax that loopholes will be left for cheaters, for chiselers, or for the manipulators of the black market."

Sitting in the Capitol as Roosevelt spoke, Senator Harry Truman was ready to do his part. Hugh Fulton would soon begin drafting the committee's Second Annual Report. "The committee is convinced that the year ahead will be the toughest and grimmest in our Nation's history," he wrote. "If we are to do the job we have set out for ourselves and cut down the loss of life in this war, this year will demand harder work, longer hours, greater sacrifices and more single-minded devotion from every American."[1]

In its watchdog role over production on the home front, the Truman Committee had to walk the same careful line as Roosevelt: pointing out the flaws and waste and mismanagement, without overlooking the genuine accomplishments made in such a short time. "While the tone of this report is critical," the report said, "the committee does not disparage what has been accomplished. War material of almost every description is now rolling off the production lines at rates which the committee is confident have not been and cannot be equaled by our enemies." Nevertheless, those accomplishments could have been greater if "the weaknesses and mistakes which have slowed our war effort during the past year" had been fixed.

The Truman Committee for two years had taken on powerful forces in business and the military who were responsible for those "weaknesses and mistakes," and emerged with hardly a bruise or scratch. In 1943, those forces, in corporate boardrooms and the War Department, would start punching back.[2]

On January 25, the Senate re-upped the committee's funding for an additional two years. The departure from the Senate of Clyde Herring of Iowa created a vacancy on the committee, filled by Homer Ferguson of Michigan three days later. In addition to preparing the Second Annual Report, Fulton and the staff were juggling several investigations.

Some were of the mundane-but-important variety, like barges—a seemingly dull topic that the committee had been looking into since the spring of 1942. But it turned out that many of the nation's fuel shortages stemmed not from a lack of petroleum but from a lack of barges to transport it. On the East Coast and around to the Gulf of Mexico and Texas, barges were desperately needed. The two options available were to convert existing barges that were originally intended for non-liquid cargos, or to build new ones made specifically for oil. Both efforts quickly ran into trouble. The government was taking forever to award contracts for converting old barges, and that program needed steel, which forced it to compete with countless other priorities. New barges required lumber and diesel engines, both of which were also in short supply. In both cases, the navy argued that the materials needed for barges interfered with other, more urgent requirements. All of which resulted in a snowstorm of paper flowing back and forth across Washington, but little real progress. "There has been unnecessary delay and confusion in carrying out a program essential to the national welfare," the committee's January 14 report on barges concluded. A week later, another dense report on farm machinery sought to untangle a similar bureaucratic knot in the production of agricultural equipment.

Other, more high-profile investigations were still months away from completion. Peter Ansberry was still poking around into complaints about training films, and questions about high-paid Hollywood executives who had gone into the military. And in February, the committee headed to Michigan to visit a place that had become a national symbol for the sheer industrial might that would shift the balance of power: Willow Run.

The giant bomber plant that Henry Ford began building outside Detroit in 1940 had immediately grabbed the public's imagination: it would be one of the biggest factories in the world under one roof, and it would produce one of the largest, most powerful airplanes in the world. And in the public's eye, it was linked with the larger-than-life mystique of Henry Ford. Now in his late seventies, Ford had built more than 15 million Model Ts and changed the American landscape in his obsession to make automobiles available and affordable for regular people, and he had become a folk hero around the world in 1914 with his announcement that he would pay workers the unbelievable sum of up to five dollars a day.

In recent years, though, both the Ford Motor Company and its famous founder had lost their edge. Ford's authoritarianism as he grew old and his bigotry had made him a dark force in the company he had built, and in the national psyche. In the 1920s, he published a newspaper, *The Dearborn Independent*, distributed nationally through his dealerships, that served as a mouthpiece for his anti-Semitic beliefs and conspiracy theories. And though he had turned over the presidency of the company to his only son and heir, Edsel, in 1919, he refused to give up control and resisted the younger Ford's attempts to modernize. Once an innovator, Ford clung to the Model T long after the design was obsolete, and he fought with violence efforts to allow labor unions into his factories, until he was forced to do so. By the 1940s, the company had long ago lost its place to General Motors as the nation's number one automaker. Edsel was now in his late forties and in poor health, and father and son were often barely on speaking terms. In a standoff between two of the richest men in the world, one sought to pull the company into the future, while the other fought hard to keep it rooted in the past.

Willow Run was in many ways the vision of Edsel Ford. It promised airplane production on a monumental scale, with an assembly line *one mile long* that would, Ford executives promised, turn out bombers by the thousands the way Model Ts had rolled off the line a quarter century earlier. The idea behind it was both monumental and simple: take the mass-production techniques Henry Ford had pioneered with automobiles—reducing costs and production time for a single car from thousands of dollars and several days, to just a few hundred dollars and about an hour and a half[3]—and apply those techniques to airplanes.

Not just any airplanes, but the army's most powerful bomber, the four-engine B-24 Liberator. Airplanes were, of course, vastly more complicated machines, and required a very different set of production skills and techniques. The aircraft industry still relied heavily on skilled labor and the hand-fitting of many parts and components. Aviation experts said mass-production principles wouldn't work for machines so complex. But Edsel Ford and his top engineers, after visiting the West Coast plant where the B-24 was made in January 1941, believed they could do it. They began drawing up plans for a huge plant, along with an airport and runways to fly the bombers in and out, on farmland Ford owned near Ypsilanti, about twenty-five miles west of Detroit. It would have under one roof a moving assembly line big enough and modern enough to produce B-24s at the rate of one bomber every hour.[4]

That was the plan, anyway. The newspapers, taken with the sheer scale of the project and the idea of the aging genius working his production magic once again—had closely followed Willow Run's progress. But so far, they had not had much progress to report: the plant was struggling—not just to meet the ambitious goals Ford's engineers had set for it, but to produce any bombers at all. By early 1943—nearly two years after construction began—the plant had delivered fewer than one hundred planes.[5] Among the many problems was the basic challenge of finding enough workers to staff it. Competition for war workers in Detroit was fierce as enlistments and the draft and "resignations for various reasons" were siphoning off the labor supply.[6] At Willow Run, tops on the list of "various reasons" was the lack of housing near the plant and the difficulty for those who lived farther away to get to work. From Detroit, it was a fifty-mile round trip, and while a highway project had been rushed through to make access easier, with gas rationed and tires scarce, it was a challenge for the plant's thirty thousand employees to make the commute.

There were other problems, too. Aluminum was not steel, and Ford's engineers had shown a reluctance to learn the different techniques that had developed for manufacturing with aluminum in the aircraft industry. And then there were the demands for modifications and changes to the plane's design. This was a problem not just at Willow Run but throughout the production effort, as the army responded to feedback coming back from the combat zones. Not just a few changes but dozens and

hundreds, as production ground to a halt while the modifications were made. The end result, according to the Office of War
Information, was that Willow Run by early 1943 was producing "only a small fraction of its ultimate potential." Truman's
colleague Mon Wallgren put it more bluntly: "apparently there
has been no production to amount to anything."[7]

The problems were so bad that the press had begun calling
it "Willit Run?" In January, Truman and Fulton began an investigation that would include a trip to Detroit, but first they
assigned Matt Connelly to a fact-finding mission. Posing as a
company vice president, Connelly quietly went undercover at
Willow Run in January with the cooperation of Ford executives, and was able to brief the committee members and the staff
in advance of their visit. On February 17, Fulton and Senator
Homer Ferguson of Michigan, the committee's newest member,
arrived at Detroit's Michigan Central Station and checked into
the Statler Hotel.[8] Truman was there as well, along with Wallgren. "We have received a great number of complaints about
this plant," Truman told the local press. "They would fill a large
file. However, we have no preconceived idea about the place.
This is purely a fact-finding investigation."[9]

The next day, the delegation met with Edsel Ford over breakfast at the Statler. He outlined the manpower situation, then
showed them a three-foot-high stack of blueprints: changes
to the B-24's design demanded by the government. Edsel and
other executives explained in detail how these changes forced
everything to halt while blueprints were drawn up, new parts
designed, new machines built, new production techniques developed, and workers trained to apply them. Then the delegation headed out to Willow Run.

Hugh Fulton had reached out to an old friend from law
school, George Meader, who was now the prosecuting attorney in Washtenaw County, just west of Willow Run, and invited him to meet the senators and come along on the inspection

tour. The facility was so huge that Ford provided a small train with open cars so they could take it all in. Edsel Ford sat near the front with Senator Kilgore. Meader was in the last car next to Fulton, behind a Ford executive who at one point turned around and urged Fulton, "if you see anything wrong as we go along, just call it to my attention." Fulton waited until the man turned around, then leaned over to whisper in Meader's ear: "If I wanted to be smart with this fellow, I would wait until we got to the end of the line and say, 'What's wrong is that there aren't enough bombers coming out of here.'"[10]

Truman was headed on to Chicago and from there another western inspection trip, but before leaving Michigan, he had one more stop to make. Accompanied by Senators Wallgren and Kilgore, he drove the few miles from Willow Run to Ann Arbor, pulling up at the small frame house at 601 Mary Court, a few blocks from the University of Michigan campus. Hugh Fulton's seventy-six-year-old mother answered the door. "I know, you're Senator Truman," she said. "Hugh sent me your pictures in the papers."[11]

Down in Room 160, the excitement had veered away from the war for a few days to focus on a wedding. Walter Hehmeyer and Shirley Key had begun dating soon after they met in the spring of 1941, when Hehmeyer came down from New York to interview with Fulton. He loved the twinkle in her eye and her Southern manners and quiet reserve; she admired this small, kind man with a love of language and a lovely voice who found pleasure in each day. The wedding took place on Saturday, February 13, at All Souls Memorial Church in Washington. Given the wartime setting, it was a less formal affair: Shirley chose a blue street-length dress and matched it with a short veil and a small lace hat. "She wore a spray of orchids," noted *The Washington Post*, "and carried a white prayer book." The groom's brother, Alexander, came down from New York to serve as best man.[12]

Hugh and Jessie Fulton gave a reception for the young couple at their apartment, where Robby Robinson casually asked Walter, "Where are you going on your honeymoon?" New Orleans, Walter said. He and Shirley would take the train down and stay in the French Quarter at the Hotel Monteleone.

"Got your reservations?" asked Robinson. Hehmeyer told him the dates and times, which was all that Robinson, the office practical joker, needed. His first attempt at a honeymoon prank—to stop the train with a telegram, failed. Western Union didn't appreciate the attempt at humor: "Got a war going on." Robinson's next try—to change their hotel reservations from a double room to two single rooms—didn't work either.[13]

So he went on their honeymoon with them.

The committee had received a complaint about a blast furnace in Texas that dated from the Civil War, when it had been used to make cannonballs, and there were questions about how it was being utilized in the war effort. Fulton told Hehmeyer that if he wanted to go check it out from New Orleans, the committee would cover half the expenses. Hehmeyer passed: "I don't want to go investigating blast furnaces on my honeymoon."

Robinson, who was working on another investigation with Franklin Parks, agreed to go. Their train passed through New Orleans, and the two investigators got off a sleeper car on the last day of February, telling Fulton they "missed" their connection to Houston. Robinson telephoned the Hotel Monteleone and asked for the Hehmeyers. When Shirley answered, an angry man demanded, "Who's this?" Flustered, she said she was Miss...no, Mrs. Hehmeyer. "I'm—I'm—I'm married." The man said he was the house detective: "What are you doing up there in that room? Now, we got a rule in this hotel, no women allowed in our guests' rooms." Shirley handed the phone to her husband, who after a short conversation said, "Robby, you son of a bitch, where are you?"

"Across the street! Come on down and have a cup of coffee."[14]

The four of them spent a day on the town: the Old Absinthe House on Bourbon Street; Sazerac cocktails at the Court of Two Sisters; a horse-and-carriage ride with Robinson driving. Walter had brought a camera along, and Robinson delighted in inserting himself into as many of the honeymoon photos as he could. "The result is that their honeymoon pictures are of Frank Parks, myself, and Shirley," he recalled, "and everybody looks at Walter and he's stopped showing them anymore. They say, 'Didn't you go on your honeymoon, Walter?'"[15]

Robinson and Parks went on to Houston, and the newlyweds continued their honeymoon, dining one night at Arnaud's and another at Restaurant Antoine—the French Quarter landmark dating back to the 1840s, famous as the birthplace of Oysters Rockefeller. Those were on the menu that night at sixty cents.[16]

COURTESY OF CHRISTOPHER HEHMEYER.

Harold Robinson with Shirley Hehmeyer and Franklin Parks on the Hehmeyers' honeymoon in New Orleans. Walter is behind the camera.

Before the couple left Washington, Fulton told Hehmeyer, "I want you to call Andrew Jackson Higgins while you're down there." Walter phoned from the hotel, and Higgins sent a car for them. "I want you to come over and see our operation." In 1940 he had expanded into a $2 million plant on City Park Avenue, a sort of Willow Run for boat construction that had become known as one of the marvels of wartime manufacturing. It was busy churning out landing craft that were soon on their way to Great Britain and the Pacific. Higgins walked them around personally, through the four parallel production lines—six hundred feet long—as workers swarmed over the boats moving down the line. Since the factory was not located on the water, Higgins showed them where the finished boats were lowered from the plant's second floor to railroad cars below. Above their heads as they walked through the plant, a giant banner read, "THE GUY WHO RELAXES IS HELPING THE AXIS!"[17]

Higgins took them back to his office, where he suddenly remembered where he'd seen Mrs. Hehmeyer before: "You're Hugh Fulton's secretary." When Shirley said yes, he handed her a notebook and put her to work, on her honeymoon, dictating a long memo to Fulton and Senator Truman. "This is a good opportunity to get all this off my chest." The memo contained confidential information, and throughout the train ride home, Shirley fretted about its safety. Coming back to Washington was a bittersweet moment: she and Walter had decided that it would be inappropriate for a married couple to work together out of the same office, and that Shirley would resign: "We thought it wouldn't be wise for a husband and wife to work like that." She would find other jobs, but none would ever be as rewarding. "I was spoiled by the excitement of the Senate Office Building. You can't work there and then easily adjust to working somewhere else. There just isn't the same excitement."[18]

In early March, Fulton was circulating drafts for the Second Annual Report, which, though it lacked the bombshell revelations about fighter planes and high-level mismanagement as the first one, nevertheless weighed in on several important issues. At the same time, a debate was heating up over the administration's goal of building the armed forces to 11 million members, and the committee was planning hearings on how labor and industry would need to adapt to meet that goal. On March 6, the newspapers carried news that the Truman Committee would soon hold hearings on this, with top officials including William S. Knudsen and Donald Nelson to appear. On the table were questions about whether to make the workweek longer, how to deal with absenteeism, and why some plants and some workers were more productive than others. Among the industry experts who would testify was the businessman who had shown more than any other American just what could be accomplished in terms of raising production and increasing efficiency: Henry J. Kaiser.

13

THE PENNY DROPS

The hearings scheduled for the week of March 8 covered a broad range of topics related to productivity and efficiency. On Monday, the senators heard about labor unions, worker loyalty, "Negroes" employed by shipbuilding companies ("found to be good workers," notes the index for that day's hearings, condescendingly), and severe housing shortages like the one in Detroit. For Tuesday, the committee summoned two industry leaders known for cutting through these problems: Jake Swirbul, the cofounder and production manager at Grumman Aircraft, which made torpedo and fighter planes for the navy, and Kaiser.

Truman was out that day, so it was Senator Carl Hatch of New Mexico who gaveled the hearing to order at 10:05 a.m. in Room 357 of the Senate Office Building. Kaiser was called first. "I think you understand," Hatch told the industrialist as things got underway, "what the committee is particularly interested in right now—the question of production efficiency. We would like to hear what you can tell us, about your own experiences and how you have achieved the efficiency you have achieved."[1]

Kaiser began by noting that, just a few years ago, "there were three or four thousand" people working in shipbuilding on the West Coast, "and now there are at least half a million." Managing that growth and raising productivity required several key ingredients, the first of which was "joy of achievement" among the workers themselves. Second was the fact that the men and women who worked in his shipyards were well supervised; his supervisors paid close attention to bottlenecks in production and could take "immediate action" to overcome them. Finally, Kaiser said an absolute necessity for all this to work was an uninterrupted flow of materials.

He prepared to move on to discuss specific assembly line techniques, but first he paused: "I don't know whether you want to go into this much detail or not."

"Yes," replied Hatch, and so Kaiser went deep into the weeds on how the teams working on a ship under construction coordinated with each other, the need for workers to know whether they were on schedule or falling behind, and how that instilled in them a competitive drive. "The amount of work they do is posted on a large blackboard at the head of the ship and the men who are going to work know the amount of tonnage they erected." Kaiser had first tried this approach on the Grand Coulee Dam project in the late thirties—splitting up his teams to see who could reach certain milestones the fastest—and it was now a mainstay of his shipyards. Next up was what Kaiser called "the most vital thing to us"—housing. The shipyards were taking on so many workers, there simply weren't enough places for them to live. "It isn't right to ask the men to work unless you provide them with a proper place to live."

On it went through the morning: absenteeism, shortages of materials, job recruitment, the draft, etc. "Look at the women!"

Kaiser noted at one point. "We have picked up ten percent of women, that will go to thirty."

On another positive note, Kaiser talked up a new benefit he'd launched that, more than seventy years later, remains his most lasting legacy. He'd built seven hospitals around his shipyards, including the Permanente Foundation in Oakland, and was allowing his workers to buy access to medical care there. "The men can voluntarily join the hospital, and for seven cents a day they get complete hospitalization up to 111 days in any one case." Many of his workers, he said, "had never seen a doctor in their lives." This new health insurance, with preventive care and simple treatments, was cutting absenteeism dramatically and saving tens of thousands of hours in lost work time.

From there, the committee moved on to labor unions and morale. Kaiser touched on the *SS Robert E. Peary*, the ship that had set the record at his Richmond, California, shipyard by being launched just four days, fifteen hours and twenty-nine minutes after the keel was laid. "Many people think that just because we get a four-and-a-half-day ship or a ten-day ship, it is a publicity stunt," he told the senators somewhat defensively. Instead, he explained, these efforts had helped raise morale, and the lessons learned were being applied to all the ships that came after.

The discussion seemed to be winding down when Senator Owen Brewster changed the subject. "There has been some conversation on the East Coast," he asked Kaiser, "about a ship breaking up and rumors about more of them. Is that difficulty a result of design or workmanship?" It was the SS *Schenectady* that Brewster was asking about, the ship that had ruptured in two in Portland the night of January 16. At this sudden turn, the industrialist grew testy.

Kaiser has grown used to being hailed as a production genius, and now he had been badly stung by weeks of bad headlines around the *Schenectady*. The man known for his miracle ships was suddenly faced with the fact that one of them had snapped in two before it ever left port. The *Schenectady*, it turned out, wasn't the only one of the new welded ships to have problems. On February 12, the deck of a new ore ship, the *Belle Isle*, cracked while sitting at its outfitting dock in Cleveland. On the 17th, the deck and part of the side of the Liberty ship *Henry Wynkoop* fractured in New York, and there were other incidents as well. Several investigations had sprung up, and there had been plenty of speculation in the press—about the design of the ships, about the use of the new welding techniques, or the emphasis on speed in the merchant shipping program. As the historian Frederick Lane notes, these fractures were not just at Kaiser's shipyards, but much of the press attention focused on the *Schenectady*, and having been "exuberantly praised, Mr. Kaiser now found himself loudly mocked."[2]

And so, when Brewster asked about it, the normally talkative industrialist was hesitant. "Do you want me to answer that question?"

"Yes," Brewster said.

Kaiser asked again: "It is the difficulty with the breaking up of a ship that you are referring to?"

"Yes," Brewster responded.

So Kaiser answered, attributing his remarks carefully. It wasn't workmanship, he said, or design: "The reports I have seen, by competent authorities, signed by competent authorities, show that the steel is very far below specification yield. The yields are very low, under the specification."

"Where it broke?" Brewster asked.

"Where it broke," Kaiser said. "The number is on the piece. The piece is Carnegie Steel Corporation, United States Steel Corporation. The steel is declared as dirty, and the letter states unquestionably it is a very great factor in the breaking of a ship."

Kaiser noted as an aside that there were likely other factors at play besides bad steel. It had been very cold that night, and there had been a sudden rise and then fall in the level of the river.

But for the Truman Committee staffers sitting there listening, a bomb had dropped. Because Bob Irvin and other investigators knew right then what Kaiser didn't: that in a room not far away, a thick file of letters told in great detail how inspectors at that very company were approving and passing along slabs of "dirty" steel just about every day.

Within hours, Irvin was on a plane to Pittsburgh. To George Dye's home on Brownsville Road.[3]

Since November, things had only gotten worse for Dye at the Irvin Works, and his letters had grown more strident. Where once he had couched his language carefully, now he was talking openly about the outright fraud he was seeing every day. On January 6, he poured out his frustrations in an eight-page, handwritten letter to Truman: "Cheating in calculating tensile properties is common practice. When the A.B.S. [American Bureau of Shipping] inspector goes to get a drink, visits an office or goes to lunch, the testers seldom fail to write in a few tests. In the event of a test failure the testers usually substitute a 'ringer' from a good heat, a practice that is jokingly referred to as 'pulling one out of the barrel for Uncle Sam.' The US Treasury inspector picks up test reports at Irvin two or three times each week and they are all fraudulent."[4]

Toward the end of the letter, he offered suggestions for fixing the problems, beginning with "a thorough purge of traitors in the metallurgical Dept and employment of an adequate force of reliable testers." He closed by including the names of several employees at the plant who were willing to confirm his information.

These latest letters were so detailed and specific that it was hard for the committee to continue to ignore them. On January 14, Rudolph Halley responded that the committee "intends vigorously to investigate the matters referred to in these letters. We are hopeful of putting an investigator on the scene in the near future." A month later, Fulton wrote Dye that he was working "to arrange things so that we can visit Pittsburgh soon with reference to this matter."[5]

But with so many investigations and the Second Annual Report in the works, no one had gotten around to it before Kaiser made his shocking revelation on March 8. Immediately, George Dye and the Carnegie-Illinois Steel Corporation became the committee's number one priority. After Irvin arrived in Pittsburgh, Fulton sent Rudolph Halley and Matt Connelly to join him. They took along a steel expert from the War Production Board, H. Leroy Whitney, as an independent advisor. Together they met with Dye in the kitchen of his home to discuss the next steps, and in his boyish enthusiasm, he showed them a map he'd drawn by hand of the mill, its offices, the location of key records, and a written plan for how to proceed: "Arrests may be in order." He'd made up a list of key officials they should talk to. They could get those records without raising suspicion, he said, by entering the plant "on pretext that you desire to examine equipment."[6]

On Tuesday morning, March 16, the three investigators and Whitney did just that, presenting themselves at the office of Lester Perry, the president of Carnegie-Illinois Steel. Perry was temporarily out that morning, and they ended up in the office of an executive vice president. There, Whitney, the steel expert, said he'd like to take the Truman Committee men out to see the Irvin Works. Halley added—truthfully—that he had never seen a continuous strip mill in action and was eager to see how one worked.[7]

Perry having now arrived, there was some general chitchat about the steel industry while the tour was arranged. "At no time did we mention any investigation," Halley told a grand jury three weeks later, "but merely a desire to see the mill." The company officials cheerfully obliged, a car was provided, and everyone piled in for the ten-mile trip to the Irvin Works.

Their first stop was the slab yard, a huge outdoor area where the incoming steel from the mills—slabs several inches thick and seven or eight feet long—were kept before moving into the works and onto the rolling line. The plant's superintendent was out of town, but an assistant superintendent, a Mr. Elliott, was on hand to show them around. He explained how each slab was earmarked with a six-digit number at the point where it was created in its original mill, with information about its origin, composition, and quality. Supposedly, these numbers were stamped into the hot steel and also painted on. It was good they had brought Whitney along to explain all this, but as Halley moved through the slab yard, he noticed that on some of the slabs he could not find any number. In other cases, the white numerals had been wiped out as the steel was cleaned and worked.

When a certain slab was ready for processing, a crane lifted it up and deposited it at the furnace, and the delegation followed one plate from the slab yard into the large room with the furnaces. As the slabs were heated, the stamped and painted numbers were of course obliterated, and so the challenge of a rolling mill like Irvin, they learned, "is to keep these slabs, once they start going into the furnace, in order."[8]

As the slabs entered the furnace, and then as they emerged, glowing, and again at various points along the continuous line, they saw men and women jotting down information and keeping track of which slab was which. Despite the reason for their tour, the visitors couldn't help being impressed. "The mill is a tremendous sight," Halley said. "They take these huge slabs and they whip through this tremendous mill faster than I can walk." At the end of the line, they observed the equally important cooling process. If the plates cooled too fast, they might be brittle. Too slow—not hard enough. Like Goldilocks with her porridge, the temperature had to be just right.

One challenge created by converting the mill from automobile production to heavy plates for shipbuilding was a lack of space for proper cooling.[9] As they observed all this, Halley grad-

ually got down to business, asking ever more pointed questions.
With so many confusing numbers and inspections, how could
the workers possibly keep track of everything? How did they
test the steel to make sure it was good quality? And, by the way,
hadn't a ship built by Henry Kaiser at one of his shipyards broken in two? And hadn't Kaiser said that the reason for that was
bad steel from Carnegie-Illinois?

They asked to see the mill's testing laboratory, where the
strength and composition of the steel were measured. After
watching a demonstration, Halley wanted to know whether the
mill kept records of these tests: "Well, do you have a book?"[10]
At first, the assistant superintendent, Elliott, told Halley that
while there was no such book, he did have records. Even so,
looking at those records wouldn't help much, he added, because
they were so complicated the committee men wouldn't understand them. And besides, there were so many records, kept in
different places, that it would take all afternoon to see them.
By this point, the company men were realizing something was
up. "Our hospitality period came to an end," said Irvin, "and
everything turned to ice."[11]

Halley said he'd like to see those records anyway. Elliott finally acknowledged that inspection books did, in fact, exist. But,
unfortunately, those records weren't available right now. It would
take all afternoon to retrieve them. Which, thanks to George
Dye and his detailed map, Halley knew was a lie: the particular
book they wanted to see was, at that moment, less than ten feet
away. "I could see the office I wanted to enter where I knew
those records were kept," Halley said later. Grudgingly, Elliott
yielded to the inevitable: "Well if you want to see it," he said, "I
will get somebody to show it to you, but I'm not going to waste
my afternoon." Since it would take some time to track down the
records, he suggested they all have lunch. "The only thing we
could gracefully do was go to lunch," Halley said, and so they
trooped "half a mile from the coveted book to a dining room."

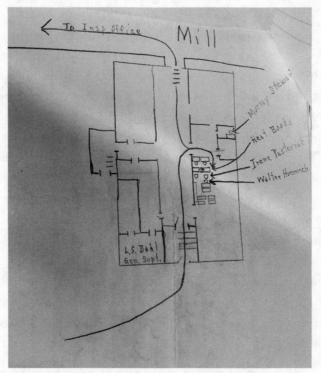

Handwritten map drawn by George Dye showing the location of key employees and heat inspection records. (Truman Committee files, National Archives.)

After lunch, the Washington men gathered with Elliott in his office, where he'd summoned several officials in charge of the record-keeping. The assistant superintendent then went off with Whitney to examine a new method for plating steel with tin, while Connelly and Halley expressed interest in learning all about the bookkeeping. A metallurgist took them right back to the room where they knew the inspection books were kept, "and the first book they pulled out was this heat analysis book." Here, too, they met the employee in charge of entries in the book, Irene Pasternak, and her boss, a Mr. Stewart. Halley invited Pasternak to sit down and walk them through the entries—the process for recording the batch, or "heat," the number of every slab, and the results of the chemical tests done on it at various points along the way. As they sat there, Halley on one side and Connelly on the other, Pasternak gave them a long explanation of the paperwork involved in tracking the steel from a particular furnace and a particular heat at the mill where it was made, through the Irvin Works and out into the world. The investigators, "knowing just what we wanted," led her along with questions.

Sometimes, Halley asked, wasn't there a finished plate, all ready for shipment, but no heat number entry in the book from its place of origin? With her boss standing right there, Pasternak hesitated a bit before answering yes. What did she do in those cases? Well, when that happened, she called the mill and got the number over the phone. Did that happen often? "Oh, no," said Pasternak, and Stewart chimed in: not often at all. Okay, continued Halley, he couldn't help but notice that while most of the entries were in ink, some were in pencil. Why was that?

Pasternak had no answer for this. She looked at Halley, and then at Stewart, who jumped in: "The pencil entries are the ones where we didn't have the chemical analysis and had to phone the mill."[12]

Then came the payoff moment. The kind of moment that lawyers and investigative reporters and writers of history live for. Halley said that he couldn't help but notice that many of the entries, especially the ones written in pencil, had an *F* next to them. A capital *F*. "How do you explain that?"

Pasternak stared nervously at Halley and Connelly, and then, without saying anything, she looked up at her boss. Who, after a pause, finally answered for her: "F means phone. That means we telephone for the analysis."

Both investigators knew that "phone" didn't start with an *F*. And besides, George Dye had told them exactly what those *F* entries meant. Halley asked to speak privately in a room with Irene Pasternak, and there he asked her bluntly to tell the truth. When she did, he took out a pencil and a piece of paper from his briefcase and asked her to write it all down. "The pencil analyses in the book are made-up analyses," she wrote. "The prefix F means fake."[13]

Halley finished up with Pasternak and got in a car to rejoin his colleagues, who had gone on to another plant a dozen miles away: the Edgar Thompson Works, one of the mills that supplied steel to the Irvin Works. Their mission: to match the numbers in the heat book with the records that mill kept from when the steel was shipped to Irvin. By this time, the steel managers had been in touch with their bosses, and Halley found himself on the phone with Lester Perry. Who told him that now that he understood an investigation was underway, he did not want the Truman Committee men to view any records until he had spoken with Senator Truman himself. Halley told him that Truman was out of town, and then Perry said he wanted to meet with Halley in his office. "I mentioned it was a matter of a long automobile ride into Pittsburgh and back, and we were right there and all we wanted to do was look at the records. But he insisted." Halley, knowing he had no real law enforcement authority in this situation, agreed.[14]

As soon as he rang off with Perry, though, Halley placed a call to Fulton in Washington. Halley told Fulton that he had stumbled into a "very bad situation," and, speaking loudly so the company managers could hear, pulled out the Truman Committee's most powerful weapon: "I don't see much point in talking about it. We will just subpoena everyone in sight for a hearing before the committee on Thursday." Fulton agreed, and since Halley had blank subpoena forms signed by Truman in his briefcase, told him to subpoena the records and anyone he thought should be summoned to Washington. The tactic worked: one of the managers left the room, and then came back a few minutes later and put Halley on the phone with Perry again, who now explained that in their earlier call, the two men had "misunderstood each other and he really thought I should look at the books."[15]

The investigators and Whitney sat down with the records
and laboriously copied the corresponding numbers of the fake
entries from the heat test book at the Irvin plant and compared
them with the original records on file at the Thompson Works.
Each time, the results were the same: wherever there was an *F*
penciled in by a heat number in the Irvin book, for a plate that
supposedly came from the Thompson mill, the records for that
mill showed no such heat, or a completely different one. For the
year 1942, for just this one mill that supplied steel to the Irvin
Works, they found more than 250 fake heat records.

*A page from the inspection book from the Irvin Works showing pencil notations marked
with the letter F. (Truman Committee files, National Archives.)*

It was now late in the day, and the four men headed back to
Perry's office in Pittsburgh, along with several of the company
officials. There Perry told them that this was all a mix-up—they
shouldn't place too much emphasis on these chemical analyses,
since what really mattered was the "tensile" or strength tests
of the steel, where a small piece of each slab was cut or sheared
off, and then that piece was put in a machine that stretched and
broke it to measure its strength. (Of course, George Dye had
explained that these tests were routinely faked as well.)

Perry then turned to the key piece of evidence, telling Halley that the heat testing book from the Irvin Works was necessary for running the plant. "Do you need it at night? Miss Pasternak goes home." Yes, Perry said, they needed it all the time. "Well, the Truman Committee has made a record of never interfering with production and we are not going to start now," he told them. "You can have the book, but I want a responsible officer of the corporation to take full responsibility for the book and keep it in his custody."[16]

They agreed to meet again the next morning and advise Perry on how their investigation would proceed.

The four men returned to their hotel, where about eight o'clock they received a phone call from George Dye. He wanted them to meet with another employee, Michael Tarella. Halley also wanted Dye to give his own written statement. And so, more than a year after he had penned that first letter to Harry Truman in Washington, George Dye was finally making himself heard:

March 16, 1943

I, George E. Dye, have been employed as Supervisor of Inspection at Irvin Works, Carnegie-Illinois Steel Corp., since January 1939. Since 1942 I have been aware that the mill was shipping badly laminated and piped plates to U.S. Navy and U.S. Maritime Shipyards and that defective steel was being supplied on U.S. Treasury Lend Lease orders. On numerous occasions I have brought this to the attention of my supervisors, D.M. Evans, Asst. Inspector Sheet Mill & John McConnell, Sheet Mill Metallurgist. My inspectors were assigned clerical duties that prevented effective control of quality; and although the fact that laminated plates were being shipped was repeatedly brought to the attention of T.W. Hunter who is jointly responsible for quality no appropriate measures were taken to prevent shipment of bad plates.

In November of 1942 I referred this matter to W.F. McGarrity
and was instructed to reject all the bad plates. Two days later John
McConnell told me that McGarrity got his ears beat back when
he brought the subject up in an operating meeting and I was in-
structed to go easy on rejections.
George E. Dye
2902 Brownsville Rd. Pgh. Pa.[17]

Tarella, who was in charge of the physical rather than chemical tests, gave a similar account. Over the past four and a half
years, he said, "from time to time I was given instructions by my
superiors to 'fake' tensile tests. Approximately 5% of these tests
pulled were false recordings."[18] So much for Perry's argument
that it was the tensile tests that really mattered.

It was nearly midnight by the time Halley and the others returned to their hotel. The next morning, Wednesday the 17th,
they were back in Perry's office, and now there was an attorney for US Steel on hand. Halley asked that they be allowed to
interview employees and ask questions. The company attorney
and Perry took the position that, since the company had not
been informed that an investigation was underway, they could
not allow interviews in private with any of their employees,
and claimed Halley had acted improperly in speaking privately
with Irene Pasternak. The investigators could only interview
employees with a company representative present. Halley said
if that were the case, he had no choice but to serve the subpoenas he had brought.

Perry said he wanted to speak to Truman first, and Halley
told him how he could reach the senator. While Perry put in the
call, the four Washington men headed back to the Irvin Works.
Once there, Halley drew up a detailed list (thanks to George
Dye) of the records he wanted to see. Tops on the list was the
heat analysis book that they had given back to the company officials the night before. One of the executives now told Halley

that the book had been turned over to a group of people who were "taking it apart and were copying notations out of it for purposes of a check he was attempting to make." Furious, Halley noted that not only the Truman Committee, but most likely the Justice Department, would very much want to see this book, "and that as a representative of the United States Government it was my duty to see that the book stayed intact."[19]

It was nearly two o'clock when finally the heat analysis book showed up, and the investigators spent the rest of the day reviewing records, relying heavily on Whitney, the steel expert, and taking detailed notes. The list of employees they'd asked for, too, finally came, but by now it was five o'clock, too late in the day to issue subpoenas since most of the workers they wanted to talk to had now gone home.

And so they headed back to Perry's office in Pittsburgh. There, with several top company officials present, Perry asked the four men from Washington what they had found. Halley turned to Whitney, who said that after examining the numbers, he just couldn't believe the steel this plant had been producing, or that the records claimed it was producing—a consistently uniform quality that no mill could possibly meet. "That's dream steel, and there just ain't no way to do it."[20]

Perry had by now spoken with Truman, who refused to get into the details until he spoke with his team. "One of the great things about the guy," Irvin said, was that Truman "wouldn't discuss it with them until he talked to his own people. And *after* he had our reports, he would be very happy to sit down and talk to them."

Nevertheless, Perry still didn't want the investigators to speak privately with employees. After some more "bickering" about whether they had misrepresented the reason for their visit, Halley told Perry that, regardless, he would be back with subpoenas the next morning and expected to serve them.

Irvin and Connelly caught a plane to Washington that night,

and Halley and Connelly headed back the next day. Perry and other company officials, scrambling to get out in front of events, headed to Washington on Thursday as well, seeking a face-to-face meeting with Truman.

It was not until the following day, Friday the 19th, that Truman—now fully briefed—gathered all the parties involved in his office: Halley and Connelly, Senator Kilgore, and Fulton, along with Perry and several company officials and lawyers. The company men argued that it would be harmful to the war effort if the investigation and its findings were made public. Truman was having none of that. Next week, he would hold public hearings.

14

FAKE STEEL

At 10:00 a.m. on Tuesday, March 23, Truman opened the hearings with five other senators: Ball, Brewster, Burton, Ferguson, and Kilgore. Hugh Fulton, characteristically, started with the smaller fry and worked his way up. First to appear was Pasternak's unfortunate boss, M.E. Stewart, of the "F means phone" explanation, and Fulton's questioning produced this notable exchange:

Fulton: How were other entries made?

Stewart: They were made in ink.

Fulton: And did you, in addition to making them in pencil, put any prefix letter in front of them?

Stewart: It was common practice to put an F.

Fulton: What did F mean?

Stewart: Fake.

Fulton: You told our investigator originally it meant phone.

Stewart: That is right.

Fulton: But now under oath you desire to state it meant fake?
Stewart: That is correct. The investigator was a stranger to
me and I was sort of pressed for something to say at
the moment.[1]

And it wasn't just faking the heat numbers. The government
had set rigid specifications, depending on the type of steel, for
the chemical composition of that steel—the proper amounts of
manganese, carbon, phosphorous, and other materials—to en-
sure it would have the needed strength or other properties when
used in a ship or bridge or building. Stewart admitted that, at
times, when the inspectors did have the correct batch number
for a given slab but the chemical tests did not meet government
specifications, fake test results were substituted, a practice known
as "pulling in."[2] Or what Dye had called "a ringer."

Irene Pasternak appeared next, but after Fulton read out loud
the written statement she had given Halley, Truman dismissed
her. From there, Fulton worked his way up the ranks, calling
inspectors and managers at the Irvin Works as well as the nearby
Homestead Works (another US Steel facility). These employees
confirmed that, as the batch numbers and chemical tests were
faked, so too were the tensile, or strength, tests. Two inspectors
confirmed under oath Tarella's estimate that as much as 5 percent of the steel shipped from the Irvin Works went out under
falsified strength numbers.[3] It had already become clear that the
steel from the *Schenectady* had not come from the Irvin Works,
but from Homestead. Of course, George Dye in his letters had
told the committee more than once that he knew for certain
that tests were being faked there, too.

Then came the big guns: Benjamin Fairless, the head of US
Steel, and Lester Perry, the president of its Carnegie-Illinois division. Perry went first and, despite a morning full of damning
testimony about the extent of the fake records and the quality
of his steel, did what he could to defend his company. "Regret-
table as these occurrences have been," he told the committee in

his opening statement, "it is reassuring to know that the plates furnished by Irvin Works have been entirely suitable for their intended uses, as shown by complete customer acceptance of this product."[4] Then he turned to the question of who was at fault. Certainly not the senior leadership. No, he said, the faked tests were the result of a few bad apples, men who "grew lax under the pressure of heavy production."

From there, Truman and the other senators let him have it with both barrels. The chairman started off, asking Perry about "your cooperation or lack of cooperation with this committee." Perry responded that on that first day, he had tried to be helpful: "We furnished transportation and did everything that we thought was cooperative. That afternoon, late, it appeared definitely that they wanted to make an investigation."

Truman cut in: "We don't send investigators to plants just for fun."

"I understand that now," Perry said. "I am telling you my state of mind at the time."

There was considerable debate that day (and in the decades since) over whether the quality of steel had anything to do with the breakup of ships. Perry's contention that it was not a factor, and that it was not the Irvin Works that made the steel that went into the *Schenectady*, was not good enough for Homer Ferguson: "I notice that you say that the break did not start in your steel. At any rate, the plate at the point where the break began was not a product of the Irvin plant?"

"That is right, Senator."

"Do you know who made that steel?"

"At this point we believe that the steel was made at our Homestead Works."

"Didn't you hear the witness testify here that he was taught how to cheat down at the Homestead Works?"

"Senator, this word 'cheat'—"

"You don't like the word 'cheat.' Have you a better one?"[5]

Through the morning and into the afternoon session, Fulton and the senators kept returning to the basic point: Carnegie-Illinois Steel had systematically and intentionally defrauded the government. At one point Perry maintained that the company had not benefited from the faked tests.

Again, Truman jumped in: "The evidence shows that you did benefit by that."

"We benefited in what way, Senator Truman?"

"By getting rid of a lot of defective steel."[6]

In one of many versions of the same question, Ferguson asked: "If a customer asks you for a strength of 60,000 pounds, and you give him a product of 57,000 pounds, is that a misrepresentation of a material fact?"

"Yes sir," Perry responded.

In that case, then, Truman wanted to know, "Have you fired anybody on the strength of the testimony that you heard this morning, most of which you had seen before it was put in this record?"

Perry stalled. "I didn't understand your question."

"Have you fired anybody?"

"We are suspending some people."

"When are you going to do it?"

"Immediately when we get through this hearing."

Truman reminded Perry that he had now known about this for days. "You didn't do anything about it and you haven't done anything about it until, after this testimony, you say you may suspend some people."

"I said we are suspending some people."

"I know what I'd have done if I had found that going on in my plant and I didn't know anything about it. I'd have fired the whole bunch."[7]

The questioning of Fairless, Perry's boss at US Steel, was less fiery. He, too, was eager to downplay what the investigators had found, arguing as Perry had that all this was the result of a few bad employees: "It would seem from the evidence that there have been misrepresentations and falsifications in one department of one plant of one of our subsidiary companies." Still, he said, "we are just as shocked to get these facts as you were, and we are just as desirous of correcting them as you are."[8]

"Steel Tests Faked on Plate For Ships" read the page one headline in *The New York Times*, and, with variations, in newspapers across the country. Developments in the story were widely reported in the days and weeks that followed. The navy announced its own investigation, and so did the War Production Board. Over and over the questions came up—Had bad steel gone into fighting ships and merchant vessels? The link with the *Schenectady* and other ships that had broken up, whether direct or not, was inescapable. National outrage ran high, and the mail poured into Room 160:

My God man our sons are over there dying, giving their all while these crooked greedy blood suckers are sending out faulty material for them to fight with and they have the gall to say they had no knowledge of what was going on. I ask in God's name what do you think we parents feel like doing when we hear of such things? I have a son over there & not only is he over there but he is turning most of his little pay back into war bonds.
Mrs. C. Morlman
Cincinnati, Ohio

On April 1, US Steel sent the committee a statement detailing the changes it was making to clean up the mess. Four high-ranking employees involved in the fake inspections had been fired, and the company had put several new men in key positions, including a chief metallurgist and chief inspector. And there was a complete overhaul of how steel plates would be inspected and shipped, and what would happen to the ones that didn't pass inspections. "All of the executives of the corporation and its subsidiaries fully agree with you," the statement concluded, "that nothing should be left undone to insure the high quality and suitability of all of the products of the Corporation."

It was a clear, undisputed victory of the kind that is so rare in Washington, or anywhere for that matter. A win for the public, a win for the government, and a win for the Truman Committee and its chairman. If the steel investigation had left even a small doubt that Harry Truman was now a national force to be reckoned with, that doubt was erased by another development that came the same week in early March that Henry Kaiser testified before the committee.

That week's issue of *Time* magazine marked its twentieth anniversary. The publication had changed journalism when it first appeared back in 1923—the first weekly newsmagazine of its kind in the US. The March 8 issue contained a personal note from the publisher, P.I. Prentice, to mark the moment. "*Time* still has only one aim," he wrote, "to help busy, intelligent people get the news and as much of its meaning as diligent reporting can discover."

The choice of a cover story that week, though, celebrated a different anniversary: "In the U.S., democratic but far from perfect, the Truman Committee celebrated its second birthday as one of the most useful Government agencies of World War II." There, in full color on the cover of one of the most influential and widely read publications in the country, was the junior senator from Missouri. The illustration by the artist Ernest Hamlin Baker portrays Truman from the shoulders up—silver hair, craggy face, wire spectacles and, of course, a cleanly knotted tie. He stands before a dark background, gazing into the distance. Behind him, the cone-shaped light from a metaphorical spotlight shines down on the Capitol building and defense plants. "INVESTIGATOR TRUMAN," read the caption: "A democracy has to keep an eye on itself."

Inside, over three pages beneath the headline "Billion-Dollar Watchdog," a largely glowing story laid out the surprising rise of Truman and his committee; a portrait in words to match Baker's image on the cover, of a serious, honest, hardworking man who had not let fame or power go to his head. If the committee members wanted to, the story said, they could raise a glass to having "served as watchdog, spotlight, conscience and spark plug to the economic war behind the lines." At the two-year mark, though, their work was far from complete: "The first annual Truman report, with its shocking evidence of all around bungling, had not spelled the end of bungling. This week the Committee worked on its second annual report, which would have to recite much the same story, chastise many of the same men, pose some of the old problems. How big should the Army be? How could the manpower tangle be solved? Where would the nation get its food this year? What was wrong with WPB?"

As for Truman himself, a "naturally shy and self-effacing man," the piece recounted the highlights of his early years—war hero, failed store owner, machine politician and Senate nobody. It told the now-familiar story of how he stood by his old Kansas City boss even when he could easily have turned his back. "Tom Pendergast never asked me to do a dishonest deed," Truman was quoted as saying. And there was plenty of color, too: "At 58, he still goes solemnly through his setting up exercises every morning, can still get into his old World War I uniform. In 1939, he dug out his old artillery maps and hung them on his office wall to help follow the fighting."

His only vices, the story said, "are small stakes poker, an occasional drink of bourbon."[9]

That line brought a telegram from his friend and former Senate colleague, Lewis Schwellenbach: "WHAT DO THEY MEAN AN OCCASIONAL DRINK OF BOURBON?" Like many of the people who wrote to Truman about the article, Schwellenbach also noted that the cover art seemed to have aged the fifty-eight-year-old senator: "HAVE YOU REALLY ACQUIRED ALL THOSE WRINKLES?" Jimmy Byrnes, the former Senate majority leader who was now serving in the administration as head of the Office of Economic Stabilization, agreed: "It really is a good picture if they would erase about 25 years."[10]

Truman, in a thank-you letter to Henry Luce, *Time*'s publisher and founder, mentioned it, too. "Thanks for the *Time* article. It had a very favorable reaction among my friends and opponents. They seem to make only one complaint, and that is that I look like I am eighty-one years old in the picture." A joke he would repeat more than a dozen times in the coming days.

Luce responded in the same spirit: "Having heard you speak at a meeting several months ago, I, too, was a little surprised that you had aged so rapidly. But you never can tell what Art will do. Let us hope that Art is prophetic and we will be able to use the same drawing when you *are* eighty."[11]

The Second Annual Report had indeed come out that week, warning of the "toughest, grimmest year" ahead for the US and its allies. It laid out three big weaknesses hindering the war effort on the home front: "inadequate overall planning within Government agencies," "conflicting authority over, and responsibility for, various phases in the war program, resulting in delays and buck-passing," and finally, "hesitancy of Government to adopt unpopular or unpleasant policies long after the facts clearly indicated such policies were necessary." In addition, the report cited many other problems, among them "confusion and bickering" over raw materials like rubber, hoarding by contractors and businesses, and labor problems including strikes and absenteeism.[12]

It was a solid report that pulled no punches with the military, the administration or big business, and a reminder that the war still had a long way to go. And while it received widespread news coverage, thanks to the committee's earlier reports, such findings were no longer a huge shock to Americans, and its revelations were soon overtaken by the Carnegie-Illinois investigation.

Already, signs of a counterattack were appearing. On April 19, the committee issued its report on the steel investigation, which, given the evidence, was a remarkably balanced one. The accompanying press release noted that the company had admitted its mistakes and that "a grand jury is sitting in Pittsburgh to determine whether criminal prosecution is warranted."[13]

This report again put the committee on the front pages. "STEEL FALSITY HIT IN TRUMAN REPORT," said *The New York Times*. But already, several stories had appeared elsewhere questioning the committee's findings and claiming the investigation had caused a nationwide slowdown in steel production. "STEEL SLUMP BLAMED ON TRUMAN," declared the *Pittsburgh Post-Gazette*, quoting unnamed officials of the War Production Board. "The net result of the Senate inquiry has been to hamstring the manufacture of steel plates so seriously that Navy and War Production Board officials believe the entire war effort may be in danger." The story gave no figures and quoted no named sources. Nor did it quote Truman or anyone from the committee. And it claimed that "there was never any question that the steel plates involved in the controversy were inadequate for safe construction of merchant vessels."[14]

Hugh Fulton had seen this coming. "It has been suggested by the Company that the steel was suitable for the uses intended," the press release noted. Then why hadn't the government agencies changed their specifications to reflect that? "Until and unless they find that it is safe to reduce their specifications, the Committee and all other government agencies expect that the steel plate furnished will be in accordance with specifications."

As to the "steel slump," the report warned manufacturers against "over-extreme cautiousness," urging them to examine their inspection procedures to make sure they weren't so rigid as to hold up production. Having said that, "the committee expects their inspections to be honestly made. There is no substitute for honesty. There is no excuse for frauds."[15]

Despite Fulton's efforts to get out in front of this, the corporate public relations machinery was now in full swing. "Press still hammering away with stories to effect that Navy never got any defective steel," Hehmeyer warned on April 21 in a long telegram to Fulton, who was in Chicago. The next day's *Washington Post* kept up the pressure: "Fairless Denies Substandard Steel Periled Lives or Safety of Ships."

And then, on May 3 and 4, the *Christian Science Monitor* ran a two-part series by reporter Harold Fleming: "Did Truman Probe Reveal All Facts in Steel Case?" The first story began with a quick recount of the investigation, and then this: "First ray of common sense was injected into the picture by Benjamin Fairless," who, the piece noted, had pointed out that the inspectors at the plant had nothing to gain personally by faking the inspections and, incredibly, that the steel company had nothing to gain.[16] Truman and Fulton, of course, had pointed out many times that getting rid of bad steel by selling it to the government at the same price as good steel was a direct and quite significant financial gain.

Anyway, the story continued, the navy and the Maritime Commission had not complained about it. No harm, no foul!

Part two continued the case for US Steel, questioning whether the investigation at the Irvin Works had been conducted properly. The committee did not check in with the management when it arrived at the plant, the story noted. "It organized a junket to Pittsburgh, apparently just to take a look-see at the plant. There the junketeers demanded access to the books. The superintendent called his boss. That was the first the executives knew."[17]

What the readers of the *Monitor* did not see was the letter of apology that its managing editor, Erwin Canham, sent to Senator Owen Brewster three weeks later. "I blame myself no end about those Fleming articles," he wrote. Canham said he was dubious about the stories at first, but told the reporter to go to Washington to check with the senators on the committee to hear their side of the story. Fleming, the editor told Brewster, assured his bosses that he had carefully checked the facts and that a trip to Washington was unnecessary.

"Now, however, we will seek to clarify the matter in print as best we can and will get in touch with you again when the time approaches that we can publish further material. In any case you will be hearing from us soon regarding the aftermath."[18]

The "steel slump" stories laid out a strategy that other companies in later investigations would take when under attack from the committee: first, stories from friendly reporters or friendly publications questioning, politely, the committee's findings. And then the counterpunch: the Truman Committee, by poking its nose into matters best left to businessmen who knew better, was slowing down production, hurting the war effort.

Was there a slump? Production figures released later by the government suggested there was not, or if there was, it was neither as serious or prolonged as the *Post-Gazette* and other papers claimed. In April, less than a month after the committee's revelations, steel production set a new record for a thirty-day period. In July, steel producers broke that record, and they did so again in August. In a radio speech in October, Truman cited the production record set in April and attacked the *Post-Gazette* and its reporting: "I wonder, and I think you will wonder, who told that newspaper there was going to be a steel slump and why was such a ridiculous rumor circulated?"[19]

15

CELLOPHANE COMMISSIONS

While the ink was still drying on the fake steel headlines, several other investigations suddenly moved off the back burner. March and April would turn out to be, for the Truman Committee, among the busiest of the war, with the Carnegie-Illinois probe, a much-publicized spat with the labor leader John L. Lewis, a mushrooming inquiry into problems at an aircraft engine factory in Ohio, and the examination of motion pictures and training films that Fulton had set in motion the previous year.

Early in the defense buildup, it became clear that in the task of training and preparing hundreds of thousands, eventually millions, of men and women to fight and serve in highly specialized jobs, movies were an effective and powerful tool. Both in teaching complex tasks in a hurry to large numbers of people, and also for shaping their ideas and attitudes about a war that would disrupt their lives and require large sacrifices.

Then as now, though, Hollywood and Washington had an

uneasy relationship—each wary of the power and influence the other wielded: the industry worried about Washington's power to regulate and restrict; and power brokers in Washington were envious and suspicious of a faraway, glamorous industry with an equal, or even greater, ability to shape public opinion. Inevitably, movies were seen as fertile soil for political manipulation, and Hollywood was often portrayed by conservatives as a dangerous, leftist influence on the country. In 1941, the industry had got caught up in the debates over isolationism and the America First movement, which was in turn intertwined with US anti-Semitism and opposition to Franklin Roosevelt. In September, a Republican senator, Gerald Nye of North Dakota, attacked Hollywood films as rife with "dangerous propaganda." Among the movies he singled out were *Sergeant York*, which starred Gary Cooper as the World War I hero and made no attempt to conceal its message of preparedness against looming threats overseas, and Charlie Chaplin's *The Great Dictator*, an open attack on fascism and dictatorship. Nye accused the industry of being influenced by "refugee or alien authors," and "refugee or alien actors," who in turn were following the orders of Roosevelt. "Are the movie moguls doing this because they like to do it," he asked, "or has the government of the United States forced them to become propaganda agencies?"[1]

This industry, so often held up as a threat to American values, became after Pearl Harbor just the opposite: a wellspring of patriotic images and ideals. Many of its biggest stars, and their bosses in the major studios, supported the war through benefits, public appearances, and fundraising drives. Jimmy Stewart and Clark Gable were among the actors who volunteered for military service; both saw combat. Feature films like William Wyler's *Mrs. Miniver* made no attempt to hide their pro-war, anti-fascist sentiments.

Several of the top directors—Wyler, Frank Capra, John Huston, John Ford, and George Stevens—left highly paid jobs and

comfortable lives in Southern California to serve as commissioned officers, and took their cameras and their skills to combat theaters around the world. John Ford was on Midway Island
for the decisive US naval victory there in 1942. On June 4, he
stationed himself and his crew on the roof of the island's power
station, with color film loaded and cameras rolling as Japanese
planes attacked. At one point he was knocked unconscious and
wounded by shrapnel as a Japanese bomb hit.[2] He used his combat footage and other film shot during the battle, along with
narration from actors including Henry Fonda, to produce a vivid
and compelling eighteen-minute documentary that received
widespread distribution throughout the US.

The Battle of Midway and other films, made by some of the
finest directors in Hollywood, brought images of the war home
in ways American had never seen before. In February 1942,
General George Marshall assigned Major Frank Capra to create a series of films that "would show the man in uniform why
he was fighting." The result, seven documentaries called Why
We Fight, laid out the case for the US involvement in the war. It
was, as the writer and historian Mark Harris put it, "the single
most important filmed propaganda of the war."[3]

In much less glamorous ways, motion pictures helped millions
of Americans adjust and adapt to military life and the strange
and complex new tasks assigned them. The industry produced
hundreds of films with titles like Fundamental Fixed Gunnery Approaches, Preflight and Daily Inspections, and Types and Components
of Cannon.[4] In 1941, Ford directed an educational film, Sex Hygiene, which graphically showed young recruits the dangers of
syphilis and gonorrhea. Traditionalists in the army opposed the
use of actors, scripts, humor or plots, in these training films, but
Marshall and others overrode those concerns. They realized recruits could be much better served by scrapping the boring lectures that made up most of the army's curriculum.[5]

As was the case in many other industries, the need was great, the urgency was high, and there was a lot of government money involved. The industry's Academy of Motion Picture Arts and Sciences had set up a nonprofit Research Council to coordinate and distribute film projects and also to bring talented film producers into the military. But as early as the summer of 1942, complaints had been coming in to the Truman Committee about the costs of these films, and about the directors, producers, and executives going into the military to make them. As with complaints in other industries, most of these proved unfounded; perhaps, in an industry famously fueled by grudges and gossip, even more so. But enough of them seemed to have merit that Fulton assigned Peter Ansberry to investigate.

The most detailed and seemingly clear-cut allegations centered around one powerful Hollywood figure. Darryl F. Zanuck had risen through the motion picture industry from its early days, writing scripts for silent films and eventually becoming head of production at Warner Bros. In 1933 he left Warner Bros. and became one of the founding partners of 20th Century Pictures. Two years later he bought out Fox studios and created 20th Century Fox. Like many in Hollywood and around the country, Zanuck, a veteran of World War I, was eager to do his part, and in January 1942, at age thirty-nine, went on active duty as a colonel in the Signal Corps,[6] which handled most of the army's movie-making. He was also the chairman of the Academy's research council.

In September, as part of his investigation, Ansberry took the train to New York to interview a captain in the Signal Corps, Ira Genet, who had formerly been a director and writer of short films for Warner Bros. Genet told Ansberry that Zanuck was still the executive vice president of 20th Century Fox and continued to draw his (very large) salary as an officer of the corporation, "and that he devoted a part of his time to managing Twentieth Century-Fox while wearing the uniform of the United States Army."

Genet alleged that, in his role overseeing the branch of the Signal Corps that was steering projects to Hollywood studios, Zanuck was directing those efforts through "a clique of 'cellophane commission' friends." Finally, he told Ansberry that Zanuck had supervised the army's purchase of short films "from his own company and from other companies managed by his friends at prices enormously in excess of their worth."[7]

Ansberry proposed, and Fulton approved, a questionnaire that would be sent to the major studios asking for data on the number of films produced, the costs, the price paid by the army and other details, with inquiries also going to the War Department to find out about its policies and procedures. That questionnaire prompted the army, in October, to begin its own investigation, sending two officers to Hollywood and launching a separate probe by the inspector general's office. "You will note," Ansberry observed in a memo, "that shortly after our investigation was instituted Colonel Zanuck was ordered to Washington."[8]

Perhaps the two were linked, but it was also the case that since going on active duty, Zanuck had chafed at the desk assignment in Los Angeles and had lobbied hard for a more challenging role that would take him to the war zones. In Washington, he was assigned to direct planning of photographic missions overseas, and used that as a launching pad to direct those missions himself. In the fall he was posted to London, and in November and December he personally directed the filming of Operation Torch, the US invasion of North Africa.

Ansberry's investigation confirmed some of those initial allegations. After Zanuck had gone on active duty in January 1942, he had also regularly showed up for work at his studio office, continued to receive his $5,000 a week salary from 20th Century Fox, and still had extensive stock holdings in the company. Since Zanuck was also head of the nonprofit research council, it appeared that he was "triple dealing"—awarding government contracts to studios including his own for the making of training films, while drawing a paycheck from both sides and chairing the organization that coordinated the projects. While the studios ostensibly charged the government only for the cost of making the films, without any profit, Ansberry noted that they still stood to gain, since the short films were generally made in a few days, between major pictures, "at a time when equipment and contract employees would otherwise be idle while running up costs."[9]

As often happened on the Truman Committee when the military stepped in to begin its own investigation, Ansberry put his inquiry on the back burner through the fall while awaiting the results of that probe. He requested a copy of the army's findings on November 11 and was told it was not yet finished. On December 11 he followed up and was again told that the report, by Major John Amen, was not finished. In February, Ansberry asked a third time, and when he learned the major was still working on his report, asked whether he could interview the officer. Again, the answer was no.[10]

Once again, Truman would have preferred to let the military clean up its own mess, quietly, without publicity. But by early 1943, the back-and-forth over access to Major (now Lieutenant Colonel) Amen's report had gone on long enough. "Several months have elapsed and the Army refuses to inform the Committee as to the results of its investigation," Fulton said in announcing a public hearing scheduled for February 16.[11]

The day before, Undersecretary of War Robert Patterson told Truman in a letter: "I feel that I must decline to make Lieutenant Colonel Amen available to your committee." The reason, he said, was that the Inspector General's office was a "confidential investigative agency" of the Secretary of War, and "it is the view of the War Department that reports of investigations should not be made available to agencies other than the Executive Branch."[12]

Nevertheless, the hearing went forward the next day in Room

457 of the Senate Office Building, and Lieutenant Colonel Amen was the first witness called. Hugh Fulton opened the questioning: "You were handed today, I believe, a subpoena on behalf of this committee?"

"I was, sir."

"Have you been given any instructions by the Army or any superior officer within the Army as to whether you should or should not testify before this committee?"

"Yes, sir."

Amen read a letter, dated that morning, instructing him to follow the guidelines set forth in Patterson's letter to Truman, "and specifically that you will give no testimony with regard to any of the facts and information that you may have gathered in the investigation."[13]

Fulton had requested Zanuck's presence that day as well, but Julius Amberg, the special assistant in the War Department assigned to congressional committees, told the committee that Zanuck was out of town, on leave in New Hampshire. Amberg promised that, given a few days' notice, he could make Zanuck available. Despite the legal debate over whether Amen should testify, Amberg and Patterson were trying to cooperate, and sent the head of the Signal Corps' moviemaking division, Colonel K.B. Lawton, to answer the committee's questions.

Hugh Fulton wasted no time in asking him about Darryl F. Zanuck: "When did you become aware that, while commissioned as an active officer in the United States Army, Colonel Zanuck was still drawing $5,000 a week pay or salary for his civilian post with Twentieth Century-Fox?"

"I don't think I ever actually knew that."

"Did you ever hear that, and if so, when?"

"No, I have never known whether he drew any money or not before August 29, when he resigned from the vice-chairmanship of Twentieth Century-Fox."[14]

Much of the testimony that day centered around whether the

studios were making a profit on the training films, or whether the films were produced at a loss, as the industry claimed. The numbers were squishy, and there were countless variables, such as how to calculate the cost of using cameras and equipment and technicians that would otherwise have had nothing to do.

Colonel Lawton argued that in many cases, the studios had lost money on these films. When Senator Ferguson wanted to know why the studios would give the United States government such a gift, Lawton responded that the patriotism of the movie people was real and that they had consciously chosen not to bill the government for every penny: "I don't know personally of any other corporation, producers of anything that is being put out for the war effort, in which they do not charge what they can."[15]

Fulton had more questions, about the officers' commissions received by executives in the movie industry: Hal Roach was a major; Arthur Loew of MGM, a major; Robert Lord of Warner Bros., a lieutenant colonel; Frank Capra, now a lieutenant colonel. But the time allotted for the hearing was running out, and it ended somewhat inconclusively, with no schedule or date for resuming. Afterward, a remark Truman made to reporters, that he believed the army uniform was "for combat soldiers, not for fellows to strut around in," made the papers the next day,[16] along with the revelations about Zanuck's $5,000-a-week salary while in uniform.

There the matter rested for several weeks while the committee dealt with the annual report and the fake steel hearings, but the question of Amen's report and Patterson's refusal to allow him to testify were still hanging out there.

Zanuck, meanwhile, had written a book about his experiences in Tunisia, and while he donated the royalties to an army relief fund, his flamboyant behavior in the combat zone, with cigars and a personal automobile, had not won him friends. His film, *At the Front in North Africa*, released in March, contained actual combat footage but also perhaps too much show business flair.

The review in *Time* suggested it "might be more appropriately titled, 'Darryl Zanuck's War.'" The review noted that Zanuck and a crew of forty-two Signal Corps photographers had captured "some of the most detailed closeups of attacking planes yet seen on the screen. These shots and the sound effects are the best things in At the Front. But Zanuck, invincibly Hollywood-minded, tried to dress up the film with arty shots of tank treads, dawns, sunsets, many another ill-placed frippery."[17]

Stung by the criticism and by the scrutiny from the Truman Committee, Zanuck requested that he be placed on inactive status, which only made things worse when the Truman Committee returned to the issue on April 3. Undersecretary Patterson had requested this hearing, to give him a chance to share new developments. His timing, though, was unfortunate: the hearing came just as news surfaced that New York City Mayor Fiorella LaGuardia was being considered for a general's commission in the army. "I know the mayor was an air officer in the last war," Truman told Patterson, "but I don't think he has any more business being a brigadier general than this fellow [Zanuck] has being a colonel." Patterson declined to comment on LaGuardia, but he told the committee that "as the result of the hearing before your committee," and of the army's own investigation, a brigadier general had been placed in charge of the Army Pictorial Service, "which is now charged with general responsibility for all photographic work of the Army Service Forces." The arrangement with the Research Council was ending, and new procedures were now in place. Patterson said, however, that the army investigations had confirmed that the council had made "no profit on the training film program." In fact, "I believe the War Department has benefitted financially by the arrangement made."[18]

He then moved to the question of commissions, and said they would no longer be awarded through the Signal Corps. And he addressed specifically the questions surrounding Darryl F.

Zanuck. "Colonel Zanuck has been commended by the Chief
Signal Officer for his courage, energy, patriotism and accomplishment. I do not believe that he is subject to any personal
criticism." Keeping his job at 20th Century Fox, Patterson acknowledged, was unwise, and under questioning from Fulton
conceded that it was "improper." But since giving up that salary, Zanuck "has made a heavy personal financial sacrifice." In
other words, he could have simply kept his high-paying Hollywood job in the first place. "The mission for which he was
originally called to active duty having now been accomplished,
he has requested that he be placed on inactive status."

Which to Truman, a former army officer, made no sense. "I
don't believe in letting fellows back out in the middle of war,"
he told Patterson. "Why don't you send him to school and make
a real soldier out of him."[19]

His comments received widespread newspaper coverage and
once again struck a chord with many Americans, including some
in the military. This was far from the last time in his life that a
throwaway comment would land Truman on the front pages.
"I have had a tremendous amount of mail as a result of a two-
sentence statement I made on Darryl Zanuck and LaGuardia and
their commissions," he wrote his friend Lewis Schwellenbach.
"People pay very little attention to the really necessary things
you do, but some personal statement like that really makes the
mail come in."[20]

Truman's attitude in many ways echoed his objections to
the dollar-a-year men: here again were highly paid, extremely
competent businessmen willing to forgo their salaries for government service, but who did not conform to the mold of a traditional military officer or government bureaucrat. Zanuck was
allowed to leave the military in June, a move that was probably
best for all, but the fact remained that many of the other directors, writers and artists who'd gone into the service had served
their country, and some would give their lives.

While the hearings over training films were taking place in Washington, the director William Wyler was in England, flying combat missions in B-17 bombers. He and his camera crews faced thick anti-aircraft fire over Germany while struggling to keep their cameras working in temperatures of sixty degrees below zero. On the night he won an Oscar, as Best Director for *Mrs. Miniver*, he was at an airfield in England, working with the bomber crews and planning for his next mission. On April 16, while gathering film for the documentary that would become *The Memphis Belle, A Story of a Flying Fortress*, one of his cameramen, Harold Tannenbaum, flying that day in a different bomber, was shot down and killed.[21]

16

BAD ENGINES

On March 22, the same day Truman, Fulton and the other senators were grilling Lester Perry and Benjamin Fairless about faked steel inspections, investigator Donald Lathrom was at his desk in Room 160, finishing up a report about another case of fraudulent inspections. This time, it was a factory that made airplane engines in Ohio.

In a pattern familiar from the movie hearings, the Truman Committee had once again uncovered serious problems, the army had vowed to conduct its own detailed investigation, and the committee agreed to wait for those findings. Fulton wrote to the senators on March 23 that Colonel Miles Knowles, a war department liaison officer, had "emphasized the importance to Army morale of the airplane crews having confidence in their engines. For that reason, he has asked the committee not to make public anything with respect to the investigation," at least for the time being.[1]

Three days later, Truman found himself again on the front pages for an entirely different matter—a bit of Washington theatrical drama notable as one of the rare times during the war that the committee went into a public hearing fistfight and came away bruised and battered. As part of a series of hearings to gather information on manpower, efficiency, and turnover, Fulton had invited several national labor leaders to testify, including William Green, president of the AFL, Phillip Murray, head of the CIO, and John L. Lewis of the United Mine Workers.

At sixty-three, Lewis looked like Hollywood's version of a gruff, scowling thunderous labor boss, and for twenty-three years as head of the mine workers union, he had been just that. In late March, Lewis was dropping hints of a strike, noting that while prices were going up, the pay of his miners was not. And that while they were spending fifty-three hours a week underground—when you counted traveling up and down the mine shafts—they were only being paid for the forty-two hours they actually spent working coal. Lewis and other labor leaders had agreed after Pearl Harbor to forgo strikes for the duration of the war, but this was an uneasy truce at best. He and others felt that a promise made by the administration—that in exchange for the no-strike pledge it would create an agency to hear and address labor's concerns—had not been met.

Lewis loved a good argument and delighted in thumbing his nose at the powers in Washington: his response to Fulton's request to appear before the committee was, maybe. "I will be glad to appear if I can, but am not able at this time to make a definite commitment." Fulton, always a little prickly, especially when he felt the committee was being disrespected, shot back: "The committee expects you to do so and desires confirmation by return mail."[2]

Lewis, enjoying himself, responded that he was shocked that Truman or his distinguished Senate colleagues could have approved of either "the peremptory tone or studied lack of courtesy" in Fulton's response. Truman put a stop to the bickering by issuing a subpoena for Lewis to appear,[3] and the curtain rose on

Friday morning, March 26, in Room 318 of the Senate Office Building. The reporters were in their seats, ready to watch the fun.

"John Lewis, last of the great ham tragedians of politics, strode to the witness stand with long, measured steps: one-two-three-four," wrote *Time* magazine's correspondent. "Two tiny spring flowers, one white, one lavender, peeped from the lapel of his flowing black coat. His broad jowls were momentarily at rest, his eyebrows arched like innocent cupid's bows."[4]

Truman started off respectfully, asking Lewis for some general thoughts about manpower and the labor situation. "We would be most happy to have your views and a statement from you on those most vital subjects that are now facing the nation." Was there something specific, Lewis asked, that he should talk about? Truman answered, what about absenteeism?

Which was all the opening Lewis needed. "I think that absenteeism occurs everywhere," he told the room, with a slight wave of his cigar. "I have been told that absenteeism is higher in Congress than it is in industry. I do not know. I know that absenteeism prevails on this committee this morning. I do not know why some of the Senators aren't here, but I am sure they are away for perfectly competent reasons."[5]

Caught off guard, Truman responded that "they are away because the Senate is in session and considering a very important bill that has to do with inflation about which I hope you will talk to us this morning."

"I am quite sure the reason is adequate, and I am quite sure if the Senators were in the factory this morning and were absent they would be absent for a perfectly good reason."

Senator Owen Brewster fared little better, asking Lewis about rising prices and wages. "Are you ready as a patriotic American to cooperate with everyone else who is seeking to hold the dikes against inflation?"

"Oh, my dear Senator, I would be very happy if anything I could do could help hold the dike against inflation."

"The country certainly believes that you have a very big finger in this dike right now."

Lewis pushed back. He noted that businesses were allowed to make profits—even fixed profits of 10 percent—on their war contracts. So why were the workers accused of contributing to inflation by asking for a raise? Thanks to those government contracts and the profits earned from them, corporations would emerge from the war with money to rebuild their factories and recondition their machinery. "And the worker in this country can't do that, because when he wears out his shoes or work clothes or tools, he can't replace those at the expense of the public."

Brewster: "Would you deny, Mr. Lewis, the right of a corporation to make any provision for depreciation?"

"Why certainly not, sir. A corporation is entitled to proper depreciation. But the worker is going to come out of this war, sir, with plant and equipment depreciated, with deferred maintenance at a high figure, older in years, weaker in body, with his assets eaten up by reason of the fact that he can't keep pace with the situation because he is asked to make a sacrifice so that the corporations of this country won't have to make a sacrifice."

John L. Lewis, left, testifies before the Truman Committee, March 26, 1943.

When Lewis noted that food prices, despite government controls, had gone up, Truman responded that control of food price inflation was a national matter that needed "the whole-hearted cooperation of the vast majority of the population."

"One way to get that cooperation," Lewis said, "is to give the workers of this country enough to eat until Congress can devise some way of restraining the rapacity of corporate industry in this country."

This was too much for Joe Ball of Minnesota. "Mr. Lewis, you are not seriously trying to tell the committee that any large number of workers in the United States don't get enough to eat? That is demagoguery, pure and simple, and you know it."

Lewis now was in full roar: "When you call me a demagogue before I can reply, I hurl it back in your face. Now hunger is a relative term. I have said it, and I say to you, sir, that the coal miners of this country are hungry because they are suffering from a dietary deficiency. Their wages will not buy enough of the proper character of foodstuffs to maintain their bodily efficiency, and malnutrition brings in its train all of the physical ills and ailments that follow it known to the medical profession. That is what is happening to the coal miners of this country and when you ask me, are the coal miners hungry? I say yes. And when you call me a demagogue, I will say you are less than a proper representative of the common people of this country when you do that."

Truman jumped in: "Now, Mr. Lewis, we won't stand for any sassy remarks to the members of this committee, and your rights will be protected here just the same as those of everybody else. I don't like that remark to a member of this committee."

"Senator, did you object when the Senator called me a demagogue?"

"Yes, it works both ways. I don't think the Senator should have called you a demagogue."

"Who cast the first stone?"

"I am stopping it right now."

"Very good, sir."

And on it went. Brewster and Lewis bickered over whether the miners' workweek could be increased, with Lewis restating his point that they were already spending fifty-three hours underground but getting paid for only forty-two. There followed considerable, highly detailed back-and-forth over the details of a coal miner's weekly pay, and whether a cost-of-living increase was enough to allow him to adequately feed a family. When challenged on just about any subject—wages, the farm bill, the dangers of coal mining, costs of clothing and health care and especially food—Lewis spoke knowledgeably and eloquently, and gave better than he got.

Homer Ferguson pressed him on the promise labor leaders had made after Pearl Harbor to refrain from strikes during the war. "Now," he asked Lewis, "do you say that one of the things that caused you to agree to it or sign it has been breached by the federal government, and therefore the agreement is no longer binding on you or your unions?"

"No, I said it wasn't *necessarily* binding."

Ferguson pressed Lewis to say that, if that agreement was off, he intended to strike, and Lewis, as he had done many times already that morning, just as firmly refused to say any such thing. "I never said anything about striking. I join with members of this committee and all other Americans in hoping that no stoppages of production will be necessary in our essential industry."

No matter how many times they asked him this question, Lewis was not going to admit that he might call a strike. Nor would he say definitively that he wouldn't. Finally, at 2:05 p.m., Truman called it a day. "Thank you, Mr. Lewis. That is all."

After a hearing that lasted three hours, the *Time* correspondent concluded, Lewis "steamed majestically from the committee room. The echoes of his blank prose died: the stage emptied. The great tragedian, whom no vegetable throwing gallery has ever been able to silence, had played another scene."[6]

★ ★ ★

The army had promised it would follow up on the complaints the committee had received in January, from army inspectors at a government-owned aircraft engine factory north of Cincinnati, Ohio. The plant, run by the Wright Aeronautical Corporation, produced several models of the air-cooled Cyclone engine used in B-25 medium bombers and other planes. After receiving those complaints, Donald Lathrom had gone out to Cincinnati and interviewed more than two dozen civilian and military employees. They told him how inspectors were not allowed to reject defective parts and engines, and that when they tried to reject them, or even to raise concerns, they faced transfer or other punishment. One of the men cried as he spoke with Lathrom, saying he had two nephews in the air force.[7]

Truman agreed to hold off on hearings or any further investigation while the company and the army conducted their own inquiries, and on March 30, the committee met in private session to hear what they had found. Brigadier General Bennett Meyers told Truman that he had sent an investigator out to the plant who, Meyers said, "advised me that there was nothing in his written report that would indicate that any action would have to be taken by me."

Which wasn't quite the same thing as saying there was nothing going on. "So you haven't really anything to offer us today," Truman asked, "by way of informing us what you found wrong with inspection or management at Wright Aeronautical in Cincinnati?"

"I haven't found anything like that to advise you on."[8]

The company officials, sitting before the committee just days after these same senators had administered a very thorough and very public spanking to Carnegie-Illinois Steel, were a bit more cautious. Truman asked the quality manager of the plant, "Have you found anything wrong?"

"Yes, there are details that are wrong."

But minutes later the overall plant manager, William Finlay, disagreed when Truman asked him the same question: "I would say that there is nothing wrong in that sense of the word. We acknowledge that we can always do a better job."

Rudolph Halley followed up: "Do you still feel that everything is in order and under control after your recent investigation?"

"Yes, we do."

Once again, the committee had given the military and a defense contractor every opportunity to clean up a bad situation—quietly and without publicity—and they had passed.* Truman sent a subcommittee to Cincinnati, and on the first three days of April, they held closed hearings. Another was held on April 8 in Washington, and finally two more, on the 13th and 14th, in Dayton. Dozens of witnesses appeared; their sworn testimony amounted to 1,286 pages.

The hearings confirmed Lathrom's investigation in every detail, and the revelations were every bit as shocking as those from the steel plant in Pittsburgh: a major corporation, with the willing cooperation of army officers, was "producing and causing the government to accept defective and substandard material." Or, as Truman put it years later in his memoirs, "These engines were causing the death of some of our student pilots."[9]

Tests had been falsified, records destroyed, inspection reports forged or skipped entirely. The committee found that the air force inspectors were far more concerned about protecting the company than ensuring that the engines supplied to the military were safe and operational. Inspectors who didn't go along were threatened, "and even during the Committee's investigation one inspector was actually transferred for the sole reason

---

* In fairness, Brigadier General Meyers, it turned out, had been misled by "Army officers and personnel later found by the committee to be obstructing the inquiry."

that he refused to accept, for the Government, an engine which was leaking gasoline."[10]

As to the claim that these engines had caused crashes and deaths, this was a hard thing to prove. The committee's report, however, methodically laid out the facts that could lead to that conclusion.

First, "engines were built and sold to the government that were leaking gasoline. The Chief of the Army's Engine and Propeller Unit testified that no engine with any kind of a gas leak should be passed."

Second, "unsafe material has been discovered in completed engines ready for shipment."

Third, "the company's own reports indicate that these parts failed in a substantial number of cases."

And fourth, "a substantial number of airplanes using this engine have had crashes in which engine failures were involved." Lathrom had provided specific details on these crashes.

The committee acknowledged that other airplanes with other engines crashed, too, and that the cause of a crash, especially when the pilot had been killed, was extremely hard to determine.[11] Nevertheless, "more than 25 percent of the engines built at the plant have consistently failed in one or more major parts during a 3-hour test run."[12]

The report found, too, that the misconduct went beyond inspections, and beyond employees of the plant. Officers in the army, specifically a lieutenant colonel who was the chief inspector for the army air forces, had deliberately lied and concealed evidence from the committee, had "attempted to intimidate witnesses, introduced evidence prepared specifically for the purpose, designed to discredit witnesses, made misstatements under oath, and otherwise attempted to impede the committee's investigation."

This time, the reaction was swifter and more decisive, at least by the military. On July 12—two days after the committee released its report—the army announced that two top inspection officials involved with the Lockland plant had been dismissed, and the Justice Department said it would convene a grand jury to consider criminal charges.

The steel hearings, the travel, the fight with Lewis, the Lockland investigation, all this had once again worn Truman down, and Bess was urging him to head back to Arkansas for some rest, and a chance for the army doctors to examine him. Before he did, though, he flew to Chicago for a speaking engagement that marked a rare diversion from his standard, fairly canned remarks about winning the war and raising production. It was also an unusual choice for a man whose private letters showed the casual use of terms like "kike" and "Hebrews."[13]

He had accepted an invitation to speak at a "Rally to Demand the Rescue of Doomed Jews." There was, by 1943, awareness in the Allied governments and extensive news coverage worldwide of the roundup and mass murder of Jews by the Nazis, yet there was also a reluctance or indifference among the Allied governments to do anything about it beyond the military effort to defeat Hitler.

As with many members of Congress, Truman's constituents had brought him firsthand knowledge of the plight of European Jews seeking to escape Nazi persecution: for years he'd been receiving letters and telegrams from Jewish families in Missouri, asking him to help a friend or relative secure a visa, or complete the proper paperwork, or make inquiries of consulate offices in Germany or France. Several of these had come through his old friend and business partner, Eddie Jacobson; often Truman used his influence when he could.

When asked about the fate of the Jews in Europe, Roosevelt said the US was doing all it could to defeat Germany, expressed support for the Jewish cause, and vowed retribution after the war for the Nazi crimes. But there were increasingly desperate calls

from Jewish leaders for the administration to do much more—
now, not after the war—to rescue Jews who were still alive, to
provide humanitarian as well as military support, to open the
nation's borders, and to draw attention to their plight.[14]

More than twenty thousand people showed for the Wednesday
night event at Chicago Stadium. Representing Congress were
Senator Wayland Brooks, Republican of Illinois, and Senator
Harry Truman of Missouri, and the keynote speaker was Rabbi
Stephen Wise of New York, president of the American Jewish
Congress.[15] Truman began his speech by drawing on his World
War I experience: "Some twenty-three years ago when we men
of America returned to this nation's shores, in our hearts was a
consuming hatred for the forces of oppression which had sought
to crush the free people of the world." Yet, now, "in conquered
Europe we find a once free people enslaved, crushed, and brutal-
ized by the iron heel of the barbarian. The people of that ancient
race, the Jews, are being herded like animals into the Ghettos,
the concentration camps, the wastelands of Europe. The men,
the women and the children of this honored people are being
starved, yes! actually murdered."[16]

He invoked Roosevelt's "four freedoms": freedom of speech,
freedom of worship, freedom from want, and freedom from fear,
and suggested that winning the war and defeating the Nazis
on the battlefield was not enough. "Today—not tomorrow—
we must do all that is humanly possible to provide a haven and
place of safety for all those who can be grasped from the hand
of the Nazi butchers. This is not a Jewish problem," he concluded, "it is an American problem, and we must and we will
face it squarely and honorably."

From there, Truman was off to Hot Springs. He quietly
checked into the Arlington Hotel, a resort not far from the military hospital where the doctors could look him over. "What did
the heart man say about you?" Bess nudged him from Washing-

ton. "I noticed you skipped that report." While he was away, the back-and-forth over the Carnegie-Illinois report and other investigations continued. Fulton was writing a preliminary report on the whole case and on April 19 sent it to Mead, who was acting chairman in Truman's absence. He was also sending it to a list of companies with large war contracts, and asked Matt Connelly to forward a copy to Truman as well in Hot Springs. "Do not tell anyone where he is."[17]

Late April was taken up with the fake steel findings, but the committee also released a lengthy report on shipbuilding that got the Truman Committee into a very public squabble with the Secretary of the Navy. Mead delivered it to the Senate on April 22, and unlike the aviation report that Fulton was beginning to pull together, this report was for the most part laudatory. "The Navy has done a magnificent job in building a first-class fighting fleet." Reporters, however, were quick to jump on a single sentence, on page four, which gave figures for the Allied shipping losses in 1942 to German submarines. "They averaged approximately 1,000,000 tons of shipping per month, and in the aggregate exceeded the new construction built by the United States and Great Britain."[18]

That revelation—the Germans were sinking merchant ships faster than the Allies could build new ones—dominated the news coverage the next day. The editorial in the Baltimore *Evening Sun* was typical: "The central, massive, and sobering fact which the committee makes public is that in 1942 we and our allies lost 12,000,000 tons of ships to the U-boats," the paper said. And while this made for "grim reading," the piece praised the committee for providing the facts "more fully and more baldly than they have been in any previous official or semi-official account."

This was, other observers then and since have noted, one of the central roles the Truman Committee played throughout the war: bringing accurate, though sometimes unwelcome, news to the American public. "There is a real value in having the record thus set plainly before us," the *Sun* told its readers, and "disclosure of the harsh figures should refocus attention here on the seriousness of this aspect of winning the war."[19]

Navy Secretary Knox not only disagreed, but he accused the committee of getting its facts wrong. "Knox Hits Report On Ship Sinkings," read the next day's *New York Times*. Knox told reporters he had already drawn Truman's attention to the "error" and accused the committee of getting the incorrect figure of a million tons a month "from some uninformed source, probably common gossip."[20]

Four days later, the secretary had to eat those words. "Knox Admits Million-Ton Net Allied Ship Loss," read page one of *The Washington Post*, with similar headlines around the country. The navy now acknowledged that, "stated in terms of gross tonnage, including all losses of Allied ships, however their loss may have been caused, there is no great difference in the Navy and the Committee figures for 1942."[21]

For the thousands of would-be inventors around the country, it was another line in the shipbuilding report that jumped out from the page. In discussing the need for new strategies and new weapons to defeat the U-boats, the committee report referenced the famous Civil War clash that marked the first-ever battle between ironclad ships—the CSS *Virginia* and the USS *Monitor*. For centuries, naval warfare had pitted large wooden ships, with rows of cannon up and down their sides, blasting away at each other. But by the Civil War, the idea was taking hold of protecting wooden ships with iron plates, and early in the war, the government received news that the Confederates were building an armor-plated ship that could threaten the US Navy squadron in Hampton Roads, Virginia. This created an urgent need for a design that could match this new ship, and the Union Navy began soliciting ideas. A Swedish inventor, John Ericsson, submitted a radical proposal for a flat, odd-looking vessel with only two guns, housed in a revolving turret designed by another inventor, Theodore Timby.

In a response that would have been familiar to Andrew Jackson Higgins eighty years later, the navy was skeptical of the new and innovative design when Ericsson proposed it, and ridiculed his design as a "cheesebox on a raft," or "Ericsson's folly." Nevertheless, with reports coming in from the South of the progress of the Confederate ironclad, his design was approved, and construction began.

Not a moment too soon, it turned out. The Confederates had used the engines and hull of a partially destroyed US Navy ship, the *Merrimack*, and converted it to an armored ship with ten cannons and an iron ram on the prow, renamed CSS *Virginia*. On March 8, 1862, *Virginia* steamed into Hampton Roads, and headed for the five wooden US Navy ships there. The cannonballs from the US ships bounced off *Virginia*'s armor plates, while the ironclad rammed the frigate USS *Cumberland*, sinking it, and then turned its guns on the frigate *Congress*, which caught fired and burned.

It was the greatest defeat up to that time in the US Navy's history (until Pearl Harbor seventy-nine years later). There were fears the seemingly invincible *Virginia* could steam up the Potomac River to attack Washington. Unless, and this seemed unlikely, the flat, unwieldy vessel now heading with all speed for Hampton Roads could do something about it. *Monitor* had only two guns—larger, heavier guns mounted in the round turret that was almost the only part of the ship above the waterline.

The next morning, as *Virginia* steamed towards USS *Minnesota* to continue the destruction, it found *Monitor* in its path. The two ships exchanged gunfire, with the shells for the most part bouncing off the iron plates, and neither able to gain an advantage over the other. After several hours, the two ships withdrew, each claiming victory. In two days, naval warfare had changed forever, and Ericsson's strange design became the model for naval warships going forward: armored vessels with revolving turrets carrying fewer but much more powerful guns. The US Navy immediately ordered ten more of them based on a larger design by Ericsson, and they became a new class of warship known as monitors.

Eighty years later, the Truman Committee in its shipbuilding report looked to Ericsson's example, suggesting that the navy once again needed to think outside the box and consider radical new ideas to counter the U-boats: "We need another 'soapbox on a raft' like the *Monitor.*"

For weeks after the report's release, the staff in Room 160 were swamped with letters from backyard tinkerers and basement scientists, many of them mentioning the "soapbox on a raft."

Dear Senator,
Enclosed find my idea to beat the U-boat. By attaching a flexible wall of floating steel plates to the bow of a ship by means of cables & booms, it would provide a steel wall say 30 feet from a ship causing a torpedo to explode far enough away so as not to blow a hole in the ship. Let me know what you think of my idea.

My dear Sir,
The attached description of the Phantom Raider shows a periscope view of the floating unit, which is designed to deal effectively with U-boats.

Dear Senator Truman,
I would like to offer an application of the radiosonde principle, now used extensively in meteorology, to the problem of submarine detection.

Most went straight into the files, with the standard form letter acknowledgment to the writer:

Dear Mr. Polhamus,
Senator Truman has asked me to thank you for your letter of April
23 regarding your invention, the submarine tank.
    Your comments on this matter have been noted with interest.
Very truly yours,
HUGH FULTON
Chief Counsel[22]

One invention that caught Hugh Fulton's eye, and which
seemed to have real potential in the fight against the U-boats,
was the helicopter. Otto Sikorsky, born in 1889 in Kiev (then
part of the Russian Empire), was an aircraft designer who had
begun experimenting with helicopters in 1909. Following the
Bolshevik Revolution, he emigrated to the United States, where
he continued his efforts to perfect a working helicopter. In 1939
he designed and flew the first successful American model, and
three years later began producing the Sikorsky R-4, the world's
first mass-produced helicopter.

The R-4 was hard to fly, and the design was in some ways
still experimental, as Sikorsky worked to develop larger, more
powerful, and more reliable models suitable for military use.[23]
Still, the coast guard early on recognized the helicopter's potential in search-and-rescue operations and possibly for spot-
ting submarines. In June 1943, Fulton wrote to Sikorsky: "The
Committee is very anxious to make sure that a good program
for the production, as soon as possible, of large numbers of helicopters is evolved. It is particularly anxious that the program
be not retarded by red tape or unnecessary difficulties." But as
with Andrew Higgins and his landing craft, the navy bureaucracy provided plenty of both. Drew Pearson reported in May
that the navy "not only has not done anything about helicopters
until the last few days, but actually has been opposing them, despite appeals from the Maritime Commission, the Coast Guard

and to some extent from the Army that helicopters are the only way to lick the submarine."[24]

If they could be produced in numbers and flown effectively, helicopters offered a potentially potent weapon against submarines—the ability for ships to carry their own search aircraft far out into the ocean, beyond the range of patrol planes. In late May, the army announced it had successfully tested a helicopter's ability to take off and land from the deck of a merchant ship.[25] But the technology was still new, and the engineering and manufacturing challenges were considerable. Helicopters would see limited use during World War II; it was not until the Korean War that they would come into their own for medical evacuations, observation, and reconnaissance.

17

COUNTERPUNCHES

"Hey, do you want a steam bath?" Joe Martinez asked Bob Irvin one day.

"What do you mean?" said Irvin. Martinez was a capable and lively addition to the investigative staff; at thirty-four, a little older than Irvin and most of the other lawyers. He had joined the committee in January, and he and Irvin had quickly become friends. Like Irvin, Martinez had only recently graduated from law school—he'd done his coursework at night while working as an administrative assistant for Senator Dennis Chavez of New Mexico. So he knew his way around the Capitol.

"We'll go down to the Senators' steam room and get a steam bath and a rub."[1]

Nope, Irvin said, that room was senators only, and one of the committee staff had already gotten in trouble for using it. "Joe, come on, man," he said, "you're liable to get us both canned."

"Oh hell no. We'll go get a rub."

Martinez, a future attorney general of the state of New Mexico, walked across the street to a liquor store and bought a pint of whiskey in a brown paper bag. At the steam room, the attendant accepted the gift and waved them off; come back in five minutes, he said, when the coast is clear. When they returned, he hurried them into the spa's little dressing cubicles, each with its own chair, a bed, and a place to hang your clothes. "Well, strip down," he told Irvin. "Wrap a sheet around you and put it over your head, and I'll come back and get you. Don't move or don't say anything."

Irvin loved a bit of fun; he'd amused his colleagues in Room 160 all summer by wearing his visitor's badge from the Pittsburgh steel plant: "Irvin Works." But here in this Senate inner sanctum, he was wondering if this would be his last day on the job. Finally, the attendant waved them in for the first steam bath of his life. "And then pretty soon he took me out into a massage room"—marble tables and hot and cold running water—for a thorough rubdown. After a while the man tossed him a sheet and shooed him back into the little cubicle: "Go ahead, take a nap."

Irvin relaxed, "stretched out very comfortably," until he heard a cheerful whistling just outside. The door to his cubicle opened and there was James Mead of New York, one of the Democrats on the committee.

"Hi, Senator," Irvin said nervously.

"I'm sorry, Bob, you just stay right there. Don't let me disturb you."

Mead closed the door and went off somewhere else, and Irvin was grateful that he never mentioned the incident. "But I never went back there either."[2]

He wasn't the only one needing a relaxing rubdown that summer. "Missed my lunch went to the Senate bath house and took a Hot Springs bath," Truman, taking a bit of a personal

day, wrote Bess on June 25. "Then went out to the Hot Shop*
ate some spaghetti and meat balls, salad, ice tea and orange ice
and went home and to bed at 6:45."[3] He was up early the next
morning for a long walk and a hot shower, then back to work.
"Feel 100% better than I have for a week. I guess I'd been worrying about all the responsibility thrust upon."

It wasn't just the demands of the committee. In the middle
of what the papers were calling the hottest June in fifty years,
Truman was tied up in two big fights in the Senate. One was an
attempt to preserve a New Deal program, the National Youth
Administration, which he lost. The other was a patronage battle with his fellow senator from Missouri over two judicial appointments, which he won. "Nomination and confirmation of
the two new judges was a personal triumph of Senator Harry
Truman over his colleague, Senator Bennett Champ Clark,"
read the front-page story in the *St. Louis Star-Times* after the
dust had settled in the Senate.[4]

Truman had apparently weathered the chill from the White
House over the *American* magazine article, since Roosevelt had
personally intervened on this matter. Truman met with the president in the White House on June 25, for only the second time in
a year,[5] and persuaded him to favor his western Missouri nomi-
nees over Clark's choices from the east. (The president was also
irked at Clark for his opposition to the administration's foreign
policy and to some elements of the New Deal.[6])

"They say I broke every precedent in the Senate getting the
job done," Truman gleefully wrote Bess. "The *Post-Dispatch* is
throwing a grand spasm as is the *Star* so I know I'm right. Had
lunch with Mr. Clark and he's about recovered."[7] It was yet another sign of how completely the pecking order in Missouri politics had flipped. Truman was now unquestionably the top dog,

---

* The Hot Shoppe, a diner on Connecticut Avenue a few blocks up from their
apartment, was a favorite spot when Bess was out of town.

and his elder colleague, facing re-election in 1944, was seen as vulnerable.

One reason Clark was "about recovered" after lunching with Truman became clear a couple of days later in the *St. Louis Globe-Democrat*. The paper noted that, until recently, political insiders had been questioning whether Clark, once a shoe-in, could win re-election in 1944. But recently his fortunes had changed, for one single reason: "That Truman is going to give Clark his complete behind-the-scenes support—and perhaps campaign openly and vigorously for him—is becoming increasingly apparent."[8]

Hugh Fulton, too, was seeking a break from the heat and the workaholic pace he set for himself. He was busy with several committee reports, as well as the exhaustive prep work needed for the hearings. Along with the large-scale investigations, there was a steady stream of smaller one-offs. In June, he and several of the senators held hearings in Kansas City about a gunpowder factory, and why the cost to build it had ballooned from $47 million to $126 million. Just getting four senators and the chief counsel in the same place at the same time in the middle of the country was a logistical challenge that involved all the complexities of rail and air travel in the 1940s. Fulton typed it up in a two-page memo for Margaret Buchholz, the efficient and hardworking administrator in Room 160 who was also tasked with travel arrangements.

On June 6 he would be in Chicago. "I believe there are several trains and would like to have one that would get me into Kansas City about 9 a.m. or before." There he would meet up with the chairman. Fulton would stay three days, then depart early enough to get him to St. Louis "in time to take the number 66, *The American*, Pennsylvania Railroad, leaving St. Louis at 9:12 a.m.," for the trip home. Meanwhile, Senator Ferguson was in Detroit. "Check the time tables and find out whether it will be possible for him to fly to Chicago late Tuesday and catch a late Santa Fe train to Kansas City that will get him there early Wednesday morning."

And if all that wasn't confusing enough, "Senator Wallgren may go along, in which event he could if necessary use the same accommodations as myself. On the return trip we may fly back in an Army plane but I think you should make the reservations anyhow."[9]

After that, Fulton was headed to Michigan to visit his mother and speak at the commencement ceremonies at Ann Arbor Senior High School. There he could also meet with the committee's newest investigator: George Meader. Fulton had invited his old law school friend to come along on the Willow Run tour back in February. Meader, the Washtenaw County prosecutor, told Fulton he'd been trying to get a commission in the military or find a way to serve in the government. At the same time, Owen Brewster had been pressuring Truman to appoint a Republican lawyer to the committee, and Meader fit the bill. He accepted Fulton's offer of assistant counsel starting July 1.[10]

From Michigan, Fulton was headed to Chicago, then to DC again for a couple of days and then off to his farm in New Jersey, where he'd invited several of the staff for a weekend getaway from the heat and, if only briefly, from the work. Throughout the spring and early summer, he had been pulling together the Lockland investigation, along with the Willow Run inquiry, a study of helicopters, and a broader look at the troubled Curtiss-Wright Corporation, into a major report on aviation that the committee would release in July. While a couple of stories about the Lockland report had leaked—Drew Pearson had gotten wind of it in May—for the most part the committee had been working with both the military and company officials behind closed doors. Pearson's column had noted many of the key details, but also that the "Truman Committee is waiting for the Army to clean up the situation completely."

Undersecretary Patterson had sent a team to Ohio, headed by Lieutenant General William Knudsen, the former OPM head and General Motors production wizard, to look into the situation. Their report agreed with many of the findings of Truman's subcommittee, but downplayed some of the most serious allegations, notably that defective engines had made their way into army planes.

In drafting the aviation report, Fulton once again had to walk a careful line, balancing constructive criticism with the very real accomplishments that had been made: airplanes were rolling off assembly lines in US factories in numbers that before the war would have been unthinkable. "We have succeeded in building an air industry in the United States which our foes cannot equal," he wrote. In 1942, 48,000 planes were produced, and now, just halfway through 1943, the number had reached 64,000. "The planes we have already produced and those produced during the next year will largely determine the result of the war."[11]

Having said that, "It is only natural that in so vast a program there have been many mistakes. Perfection must not be expected in war where it is better to use wasteful methods than to risk having too little. All that can be fairly asked is that reasonable care should be taken and common sense exercised to keep waste and mistakes at a minimum." The report directly addressed the criticism aimed at the committee's earlier reports, and which Fulton knew would target this one: that pointing out "mistakes and difficulties" could be "misconstrued as a condemnation by the committee of a program which as a whole has been unequalled anywhere in the world. However we should not judge our efficiency simply by comparison with what others have done, but should also take into consideration what could have been accomplished. In a great many instances we could have done much better than we have."[12]

From there, Fulton got down to business. For the most part, the news was good: modern and efficient planes—many of them now superior to the ones flown by the Germans and Japanese—were reaching the front lines in significant numbers. The B-17 Flying Fortress and the B-24 Liberator—long-range, four-engine bombers—were as good or better than any in the world, and hundreds of them were now attacking Germany almost every day. And while production of those planes by Boeing and Consolidated "has been excellent," there was, on the other hand, Willow Run.

"The Ford Motor Co. was relatively much slower than had been expected in getting into production" with the B-24. Several times the committee had checked in with the company "and insisted that additional action be taken to expedite production." The problems were many, starting with the fact that Ford had tried to build such a complex and complicated piece of equipment using the methods of an automobile assembly line, "despite the warnings of many experienced aircraftmen." Nor had the company tried to learn from the designers and engineers on the West Coast who were already building the Liberator. And then, as the committee learned on its inspection tour of the plant, hundreds of design changes demanded by the government had forced delays in training and retooling. Finally, there were the problems with the lack of transportation and housing for the thirty thousand workers needed to make the plant run.

All of this added up, the report said, to the startling fact that Fulton, Meader, and the senators had seen for themselves back in February: "the Ford Motor Co. had not produced at Willow Run a plane which was capable of use at the front." What the report did not note, but was also a factor, was the disarray in the company's top management. In May, Edsel Ford had died suddenly, of stomach cancer, at age forty-nine, leaving control of the company once again solely in the hands of its aging and increasingly erratic founder, now seventy-nine years old.

The committee had kept in close touch with Ford executives since the February visit, and since then, "great progress has been made," notably by using other Ford plants to make subassemblies that would then be shipped to Willow Run. The plant and its mile-long assembly line would soon live up to the potential

that Edsel Ford, Charles Sorenson and the company's top engineers and designers had envisioned when they first drew up
the plans back in 1940.

On some developments in the heavy-bomber program, the
Truman Committee was silent: "There are matters with respect
to four-engine bombers and improvements thereon which the
committee has studied but to which it cannot refer in a public
report for matters of security."[13] This was a reference to the Boeing B-29 Superfortress—a plane that could fly higher, faster, and
farther and carry a heavier load than any bomber in the world. It
would incorporate modern innovations like a pressurized cabin
and remote-controlled gun turrets, and would eventually enable the long-range bombing of Japan. But the plane was vastly
more complex than any currently in existence, and would not
become operational until mid-1944.

Across the board, newer models were in full production that
were among the finest combat airplanes in the world: fighter
planes including the twin-engine P-38 Lightning and the P-47
Thunderbolt; and the P-51 Mustang, considered the best all-
around fighter of the war. The navy's new F6F Hellcat and F4U
Corsair fighters would prove more than a match for the Japanese Zero.

Once again, though, the committee raised concerns about
the Curtiss P-40 Warhawk, which despite the availability of
the newer fighters was still being made in large numbers. The
plane had been used successfully by nearly every Allied nation
and in nearly every theater of war. Pilots had shown that when
it was properly flown, it could hold its own against older German and Japanese fighters, and it had proven to be effective in a
low-level, ground-support role. But despite efforts to upgrade its
performance, the Warhawk could not compete with the newer
models and would be phased out of production in 1944. "In the
opinion of the committee, it would have been preferable to in-

crease the production of Mustangs and decrease the production of Curtiss Warhawks."

From there the report turned to another troubled Curtiss-Wright plane, the SB2C Helldiver. On paper, the dive-bomber was better than the navy's current model, the Douglas Dauntless, but its early development had been hampered by production delays and performance difficulties. And while those bugs were being worked out, it was becoming clear that the tactics of aerial warfare and anti-aircraft defense were shifting. Some recent reports from the battle lines indicated that "dive bombers have very definite limitations even for naval use." Nevertheless, the navy said it needed the new dive-bomber and, as always, the committee deferred to the military when it came to combat requirements.

Still, the Helldiver program was a mess. The committee had received dozens of complaints from the factory built to produce the plane in Columbus, Ohio: construction delays, late modifications, idled assembly lines, waste, and inefficiency. Production "has been hopelessly behind schedule and to date Curtiss-Wright has not succeeded in producing a single SB2C which the Navy considers to be usable as a combat airplane." Meanwhile, the costs at the plant were soaring—the payroll was nearly $1 million dollars a week. Often its 21,000 workers, many of them "diverted from farming or industrial work," found themselves with nothing to do. The "knowledge of the inactivity at the plant has become widely known among the friends and relatives of the workmen there and throughout the area adjacent to Columbus and has had a bad effect on morale in that area."[14]

The Helldiver was a troubled plane: way behind schedule, disliked by some pilots, unproven in combat, and possibly not even needed anymore. On top of all this was the fact—which the Truman Committee noted with barely concealed outrage—that "Curtiss-Wright has advertised the Helldiver plane as 'the world's best dive bomber.'" So far, the company had spent more than

$12,000 "in such eulogistic self-praise of the Helldiver," part of the company's overall advertising budget in 1943 of $872,000. The bulk of that cost, the committee noted with gritted teeth, "will be borne by the Federal Government."

The sections on the P-40 and the Helldiver were followed by a lengthy and highly critical chapter on the Curtiss-Wright Corporation, which was second only to General Motors in the amount of war contracts received: $4.4 billion. This was a huge amount for a company much smaller than GM, and one that had needed government help to pay for the construction of new facilities. The Helldiver plant in Columbus had cost the taxpayers $27 million. Engines for the plane were to be built in Canada, and the army version of the plane at an existing plant in St. Louis. All this "was a most unfortunate decision as a result of which many tens of millions of dollars have been wasted." The army, no longer interested in dive-bombers, was backing away from the St. Louis contracts. That facility would shift to producing cargo planes—the successful Curtiss C-46.

On the issue of advertising—which would soon become an even bigger issue with Curtiss-Wright—Fulton lingered for some time. Of course companies needed to advertise, and it should properly be recognized as a legitimate business expense. But in this case, "The committee particularly condemns advertising which was intended to give the public the erroneous impression that the Curtiss Helldiver was the world's finest dive bomber and making a substantial contribution to the war effort when the fact is that no usable plane has yet been produced and that the dive bombers in use by the Navy were produced by Douglas Aircraft Co. and not by Curtiss-Wright."[15]

All of which added up to the fact that, "through the excessive ability and zeal of its salesmen," Curtiss-Wright had received far more contracts from the army and navy than warranted by the quality of its products or its ability to produce them. And it was guilty of "gross negligence" in the management and operation of the Lockland plant. "The committee is disappointed at the over all performance of Curtiss-Wright."[16]

The War Department was to blame as well, and here, perhaps understandably, Fulton indulged in a bit of "I told you so" finger-wagging: "Members of Congress have been constantly advised by the Army and Navy that they and they alone were capable of producing safe and satisfactory material for the fighting forces and that for that reason no civilian agency should ever have anything to say with reference to such matters." Perhaps, the report suggested, the military should worry less about shoring up production at questionable facilities, and more about "the procurement of quality material for the fighting forces."

And then, in fairness, the committee nodded to the other side of the ledger: both the military and Curtiss-Wright had taken steps to clean up the messes and, "despite its difficulties and failings Curtiss-Wright has, like all corporations, made signal contributions to the war effort." The bottom line in all this? "The committee recommends to the War Department that it take prompt and effective action to renegotiate the contracts of Curtiss-Wright."

The aircraft report concluded with an enthusiastic endorsement of the helicopter, dinging the navy for being slow to recognize its potential, especially in antisubmarine warfare. The committee had found a navy memo from 1938 that all but dismissed the invention as a "minor application which hardly justifies expenditure of experimental funds."[17]

Senator Mon Wallgren delivered the report on July 10, and predictably, it made headlines around the country. Once again, many of the stories focused on the clear, accurate information the Truman Committee had provided to a public that was hungry for it—as the Associated Press put it, lifting "some of the secrecy surrounding America's newest warplanes."

"Navy Disclosed To Have 'Exceptional' Fighter in Grumman Hellcat—Corsair 'Fine Model,'" read the headlines in the

St. Louis Post-Dispatch. "VERDICT ON MOST TYPES FA-VORABLE—Committee Finds Mustang Is Superior to P-40, Praises Thunderbolt and Lighting."[18]

The New York Times, in its page one story, focused first on the revelations that "one of the country's largest plane-makers, caused the Government, through falsification, to accept defective materials." The story noted that "while many other planes were praised, almost the only kind words for Curtiss-Wright airplanes were for cargo planes." The *Times* reported too the news that the government had filed a lawsuit in federal court in New Jersey, charging Wright Aeronautical and eight corporate officers "over the alleged sale of 'defective, sub-standard and unsatisfactory' airplane motor materials."[19]

As with previous reports, Truman had sent copies of the pertinent sections to the companies it named in advance. Curtiss-Wright on July 7 sent a four-page response saying it "emphatically denied" several of the charges, notably that bad engines were sold to the government, and that crashes were caused by those bad engines. The early notice also enabled Curtiss-Wright to do some damage control. "CURTISS-WRIGHT HEAD SAYS PLANES SPEAK FOR THEMSELVES" said the *St. Louis Post-Dispatch,* one of many papers that printed the full text of a lengthy statement by Guy Vaughn, president of Curtiss-Wright: "It is unfortunate the Truman Committee has misrepresented standard and recognized manufacturing and inspection procedures which have led them to conclude that the engines turned out by our Lockland plant are not up to the high standards we have always maintained." The statement cited the army's report by Knudsen, and also claimed (wrongly) that the engines made at the Lockland plant "powered the North American B-25s that bombed Tokyo" in the famous Doolittle raid of April 18, 1942.

So far, this investigation, and the response, had roughly followed the path of the aluminum and rubber probes, fake steel, and others: with polite-but-firm pushback from the company involved, attempts to deflect the criticism, suggestions that the committee's findings could hinder production, and promises to do better. This time, it would be different. The battle over the Lockland plant was about to turn ugly, and over the next few weeks, it would play out in the national news media and in sworn testimony before the committee—a four-way brawl involving the Truman Committee, the Curtiss-Wright Corporation, the War Department, and the press—notably *The New York Times*.

It began the next morning, when readers of *The Cincinnati Enquirer* opened their newspapers to page eleven: "To the Employees of Wright Aeronautical Corporation," read the large headline on a full-page advertisement. "The special committee to investigate the national defense program, sometimes known as the Truman Committee, has accused this corporation of supplying materials which are defective and substandard in connection with the delivery of engines from our Cincinnati plant to the Army Air Forces. As patriotic citizens and loyal employees of this corporation, you should know certain facts in connection with this matter." The ad went on to say that in no way had the company shipped defective parts and materials. "We are prepared to fight these unjust charges to their finish. I, as general manager, assure you that this corporation has been unjustly accused. Regardless of obstacles beyond our control, we as patriotic and loyal employees, will continue to do our part to supply the material so urgently needed to win the war.—M.B. Gordon."[20]

That same day, editorials in several newspapers, including *The New York Times*, the Washington *Evening Star*, and *The Baltimore Sun*, criticized the committee's conclusions, notably on the P-40 fighter plane, arguing that it had performed well in combat in virtually every theater of the war. The *Sun* called the critique "an ancient bugaboo" of the committee; the *Times* urged readers not to "leap to unwarranted conclusions and condemn the performance of Curtiss-Wright materials as a whole."[21]

Over the next few weeks, charges and countercharges flew

back and forth: Undersecretary Patterson said on July 12, the day the full-page ad appeared, that conditions at the plant "have been much less sensational than some of the instances drawn in recently published statements." He cited Knudsen's finding that "no instance was found where any engines known to be defective were ever placed in service." But Patterson also acknowledged the removal of the two officers from their posts as part of "vigorous remedial action" over the last several months.

Truman shot back the next day: the committee's report, he said, "was exceedingly temperate in comparison with the 1,286 pages of sworn testimony on which it was based."[22] As reports continued to filter back about problems at the plant, Truman sent a subcommittee to Cincinnati to see for themselves. The senators—and Fulton and the staff—were still seething over the full-page ads and the company's denials. On top of that, this latest visit to the plant found that not only had things not improved, but engine production had fallen dramatically—by a staggering 85 percent.[23]

To find out why, Truman called a public hearing for August 20 at the federal courthouse in Cincinnati, and summoned Guy Vaughn, the president of Curtiss-Wright, to testify. After all the committee's careful deference to the army and to the company, this time things would be different. Truman flew in from Las Vegas, meeting up with Fulton and Senators Wallgren, Kilgore, and Ferguson, as well as Rudolph Halley and investigator Donald Lathrom. It would prove to be among the committee's most remarkable hearings of the war.

As always, Fulton built his case carefully. First up was Major General Oliver Echols, the assistant chief of the army procurement department in Washington that, ultimately, had responsibility over the Lockland plant. After the preliminaries, Fulton got right to the point, asking bluntly whether the plant had been well managed or not. "My opinion," Echols said, "is that the management has not been strong enough to accomplish the job."[24]

Then came the question of why the number of engines being made had plummeted in the weeks since the investigations by the committee and the army. Echols named the actual numbers, but Truman told the reporters present that "these figures are not for public use because it is a strategic matter." The figures were deleted from the official transcript, too, replaced by an underlined blank space: ____. Regardless of the exact figures, though, output had fallen, and Fulton wanted to know why: "Was that due to hypertechnical Army inspection or was it due to the inability of the company as then managed to produce ____ engines which would conform to Army specifications when there was a thorough inspection?"

Echols: "To answer your question, I am adequately satisfied in my own mind that production did not fall off due to unduly tight or picayunish inspection on the part of the Army."

Senator Homer Ferguson followed up: "General, what was the cause, in your opinion, of such a drop?"

Echols ticked off several reasons, notably that "the management of the plant persisted in trying to blame the Army for interfering with production."

Fulton's next witness could speak to that directly. Major Frank LaVista was a mechanical engineer who in late July had become the army's in-house representative at the plant, overseeing all inspections, and had recently written a detailed report about production there. Fulton asked about the company's claim that army inspectors were the cause. LaVista said he had asked four top company officials at the plant to provide specific examples, but they could not cite any.

Then Fulton moved on to one of the main reasons LaVista had found for the plant's low production: that four hundred completed engines were rejected and sent back to be rebuilt, not because of rigid demands by the army but because they had not been assembled properly.

In another troubling finding, LaVista described how three

defective engines had been discovered that were already "on the shipping dock, finally inspected and sealed, ready to ship to the destination."

Does that mean, Fulton asked, "that those engines, unless they had been picked up and given an unusual inspection, would have gone out into service?"

LaVista: "Yes, sir."

Fulton continued, reading from the major's report: "Every one of the three engines were found to be in such a condition that they could not have been installed in an airplane." Which led the company to reexamine eighty-nine more engines that were ready to ship, sending them back to be taken apart completely and reassembled.

"I take it that in your opinion," Fulton said, "as in General Echols', there is nothing to the contention that inspection procedures and the requirement of living up to them have been the cause of the production difficulties."

"At no time," LaVista answered, "will I permit, in carrying out my duties, any ridiculous inspection."

These first witnesses had set the stage for the main event. Truman called the company president, Guy Vaughn. "Mr. Vaughn, have you anybody you want to sit with you? I thought you might want your attorney."

"No, I won't need an attorney."

With that, Hugh Fulton picked up where he had left off: Was Curtiss-Wright, he asked, officially and on the record saying that "the Army inspection service is blocking production by its inspection procedure?"

"No, it could not." Vaughn answered. "We don't want to take that position."

Had he authorized any newspaper articles to that effect? Or allowed company officials to do so? "No, certainly not. We haven't contacted newspapers."

Fulton then moved on to questions about why production

had fallen so abruptly, how so many problems had been found in so many completed engines, and why the company was still claiming it had not produced defective materials.

He asked Vaughn specifically about the three mentioned in LaVista's report—the ones packed and ready to ship. Vaughn wanted to know, exactly, what was wrong with them, and Fulton asked LaVista, who was still in the room. One of them had a "lock wire" missing from a gear, LaVista said, another "had five cylinders that were perfectly dry and three were corroded, and the third one had a clutch retainer that was damaged in assembly, a drive shaft gear with one tooth broken, and the magneto flooded with slushing compound so it was inoperative."

Fulton turned back to the company president: "In light of that testimony, Mr. Vaughn, do you still take the position that your inspection procedures are such that no matter how lax you may be in any given part of the work, a finished engine which is defective cannot get through and does not get through?"

"Well, I say there is no record of any engine that we know of—"

Fulton interrupted: "But you have three now."

"I don't know whether you are thoroughly familiar with motors, but I wouldn't call it a defective engine in that sense."

"Would you put those three motors, with defects of the character described by Major LaVista, into an airplane?"

"No sir, not if I had found them."

"And you hadn't found them, had you?"

"Apparently, not from the records."

Having wrung this startling admission from the president of the company, Fulton moved on to that advertisement. "Here are cases, three engines specifically, eighty-nine others, which Major LaVista has characterized as having defects. Do you still take the position on behalf of Curtiss Wright and Wright Aeronautical that defective engines or engines with defective parts did not get out into service?"

Backed into a corner, Vaughn resorted to splitting hairs. An engine "is made up of several thousand parts, and if there is a little corrosion on one piece, it is highly technical to call it a defect."

"What do you call it?"

"I call it an oversight that has got to be fixed before it goes in an airplane."

And besides, he noted, those three engines *weren't* actually shipped.

Fulton was incredulous: "They weren't shipped solely because a new and second and unusual inspection was ordered. You understood that, didn't you?"

"Oh yes, I understood that."

"And you understood that they would have been shipped except for that."

"Probably. They were on the shipping platform. I can't argue against that either."

The senators had been waiting their turns, and now Truman stepped in. He showed Vaughn a copy of the newspaper ad. "Mr. Vaughn, do you know just how many full-page advertisements, such as this, went into newspapers around the country after the report of this committee was made?"

Again, Vaughn hedged. He didn't know, and the company had "long ago contracted for the advertising campaign we put on."

Yet clearly, Truman pointed out, the ads were written quite recently. Vaughn, not really answering, responded that they were placed in cities where the company had factories, to "bring up the morale of the men." Truman pounced: "Wasn't the best way to put somebody in there competent to manage the plant and make it operate? That is the best way to build the morale of the men."

Vaughn: "I won't argue about that."

For more details about where the ads had appeared and how much they cost, another company official was called, William

Finlay (the same official who, in March, had told the committee there was nothing wrong with inspections at the plant). He
explained that the ads appeared in several papers in Cincinnati
and New Jersey, where the company had plants, at a cost of
about $5,000. Mon Wallgren asked him about the claim that the
Lockland plant made the engines flown on the Doolittle raid.

"Your ads carrying the story about Lockland motors being in
the Tokyo raid just don't seem to fit in here very well. Your plant
opened, when, in 1941? And they took those motors out of there
and used them in the following April in the raid on Tokyo?"

Finlay wasn't sure. "That is the story I get, but you would
have to get a record of the motor numbers."

Fulton resumed his questioning of Guy Vaughn: "Wasn't this
full-page ad intended to make people, and company stockhold-
ers, believe that your company had been unjustly accused of having defective parts and lax inspection procedures?"

No, Vaughn replied: "I can assure you that was for the effect
it had on the employees of the plant."

"And not for other purposes?"

"Not for the public."

"And it was just for happenstance that it went to the public
in addition to your employees."

Vaughn: "That is correct."

Often in hearings like this, the senators were content to let
Fulton follow his methodical line of questioning, but in these
ads, the committee and its work had been publicly attacked,
and one by one they kept jumping in. Next up was Homer Ferguson: "Here is what I want to get at. Do you admit now that
you have defective inspection?" Yes, Vaughn replied, "I have
admitted that straight along. I don't know whether you call it
defective inspection, but it was not as efficient as it should be,
by any manner of means, and I have never said anything else."

"Then you claim this advertisement is true?"

Yes, said Vaughn, this time splitting hairs under a microscope:

"I think it is true that we never knowingly have shipped any-thing defective to anybody."

"In other words," Ferguson said, "the whole ad centers down on the word 'knowingly.'"

Fulton now returned to Vaughn's argument that the ads were intended to raise worker morale. "Will you show us the ads that are in accordance with your testimony today, that your com-pany did have lax inspection procedures which this commit-tee and the Army, through their investigation have corrected?"

"Do you think it would do any good?"

"I do, because it would show that you were now not doing what caused several scores of your people to write to the Tru-man Committee."

This went on for more than an hour: What if those engines had been shipped and put in an airplane? Why hadn't the man-agement found any of those other eighty-nine engines? Wasn't the company endangering the lives of pilots? If a plane crashed with one of the company's defective engines, wouldn't it likely get blamed on the pilot and not the engine? "Because the poor pilot can't be there to tell you what happened to his engine."

The head of a major defense corporation, in charge of tens of thousands of workers making vital materials for the war effort, had been treated like a misbehaving student sent to the prin-cipal's office. It was past noon when Truman ended it with a final scolding: "I want to say this to you on behalf of the com-mittee: That if you have any further statement or any brief that you want to submit to the committee, we will make it a part of the record. But it is the opinion of the committee that it is up to you to put the proper management in that plant and to get production up to the point where it should be. We shall expect to continue to be available to find out whether that is done or not—and that is not a threat; it is merely a statement of fact."

There would be more charges and countercharges in the coming weeks: Truman suggested after the hearing that if the plant didn't improve, the government might step in and take over. News stories noted that production at Lockland had climbed back up to 50 percent. And in early September, *The New York Times* ran a three-part series by reporter Turner Catledge claiming the committee's report and the resulting slump cost the army and navy "10,000 engines." The investigation had "demoralized" the facility and its workers: "In short, the whole inspection procedure at the plant closed in like a bottleneck, tightening with each new flood of rumors that the Truman Committee or the Army was in and around the plant." The first installment said the committee's report "was more sensational in its implications than in its citations" and repeated the claim that engines from the plant were used in the Doolittle raid. (Guy Vaughn wrote to Wallgren a week later with an apology and a correction: the engines flown on the raid were, in fact, not made at Lockland.)

The next day's piece said industry leaders were worried that overreaction caused by the Truman Committee's investigation and the resulting drop in production could spread to other companies and other plants. And the third story quoted union leaders defending Curtiss-Wright, with the headline, "Union Organizers Assert Truman Report on Plane Engines Was Blow to National Morale." Catledge again characterized the committee's report as "highly sensational."[25]

On September 1, the day the first piece ran in the *Times*, a reporter reached Truman by telephone in Missouri to ask him about it. "The facts are that they were turning out phony engines and I have no doubt a lot of kids in training planes were killed as a result," Truman said. "The committee was conservative in its report in order to prevent too much alarm over the situation." The drop in production "was put on by the company for the purpose of just such articles as that one. The company was holding back engines so that production would jump when the committee got out of the way."[26]

The Washington Post weighed in on September 5: the committee, it said, had rendered "a unique service to the country" by investigating the Lockland plant. "We venture to assert that but for the unpleasant publicity given these conditions, reforms there might have been delayed indefinitely."[27]

At his apartment on E Street Northwest, Wilbur Sparks cut these and other stories out of newspapers and magazines and pasted them into a scrapbook he was keeping about his time on the Truman Committee. These are the last two clippings on the Lockland investigation.

From October 6, 1943, in the New York newspaper *PM*: "Bad-Plane Figures Censored, But Army Finds Truman Right." It reported that Truman had threatened to call another hearing, and summon Undersecretary Patterson to testify, after the army censored a nationwide radio speech Truman was scheduled to give. In it, he planned to reveal the actual production numbers for the plant. The two men had instead reached a compromise: Truman kept the production numbers out of his speech and called off the hearing, while Patterson acknowledged that "the Truman Committee's findings—so widely attacked by *The New York Times* and other newspapers and radio commentators—were correct."

And finally, an Associated Press clipping from March 7, 1944, noting that the Army Air Forces had ordered a general court martial for three officers "on charges of neglect of duty in the inspection of airplane engines produced at the Wright Aeronautical Plant at Lockland, Ohio."[28]

18

BEYOND THE SENATE

"It was in the early summer of 1943," writes historian David McCullough, "one year in advance of the Democratic National Convention, that Senator Truman recorded on paper for the first time that in some circles he was being talked of as a candidate for Vice President, assuming the President were to run for a fourth term."[1]

The subject came up on Sunday, July 11, over a roast beef lunch at the home of Senator Joseph Guffey, Democrat of Pennsylvania and a reliable soldier for the New Deal. After the meal, Guffey took Truman out into the backyard, away from the other guests, to ask him a confidential question: What did he think of Vice President Henry Wallace? "I told him that Henry is the best secretary of agriculture we ever did have," Truman wrote Bess the next day. "He laughed and said that is what he thinks." Then, Guffey wanted to know "if I would help out the ticket if it became necessary by accepting the nomination for Vice President. I told him in words of one syllable that I would not—that

I had only recently become a Senator and that I wanted to work at it for about ten years."[2]

Which was what he would say nearly every time over the next year when the subject came up, almost right up until the time he accepted the nomination. "The Vice President simply presides over the Senate and sits around hoping for a funeral," he wrote a political acquaintance in Missouri. "It is a very high office which consists entirely of honor and I don't have any ambition to hold an office like that."[3]

Of course, many politicians before and since have said much the same thing, but there is no real reason at this point to doubt him. And the possibility in 1943 must have seemed a remote one. Truman had never had the slightest indication of Roosevelt's affection or even interest in him. Just three years earlier, the president had favored Lloyd Stark in Truman's bid for a second term, and since then he had met with Roosevelt just five times.[4]

Nevertheless, as the months went by, he found himself answering this question more often. While it was still far from clear whether Roosevelt himself would run again, leading Democrats hoped he would, and many of them hoped he would do so without Henry Wallace.

In hindsight, it seems inevitable that Roosevelt would again seek re-election. That having led the country out of depression and through the disaster of Pearl Harbor, with the United States caught up in a terrible and devastating world war and the tide only beginning to turn, he would want to see it through. It seemed inevitable to many people at the time, too. "Everybody knows," said Senator Guffey, one of FDR's biggest champions, in a speech in April, "that if the war is still raging in 1944, the American people will renominate and re-elect President Roosevelt to a fourth term."[5]

But a fourth term was by no means as certain as Guffey implied. No one in the nation's history had served that long, and there were genuine worries that a single president serving for sixteen years would be dangerous for the democracy. "Not unless we are ready to accept dictatorship and give up the America we have known and loved," argued Senator Styles Bridges, Republican of New Hampshire, "should the President of the United States have a fourth term."[6]

Already, some were talking about a constitutional amendment that would limit a president to two terms, though it soon became clear that such an amendment could not possibly be ratified before the 1944 election. And then there was the speculation and concern, mostly whispered, about the president's declining health.

Through it all, Roosevelt wasn't talking. "Clearly Mr. Roosevelt, as long as he can, is going to keep the people and the politicians in a state of uncertainty as to whether or not he will seek a fourth term," declared *The Wall Street Journal* in December. "That is what he did four years ago and that is what he will do now."[7]

There were political calculations involved as well. If Roosevelt chose to run for a fourth term, it would not be a cakewalk. There were huge unknowns—the military situation could darken at any moment, or the economy could slide back into depression. "If he wants the nomination," said the *Journal*, "he will have to go after it with all he has."

Regardless of what the president was or wasn't thinking, the topic was endlessly fascinating to the press, undeterred by the absence of any solid information. Through 1943 and into 1944, there were stories and columns and radio commentaries on it just about every week. Equally enthralling for the media and for the power brokers in both parties was the question of who—if Roosevelt did run—would be his running mate.

Vice President Henry Wallace was a fascinating figure—second only to Roosevelt in popularity among Democrats.[8] He had been a farmer, a journalist, a pioneer in the development of hybrid seed corn, and as Secretary of Agriculture from 1933 to 1940, a driving force behind the agricultural reforms of the

New Deal. While both Franklin and Eleanor Roosevelt liked and respected him, he was unpopular with the more conservative elements of the party, and by 1943 there was widespread speculation in the press about the pressure to nudge him aside.

Oddly, it was Senator Guffey, just two weeks after asking Truman if he would consider replacing Wallace, who became the first high-ranking Democrat to say publicly he favored keeping the vice president on the ticket: "I'm for Roosevelt and Wallace as a Democratic ticket in 1944."[9]

That contrast—public support and private criticism—was typical of Wallace's standing among many of the party's leaders, especially the more pragmatic ones. "There is a vast gulf between Wallace and the state, county and city chairmen of the party's organization," the Washington reporter for *The Louisville Courier-Journal* wrote a few days after Guffey's endorsement. In three years as vice president, "he has done little or nothing to bridge that gap. If anything he has widened the chasm by making speeches which the New Deal's enemies have seized upon as evidence of the dreamy-eyed impracticability of the Roosevelt Administration."

That, in a nutshell, was the beef with Wallace: he was too intellectual, too liberal, his head in the clouds, awkward and uncomfortable with the messy business of politics. No political figure in America, the *Courier-Journal* reporter, Robert Riggs, continued, "is so politically naive as the Vice President. People who have talked with him about the problems of building up a political organization say he knows nothing at all about the mechanics by which such groups get their supporters to the polls."[10]

While Truman's name came up occasionally, and more often as time passed, he was considered at best a long shot. There were others—Jimmy Byrnes, Kentucky Senator Alben Barkley, Speaker of the House Sam Rayburn, even Henry J. Kaiser—who were thought to be much more likely to get the nod from Roosevelt.

★ ★ ★

Everywhere, the pace of Truman's life was accelerating. Magazine covers and articles. "They are getting up an article in *Life* on your old man," he wrote Bess in June. "Ain't it awful? *Time, Life, Satdy Evenin Post, Click.* What can I do?" The best-selling magazine in America, *Reader's Digest,* did a big article on him, borrowing *Time's* headline from March: "Billion Dollar Watchdog." He was regularly asked to give radio broadcasts, and the number of invitations and speaking requests his office received now ran to more than one a day.[11]

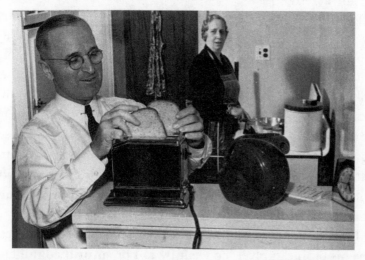

Harry and Bess Truman in their apartment at 4701 Connecticut Avenue, N.W.

The demands on his time were causing problems in his home life. Bess had never cared much for Washington, and the back-and-forth from Missouri to DC was even more difficult now as her mother aged and grew frail. It was decided that, since Bess was away so often, Grandmother Wallace could no longer live on her own in the big house on North Delaware street. Initially, they moved her to a small apartment nearby, but eventually the family decided Mrs. Wallace would be better off living in Denver with Bess's brother, Fred, and his family.[12]

In June, Bess and Margaret, who was on summer break after her freshman year at George Washington University, went out to Independence to help with the move. They remained in Denver for several weeks, and during that time, Margaret got a chance to "dip my toe into show business" by auditioning for a small part in a local production of an operetta, *Countess Maritza.*[13]

It was agreed that Truman would come out to spend time with them, and hopefully see his daughter perform. But he was "up to his eyeballs in committee and legislative business," and letter after letter brought news of another delay, including a couple of days while he dealt with a staff member who had disappeared on a drinking binge. "His trouble is scotch and soda," he told Bess, "or just scotch, soda never hurt anyone." On July 10, Truman was almost ready to leave. He would stop in Kansas City and Independence along the way to see his own mother. "Should be in K.C. by Tuesday and I hope after seeing mamma I can come on to Denver." Already, though, the timing meant he would miss seeing Margaret's debut. "I sure wish I could see you and hear you in that opera but I can't," he apologized in a letter to her the next day, written just after his lunch meeting with Joe Guffey. With all the delays and the stop in Missouri, "I expect it will be Friday after next before I get there."[14]

Finally, on July 15, he was in the old coupe, on his way west. For his business travel, he went by rail or air or used military transportation, but for his personal trips he was on his own, another reminder of the wealth gap that separated him from most senators. He made it to Uniontown, Pennsylvania, the first day. Another long day's drive got him to Indianapolis. As always, he loved a good road trip, and that night he delighted in telling Bess all about it:

I've had quite a day. If you can imagine me leaving Uniontown at 7:00 A.M. after having breakfast at six-thirty and driving all day in the hot sunshine—keeping the speed indicator below forty most all the time and never more than forty plus, you can under-

stand why I could hardly write my name on the register when I arrived about six o'clock. It was actually eleven hours driving to make exactly 370 miles.

I still had some of the grand box lunch Mrs. Boyle made for me and I didn't have to stop only at roadside parks to eat. I don't know whether I told you yesterday she sent over a shoebox with six deviled-eggs, a whole fried chicken, six bread-and-butter sandwiches, and some cupcakes sealed up in this Cellophane. I ate chicken, a deviled-egg, and a bread-and-butter sandwich for supper last night in Frostburg. Then I had my usual breakfast in Uniontown—a big tomato juice, Post Toasties (couldn't get oatmeal), toast and milk. Well by ten-thirty this morning I was hungry as a bear. So I stopped at one of Ohio's roadside parks west of St. Clairsville and ate a deviled-egg, a couple of pieces of chicken, and a bread-and-butter sandwich out of Mrs. Boyle's shoebox.

I stopped in St. Clairsville to get the old car tightened up. I had cultivated a rattle underneath that sounded as if I was going to lose the running gear. Fortunately I stopped at the right place and found a fellow. So he tightened up everything for $1.68.

When I registered at the White Swan last night the clerk said he hoped I wouldn't investigate him. The Lincoln clerk said the same thing. Ain't that an awful reputation?

Well I stopped at another Ohio park on the east side of one of those dams west of Springfield and ate the rest of the chicken and deviled-eggs but I still have some cupcakes and bread-and-butter sandwiches left—and I'm hungry now. So I'll have to go buy a meal I guess.

If all goes well, I'll get to St. Louis tomorrow—go and see John Snyder who is in the hospital having his rupture sewed up, and then go to Jefferson City and stay all night. I'll see Dick Nacy and then go to Kansas City. See all the folks and come to Colorado soon as possible. Kiss Margie. Love to you. My best to your mother, Chris, and the kids.
Harry.[15]

★ ★ ★

The next day, all did not go well, as he told his increasingly frustrated wife in a letter from Vandalia, Illinois. "I stripped the gears in the old coupe. And what I mean I stripped 'em right." He was stuck in Illinois with the car in the shop, and the nearest parts were in St. Louis. He arranged to have the car towed there the next day and for his aide Fred Canfil to drive him to Kansas City. "We ought to leave there about Tuesday noon or Wednesday morning and I should be in Denver Thursday or Friday."[16]

With all these delays, and her recurring frustrations with the demands on her husband's time, "Bess did a slow burn," Margaret wrote. "There are times when every woman feels neglected and unappreciated, and this was one of them. Senator Truman seemed to be putting everything in the world ahead of his family." When he did finally make it to Denver, "Bess let him have it with both barrels. Dad was so upset, he told mother he almost wished he had never become a Senator." But as always with the woman he fondly referred to as "the Boss," he did not push back. After a brief visit, he put his wife and daughter on a train to Missouri and headed off for a long speaking tour, still feeling the sting of Bess's words. He'd been hoping to get away again to Hot Springs for a short rest, but Democratic leaders had roped him into a series of appearances across three states, and he felt he couldn't get out of it. He wrote Margaret hoping her mother was "all thawed out from Colorado."[17]

His daughter believed there was another reason for Bess's outburst, beyond the delays and missing his daughter's performance: he had written Bess about that lunch with Joe Guffey, and the discussion of the vice presidency—an idea that was "going to wreak havoc in Bess' life."[18]

In the midst of this hectic summer, Truman's investigators had stumbled across the biggest, most highly guarded secret of World War II: the Manhattan Project. The program to create an atomic bomb grew out of discoveries by physicists in the late 1930s. Their research made such a weapon more than just a theoretical possibility. By the early 1940s it was clear that such a fantastical-sounding device could produce an explosion that could destroy an entire city.

Top scientists in the US and Great Britain were working on this research, but so were physicists in Germany, and in 1942, Franklin Roosevelt approved the massive, secret effort to make sure the US and its allies got there first. The government began acquiring more than fifty thousand acres at a site west of Knoxville, Tennessee, for a facility devoted to the enrichment of uranium, displacing farmers and making the whole area off-limits. Another site near the towns of Hanford and Pasco, in Washington State, was identified for the creation of the world's first plutonium reactor, and the government began buying up more than forty thousand acres there. The actual bombs themselves would be designed at another laboratory in Los Alamos, New Mexico. Eventually, these sites and others would employ more than 130,000 people, and the project would eventually run to nearly $2 billion—the most expensive weapons program to that time in history.

Which could not have failed, sooner or later, to come to the attention of the Truman Committee. In the spring of 1943, a complaint had come in about some equipment taken from a plant in Minnesota, where it had never been used, and moved to the Pasco site in Washington State. The committee investigators found this confusing, and Rudolph Halley wrote to the War Department in June to ask about it.

Which set alarm bells ringing at the highest levels. George Marshall, the Army Chief of Staff, vowed on June 14 to reach out to Truman and "have him instruct his counsel to drop any investigation of the Pasco plant."[19] He may have already done so when, three days later, Secretary of War Henry Stimson brought it up on a phone call with Truman: "I think I've had a letter from Mr. Halley, I think, who is an assistant of Mr. Fulton of your office," Stimson said.

"That's right."

"In connection with the plant at Pasco, Washington."

"That's right."

"Now that's a matter which I know all about personally, and I am one of the group of two or three men in the whole world who know about it."

"I see."

"It's part of a very important secret development."

Which was enough for Truman. "I herewith see the situation, Mr. Secretary, and you won't have to say another word to me. Whenever you say that to me, that's all I want to hear."

"All right."[20]

With that, Truman agreed to back off—for now at least—and remain in the dark about a project he may not have needed to know about as a senator, but one he would very much need to know about as President of the United States. Nevertheless, he had gleaned some idea of what the project was for—possibly from Marshall—because, four weeks later, he told his old friend Lewis Schwellenbach about it in a letter. The former senator, now a federal judge in Spokane, had written to Truman, urging him to investigate the huge federal land grab in his home state. "I know something about that tremendous real estate deal," Truman responded, "and I have been informed that it is for the construction of a plant to make a terrific explosion for a secret weapon that will be a wonder. I hope it works."[21]

General Marshall and Secretary Stimson would no doubt have been stunned to know that, not only did Truman spill the biggest secret of the war in a personal letter sent through the US mail, but he dictated it to his secretary, Mildred Dryden, letting her in on the highly classified information as well.

Truman initially kept his promise, but the letters and complaints from Hanford and from the site near Knoxville continued to arrive in Room 160, with incredible-sounding descriptions of waste and expenditures. In late 1943 and early 1944, Truman and the committee would again start poking around in Washington State, and would run into a brick wall of secrecy.

In early September, once more exhausted from the speeches and dinners and demands of his road trip, Truman did make it down to Hot Springs for one of his much-needed rest breaks—a few days of quiet at a resort hotel and a checkup with the army doctors at the hospital. This time it was sinus trouble and the recurring headaches brought on by stress, work and—his perennial problem—sleep deprivation. But he was able to report to Bess good news on all fronts: "This was a banner day—two letters and the doctor over at the hospital said the sinus trouble was not serious and that 3 days in a dry climate would stop it. It has cleared up almost completely and I haven't had a headache since I've been here—been asleep most of the time, guess that's the reason. Took two sun baths yesterday and will take two today and start home in the morning. Love to you, Harry."[22]

He was back in Hot Springs again six weeks later, exhausted after another trip out to Missouri, worries about his mother's health, and the stress of his big national radio speech on the Curtiss-Wright investigation. This time, he was also suffering from a bad tooth, and told Bess he would have to remain in Arkansas until it was fixed. This time, he made sure to apologize in advance: "Please don't sue me for desertion—I hate it as badly as you do."[23]

While he was there, waiting for the "tooth man" to finish up, his thoughts turned to the eventual Allied victory and what the world—and the United States—should look like afterwards. He had a speech to make in St. Louis to a group of state officials from around the country, and he wanted Bess's advice on shaping it toward a discussion of the postwar future. "I am just as certain as I can be the struggle to maintain what we are fighting for after we win the war will be much harder than the war itself."[24]

While that victory was beginning to seem more and more certain, it was by no means imminent. The Allies had in September finally launched an invasion of mainland Europe. Not the long-awaited attack on France, which was still months away, but a strike at Italy—in Winston Churchill's famous words, the continent's "soft underbelly." Landings began in the toe of the Italian boot on September 3, followed by the main invasion at Salerno on the 9th, and thus began a long and costly battle by British, Canadian, and American forces to push their way up the peninsula. On September 8, the Italian government announced its surrender, leaving Nazi Germany fighting on its own. The Germans immediately sent 35,000 troops into Italy (where they quickly began rounding up and deporting Jews), and beyond that, Hitler's forces remained in control of vast hunks of Europe. On the Eastern Front, where the Soviet Union had been battling millions of Germans in a massive land war for more than two years, Soviet forces were moving forward, but Berlin was still a thousand miles away, and Hitler still had three hundred divisions to defend the fatherland.[25]

In the Pacific, where the distances were even greater, the Allies significantly were no longer on the defensive. After the hard-won victory at Guadalcanal in February, American and Allied forces under General Douglas MacArthur were now pushing the Japanese back on Papua New Guinea in their drive toward MacArthur's goal of eventually reclaiming the Philippines. In the Atlantic, the Liberty ships and new weapons and tactics, including long-range air patrols, developments in radar, and British codebreaking, were finally turning the tide against the U-boats. The loss of shipping each month had declined significantly from its peak.[26]

There was still long, hard fighting ahead, but it was by now becoming clearer to the Allied leaders that Germany and Japan could not win.

"With the steady march of the Allied Armies on the Southern and Eastern fronts in Europe, with the new advance in the Southwest Pacific—the fortunes of our armies are heartening," Truman said in his speech to the secretaries of state in St. Louis.

Americans had come together on the home front to meet the challenge, he said, but there were cracks in the sense of shared purpose: "Conflict has arisen between Management and Labor, Congress and Labor, race and race, Democrats and Republicans, and even at times between the federal and state governments." Once the common enemy was gone, "our national unity must go deep enough to carry us into the post-war world—trained to think and work together."[27]

Before the country could reach that postwar world, some big decisions had to be made. Truman and his committee were about to release a report that looked ahead with clear eyes and concrete suggestions to one of the biggest: having converted the entire national economy to war production, how the government should reverse that transformation and convert it back once again to civilian goods. US production had reached such levels that, as victory approached, there would come a point when factories and shipyards would be producing material that might not be needed months later when the war was over.

Truman delivered the report to the Senate on November 5: "The population of the United States have been reshuffled from one end of the country to another, and today millions of people live in communities different from those where they lived before the war. Some of these communities grew up around war plants, and many more are largely dependent on war plants for jobs for their people. It is no answer to say that they might return to their former jobs, because tens of thousands of small businesses by which they were formerly employed are now out of business. Some communities with war industries will become ghost towns, and others will lose most of their increase in population."[28]

The report noted that there was no going back to the prewar economy, where in 1939 the nation had nine million people out of work, and accurately predicted the postwar economic boom that was coming. Millions of families during the war had been able to pay off their debts and increase their savings at a time when consumer goods were scarce: "Thus, we will have the plants, the tools, the labor, the new materials and the purchasing power on which to base the greatest and soundest era of prosperity that this nation ever enjoyed."

Truman and the committee offered no grand vision for a postwar world. Instead, they raised a series of questions for the government to consider: How should war contracts be terminated? How should industry be notified of those terminations? What should happen to government-owned machines and property as factories shifted to making civilian goods? How should the government lease or sell plants and facilities built for war production?

Having raised these questions, the committee would hold hearings in the coming months to solicit answers from the leaders of government, industry, and labor: "Even if the solutions are not entirely satisfactory, it is important that certainty be substituted for the doubt that now prevents business from making its plans."[29]

19

CANOL

I n the fall of 1943, twenty-five-year-old Allen Drury was
fresh out of the army, discharged due to an old back in-
jury. He had graduated from Stanford in 1939 and worked
in newspapers in California before enlisting in 1942. After his
discharge, he headed east to look for a job and found work as
a reporter with the United Press in Washington, where he was
assigned to cover the Senate. With the chance to observe the
government at work up close, he "soon realized how little most
Americans know about the very human institution which makes
their laws and in large measure runs their country."[1]

In addition to filing his stories every day, Drury began keeping a diary,* recording his thoughts on the issues and the people
and the personalities—the senators themselves and "the people
from downtown who came to the Hill to testify: Frank Knox,
Donald Nelson, James Forrestal, Henry Stimson, General Brehon Somervell..."[2]

---

* Published in 1963 as *A Senate Journal 1943-45*.

Drury's list of notables continued, to include Franklin Roosevelt and others, but it is worth pausing there at General Somervell.

Brehon B. Somervell was one of the most capable and efficient administrators in the army. As the chief supply and logistics officer throughout the war, he commanded a vast logistical and construction bureaucracy involving tens of billions of dollars. His realm included construction of the Pentagon, hundreds of army camps and facilities, management of ports and depots, and the Manhattan Project. He was a ruthless and aggressive force—"one of the most adept empire builders in the modern history of the Army"—who could get things done and get them done quickly.[3]

Born in 1892 in Little Rock, Arkansas, Somervell graduated sixth in his class from West Point in 1914 and was commissioned a second lieutenant in the Corps of Engineers.[4] He served in France in World War I, where he gained a reputation as a capable and talented engineer on construction projects, and won the Distinguished Service Cross. After the war, he moved up through increasingly important roles in supply and construction projects. In 1935, he took on the massive job of running the Works Progress Administration in New York City, demonstrating an ability to manage a complex and vast public works project. In 1940, Colonel Somervell was given command of the construction division of the Quartermaster Corps, which handled all of the army's needs for supply, logistics, and construction. Staring out from the cover of *Life* in April 1942, he looks very much the square-jawed, steely-eyed military leader. From his vantage point in the Senate press gallery, Allen Drury described him as "handsome, dynamic, suave, striking, forceful, dramatic, incisive—and all the other adjectives customarily fawned upon him" by the news media.[5]

Somervell was also combative, prickly and short-tempered. He knew how to carry a grudge and did so aggressively with just about anyone who disagreed with him. "Working at a non-

stop pace and demanding that others do the same, insisting that
military necessity must prevail, ruthlessly eliminating dead wood
and cutting red tape, intolerant of indecision and ready to run
down those who got in his way, he attacked projects without
regard for costs," wrote his biographer, John Kennedy Ohl.[6] If
the Truman committee in World War II had an archenemy, it
was Brehon Somervell.

General Brehon B. Somervell.

"General Somervell was a brilliant general," said Matt Connelly. "But he was also a martinet, and resented any intrusion or
stepping on his toes."[7] Harry Truman did not dispute Somervell's
abilities, but disdained his methods: "I will say this for General

Somervell: He will get the stuff, but it will be hell on the tax-payer."[8]

From his time in France, Truman resented what he considered the snobbish and elitist attitude of West Pointers like Somervell toward reserve officers like himself.[9] (In 1925 and 1926, then-Major Somervell attended the army War College, where he co-authored an infamous report on "the use of negro man power in war" that condemned Black soldiers as unfit for combat or leadership roles, "mentally inferior to the white man."[10])

Now, years later, Somervell personified all of Truman's suspicions about military power and wasteful spending: "I had known Somervell in the Army," he told the journalist Jonathan Daniels, "and I knew he cared absolutely nothing about money." In June 1942, Truman watched Somervell and other generals at an appropriations hearing and came away disgusted: "They are asking for $43 billion," he wrote Bess, "and they'll get it without a whimper to waste and riot and create a fascist government if Somervell can manage it. I want to keep the strings on them, just as we do the others."[11]

Somervell, now a lieutenant general, had first appeared before the committee on the army camp hearings in 1941, where he had openly acknowledged the problems and was the source of the widely cited figure that the program had squandered $100 million. (The mismanagement and corruption had not been on his watch—he'd been placed in charge of the Quartermaster Corps after most of the damage was done—and had moved quickly to clean things up.)

From that investigation onward, though, Truman and Somervell despised each other. For his part, Somervell's principle was that "you can't save time and money at the same time," and his view of congressional investigations like Truman's was that they sucked away valuable time from the job of winning the war. He believed the Truman Committee was "formed in iniquity for political purposes," and that Truman carried a personal grudge against him for once declining to award a contract to a St. Louis company that Truman had favored.[12]

Somervell was a forceful adversary, and when he and the Truman Committee clashed again in December 1943, Allen Drury had a ringside seat. This time, the fight was over a government boondoggle of epic proportions, with waste and mismanagement to rival even the army camp mess—and it was one Somervell had created entirely on his own. In this investigation, a bigger issue arose, one that down through the decades has come up repeatedly and grown in importance: the conflict between the role of Congress (or the news media) in monitoring the activities of the government, and the military's efforts to conceal those activities from scrutiny behind a shield of "national security."

The seeds of the confrontation were planted in April 1942. After Pearl Harbor, the territory of Alaska was suddenly of strategic importance—as a potential route for ferrying airplanes to the Soviet Union and as a possible staging area for attacks on Japan. Amid the bleak military outlook in the war's early months, worries grew about the ability to supply the territory if the sea lanes were dominated by the Japanese. Plans were developed to build a road through Canada to Alaska, known as the Alcan Highway.[13] That 1,500-mile-long road, and an existing string of airfields along the route, would need a supply of oil and gasoline, and Somervell as head of supply began looking for ways to provide it. In January 1942, he asked James Graham, a dollar-a-year adviser who was also dean of the Engineering School of the University of Kentucky, to look into the problem. Graham spoke with an Arctic explorer who suggested he check out a small, remote oilfield at Norman Wells, in Canada's Northwest Territory.

On April 29, Graham held a meeting with several oil officials and high-ranking army officers to discuss the possibility of increasing production at Norman Wells, from its current level of about four hundred barrels a day to about three thousand,

enough to supply the highway and the airfields. In the meeting
were representatives of Standard Oil of New Jersey, and Imperial Oil of Canada, a Standard Oil subsidiary that ran the Norman Wells operation. While those officials agreed it might be
possible to get that much oil, "they were not optimistic."[14]

The army officers at the meeting, however, were enthusiastic,
and at the end of the meeting, Graham wrote a one-page memo
to Somervell outlining his proposal: the Army Corps of Engineers would expand the Norman Wells operation by drilling
more wells; constructing a four-inch pipeline about 550 miles
long from Norman Wells to Whitehorse, in the Yukon Territory;
setting up a refining operation in Whitehorse using equipment
relocated from the United States; and creating a transportation
system from Whitehorse to Waterways, Alberta. This would all
be completed, Graham's memo said, by October 1, 1942—just
five months away.[15]

To accompany his memo, Graham provided no documents,
no charts or tables, no cost estimates or maps. He forwarded no
survey of the proposed route and "no knowledge of the conditions to be met there except that mountainous terrain, muskeg
[a type of swamp or bog], and extremely cold winter conditions
would present very difficult problems." Nor did he consult with
the navy about whether it could do the job by sea (which would
have made the whole project unnecessary), or with the Roosevelt administration's petroleum administrator, or any "other
agencies affected by the decision."[16]

As historian Donald Riddle put it, "it was a set of bare recommendations as simple as though he had recommended, 'Build
a bridge from New York to London.'"[17] Nevertheless, Somervell
approved the memo that same day on his own authority, and
the next day ordered the Army's Chief of Engineers to get
started. Eventually, that decision would cost the US taxpayers
more than $134 million. Looking back, Riddle wrote, "it is

difficult to understand the offhand manner in which he made such a decision."[18]

Almost immediately, the serious flaws in the plan started to appear. Imperial Oil questioned the overall feasibility of the idea and suggested that gasoline and oil might better be shipped by plane. An army general suggested that barges could transport the equivalent amount of oil at less cost from the mainland. Standard Oil of California, hired as a technical advisor, warned that the pipeline would not be completed on schedule.[19]

Nevertheless, in May, $25 million was quietly added to the War Department budget for fiscal 1943.[20] Harold Ickes, the Secretary of the Interior and the administration's Petroleum Administrator for War, got wind of it soon after and flatly opposed it, noting that it would be late 1943 at the earliest before the project would be finished, and that cheaper and faster alternatives were available. The Canadian government, when notified about the project, raised similar doubts.[21]

Despite these red flags, Somervell pushed ahead, securing along the way the backing of Secretary of War Stimson and Undersecretary Patterson by presenting them with some, but not all, of the facts. Stimson, in turn, persuaded Roosevelt that the project was a military necessity and, for now, that was that.

As so many had predicted, the project quickly stalled. Terrain and weather proved, not surprisingly, to be major obstacles. Before work could even begin, the challenge of transporting 55,000 tons of equipment and cargo, along with hundreds of military and civilian workers hundreds of miles to the remote location, had to be met.[22] Yet Somervell after visiting the site in August became even more convinced of its value and increased his demands for men, supplies, and money. In some cases—a testament to his drive and energy and the work done by the engineers and technicians working in very difficult conditions—the project moved forward. Some sections of what became known as "Canol"—short for Canadian Oil—were finished in early 1943.[23]

The costs, meanwhile, had now soared above $80 million, and the War Department sent two investigators to look into it. Their report in June 1943 predicted that the cost would balloon to $120 million and recommended that, since the military situation had now changed and the perceived Japanese threat to Alaska had faded, the project should be reevaluated and possibly abandoned.

Somervell's response was to double down. Given the threat to oil supplies around the world and the discovery of additional oil at Norman Wells, he argued, Canol should continue and, if possible, grow larger. "Supremely self-confident in his own judgment," his biographer John Kennedy Ohl writes, "temperamentally incapable of admitting his own mistakes, and regarding himself above criticism, he was ready to defend Canol against all critics."[24]

Of course, it was inevitable that huge problems in a project of this magnitude would reach the ears of Harry Truman and his committee. Senator Harley Kilgore, appointed by Truman to head a subcommittee to investigate, went to Alaska in September to see for himself, along with Colonel Miles Knowles, the committee's liaison in the War Department. Knowles conducted his own investigation and, like virtually everyone else but Somervell and his superiors, concluded the project was not worth it.

The question, especially now that the Truman Committee had picked up the scent, was whether the army should cut its losses and abandon Canol, or push forward and pump even more money into it. Jimmy Byrnes, as head of the Office of War Mobilization, asked the Joint Chiefs of Staff for yet another investigation, and they reported back in July, without much real discussion, that it was of strategic importance and should be completed as "necessary to the war effort." When Truman later asked for the justification behind this, he was turned down for reasons of "national security."

This provided Somervell with the vital cover he needed: instead of being just a pet project of a single general, now Canol had the approval of the high command. And by designating it a national security issue, the War Department and Somervell were now able to deflect questions about it, or simply refuse to answer them.

Which left Truman with no option but to call for public hearings. These began in late November, with several officials including Harold Ickes testifying against the project. On the 23rd, the committee called James Graham, the dollar-a-year adviser to Somervell who was the author of that original one-page memo.

Fulton walked Graham through more than an hour of testimony that mostly elicited a long list of the facts he didn't know, and the officials and experts he hadn't consulted, at the time he wrote that memo. In response to many of Fulton's questions about the actual costs or details of the project, Graham repeatedly reminded Fulton that he had not had anything to do with Canol since writing it. And besides, given the urgency of the situation, he wasn't at all concerned about the costs: "I never consider cost in war."[25] He told Fulton that all he had done in that memorandum was to make a recommendation. "They could take it or leave it. General Somervell himself could take it or leave it."

As Somervell was out of the country, Undersecretary Patterson appeared for the War Department; he not only defended the project but, from the very first sentence of his opening statement, praised it: "The War Department is proud of Canol. Canol was a bold undertaking. The results so far have surpassed our hopes. We are confident that even greater success lies ahead. This job of strategic importance for the war effort has been approved by the Joint Chiefs of Staff. That should settle any doubts."[26]

It did not, and Patterson was in for a long morning. At one point, as Harley Kilgore questioned him about the statistics he had cited for how much oil could be produced, and "really how much of an aid that aviation gasoline would be to the strategy of defending Alaska," Patterson began to answer: "Any supply you could get at the source—what are you laughing at, Mr. Fulton?"

"No matter," Fulton responded.

"You have been laughing all through this. I haven't seen the humor in it yet."

Fulton: "I have been laughing at the concept that any supply, no matter what it was, would be valuable, without regard to the cost in man-hours and materials together."

Tom Connally of Texas, the committee's staunchest defender of the Roosevelt administration, at one point objected to Fulton's tone. The chief counsel had asked Patterson if he was aware that a top general charged with building the project had never made any estimates of how much it would cost. Patterson began to answer when Fulton cut him off: "That means nothing to you as a matter of—"

Here Connally broke in. "I don't mind the counselor asking questions, but I don't think it is quite fair to a witness like this to say, 'That doesn't mean anything to you?' I don't think that is quite courteous."

Truman shot back, "I think it ought to mean something."

Connally: "It does, I am sure, and as I understand the Secretary, he is not trying to justify this on a long-time, peace basis, but he is trying to justify it as a military project, that if you need a gallon of gasoline to save a life, you are willing to pay anything that is necessary to get that gallon of gas."

"I think we are all in that frame of mind, Senator," Truman said. "But I don't think it was necessary to take this 134 million dollars to get a prospective 1,500 gallons of high-octane gas. The way the plant is set up now we won't get over 450 barrels."[27]

Over and over, Fulton forced Patterson into the position of acknowledging how little he or any of the War Department leadership knew about Canol until the project was well underway, and how little attention Somervell had paid to the huge obstacles, the likely costs, and the many warnings about the quality and quantity of oil it would produce: "You are familiar, I take it, Mr. Under Secretary, with General Robbins' statement on behalf of the Chief of Engineers when he received this directive of General Somervell to the effect that he thought they ought to use barges and could take 10 times the gasoline up in one-tenth the time?"

Patterson: "No, I did not know that was General Robbins' opinion."[28]

Nor did he have much of an answer to this question: "Why was it necessary to decide this in one day by General Somervell on a one-page memorandum after one conference in which the only experts who had knowledge expressed considerable doubt as to whether they could get oil?"[29]

And so it went until 1:30 p.m. While it was now clear to just about everyone that Somervell had committed the government to a massive and costly blunder without serious thought or study, it was also becoming clear that there wasn't much the Truman Committee could do about it. "Interestingly," writes Ohl, "what had begun as a project to provide fuel for airplanes and trucks in Canada and Alaska was now being defended as potentially a major element in the war against Japan."[30]

On December 9, at Truman's request, several key administration officials including Donald Nelson, head of the Office of Production Management; Patterson; Secretary of the Navy Knox; and Ickes met to discuss the project. Knox, Ickes, and Nelson were for cutting the government's losses. "It is my opinion," Nelson wrote Hugh Fulton afterwards, "that it would be the lesser of the two evils to put a stop to the Canol project," thus saving the $30 million that had not yet been spent, "and that every effort should be made to salvage as much materials and equipment as possible."[31]

Nevertheless, with their blanket of protection from the Joint Chiefs, Somervell and the War Department had shown the limits of how far a congressional investigation could go. By the time the general himself testified on December 20, the whole thing had a sense of inevitability to it. Kilgore and the subcommittee had already drafted their preliminary report; most of the facts, damning as they were, were already out there. And Somervell had plenty of time to prepare.

He arrived in Room 318 with an entourage of officers and plenty of facts and figures, opening with a long statement not only defending Canol but now claiming it was an oil bonanza that wildly exceeded anyone's expectations. The senators and Fulton pressed him on many of the same questionable decisions and shaky facts that had made Patterson squirm, but Somervell was a veteran soldier who knew how to dig an entrenched position and hold it against repeated attacks.

Allen Drury was among the reporters on hand to watch the show, and in his diary that day captured the sense of anticlimax. "General Brehon B. Somervell got put on the griddle by the Truman Committee this morning," he wrote. "And emerged from the ordeal still handsome, dynamic, suave, etc., albeit a trifle limp."[32] After weeks of back-and-forth in the press over Canol, Drury realized that Somervell's testimony was unlikely to change much.

Nevertheless, he still found it entertaining. Here was Somervell in dress uniform, three stars on his shoulder and an entourage of brigadier generals and majors behind him. At one point, Drury watched with delight as Somervell asked for a glass of water, turning to hand his glass to a brigadier general. "The brigadier promptly handed it to a major. The major looked around desperately for somebody lower down; finding no one, he filled it up and returned it to the brigadier, who returned it to the general. All very correct, right in line with regulations, and strictly conforming to the chain of command. I was glad to see that the finer things of life are still being treasured in the service."[33]

The hearing also gave Drury an up-close look at the committee's chairman: "Truman has very thick glasses, a conservative appearance, and a quick, humorous way of speaking. He seems to be a generally good man, probably deserving of his reputation."[34]

There were moments of spark, as Kilgore forced Somervell to fess up to some of the wild claims about the project, for example the notion that Canol could be completed in a few months. "That was a very optimistic date," Somervell admitted, acknowledging that even he didn't really believe it at the time. "I didn't think we could."

But the questioning was highly technical, and as Drury noted, "the committee got off base somewhat by concentrating on the project itself instead of on the way it was handled. Few intelligent people can disagree with most of the objectives. The fault lies in the wasteful, sloppy, irresponsible methods." In his diary, the young reporter summed up the sad inevitability of the whole mess: "The committee damns it up and down while the War Department is as usual scrambling desperately to save face instead of having the guts to admit a mistake frankly and go on from there. In all this controversy Brehon B. occupies the central spot and today, his three stars glittering, was brought to book. Not much was gained by the whole business."[35]

As just about everyone expected, the committee's report when Kilgore delivered it to the Senate on January 8 was harshly critical of Canol and of Somervell, saying the project should never have been started, and once the problems became apparent should not have been allowed to continue. Yet the committee was fully aware that not much could be done about it. "What has been done, has been done. It is too late now to go back and rectify past mistakes."[36]

The report acknowledged the hard work of the engineers and workmen who had accomplished so much under "almost insufferable conditions." But with all that work, all that money, essentially wasted, what to do now? On that question, the committee threw up its hands: "This project was undertaken by the

War Department and has been so largely completed that only a small amount, proportionately, could be saved by abandoning it now. The committee therefore believes that the decision as to whether to abandon it now should be made by the War Department."[37]

For nearly three years, the Truman Committee had shown what could be accomplished by honest, aggressive, bipartisan inquiry aimed at protecting the public interest. In the process, it had become the most powerful congressional investigating panel in the nation's history. Canol showed the limits of that power when going up against what later became known as the "military industrial complex."

The project, and the committee's criticism of it, would continue well beyond Truman's time as chairman and even the end of the war. The pipeline was finally completed in February 1944, and refining operations began in April. Not long after that, the government began shutting it down. In 1947, the refinery, which had cost the United States more than $68 million, was sold off to Imperial Oil for $1 million. The company dismantled it and shipped it elsewhere. The pipeline was put up for auction as scrap, and sold for $700,000.[38]

20

THE DOCTRINE OF
APPARENT FRANKNESS

On November 23, 1943, the day Undersecretary Patterson testified on Canol, one of the people observing the hearing was a young naval officer. Three months earlier, Lieutenant John Tolan Jr. had been assigned to a new team in the office of the Chief of Naval Operations that would function as a bridge between the navy and the Truman Committee. This was part of a growing effort by the navy and the War Department (Miles Knowles had a similar role there) to engage and cooperate with the various congressional investigations, especially Truman's.

At thirty-three, Tolan was well-suited for his new assignment: he was the son of Congressman John H. Tolan of California, who chaired a similar investigating committee in the House. These liaison roles were tricky, though. The job involved responding to the needs and requests of the civilians in Congress, or at least appearing to do so, while also protecting the military from embarrassing revelations. This often put these officers in a tough spot with other departments, since usually they arrived bearing annoying, time-consuming, seemingly petty requests for documents or evidence. "It was our somewhat melancholy and unpleasant duty," said Lieutenant John Abbott, another member of the team, "to tromp down the hall and tell some senior admiral that the Truman Committee thought he was doing a very poor job."[1]

Abbott was a former reporter with the Associated Press who had worked on the House side as chief investigator with the Tolan Committee before entering the navy in 1942. He was initially assigned to shipboard duty, but the younger Tolan, aware of Abbot's Capitol Hill experience, asked his boss, Captain John A. Kennedy, to bring him to Washington.[2]

With their superiors in the navy, they were "something like the ancient messengers who come to the king with bad news," Abbott said. "Only, in those days, they chopped off the head of the messengers who brought the bad news. So far we've escaped that." On the other hand, if they came back from the navy "empty handed to the enquiring Senators, we got an unusually frosty reception."[3]

In laying out for Tolan his duties in his new assignment, Captain Kennedy instructed him to "practically live on Capitol Hill, get to know every member of the committees and each of the staff." Kennedy wanted him to learn everything he could about the investigations, analyzing the requests for documents or information, anticipating lines of questioning, and visiting shipyards or bases in advance of the congressional fact-finding trips that made such good photos and headlines. By now, the navy had been burned many times; Kennedy's plan was to "get out in front and clean things up before formal hearings or the issuance of subpoenas."[4]

Captain Kennedy was, in many ways, even more plugged in to Washington than Tolan. He had spent years in the Washington press corps as a correspondent, had owned radio stations in West Virginia, and was a close friend of Senator Harley Kilgore. He'd known Truman personally since his days as a rookie senator, and he seemed to know just about everyone on the Hill who was anybody. Soon after he joined the navy, Kennedy had come down to Washington for a few days from Philadelphia where he was serving, and ran into Secretary Knox at the Chevy Chase Club. Knox immediately had him transferred to Washington and assigned him to work with the Truman Committee.[5]

Most of the time, this new approach worked, as Truman for his part preferred to avoid embarrassing the military. "He always gave them a chance to clean up their act, particularly if they took the blame when the blame was theirs," said Tolan.[6]

The Canol hearings gave Tolan his first chance to see the Truman Committee and its chairman in action. Kennedy had received a question from someone in Room 160: Had the navy ever signed off on Canol? He dug up a letter suggesting that the navy thought the project was unnecessary, and called Tolan and Abbott into his office. "The Army is in real trouble on this," he told them. "They may try to shift some of the blame on the Navy. Get up on the Hill and follow this investigation as close as possible. Keep the Navy out of it, but if the Committee or the Army tries to pull us in, then pass the word and I'll inform Vice Admiral Horne and Secretary Knox."[7]

So Tolan was there in Room 318 when Patterson appeared. Having sat through many hearings on his father's committees in the House, he was surprised at how the War Department's second-highest-ranking official handled it. Patterson seemed unaware of the shaky ground Somervell was on with Canol, and unprepared for the questions Fulton and the senators were asking. When Patterson made his testy comment to the chief counsel— "What are you laughing at, Mr. Fulton?"—Tolan knew it was a mistake. "It is almost the first rule of congressional hearings that no matter how hard-pressed you become, you *never* pick on the committee staff."

But it was Patterson's opening statement—in which he not only defended Canol *but praised it*—that really shocked Tolan: "I could hardly believe what was being said." When it was over, he rushed back across town and into Kennedy's office: "You won't believe how Patterson started off his defense of General Somervell. He came out with the flat-footed statement that the Army is proud of Canol."[8]

Kennedy looked up and replied, "That's the Doctrine of Apparent Frankness." Delighted, Tolan repeated the story and Kennedy's comment to Abbott, who also thought it was funny. Tolan said, "Let's think up some more doctrines," and they began making a list. Their assignment from Kennedy: "Visit naval installations in advance of proposed Committee field trips," was in essence an early warning that gave officials on the ground time to clean things up. This became known as "Paul Revere-ing."

Their counterparts on the committee—who had by now sat through hundreds of hours of these hearings—found all this hilarious, too. Bob Irvin had seen the Doctrine of Apparent Frankness in action many times: "The witness would say, 'Senator, I'm glad you asked that question, and I want to explain it to you in complete detail.' And then he'd launch into such a complicated, endless explanation that by the time he finished, everyone would be so confused, the original question would be lost."[9]

He especially enjoyed the "Statue of Liberty play"—named after a football maneuver in which the quarterback pretends to throw the ball downfield by raising one arm in the air, resembling Lady Liberty, while secretly handing it off to another player with the other hand. "Say there was a General testifying, or an Admiral," Irvin explained. "And if he didn't know the answer to that question, he'd raise his hand and say, 'Well, I have Captain so and so in the room who will be glad to answer this question later,' and Captain so and so again would raise his hand and say, 'Well, Lieutenant so and so has the answer to that question and will be happy to provide you.'"*

Another common tactic for dodging a question became the

---

*   The play has a long and storied history in football. Its most famous recent use was by Boise State to defeat Oklahoma in the 2007 Fiesta Bowl.

Doctrine of Studied Delay: "Senator, I'm going to cover that later in my testimony if you don't mind, and with your permission I would like to defer my answer…" Meanwhile, the discussion moved on to other topics, "and pretty soon the hearing was adjourned, and that question was never answered."[10]

Rudolph Halley's contribution to the list was the "Super-Abundant Luncheon." This was when the senators would show up to inspect a defense plant or military base—or, in the example Tolan gave, a shipyard. There, the commandant would greet the visiting dignitaries "with appropriate fanfare" and in a spirit of goodwill show them to a table piled high with food, inviting everyone to have lunch before getting down to business. Halley, seeing these meals drag on and on, put a stop to them, "because by 2:30 the Senators were not nearly as much in a mood for records investigation, particularly tours of the shipyard that would involve long hours of walking and climbing up and down ships."[11]

Even the senators got into the act. The two navy lieutenants shared a laugh one day in early 1945 when their game made it into the *Congressional Record*: James Mead was on the Senate floor, describing efforts by the navy to cover up a bad situation at the Norfolk Navy Yard: "When investigators go through the men are warned in advance to look busy," he said. "A few minutes before the investigators actually appear, another warning is given by a 'Paul Revere' who tears through the shop just ahead of the investigators." Homer Ferguson was so tickled with the doctrines that he wrote an article about them and sent it to *Liberty* magazine, which ran it with the headline, "You Can't Fool Us Senators."[12]

When these liaison relationships worked, they could help both the committee get things done and the army or the navy deal with a problem quietly, and also cut down on the amount of time that Knox or Patterson or other high officials had to spend answering questions on Capitol Hill. In many cases, the relations were good:

Knox had chosen Kennedy because of his connections with two of the Truman Committee senators, and Abbott and Tolan became friends with several of the investigators in Room 160. Both sides knew there was a game being played, said Irvin, and "there was always a lot of jockeying of wits and strategies to either conceal the facts or disguise them or divert you in other directions."[13]

Still, throughout the military and the cabinet bureaucracies, there was deep resentment at what seemed like endless and pointless requests from various congressional committees. Every time Tolan showed up at the Bureau of Ships, for example, his counterpart there would "open the bottom drawer of his desk and throw the Committee request into it, slam the door and glance up at me with a guileless smirk."[14]

Which, Tolan knew, just made things worse. It was much better to at least give the appearance of responding. When a request came in, it was easy just to call Hugh Fulton or Rudolph Halley and tell them the navy was looking into it, but that it would take some time to get all the materials together. "That will give you a month, easily," Tolan said. "I had used this 'we will get right on it' method quite successfully."

Thanksgiving Day 1943 found George Meader in his office, feeling a bit lonely and homesick for Ann Arbor. "Here I am," he wrote his wife, Elizabeth, from his desk, "doing some work on a rough draft of the transportation report (60 mimeographed pages so far)." He was invited to Matt Connelly's house later for turkey dinner, and then to Hugh and Jessie Fulton's, but he couldn't help thinking of his wife and three children. "How I wish I were there right now and I could spend the day with my family." Despite missing them, Meader was for the most part loving his new job and the chance to work with his old law school friend. "He has surely been swell to me, and I admire and respect him more, the better I know him."

From his previous life as a county prosecutor in Michigan,

wartime Washington was a huge change, and it was hard not to get swept up in the work and the excitement of it. On the night before Thanksgiving, he'd gone to dinner with Truman and four senators, as well as Fulton and Halley, and listened as Donald Nelson told the story of his recent trip to the Soviet Union. Just a week earlier, Fulton had come down sick and asked Meader to take over and run a hearing, on a Philadelphia shipyard that was having labor problems. "I guess I handled it all right," he wrote Elizabeth. He had hoped to get home for the holidays, but Fulton had assigned him another investigation, and he couldn't get away. On Saturday night, he dined again with Connelly, and played chess with Rudolph Halley. "I can beat him at that but I feel I am way below both Fulton and him as an investigator or lawyer."[15]

The social season as the holidays approached allowed some respite from the work. On December 1, Truman invited all the committee staff and their spouses, along with the other senators, to dinner in the senate restaurant in the Capitol.

The committee was in the thick of several investigations—transportation, wartime reconversion, Canol, the Third Annual Report—and there were still those complaints coming in from Tennessee and Washington State. On December 3, Harold Robinson wrote a memo reminding Truman that General Marshall had spoken to him about the "highly secret nature of this project." Nevertheless, "within the past two or three weeks complaints have been chronic with respect to waste, inefficiency and lack of a definite construction program." Robinson felt the committee was "handicapped" by Truman's hands-off agreement with the War Department: "In my humble opinion, this is another 'Canol,' wherein the guise of secrecy is being resorted to by the War Department to cover what well may be another shocking example when the lid is taken off."[16]

Truman agreed, and sent his old Missouri crony Fred Canfil—nominally an investigator on the committee but in practice more of a personal assistant—up to Washington State to look

around. But soon after Canfil arrived and began asking ques-
tions, the doors slammed shut. Officers and civilian engineers
in the region had been told, he told Truman in a telegram from
Walla Walla, "THAT NO SENATOR OR ANYONE CON-
NECTED WITH THE SENATE WAS TO BE GIVEN ANY
INFORMATION ABOUT THE PROJECT."[17]

As 1943 drew to a close, the United States entered its third
full year of war. The background noise of national politics grew
louder every day, and speculation grew around whether Franklin Roosevelt would seek a fourth term. As Truman's schedule
filled up with more hearings and investigations, more invitations, more requests for speeches and radio appearances, he and
his family could look forward to a rare and exciting break. For
nearly three years, Margaret Truman had watched as her father
"zoomed around the country," traveling thousands of miles.
Early in the new year, Margaret would get to join him on one
of these trips, and for once Harry and Bess would be watching
from the side as their daughter was the center of attention. It
would be the adventure of her young life.[18]

In January 1941, the navy laid down the keel for the latest of
its fast, powerful battleships at the Brooklyn Navy Yard in New
York City, and three years later the ship was nearly finished. This
one, like the other battleships in the fleet, would be named after
a state, and it was Missouri's turn. Typically in these situations,
the navy allowed the governor of the chosen state to select the
woman who would have the honor of christening the ship, but
with a Republican now occupying that office, and the state's
junior senator running a powerful war investigating committee,
Navy Secretary Knox broke precedent and invited nineteen-
year-old Margaret Truman to do the honors.

Both father and daughter had been looking forward to the
event for more than a year. "Tell Margie I'd sent her a letter on
the same day she mailed me one. Also tell her *Missouri* is still to

be launched," Truman wrote Bess the summer before. "So she'd better commence breaking bottles on the corner of the barn so as to be in practice."[19]

As the big day drew near, invitations and memos flew from the typewriters in Truman's office: Could the navy find this or that politician a seat at the launching? Could this many of Margaret's friends be accommodated? The itinerary was laid out in meticulous detail: everyone would board the train in Washington at 1:30 p.m. on January 28 for New York, where they would be met by government cars to take them to the Waldorf-Astoria, and from there they'd be driven the next morning to the Navy Yard.

"It was my first real visit to New York," Margaret wrote. She was allowed to take along two close friends as maids of honor: Drucie Snyder, the daughter of Truman's longtime friend John Snyder, and Jane Lingo, a classmate from Gunston Hall and a fellow sophomore at George Washington University. The night before the launching, the three young women had tickets to see the hottest show in town—the Rodgers and Hammerstein hit *Oklahoma*. It was their first Broadway show, and the three girls were so excited they barely slept that night.[20]

The *Iowa*-class ships were the largest and fastest battleships ever built by the United States, and the 45,000-ton *Missouri* would be the last of them. Though Pearl Harbor and Midway had made clear that aircraft carriers now ruled the high seas, *Missouri* was a fearsome and formidable weapon: its sixteen-inch main guns could fire shells weighing 2,700 pounds a distance of twenty-four miles. *Missouri* had nine of them. In addition, there were twenty smaller five-inch guns, and 129 anti-aircraft guns. The battleship was 887 feet long; a floating city home to more than 1,800 men, powered by steam turbines that generated more than two hundred thousand horsepower.

As with Truman's senatorial brush with the Manhattan Project, his role in the launching of *Missouri* is one of those accidents of history that, in hindsight, seems almost a foreshadowing of events to come. None of the thirty thousand people who made their way to the Brooklyn Navy Yard that cold, gray morning of January 29 could have known that, eighteen months later, on the deck of this very ship in Tokyo Bay, the Japanese would sign the formal surrender to end World War II; and that the politician up on the platform, the one with glasses, fidgeting nervously as he prepared to make a speech, would be President of the United States.

As a cold wind blew in from the East River, Margaret and her friends shivered on a platform constructed at the base of the ship, which towered fifteen stories above them and was poised to slide down two massive "slipways" and into the water. Facing them on the platform was "a tremendous battery of cameras," including, said *The New York Times*, "'television instruments' that would enable hundreds of General Electric workers at plants in Schenectady, where much of the machinery and equipment that powered *Missouri* was built, to watch the launch 'through the magic of this 'seeing eye.'"[21]

Harry, Margaret and Bess, along with Rear Admiral Monroe Kelly, at the launching of the USS Missouri, *Brooklyn Navy Yard, January 29, 1944.*

Rear Admiral Monroe Kelly, commandant of the Navy Yard, made a speech, and messages were read from other admirals. Then it was Truman's turn, but there was a hitch. Launching a ship that size was a highly complex operation, requiring meticulous timing—the itinerary had been planned down to the half minute—and delays caused by wind and tides forced the officials in charge to advance the schedule by a few minutes. As a result, some of the prepared messages had to be cut from the program, and Truman was told he needed to speed things up. ("I am glad you liked my speech," he told an acquaintance a few days later. "The Navy pushed me up at such a rate I had to rattle it off like a sideshow barker."[22]) Nevertheless, he made it all the way through, noting proudly that the ship had been finished months ahead of schedule, part of a massive building program that made the US Navy "beyond question master of the seas." Then, in a prophetic statement, he told the crowd that "the time is surely coming when the people of Missouri can thrill with pride as the *Missouri* and her sister ships, with batteries blazing, sail into Tokyo Bay." Truman finished his remarks, "talking in a gallop," just as three sharp whistle blasts signaled the big moment.[23]

With her proud parents watching, Margaret was ready on the platform, holding a bottle of "champagne" made from Missouri grapes. The navy band struck up "Anchors Aweigh" as "I gave a mighty bash with my magnum," but nothing happened. The *Missouri* stayed put. "Playfully I put my hand on the bow and gave her a shove. Meanwhile I was getting a champagne shower." Normally, the broken bottle would be dragged down the ways with the ship, but the short delay meant it just hung there as champagne dripped down on Margaret and Admiral Kelly.[24]

Finally, the ship began to slide down the slipways—"coated with almost fifty tons of special greases"—toward the river. Just as the ship entered the river, "the sun came out," Margaret wrote. "All the navy men solemnly agreed that it was a good omen."[25]

If Truman was irritable after having to rush his speech, "his dizzy daughter and her equally dizzy friends restored his good humor" over dinner back at the Waldorf. At the end of the long meal, as the waiters in the Empire Room served crêpes suzette for dessert, the three young women, exhausted from the excitement and from staying up all night, fell asleep in their chairs. While everyone enjoyed a laugh, "Mother politely suggested that we ought to go to bed. We nodded, abandoned our crêpes, went upstairs, and collapsed."

21

A CHANGE IN THE WIND

Back in Washington, Truman, Fulton, and the rest of the committee picked up where they had left off—dealing with the mail, requests for investigations from other members of Congress, a request to the Senate for more money (granted), working on the Third Annual Report, and looking ahead to the challenges of the postwar economy. The launching of *Missouri* was one of many signs of the growing US and Allied military superiority, and while there were still huge challenges ahead on the battlefield—notably the long-expected invasion of France—the new year brought a growing certainty that the Allies would eventually prevail. "What has been described as the 'beginning of the end' seems at hand," Truman said in late March. "None of us at home has any real basis for prediction of the military deployments that are certainly impending. We can only surmise that actions of great moment are an immediate prospect."[1]

The committee's brief November report on reconversion,

while accurately looking ahead to many of the postwar challenges, had met with stiff opposition from the military. More
hearings had been held in November and December, with key
labor and business leaders appearing, and the committee returned to the topic in its Third Annual Report. The 210-page
document, which Truman presented to the Senate on March 4,
noted that while the "problem to date has been to produce as
much war material as possible," now the challenge was to produce only as much as necessary, while beginning to look ahead
to the needs of the peacetime economy. The scars left by a decade
of depression were still fresh, and the committee worried that if
the transition wasn't managed right, those years of hardship and
hunger could return. "We are determined that the aftermath of
this war shall not be a depression in which our returning soldiers
and our war workers will be without employment."[2]

Before it explored those challenges, however, the Third Annual Report paused to mark the accomplishments of the past
three years: 153,000 airplanes, 746 warships, 28,000 "subsidiary naval vessels," 1,899 Liberty ships, 1.5 million trucks, and
equipment and clothing for 10 million men. "This astounding
performance exceeds anything of its kind ever achieved in the
history of the world." Significantly, the United States had also
built "nearly 20 billion dollars worth of the best and most modern plant facilities in the world equipped with the finest machine
tools that can be designed"—facilities that could form the basis
of a postwar economic juggernaut.

The senators on the Truman Committee weren't the only
ones looking ahead. Roosevelt had brought up the challenges of
reconversion in a speech in July, and across the government and
the news media and in corporate boardrooms and union halls,
the question of how and when reconversion would happen were
front and center. As historian Maury Klein writes, there were
much bigger issues at stake than the simple question of when to
switch from tanks to typewriters: "Convert the economy back

to—what?" Klein asked. The depression-riddled economy that existed before the war? "Some more powerful vision of a better society grounded in lessons learned from the war? Any one of a dozen variations on these themes?"[3]

Not surprisingly, a fierce fight broke out within the administration over who would be in charge of reconversion. Donald Nelson wanted it, Jimmy Byrnes wanted it, and the military wanted to control production and allocation until the last shot was fired. Suggestions to ease the restrictions on producing civilian goods drew strong opposition from Patterson in the War Department, and military leaders often expressed the idea that even talking about life after the war could distract Americans from the very serious fighting still to come. Byrnes in November had assigned the financier Bernard Baruch and John Hancock of Lehman Brothers to devise a plan for reconversion, and this much-anticipated report was finally made public in February, aligning closely with many of the points the Truman Committee would make weeks later—notably that planning should begin sooner rather than later.

"It is an easier task to convert from peace to war than war to peace," the Baruch report warned,[4] and there was great potential for danger and hardship in the changeover. Already, the War Department and the navy had cut back on nearly $13 billion in contracts.[5] In fact, the US economy had peaked in terms of wartime production in November 1943; from then on it would steadily decline. Canceling contracts meant shutting down factories, and layoffs and unemployment. Should those idle factories and workers then be allowed to make civilian goods? The military's view was no—that workers displaced from one aspect of wartime production would gradually shift to another. That notion—that such unemployment was "desirable because it would tend to force some of the unemployed to migrate to areas of manpower shortages"—the Truman Committee found dubious: "It is not so easy for workmen to transfer their homes."

For one thing, "many women and older men who were not employed before the war would be lost to the labor force, because
they would be forced to stop work and would not be willing,
or in many cases able, to move to areas where additional manpower was needed."[6]

The United States, in becoming the "arsenal of democracy,"
had also maintained during the war a much higher standard of
living than most other combatant nations. The challenges of
drawing down war production, avoiding unemployment, and
shifting over to a civilian economy—all while the war was still
on—were incredibly complex. Echoing the Baruch report, the
committee came down hard on the need to get started right
away: "FREER INDUSTRY URGED BY TRUMAN," read
The New York Times headline. "Committee's Report to Senate
Stresses Quickest Possible Return to Competition."[7]

As confidence grew that the Allies would eventually win, the
feeling of national unity and sacrifice that had brought people,
and Congress, together after Pearl Harbor began to fade. This
was becoming more evident as 1943 gave way to the election
year of 1944, and political divisions that the national crisis had
suppressed began to reassert themselves.

Allen Drury could see it happening in the Senate. In early
March, he covered a Truman Committee hearing about defects
in Liberty ships. In the year since the *Schenectady* broke up in Portland, cracks and structural problems had been found in dozens
more (out of more than two thousand built during the war), and
several Liberty ships had broken apart at sea. Now cracks began
to show, too, in the bipartisan unity of the Truman Committee. During the hearing, the president of the National Maritime
Union, Joseph Curran, made the point that the Liberty ships
overall were serving their purpose and that cracks were few. At
one point in his testimony, he remarked that some newspapers
were sensationalizing the story about the ship defects, "using this
hearing for their own political ends." Two Republicans on the

committee, Homer Ferguson and Owen Brewster, bristled at this. "What political purpose could be served?" Ferguson wanted to know. Curran answered that there might be an attempt "to smear the administration." Brewster reminded him that among the lawmakers raising questions about the Liberty ships were two Democrats, Senator Mon Wallgren and Representative Warren Magnuson.

From there, the increasingly heated questioning by Ferguson and Brewster became personal, as they asked Curran about his draft status, implying that he had avoided military service by being classified as an "essential worker." That forced the union president to defend himself, saying the classification was made by his local draft board and was not something he had requested. "Tempers flared at Senate Truman committee hearing today," read the story Drury wrote that went out over the United Press wire: Curran "started off by praising the Liberty ship as a sound cargo vessel and finished up defending his 2-A draft status in a clash with two Republican senators."[8]

In his diary that night, Drury described Truman's simmering anger as he watched his two colleagues derail the hearing, knowing full well it would dominate the headlines the next day. Curran kept his temper, "but Truman got mad, a lot of hot words were exchanged." The remark about newspapers playing up the story for political reasons, pretty standard media-bashing that might otherwise have passed unnoticed, was now "lifted into the class of news and spread across the country. Truman twice tried to shut his irrepressible colleagues up, each time growing angrier."

Ferguson refused to drop the issue, and Brewster had then made it personal. "It was this more than anything else that seemed to annoy Truman," wrote Drury, who after several months now of watching the Missourian had come to like and admire him. "The chairman is a fine fellow, presiding like some trim, efficient, keen-minded businessman, which is just what he looks like, with his neat appearance, heavy-lensed glasses, and quick, good-humored smile." And then, in the privacy of his diary, Drury let slip for a moment the facade of the cynical reporter: "There are a number of times, in fact, sentimental though it may seem, when it is quite easy to find oneself thanking whatever powers there be that the country has Harry Truman in the Senate. He is an excellent man, a fine Senator and sound American. The debt the public owes to him is great indeed."[9]

Two weeks later, Drury saw the divisions widening. "The Truman Committee is beginning to succumb like everything else to the virus of politics."[10] This time, it was Truman himself who set off a partisan fight within the committee, by endorsing a fourth term for Franklin Roosevelt. In a statement on March 26—the same one in which he noted that the "beginning of the end" was approaching—Truman also expressed his "complete confidence in our leadership, both civilian and military. I think the country realizes that we have wise and experienced leadership. And I am further convinced that this leadership will be continued until the job at hand is completed."[11]

It was yet another sign that he was no longer just a lawmaker going about his business, but a powerful leader of the Democratic party. The New York Times story the next day saw it as a strong endorsement by Truman of a fourth term and that it was "generally agreed that Mr. Truman's statement, which has the effect of giving a stamp of approval to the nation's war leaders and war program from a source which commands considerable respect, is an important boost both for President Roosevelt's nomination and for his chances with the electorate in November."[12]

His Republican colleagues on the committee took immediate offense, for exactly that reason: that Truman was using the bipartisan reputation of the Truman Committee to advance the political aims of the administration. Owen Brewster, Homer Ferguson, and Joseph Ball responded with their own statement the same day: "Senator Truman has a perfect right to state his political position as an individual, but it should be emphasized that he does not speak for this special committee." They noted that the committee had many times criticized the administration's handling of the war effort, findings that were "strongly at variance with those expressed by Senator Truman in his statement."[13]

Drury believed it was Owen Brewster, "one of the touchiest men in the Senate," who roped Ferguson and Ball into "the stern reminder to the chairman that he can back Roosevelt as a senator if he wants to, but not as the chairman of the committee." What Truman made of this criticism, Drury couldn't say, because the chairman had left for Seattle and an inspection tour. "Perhaps when he returns oil will flow on the waters and all will be well. This is not too certain, however."[14]

The very next paragraph of Drury's diary that day confronted the other end-of-an-era upheaval looming over Washington: the declining health of the president, who now had been in the White House for more than a decade, longer than any other occupant. Aubrey Williams, a staunch New Dealer who had headed the National Youth Administration and was now with the National Farmer's Union, had visited Roosevelt and Drury had read a piece Williams had written about it for *The Atlanta Journal*, in which he described his shock at seeing Roosevelt looking ill and tired.[15]

From now on, every move Truman made, every word he uttered, would take place in this politically charged atmosphere, and the committee's work now had what Drury called the "cancer of politics" hanging over it.[16]

The committee staff was feeling the change, too. Hugh Fulton had long chafed at the salary required of a government lawyer, and he was already looking to a future beyond the committee. "As least as far as I am concerned," he told John Cahill, a friend and prominent New York attorney, "I expect to continue in my

present work, at least until the fall of Germany, and then hope
to go into private practice." He had been offered positions elsewhere in the administration, but "I am not much interested in
any other governmental job."[17] Fulton said much the same thing
to George Meader: "He is impatient to get into private practice,"
Meader wrote his wife, "where he will have a chance to earn the
kind of money he continuously sees less able lawyers making."[18]

On board a Catalina flying boat to Maine for an inspection
tour, Meader bet Harry Vaughan, Truman's old friend and now
an army liaison officer with the committee, a bottle of bourbon
that Truman would be nominated vice president. Meader had
recently gotten a chance to work closely with Truman, writing
a speech on transportation that Truman was scheduled to give
in Baltimore. He spent a couple of days on a draft and gave the
manuscript to Truman, who took it home and read it to Bess.
"The next morning he gave it back to me saying both he and
his wife liked the speech." Truman had just two suggestions:
Meader had used the Latin phrase *sine qua non*. "He said, 'Put
that in English.'" And here and there in the draft, Meader had
hedged some statements with phrases like "in my opinion," or
"probably." Cut them out, Truman said: "If it's true, don't qual-
ify it. If it's not, or you are unsure, don't say it."[19]

At times, Meader was working so hard it was affecting his
health, he wrote his wife. He had migraines and occasional dizzy
spells. He suffered a mild one on April 11 while playing cribbage
on a train with Hugh Fulton, and then a worse one the next day
at the office. He suspected poor diet was a factor, and also, he
told Elizabeth, "the fact that I had stayed at the office until 11
p.m. Thursday night without eating anything."[20] He saw an eye
doctor, who diagnosed migraines and told him not to worry.

To save money, Meader was about to give up his apartment
and move in with Joe Martinez—the investigator from New
Mexico who had treated Bob Irvin to a steam bath. Martinez's
wife was leaving for New Mexico to have a baby, and Meader,

who spoke several languages, was looking forward to the chance to brush up on his Spanish.[21]

Along with the distractions of politics, the committee was swamped with work. Meader was deep into an investigation into "incompetence and stupidity and mismanagement in the War Food Administration."[22] The committee was also examining the acquisition of hotels by the military in Florida; Fulton was monitoring the progress of court-martial proceedings against the officers implicated in the Curtiss-Wright scandal; reports on magnesium and merchant shipping were in the pipeline. There were staffing changes, too. A new investigator, a promising attorney named Agnes Strauss, had joined the committee in November. Fred Canfil resigned in January to become a US marshal. Most of the staff in Room 160 hadn't really known what he did anyway. Hugh Fulton was suffering from gout, which forced him to take a couple of weeks off. In March, Matt Connelly left the committee to work in Truman's Senate office as executive assistant. Harold Robinson was named chief investigator, and Wilbur Sparks was promoted to take over Connelly's duties in charge of Room 160, supervising the clerical staff and assigning routine investigations.[23]

And then there was the case of Corrigan, Osburne & Wells. For some time, the committee had been looking into complaints that a navy officer had been improperly using his position to steer business to a consulting firm in which he was also a partner. In the grand scheme of billions of dollars in wartime spending, it was a small case, but it was a bold and blatant example of corruption that provided the Truman Committee with some of its most dramatic public hearings—and testimony—of the war.

Commander John D. Corrigan—US Naval Academy, class of 1920—had gone into business in 1938 with a partner, Robert Wells, to create the consulting firm of Corrigan, Osburne & Wells. Corrigan was recalled to active service in April of 1942 and, ostensibly, resigned from the company at that time.[24] Back in uniform, he was assigned to the ordnance department as a troubleshooter to identify and correct problems at facilities or companies with navy contracts. The complaints to the committee charged that he used his position to tell contractors that, if they wanted to continue to do business with the navy, the best way to solve their problems was to hire the firm of Corrigan, Osburne & Wells.[25] And that, despite his having "resigned," he was still receiving pay and owned 50 percent of the company's stock.

This was still another case where, before going public, the committee turned to the navy first in an effort to clean the situation up quietly. Lieutenant John Tolan, the liaison officer, was in his office one day when he got a call from Rudolph Halley. Could Tolan come see him? "I have a real need for some cooperation from the Navy," Halley told him when he arrived in the Senate Office Building. "You have a Commander John D. Corrigan in the Bureau of Ordnance." Halley explained that Corrigan and his inspection team had been very critical of Remington-Rand, the typewriter company, for work it was doing for manufacturing the top-secret Norden bombsight. Company executives had gotten the strong impression that the criticism would disappear if they hired the consulting firm, and as a result had hired private detectives to investigate the activities of Corrigan and his firm. Those detectives had found evidence, Halley said, that Corrigan was passing confidential information about navy contracts to his partner, Wells, who would then call on the companies involved to offer his services.[26]

That evidence was now in the possession of the Truman Committee, Halley said, and the next step was to obtain Corrigan's own files. "We want the contents of Commander Corrigan's locked desk in the Bureau of Ordnance. We want all his personal correspondence. We want it now."

"How do you expect me to get his files?" Tolan asked.

"Move immediately. We know the evidence is in his desk. If

you don't make a real effort to clean this up right now, the committee will send investigators, with Senate subpoenas. We'll get the information anyway. However, we are giving the Navy an opportunity to cooperate."[27]

Tolan took this back to his superior, Captain Kennedy, who didn't see anything wrong with the request. Later that day, Corrigan's desk was opened by navy investigators, and indeed it contained copies of letters Corrigan had sent to his company that contained confidential information. By the next morning, though, higher officials had become involved, and Tolan found himself in a meeting with Admiral Thomas Gatch, the navy's Judge Advocate General. Gatch felt the case should be investigated by the Justice Department for possible criminal charges: "I don't believe we can hand any evidence to the committee," he told Tolan. "I think that the Department of Justice would agree with me that this might prevent the successful prosecution of the case."[28]

One thing Tolan had learned about military service was that "lieutenants don't argue with admirals." He reported back to Kennedy that the navy was about to be "in deep trouble with the Truman Committee staff and very likely with Senator Truman himself." Kennedy appealed to Undersecretary James Forrestal to try to reverse the decision. Forrestal reported back that senior officials had talked it over and agreed with Admiral Gatch—the committee would not get the documents. It was left to Kennedy to relay the news. Halley, furious, said he would call back and hung up.[29]

About twenty minutes later, Kennedy's phone rang. It was Halley and Hugh Fulton. Their message was short and to the point: "Chairman Truman wants Admiral Gatch to meet with the full committee in the Capitol at 3 p.m. Bring the evidence. If you want a subpoena, we'll send one down. It may not be just for Admiral Gatch. It will probably include the Secretary."[30]

Once again, the military had pushed Truman's buttons and

paid the price for it. Eventually, the navy surrendered the documents, but Truman had by now scheduled hearings—both a private session and two days of public testimony, at which Corrigan would be summoned. When the hearings began on May 25, Tolan, Abbott, and Kennedy were there for the fireworks.

On the first day, May 25, the accountant for Corrigan, Osburne & Wells testified in detail, notably about the fact that while Corrigan was on active service with the navy in 1943, the company had paid him $12,000 in salary and that he owned half of its stock. Then came Corrigan's turn. Wearing his navy uniform, he took his seat before the committee as Fulton informed him that a grand jury in New York would begin considering the case the following day in New York: "I wanted you to be particularly aware of your constitutional rights against answering any question that you might consider would tend to incriminate you. Now do you know that if you wish to claim that right, this committee will not ask you any further questions?"[31]

"I do not wish to claim that right."

With that, Commander Corrigan was in for a very long couple of days. The committee allowed him to read a lengthy statement, laying out his case that his company had saved the country millions of dollars by fixing problems in vital war plants, and that he personally had cleared up many production bottlenecks and delays: "I sincerely believe that my own work in the Navy has been of great assistance to the prosecution of the war." He claimed also that he had fully informed his superiors of any potential conflicts with Corrigan, Osburne & Wells.

As he described at great length the work his company had done, and his many suggestions for improving efficiency and reducing costs, it's easy to imagine Lieutenants Tolan and Abbott exchanging with Captain Kennedy knowing smiles at what must have seemed a prime example of the Doctrine of Apparent Frankness in action. Little of what Corrigan said had any bearing on the question of whether he had drawn double pay from the navy and his company or used his position to steer business to his firm.

When he was finished, Hugh Fulton went to work, playing hardball right from the start. "Mr. Corrigan, what is your status with the Navy department now?"

"I have been suspended."

"As of when?"

"As of the night the Truman committee announced that this meeting would be held today."

Fulton then walked him through a detailed history of Corrigan, Osburne & Wells, which, to the amusement of everyone present, revealed the fact that there was no Osburne.

"There never was an Osburne in the company," Corrigan said.

Fulton, understandably, wanted to know, "Why did you put in the name a fictitious name of Osburne when there wasn't any Osburne that you expected to have as a partner or whom you never had had?"[32]

Corrigan explained that most firms operating as consultants at that time had three names. And so, when he and Wells had formed the company in 1938, they added the fictional Osburne with the intention that, sooner or later, the name would be dropped when a real third partner came on board. With that detail cleared up, Fulton moved on to the accountant's testimony that the firm, from 1938 until the date when Corrigan reentered navy service, had lost money. But "since you went into the Navy these firms which have had occasion at least to be visited by you have been employers of your company to the extent of $319,000?"

Corrigan: "I never knew the amount of money."

Fulton: "Have you any reason to think that Mr. Wagner's computations are in any way inaccurate?"

Corrigan: "No, I haven't any reason to think it."[33]

And so on, throughout the morning and into a long afternoon session. From Corrigan's own words, his duties in the navy were "the investigation and analysis of firms who manufacture ordnance material, particularly those firms who are behind schedule on needed ordnance material, to determine what must be done to get production out of that plant." Time and time again, it emerged that the answer to "what must be done" for those firms was to hire Corrigan, Osburne & Wells.

Almost from the start, Fulton's careful questioning forced Corrigan to backtrack on previous statements, or led him into outright contradictions.

"Did you ever in any way participate in the decisions," Fulton asked, "made by the Chicago office of your company?"

Corrigan: "I never have."

Would Corrigan be surprised to learn that his papers in his desk at the Navy Department indicated otherwise? "Yes, very much so."

Fulton: "You have just denied that you had any contact."

"That is right. I didn't deny I had any correspondence. I said I did not recall any correspondence."

"You mean your memory may be bad?"

"It could be on that. I cannot remember details. I never have—never tried to."

"Now I will perhaps be able to refresh your recollection somewhat from the files of your Chicago office."

He then read a letter from Corrigan's partner, Wells, to the president of one the firm's clients, Danly Machine Specialties Co., dated May 23, 1942: "Mr. Corrigan of our organization may be in Chicago next week and he will call on you at that time if possible."

Fulton then read from another letter from an employee, this one from November 1942: "Apparently the Danly job will continue for a while and I have since talked to Jack Corrigan in connection with his visit and the general reaction to our work at Danly."

And so on.

Fulton: "We talked about that a minute or two ago, whether you told your Chicago man, Evans, that you discussed with Danly whether the Corrigan, Osburne, Wells firm was doing a good job and he seemed satisfied with the work of your firm. Did you tell Mr. Evans that?"

"I did not."

"Did he make this up when he said, as in this first sentence..."

"He was making it up."

"In other words, he was making a false report to Mr. Wells."

"Apparently."

With Fulton pressing, and Corrigan twisting himself in knots, Senator Carl Hatch stepped in, leading Corrigan to one of many contradictions of something he had just said: "You were pleased with the activities of the Chicago office, were you not?"

"I said, 'I think you are doing a swell job, fellows.' That's all."

"There is nothing in Mr. Evans' letter that wasn't true, then."[34]

"I wouldn't think so," said Corrigan, who had just told Fulton that that same letter was a false report.

A few minutes later, Corrigan was once again back to claiming the statements were false. From there it got worse, as Fulton moved on to the evidence that Corrigan had sent restricted information from his navy office to Wells at the company.

"Did you ever tell anybody in Corrigan, Osburne & Wells to destroy by fire any papers that you sent them?"

"I don't recall."[35]

By now it was well into the afternoon, and Corrigan was excused until the next morning. This answer, too, would come back around on him the next day.

Harry Truman had not been present for the first day of the hearings, but spent the evening reviewing the case and the testimony with Hugh Fulton, and he was in the chair the next morning at 10:35 when the questioning resumed.[36] If things had gone badly the first day, today started off even worse, as Homer

Ferguson presented Corrigan with a letter he had written from his navy office to an employee named David Amour. (The day before, when Fulton had asked Corrigan about this man, Corrigan responded, "I never heard of him."[37])

"Dear Dave," the letter began. "Enclosed you will find a list" of companies the navy had given money to for plant facilities. "After you have looked this over and taken whatever data you want off it, will you be kind enough to see that it is destroyed by fire. You will notice at the top it says 'Restricted,' which means it is not for general distribution. So when you get all the information you want off it, please destroy it. But do yourself and your country a favor by selling some of these people on here a job and then proceed to get them the results you gave Danly."

Ferguson then asked, "How is it signed?"

Corrigan read the signature: "John D. Corrigan, lieutenant commander, United States Naval Reserve."[38]

After a discussion about what "restricted" meant, with Corrigan admitting it meant that such documents were not to be shared outside the navy, Truman stepped in for the first time: "If that is a restricted document, Commander, why did you send it to your private office?"

"I don't recall at the time, Senator, why it was done."

Homer Ferguson had a pretty good idea of why it was done. "It would be very valuable to you personally to have your company get it because you were on a $12,000-a-year salary."

"That is right."

More letters, more incriminating evidence, more evasions and admissions, including a statement to a skeptical Fulton that, although his business partner was often in Washington, staying at Corrigan's apartment, he never once talked with Wells about how much money their company was making. "No, I never did."

"Do you wish us to believe that?"

"I do."

This was the last straw for Truman. "We will excuse you for the time being, Mr. Corrigan. You are subject to further call."

Lieutenant Abbott of the navy liaison office was seated that day close to the table where Truman and the other senators were asking their questions—close enough to hear as Truman leaned over and told Senator Kilgore: "Harley, this son of a bitch is as crooked as a dog's hind leg, and I'm going to move to court-martial him."[39]

With that, as Corrigan stood to leave, Truman pointed a finger at him and said, "I want to make this announcement now. To my viewpoint, I think that Commander Corrigan should be immediately court-martialed by the United States Navy. I think it is the most flagrant violation of the rules and regulations of the Navy that I have seen since this committee has been at work."

Homer Ferguson voiced his agreement, and with that, said *The Washington Post,* Corrigan "reddened and walked away."[40]

22

CHICAGO

Truman continued to tell anyone and everyone that he was not interested in the job of vice president, and all indications were that he actually meant it. He loved the Senate and his place in it, and he knew the weaknesses and the frustrations of the vice presidency. At the same time, though, pieces were falling into place. Significantly, his close friend and Missouri political ally, Bob Hannegan, in January became chairman of the Democratic National Committee.

With each passing day, Truman was having to face the question more often. In one of many such letters he wrote in 1944, he told a Florida state senator in March, "I have just gotten to the point in the Senate where I can be of use to the people of Missouri and the country, and I would hate to give up that job for one that is purely decorative. While I think that it is a very high honor to be Vice President, actually he does not have anything to do, and I don't want a job of that kind."[1]

As the political season heated up, the demands on Truman

as one of the party's rising stars kept him on the road. In his speeches, he came out as a forceful backer of a fourth term, which Roosevelt had not yet, officially, agreed to. "To entrust the winning of the war and the framing of the peace into the hands of any man with a limited outlook and without the experience for such a job would be the sheerest folly," Truman said in one of many speeches during these months, this one to a Democratic audience in Topeka.[2]

Among the other names floated as a possible running mate was Senator Alben Barkley of Kentucky, considered in May about on par with Truman as a long shot. Ahead of them were, at least the newspaper speculation had it, Jimmy Byrnes, the former senator and Supreme Court justice, now head of the Office of War Mobilization; and the vice president himself. Henry Wallace had not given up, and continued to receive encouragement and, at least to his face, support from Roosevelt. (Roosevelt in May also sent Byrnes on a long trip to China and Siberia, which many interpreted as a signal that he was out of the running.)

Byrnes was close to Roosevelt, and the papers often called him the "Assistant President." Working against him, though, was his record as an established segregationist who came from South Carolina, a "poll tax" state. After the Fifteenth Amendment in 1870 extended to Black men the right to vote, many Southern states adopted a poll tax as a way to freeze out these men, most of whom were too poor to pay it. By the 1940s, abolishing the poll tax had become a key civil rights issue, and to say a politician was from a "poll tax state" was a euphemism in the press for white Southerners like Byrnes. Since 1939, Congress had been considering a bill that would ban poll taxes as a requirement for voting in federal elections, and the NAACP and other organizations had been pushing for its passage. Despite many pleas to Roosevelt for help, the president was more concerned about needing to carry Southern states to win nationally, and largely

ducked the issue. In November 1942, asked at a news conference whether he thought the poll tax bill should pass, Roosevelt
"reiterated that he knew nothing about it, had talked to no one
about it, and therefore could not express an opinion."[3]

But it was growing more evident that civil rights and the
Black vote would be important in 1944 and would be a factor in
the selection of a running mate. In May, Southern-state Democrats joined with thirteen Northern Republicans to deny a vote
on the bill in the Senate. "Thus, for this session of Congress
anti poll tax legislation is dead," declared *The Chicago Defender*,
a prominent Black newspaper, "and the 13 million poor Negroes and whites living in eight southern poll tax states remain
disfranchised in the world's greatest democracy." The *Defender*
printed the names of all the senators who voted to kill the bill.
Harry Truman's name was not among them.

While Truman was now widely viewed as a staunch ally of
the president, he had not spoken with Franklin Roosevelt since
June 1943.[4] Over and over, Truman said to anyone who asked
that he did not want the job. In early May, with two months to
go before the convention in Chicago, the Associated Press reported that "the Democratic second place contest has assumed
the aspects of a five-man race," with those five being Speaker
of the House Sam Rayburn, Wallace, Truman and Barkley,
and Governor J. Melville Broughton of North Carolina. Other
names out there included Jimmy Byrnes, who believed he had
Roosevelt's blessing, Supreme Court Justice William O. Douglas,[5] and Henry Kaiser.[6]

Roosevelt, true to form, was sending mixed messages. At one
point in June, he had seemed to favor Byrnes: "That suits me
fine," he told Robert Hannegan, but even Byrnes knew that
didn't mean anything. At another meeting that same month,
Roosevelt said, "everyone knows I am for Henry Wallace."
Asked about Truman, he said he didn't really know the man,

but agreed that his committee had done a good job and gained a lot of favorable press.[7]

Overshadowing the domestic politics was an even greater drama playing out in Europe. On June 6, more than 150,000 British, American, and Canadian troops (many in the Higgins boats and tank lighters the Truman Committee had worked so hard to procure for them) fought their way ashore on the beaches of Normandy in the largest seaborne invasion in history.

From the perspective of nearly eight decades on, and familiarity born of countless films and documentaries, the outcome of D-Day seems inevitable. But at the time, success was by no means a sure thing, as illustrated by the penciled note that General Dwight D. Eisenhower, the Supreme Allied Commander in Europe, wrote the day before and put into his wallet in case he needed it: "Our landings in the Cherbourg-Havre area have failed to gain a satisfactory foothold and I have withdrawn the troops. My decision to attack at this time and place was based on the best information available. The troops, the air and the Navy did all that Bravery and devotion to duty could do. If any blame or fault attaches to the attempt it is mine alone."

The landings did succeed, and despite heavy casualties—especially among the American troops at Omaha Beach—the Allies established a beachhead and began to push inland. In the coming months, the massive buildup of troops and supplies in Great Britain over the past few months—weapons and ammunition and equipment stretching back thousands of miles to factories and workshops in the United States—would prove overwhelming on the battlefield.

The Normandy invasion brought much-needed relief for the Soviet troops pushing steadily westward toward Germany, while Allied forces pushed their way up the Italian peninsula and British and American bombers attacked German industrial cities by day and night. There were months of hard fighting ahead in Europe, and then the planned invasion of Japan after Hitler's defeat, but from D-Day onward, it seemed no longer a question of whether the Allies would win, but when.

In late June, the Republicans met for their convention in Chicago, staying in many of the same hotels the Democrats would use a month later. The party nominated forty-two-year-old Thomas E. Dewey, governor of New York, for president, with Ohio Governor John Bricker rounding out the ticket. The Republicans in their platform opposed the poll tax, condemned racial prejudice, and vowed a congressional inquiry into discrimination against Black people serving in the armed services[8]—something the Truman Committee had still not gotten around to. Dewey, a former prosecutor and district attorney, had sought the Republican nomination in 1940, at age thirty-eight, but was edged out by Wendell Willkie. He was considered an effective governor, and was a leader of the moderate wing of the GOP, supporting, among other things, Social Security and other pillars of the New Deal. His campaign would center on smaller government and opposition to what the Republicans portrayed as corruption and inefficiency in the New Deal and the Roosevelt administration.

As June turned to July and the Democratic convention approached, the plotting and speculation in the press and in the leadership circles of the Democratic party continued, fueled by the vague and contradictory signals coming from Roosevelt himself, and bitter fighting among the factions seeking to either keep Wallace on the ticket or dump him. On July 6, the New York Democratic leader Ed Flynn warned Roosevelt that having Byrnes as the vice-presidential nominee could cost the Democrats enough Black voters that Roosevelt might lose his home state in November. Roosevelt met with Wallace upon the vice president's return from Asia on July 10 and gave the vice president the impression that he would stay on the ticket: "I hope it will be the same old team."[9] But the next day, the president told Harry Hopkins that Jimmy Byrnes had the strongest chance. Roosevelt, despite his failing health and his constant weariness, still controlled his party and his administration. "Only he could have a clear picture of where the game was headed," writes historian Joseph Lelyveld. "Exercising his mastery over his party yet again was one way of convincing himself he still might be equal to the tasks ahead."[10]

On July 11, Roosevelt formally announced that "reluctantly but as a good soldier"—he would accept the nomination for a fourth term.[11] Drury described in his diary how he had observed three Democratic senators that day as they heard the news: "It was as though the sun had burst from the clouds and glory surrounded the world. Relief, and I mean relief, was written on every face. The meal ticket was still the meal ticket and all was well with the party. They almost sang out loud."[12]

Later that night, on a hot Washington summer evening, the president met with several party leaders, including Hannegan; the New York party leader Ed Flynn; Edwin Pauley, treasurer of the DNC; Postmaster General Frank Walker; George Allen, a Washington insider; and Mayor Ed Kelly of Chicago. They gathered in the second-floor study of the White House to talk over the various choices for vice president. Everyone was in their shirtsleeves as drinks were handed around, and it quickly became clear at this meeting that for Roosevelt, Wallace was no longer in contention. The various names were considered, with Roosevelt, looking tired and for once not leading the conversation, listening for the most part. Accounts of the various participants differ, but there is general agreement that Truman's name came up last, that Roosevelt acted "as if he were hearing the idea for the first time"[13] and spoke favorably about Truman and his investigating committee.

Finally, the meeting ended with Roosevelt saying to Hannegan, "Bob, I think you and everyone else here want Truman." The meeting wrapped up quickly as those present sought to leave before the president could change his mind.[14]

Hannegan circled back and, possibly on this same night, or in the next few days in Washington, or possibly in Chicago several days later, obtained from Roosevelt this note, dated July 19, the first day of the convention:

Dear Bob:
You have written me about Harry Truman and Bill Douglas. I should, of course, be very glad to run with either of them and believe that either one of them would bring real strength to the ticket. Always sincerely,
Franklin D. Roosevelt[15]

Even that was by no means final, and journalists and participants at the time, and historians in the decades since, have been unable to sort out the exact sequence of events, or Roosevelt's true intentions. The president had encouraged both Wallace and Byrnes, to their faces, while urging aides to deliver the bad news to both men, and he had seemed to favor Truman at the end of the July 11 meeting. But he had also written a letter that seemed to support Wallace while also appearing to give delegates an option to bypass him.[16] Both Byrnes and Wallace headed to Chicago still determined to fight. Truman, meanwhile, was saying to anyone who asked—even his own daughter—that he did not want the job. Margaret, who was in Denver with Bess, had seen one of the many newspaper stories speculating about her father's chances, and written him to ask about it. "Yes, they are plotting against your dad," he responded on July 9. "Every columnist and prognosticator is trying to make him V.P. against his will. It is funny how some people would give a fortune to be as close as I am to it and I don't want it."[17]

Right up until the eve of the convention, he was saying the same thing, and apparently still unaware of the July 11 White House meeting that had put him in the pole position.[18] Margaret showed his letter to her mother, as he likely hoped she would, since the one person even less enthusiastic than Truman about him becoming vice president was his wife.

Truman was at the President Hotel in Kansas City, where he would stay and do some political work until heading to Chicago for the convention. Bennett Clark, his Missouri colleague in the Senate, was up for re-election and seemed likely to lose—a political decline as surprising and precipitous as Truman's rise over the past four years—but Truman had promised to support him. On July 13 he wrote Bess, once again reassuring her: "Just gave Mr. Roberts* a tough interview saying I didn't want the V.P. Also told the West Va. and Okla. delegations to go for Barkley. Also told Downey I didn't want the California delegation. Mr. Roberts says I have it in the bag if I don't say no—and I've said it as tough as I can."

On July 14, Byrnes, still believing he would get the nod from Roosevelt, called Truman in Missouri to ask him to make the nominating speech on his behalf. Byrnes had made a strong personal appeal to Roosevelt, making the odd argument that as a Southerner from a poll tax state, he would not hurt FDR's chances with Black voters, but could actually help by giving support to an effort to end the poll tax. "This is a serious problem, but it will have to be solved by the white people of the South."[19]

He asked Roosevelt to keep the choice open, and Roosevelt had, once again, appeared to agree.

Truman said yes to Byrnes, and no sooner had he hung up the phone than Alben Barkley called to ask him the same thing. Truman told him Byrnes had gotten there first.[20]

In the days leading up to the convention, newspaper speculation built to a frenzy. The arrival of Bob Hannegan in Chicago came as word leaked out that he was carrying letters from the White House indicating Roosevelt's choice. The International News Service reported on July 15 that Hannegan carried a letter from Roosevelt in support of Wallace. The papers that day also carried news of a Gallup poll showing strong support for Wallace among rank-and-file Democrats: "He receives more than four

---

* Roy Roberts of *The Kansas City Star.*

times as many votes as the next popular man, Senator Alben W. Barkley." Truman, Byrnes, and several other names ranked far behind—Byrnes with 3 percent and Truman with 2. On Saturday the 15th—the day Truman left Kansas City—Hannegan denied any knowledge of the letter supporting Wallace, but when asked whether he was carrying any letters from the White House on the subject of the vice-presidential choice, he had no comment.[21]

Truman, arriving in Chicago, met for breakfast with the powerful labor leader Sidney Hillman. Truman asked Hillman whether he was for Byrnes. Hillman said he was not—there were only two men besides Wallace he would support: "They were William O. Douglas, justice of the Supreme Court, and Harry S. Truman, U.S. senator from Missouri." Truman told Hillman he didn't want it, but later that day in meetings with Philip Murray, head of the CIO, and Alexander Whitney of the Brotherhood of Railroad Trainmen, Truman heard much the same thing.[22]

He related these meetings to Byrnes, who told him not to worry, that Roosevelt would soon make everything clear. Nothing became clear as the convention began, except that it was more and more evident to Byrnes and everyone else that he was not going to get the nod. Truman continued to hold out, likely out of his knowledge that Bess, who was scheduled to arrive with Margaret on Tuesday the 18th, did not want him to be vice president. Margaret believed that her father was worried about newspaper criticism of Bess being on his Senate payroll, and also that the press would dig up and rehash her father's suicide. Though Bess feared what, it now seemed clear, was about to happen, she did not put her foot down and forbid him to take the nomination.[23]

Beyond his concerns about Bess, writes Alonzo Hamby, Truman may have been determined before making any commitment "to get definitive word from Roosevelt himself." Even a handwritten note Hannegan showed him, written on a White House notepad—"Bob it's Truman, FDR"—did not change his mind. "I still could not be sure that this was Roosevelt's intent," since he also knew of statements Roosevelt made in support of Wallace.[24]

That definitive word finally came on Thursday, July 20.[25] Bess and Margaret were staying at the Morrison Hotel, but Truman had a suite at the Stevens Hotel.[26] There, that afternoon, he received a summons to come to Hannegan's suite at the Blackstone. When he arrived, the room was full of party bosses. Hannegan put through a transcontinental call to the president in San Diego. Truman sat quietly on one twin bed, Hannegan on the other, as the familiar, booming voice of Franklin Roosevelt came down the line, loud enough for Truman to hear clearly.

"Bob, have you got that fellow lined up yet?"

"No," said Hannegan. "He is the contrariest Missouri mule I've ever dealt with."

"Well, you tell him if he wants to break up the Democratic party in the middle of a war, that's his responsibility."[27]

With that, there was a click on the line as Roosevelt "banged down the phone." Truman sat there, "completely stunned," and after a minute or two stood up and began pacing while those in the room watched him in silence. As Joseph Lelyveld writes, "by one account, the first words out of Truman's mouth were 'Oh, shit.' By another, they were 'Jesus Christ.'"[28] In Truman's version, he eventually said, "Well, if that is the situation, I'll have to say yes, but why the hell didn't he tell me in the first place?"[29]

There was still convention drama to come, and a push later that Thursday by Wallace supporters to secure the nomination, but the powerful men who were in the room with Truman and Hannegan that day stepped in. On Friday, when the delegates voted, Wallace led after the first ballot, but Truman went over the top on the second vote, 1,031 to 105.[30] Bess and Margaret were there to watch as he made one of the shortest—and least memorable—acceptance speeches in history: fewer than a hundred words. In three years on the Truman Committee, he had grown used to being a national figure, but now, suddenly and forever, he had stepped onto a much bigger stage.

He finished his short remarks and made his way through the crowd to the box where Margaret and Bess were sitting. There, they were swamped by photographers and a crowd of emotional supporters. Truman asked for police help to push their way through the crowd and outside to a waiting limousine. As they got into the car, Bess looked over at her husband: "Are we going to have to go through this for the rest of our lives?"[31]

The next day brought further evidence of how much their world had changed. Bess gave a news conference, "and answered as patiently as she could all sorts of silly questions about Dad's eating habits, clothing styles, work routines and the like." As they packed and readied for a quick trip to Independence, Truman gave Margaret a souvenir: a telegram he'd received from the president just before Roosevelt boarded a navy warship for Hawaii: "I send you my heartiest congratulations on your victory. I am, of course, very happy to have you run with me. Let me know your plans. I shall see you soon. Franklin D. Roosevelt."[32]

Truman would not stay long in Missouri before heading back to Washington. It was becoming clear that he and not Roosevelt would do most of the work of campaigning. The president's health and his status as commander-in-chief as the war entered its crucial final phases meant that the vice-presidential nominee would be on the road almost constantly. Of the many decisions and changes Truman faced in the weeks ahead, one that came up immediately was whether he should continue as head of the Senate investigating committee.

From Washington, George Meader had followed the Democratic convention on the radio, listening as his boss was nominated to become vice president. "I don't have any inside dope of course," he wrote his wife on the 22nd, but "I was a little

surprised that Truman had told his first press conference that
he would resign as chairman of the committee."

Hugh Fulton, Meader wrote, "is anxious to get into private
practice where he can make some money. I will be interested to
find out how he sizes up the situation now that Truman's nomination is a fact." And then Meader touched on a question that
would come up often in the next few months: how much of the
Truman Committee's success was due to its chairman, and how
much was the result of its chief counsel. "Probably, neither Hugh
nor Harry really know themselves. Personally, I think that both
of them know they can accomplish more together than either
could without the other."[33]

Meader wasn't the only one wondering if Truman would
stay on with the committee. On July 25, Fulton sent a telegram
from Washington to Truman in Independence: MEAD AND
HATCH OFFICES BOTH HAVE INQUIRED CONCERN-
ING POSSIBLE RESIGNATION. I HAVE INFORMED
THEM WHOLE SUBJECT OF FUTURE COMMITTEE
WOULD BE DISCUSSED ON THURSDAY.[34]

As Truman returned to Washington, Fulton joined his train
in Martinsburg, West Virginia, to urge him to change his mind
and stay on as committee chair. For three hours they talked it
over, but the senator ended up persuading Fulton that resigning was the only option. Back in the Capitol, he gathered the
committee members in the Doghouse on Thursday, August 3.
Some of the members—including the Republicans—urged him
to reconsider, saying they could carry on the work while he
campaigned. And then, they argued, if Roosevelt won, it might
be time to resign. Truman wasn't budging. The committee had
for the most part avoided politics, he told them, and if he stayed
on, that would not be possible. "It will be attacked and I will
be attacked for remaining as chairman."[35]

He was deeply upset by the fact that he had to resign, and
moved nearly to tears by the efforts to persuade him to stay. "I

had never in my life wanted to sit down and really blubber like I did when I told 'em I was quitting," he wrote Bess the next day. "I didn't do it—but they did."[36] He came out of the meeting carrying copies of the resignation letter he'd written to Henry Wallace, the man he would be replacing as vice president, in Wallace's role as President of the Senate:

Dear Mr. President,

I herewith submit my resignation as Chairman and a member of the Special Committee of the United States Senate Investigating the National Defense Program.

The accomplishments of the committee in the past largely have been due to the fact that all its members, Democrat and Republican alike, were able to work together in harmony without partisanship. I know they would all try sincerely to continue this, and I appreciate the great compliment which the Republican members have paid me by requesting me to continue and pledging me their support.

However, I have been nominated for the office of Vice President of the United States by the Democratic party, and as candidate for that office it is my obligation to present to the people the accomplishments of the Democratic Party and the reasons why it should continue to be entrusted with the administration of the government in this great national emergency.

I do not want even the shadow of suspicion that the Committee's activities in any way are determined or influenced by political considerations.

Sincerely yours,

Harry S. Truman, Chairman[37]

He told reporters, including Allen Drury, that he had "considered all the angles and my mind is made up."[38]

A few days later, Drury popped in to see Truman in his office, and in his diary that night left a sketch of the man who he now realized might be the next vice president, or even president. "No pomp and circumstance for Harry Truman and no hesitation about telling you what he thinks. He is so frank, in fact, that unfortunately nine-tenths of it must remain off the record, but it certainly makes him an enjoyable man to talk to. He talks rapidly, laughs often, is entirely natural and completely likable. And the press, without exception, eats out of his hand, principally because his best stories are on himself."[39]

On August 3, the same day Truman wrote to Wallace, Hugh Fulton resigned. Four days later, Truman addressed the Senate for the last time as chairman, calling his decision to resign "one of the most difficult decisions I have ever had to make."

"My colleagues have deeply honored me by referring to it as the Truman committee, and I have worked hard to make it a success. But I want to emphasize again, as I have so often done in the past, that the accomplishments of the special committee have not been those of one man. They are due to the splendid teamwork of 10 members, who have given unsparingly of their time and energy, and to the work of what I think is the ablest staff ever assembled by a congressional committee." He went on to name the senators, with special praise for his Republican colleagues: Burton, Ball, Ferguson and Brewster. And then the senior members of the staff—Fulton and Meader, Rudolph Halley, Matt Connelly, Bill Boyle, and Harold Robinson. From there he named the investigators, "most of them young lawyers and accountants. They have all done good work, and I want to refer to them by name: Wilbur Sparks, Donald Lathrom, Franklin Parks, William Cole, Walter Hehmeyer, Robert Irvin, Russell Searl, Joe Martinez, Harry Magee, Haven Sawyer, Marion Toomey, and Agnes Strauss." Then he thanked the stenographers and clerks, specifically Lydia Lee and Margaret Buchholz, who had made Room 160 hum with efficiency.* He closed by not-

---

★ When copies of that week's *Congressional Record* came in, with the text of the speech and the names of the staff members printed, Truman personally autographed a copy for each staffer.

ing that the days when a single senator or representative could
master all the details of a bill or program were gone forever, and
noted that his committee showed what could be accomplished
"by making a factual investigation with a good staff. The cost
of a good investigation is negligible when compared with the
results which can be obtained."[40]

After Truman finished his remarks, he went down to Room
160 to meet with the staff and thank them. He told everyone
he didn't really want to go to Chicago, "but that he had been
nominated and that he was going to run and do his best to win."
He said how proud he was of their work and how disappointed
he was to leave the committee. "And when he got all through
there was a sort of a silence and everybody in the room stood at
their desks." There were no reporters and no crowds, said Walter Hehmeyer. "It was just very personal." He watched as Truman went around "and shook hands with every single person
in the room, including the office boy."[41]

23

AFTERMATH

The Truman Committee would continue, for another four years, with Senator James Mead of New York as chairman and then others. Rudolph Halley succeeded Hugh Fulton as chief counsel, and George Meader took over Halley's duties. Of course it wouldn't be called the Truman Committee anymore, and pretty much everyone knew that it wasn't the same. Without him, the fire had gone out. "When Truman left the basic idea did not depart but the committee's accomplishment was completed," wrote Jonathan Daniels. "Three months after Truman left, according to a man above all others who should know, 'it had gone to the dogs.'"[1]

Truman himself said it to Bess the day after he resigned as chairman: "Its major job is done and when peace comes it will require another approach to things."[2]

In many ways this story, the story of the Truman Committee, ends just as the story of Harry Truman takes off in dramatic new directions. A national campaign, Franklin Roosevelt's election to a fourth term, and then, on a snowy day in January 1945, taking the oath of office as vice president and then standing by the aging president on the South Portico of the White House as Roosevelt was sworn in for a historic fourth term.

In the end, he was vice president for only eighty-two days. On the afternoon of April 12, 1945, he was back in the Senate chamber, writing to his mother and sister:

"Dear Mamma and Mary—I am trying to write you a letter today from the desk of President of the Senate while a windy Senator from Wisconsin is making a speech on a subject with which he is in no way familiar."[3]

Just before 5:00 p.m., the Senate went into recess. Truman, as he often did in the afternoons, walked to the other end of the Capitol building to Sam Rayburn's hideaway office, known as the "Board of Education," where the House Speaker met in the afternoons with other regulars for a drink. Truman, wearing a double-breasted gray suit and a crisp bow tie, was just about to sit down when Rayburn told him there was a message from the White House press secretary: "Steve Early wants you to call him right away." Truman mixed himself a drink while he dialed the White House: "This is the Vice President." Truman listened for a bit, said, "all right" and put the phone down. He looked around, the color gone from his face, and among the several versions of what he said next is, "Jesus Christ and General Jackson." Come to the White House, Early had told him, as quickly and quietly as possible.[4]

He arrived at 5:25 p.m. In the living quarters on the second floor, Eleanor Roosevelt stood waiting for him. She put her arm on his shoulder: "Harry, the President is dead."[5]

It could have been Alben Barkley, or Jimmy Byrnes, or even Henry Wallace standing there that day. But it was Harry Truman, and many Americans, facing the loss of the man who had been their leader for much of their lives, struggled in the days to come to figure out how this relatively unknown Missourian had taken Roosevelt's place.

In the piece they started writing soon after for *Harper's Magazine*, the two journalists, Wesley McCune and John Beal, had a ready answer: it was his "performance as an investigator" that, above all other reasons, lifted Truman into the White House.[6] They noted that "plenty of other investigators were running investigations at about the same time, in fields as important as Truman's. Yet none was able to build himself into a national political figure."

It is in this context that the story of the Truman Committee is most often told—how it vaulted Truman into national leadership and, ultimately, the vice presidency. But there are other accomplishments as well. Of course the one most often cited—by Truman and many others—is that it saved the country billions of dollars, and the lives of thousands of soldiers and sailors and airmen. And it likely did both of those things, though each is impossible to quantify with actual numbers. "There is no doubt," wrote Marquis Childs, the Washington reporter for the *St. Louis Post-Dispatch*, "that it has saved billions—yes billions—of dollars."[7] Historian Donald Riddle agrees: the figure was "no doubt" in the billions, he wrote, noting along the way (as Truman loved to point out) that those billions were a "gratifying return on the investment of less than a million dollars in the Committee's work."[8] Truman and others often put the number at $15 billion, though no one seems to know where that number came from. With so many intangibles, it is probably as good, or bad, as any other.

The army camp report, General Somervell acknowledged, found $100 million in waste (though the figure was almost certainly a guess by Somervell, and *Time* quoted him saying it was probably closer to $250 million[9]). Did that mean the committee really "saved" that money? Perhaps not, but the committee's report did lead to an overhaul of the system for awarding such contracts going forward, which may have saved the country that much or even more.[10] Some actual numbers can be found in the area of renegotiating war contracts. The committee had highlighted the need for this in its First Annual Report, and pushed hard for it afterwards. Here's how Truman explained the idea: "Renegotiation is a poor word," he said. "We should call it repricing. For all it amounts to is sitting down calmly and refiguring the cost of war contracts on a mass-production basis. Many of the things we needed in vast quantities had never been made that way before; nobody could know what they cost." As a result, contracts had been awarded based on guesses of what the costs would be. "But now we have the leisure to recheck, and it is our duty to do so."[11]

Soon after that first report, Congress passed a law allowing for renegotiation, and it was used many times to reclaim excessive profits. The Truman Committee's Third Annual Report in 1944 put some hard numbers on the savings, by examining companies with the largest volume of war business and comparing their prewar profits with what they had made in 1942. Even after taxes, many of them had shown huge profits, several times what they had ever made before.

In the prewar period, for example, a "small airplane manufacturing company in Pennsylvania" had been operating at a loss of more than $70,000 a year. In 1942, the report said, that company showed an operating profit—after paying its taxes—of nearly $3 million. Renegotiation returned to the taxpayers more than $1.2 million.

Then there was one of the "larger and more successful prewar airplane builders," which had earned an average $432,000 in profits after taxes before the war. In 1942, that company made more than ten times that—$5.5 million. Renegotiation "stepped in to recover" $2 million.[12] The list went on and on. So here, clearly, were actual billions of dollars in savings. But could the committee claim all the credit? Certainly the First Annual Report had led the charge, but it is also true that other congressional committees had examined the problem; other members of Congress had written and passed the bill; and accountants and bureaucrats across the government had examined the books and negotiated the savings.

It is equally impossible to calculate the savings in human lives. Impossible to say how many more tons of bad steel would have found its way into ships, how many more of those ships might have broken up at sea, whether the steel would have been the cause, and how many sailors might have died as a result. The same goes for defective airplane engines. No one could say how many engines from that plant had already wound up in airplanes, causing, as Truman put it, "the death of some of our student pilots." How many more such engines would have been shipped? How many soldiers or marines might have perished on tank lighters of that inferior navy design, foundering in heavy seas off the coast of Normandy, or drowning before they ever made it ashore on some island beach in the Pacific?

Beyond those well-known examples, how much more money was saved, or how many more lives, because Hugh Fulton or Rudolph Halley made a phone call, or Harry Truman called a hearing or threatened a subpoena? Just about everyone agrees that those hidden savings were just as real; that fear of scrutiny by the Truman Committee kept both the military and defense contractors on their toes. *Time*, in its 1943 cover story on Truman and his committee, said the billions in savings stemmed "partly because of what their agents ferreted out, partly because their hooting curiosity was a great deterrent to waste."[13]

The Truman Committee, of course, wasn't all about rooting out fraud and corruption, though it was those investigations that got the biggest headlines. "Probably the committee's most constructive work," concludes Donald Riddle, "was its studies of continuing problems of mobilization together with the arbitration of conflicts." Sorting out the shifting alphabet soup of Roosevelt's mobilization bureaucracy—OPM, WPB, etc.—and examining shortages of critical materials including magnesium, rubber, and steel, these investigations were the important but less glamorous work of the committee and take up thousands of pages of its reports and hearing testimony. "Most of these problems," Riddle notes, also "received attention from other Congressional committees, sometimes with conflicting conclusions." Ten or twelve committees, for example, at some point looked into the rubber shortage, which was "probably the most studied supply problem of the war."[14]

Inevitably, there were mistakes—of both omission and commission. Truman's emphasis on steering contracts away from giant corporations to "the little fellow," while making for good headlines, never really came to much. "His efforts enjoyed scant success and at times did him little credit," writes Alonzo Hamby. The idea "of bringing maximum efficiency to the war effort by involving tens of thousands of small enterprises was never feasible. Inexorably, the war made big manufacturing bigger."[15]

Matt Connelly's investigation into Senator Chandler's swimming pool, and the report that followed, was an old-fashioned political whitewash, pure and simple. The attempt to stop Canol was a failure—not for lack of trying, but because the committee had reached the limits of what a congressional inquiry could accomplish.

And despite its early promises to do so, the committee never did investigate discrimination against Black workers in war industries or against Black servicemen and women in the military. Several times throughout the war, leaders and everyday citizens from around the country pleaded with Truman to do so. No sooner had he accepted the vice-presidential nomination than Republicans—and the Black press—pointed this out. "GOP to Use Truman's Nomination as a Weapon," read the headline in the Baltimore *Afro-American* on August 5. The story noted the "failure" of the Truman Committee over three years to investigate discrimination in the armed services and in defense industries. And yet, the piece went on to note that, overall, "Senator Truman's record of votes on legislation sought to benefit colored people, directly or indirectly, is good."[16]

Another area the committee never looked into, possibly because no one asked it to, was the role played by the millions of women who entered the workforce during the war. "Women had moved into almost every imaginable job," writes Maury Klein, from taxi drivers to steelworkers.[17] Their presence created challenges and changes that most factory managers had never thought of—among them finding work clothing and protective gear that would fit, such as heavy gloves. There were issues of pregnancy and menstruation and health care. And then, at the end of the workday, many of these workers had to go home to cook and clean and care for their children.

Despite the contributions they had made and the evidence for all to see that women could handle any job they were asked to do, it was widely assumed during the war that, as one newspaper put it, "many of the women who now work in war plants will return to housekeeping."[18] Employers who had welcomed them when the need was great let them go afterwards in the widespread belief that they should make way for returning servicemen. The Truman Committee wasn't so sure. While it never conducted a full investigation or held hearings on the issue, the October 1943 report on postwar planning—considered by Alonzo Hamby "the most farsighted of all the Truman committee reports"—had come close: "Many of the women who have gone into our factories and done such splendid work during the war, will want to continue working and they are entitled to a chance to earn a good living at jobs they have shown they can do. The last war put women into the offices on a large scale. This war put them into the factories. They are there to stay."[19]

Why the Truman Committee? There were other investigations, other committees in the House and Senate, other reports examining many of these same issues. But only one was almost automatically considered front-page news. Only one polevaulted its chairman into the White House.

One answer is that, right from the start, Truman and Hugh Fulton set out to do things differently from those other investigations and from the way that congressional committees had always operated. Some of the innovations they put in place, right from the earliest days in 1941, turned out to be key factors in their success. "Truman's unorthodox formula for running a Congressional inquiry surprised everyone—including the committee members," wrote the reporters McCune and Beal in *Harper's*. "All too often such inquires begin with a fanfare of publicity, and then dribble away into confusion, bickering, and impotence."

For starters, the committee "went to unheard-of lengths" to get the facts straight.[20] Its files contain voluminous back-and-forths with bureaucrats in the government or with company officials—Edsel Ford, Lester Perry, Henry Kaiser, Andrew Higgins, Robert Patterson, and many others—discussing proposed corrections or changes. It was Fulton's policy to make the final versions as bulletproof as possible, and Truman's interest in grounding those reports in the realm of facts and not opinions that were subject to debate or partisanship.

In another nod to fairness—and another departure from the way investigations had previously been run—Fulton notified witnesses in advance when they would be scheduled to appear, and gave them a chance to prepare and read an opening statement.[21]

Long afterwards, Truman spoke with the journalist and author Merle Miller in a series of tape-recorded interviews, which Miller eventually turned into a best-selling book, *Plain Speaking*. Miller asked about the committee and its accomplishments, and one of the things Truman said he was proudest of "was the fact that we never issued a report that wasn't unanimously approved by every single member of the committee." Even for that time, but especially from the perspective of anyone familiar with the toxic partisanship of Washington today, this is a remarkable achievement, and bears repeating: while Truman was chairman, his committee issued thirty-two reports, running into the thousands of pages. Every one was delivered to the Senate, and to the public, with the unanimous agreement of its Democratic and Republican members.

The display of bipartisanship is almost always attributed to Truman's deft and skillful leadership, his willingness to park his own ego and share the credit, as well as a lot of hard work by the senators in the Doghouse, hashing out the disagreements and reaching compromises over "bourbon and branch water." But, as Riddle and others note, this should not be taken to mean that the Truman Committee was somehow "nonpolitical" or "above politics." Truman, like his fellow senators, was a politician. A Democratic politician and a loyal soldier for Franklin Roosevelt and the New Deal. Through the war, he carefully avoided direct criticism of the president, and on the couple of occasions when he slipped—notably the *American Magazine* article—it brought Franklin Roosevelt's cold disapproval. Beyond that, the Truman Committee existed in a purely political environment—the United States Senate. Reaching unanimity on those reports took a lot of hard work and a lot of compromise—but without such political compromises, those reports might otherwise have been harsher, or told fuller truths. And then, of course, there was Happy Chandler's swimming pool.

Another thing Truman was proud of, he told Merle Miller's tape recorder, was this: "We didn't give a hoot in hell about publicity. My goodness, if I'd got into the committee to make headlines, I could have made enough to cover the whole of this

room, but I didn't do it. We didn't give anything to the reporters unless the case was closed down tight."[22] While Truman of
course cared a lot about publicity, in one sense he was right: he,
and through him Walter Hehmeyer as the committee's press man,
did not sensationalize the findings or play up the reports or leak
them to favored journalists to get splashier play. In the one or
two instances when information did leak, usually to Drew Pearson, Truman was furious. One thing guaranteed to get staffers
in hot water with Fulton or the chairman was talking too freely
to a reporter. Hehmeyer's job was to keep the press informed
and up-to-date, and he did so "quietly and honestly, with none
of the synthetic fireworks which characterized some other Congressional investigations."[23] He worked the phones and attended
all the hearings, and whenever there was a break or recess, Wilbur Sparks remembered, "there was often a newspaper man sitting at his desk trying to find out what to write about next."[24]

As a by-product of not seeking publicity, the Truman Committee got lots of it. Newsmen warmed to the committee's even-
handed approach, and also to the honest and open personality of
the chairman, so unlike most of the lawmakers they dealt with
every day. As Allen Drury put it, "the press, without exception,
eats out of his hand."[25]

It wasn't just personality and good public relations. Over and
over again, the committee brought to the press, and to the
American people, news that they weren't hearing anywhere
else—facts that at times were hard for them to accept, but that
at least made them feel like they were getting the truth. Governments, of course, are often secretive, even more so in wartime. And they are especially likely to withhold information that
makes them look bad. The Truman Committee, said Riddle,
"constantly exerted pressure upon public officials, both civilian
and military, to give the public maximum information about
the conduct of the war at home and abroad and forced them to
justify withholding of information."[26]

And so, Americans learned that army camps had been "built along Civil War lines," and that some of the contractors building them had soaked the taxpayers for millions. That Roosevelt's leadership structure for managing war mobilization and allocating resources was a hot mess. That US pilots in 1942 were taking to the skies in fighter planes that were not as good as the ones flown by their opponents. That navy shipyards and merchant shipyards were receiving steel that had failed inspections. That the number of ships sunk by U-boats in the Atlantic was far greater than the public had been led to believe. That the navy had for some reason rejected a much better landing boat in favor of its own inferior and dangerous design. That a factory in Ohio was shipping defective airplane engines to the military, and lying about it.

In their work, Truman and the committee built a level of public trust and confidence that, compared with the contempt people have for their elected leaders in Washington today, seems unimaginable. Americans read about the Senator from Missouri in the paper, or heard his flat voice on the radio, and came away believing that here was someone who was looking out for them and for their sons fighting overseas. Thousands of times during the war, those people—George Dye of Brownsville Road in Pittsburgh, Mrs. C. Morlman on Hickman Street in Cincinnati, Vivian Barry of East 44th Street in Manhattan—picked up a pencil or pen, or sat down at a typewriter, to tell him what they thought:

March 27, 1943

My dear Senator Truman,
On behalf of myself and I am sure millions of other fathers who have boys in actual combat service I want to congratulate you and your Committee on the wonderful public service you have rendered the nation.

I have two sons, a brother and a son-in-law in the combat forces of the nation, two are at present overseas and the others will probably go in due time. It's one hell of a situation when you and myself and millions of others who have boys risking their lives are compelled to submit to a thing of this sort that additional profits might fall into the coffers of the steel company. Stay in there and pitch, Senator, you and your Committee have done a swell job. Very respectfully yours,
John Duggan, Jr.[27]

It was a time, however brief, when Washington worked.

EPILOGUE

On the morning of Harry Truman's first full day as President of the United States, he met with Hugh Fulton before seeing anybody else. Since his resignation from the committee, Fulton had done what he'd been talking about for more than a year—gone into private practice, opening the firm of Fulton and Walter, with offices in New York and Washington.

In the days after his resignation, he sent out dozens of letters, to famous and prominent people in law firms, large corporations, and the government, informing them of his resignation and his new private venture. The letters noted that "this will leave me free to help elect Harry Truman in any way I can."[1]

In August, he headed to Kansas City to work with Truman and other staffers on major speeches and policy matters. Then, once Truman was elected in November, Fulton returned full-time to building his practice and setting up the New York office at 30 Rockefeller Plaza. Joining him initially in the new firm were Marion Toomey and Harold Robinson. His partner, George Walter, was a colleague and friend from his New York law days.

There are several different versions of that early morning meeting on April 13, 1945. Some say Fulton came to the apartment at 4701 Connecticut. Others have him riding in the car with Truman to the White House that day. What isn't known is what the two men talked about—neither man ever described it in detail.

One thing that definitely did *not* happen, though, was an offer from Truman for Fulton to join his administration. For several weeks, there was widespread speculation in the press that Fulton would have a key job, and Fulton himself had gotten the impression that he would be named attorney general.[2]

Yet as the weeks went by, there was no announcement, no big job for Fulton. And speculation mounted as to why the man who'd worked so closely with Truman to make the committee a success had been shut out. "The question 'Where's Fulton?' echoed around the Capitol yesterday," reported *The Washington Post* in late April. The paper described the early handicapping that had Fulton as a favorite for a top job, "but recently, high-placed friends of the President have thrown the coldest water they could on such speculation."[3]

A hint comes in the way Truman, years later, would describe his first day as president: "I got up a little later than usual, around 6:30, and I didn't take my morning walk. I had breakfast with… I'd just as soon not mention the gentleman's name."[4]

Clearly, something had gone wrong between the two men, and for years no one really wanted to talk about it. "I've had so many people say, 'Well what happened to Hugh Fulton?'" said Mildred Dryden, Truman's longtime personal secretary. "And if I did know, I wouldn't have told them, but I don't know."[5]

Elements of the story can be pieced together from several sources, though it's likely that none of them give the full picture. Some said Fulton was too quick to agree with those who said he was the real brains behind the committee, that Truman was just a figurehead.

"A lot of myths have grown up around that committee," Drew Pearson wrote in his "Merry-Go-Round" column a week after Truman became president, "chiefly that it was run by Hugh Fulton, its counsel. Fulton was a good fact-finder, but it's sheer baloney that he ran the committee."[6]

The next day, April 20, Pearson had more to say on the subject: while Fulton was a top-notch lawyer and prosecutor, he was "otherwise stodgy and conceited. He showed no aptitude for knitting his facts into the broad picture of political issues and social trends."[7]

Some of this may have been true, but it also smells of the kind of back-stabbing Washington is known for.

Others more supportive of Fulton acknowledged, too, that during the vice-presidential campaign, he had come on too strong, and that he lacked the touch for writing political speeches. "Hugh Fulton was not a politician," said Walter Hehmeyer. "He didn't understand how politics worked. Often he didn't understand human motives. He misjudged people."

Another likely factor was that Matt Connelly had moved into Truman's inner circle as one of his key political advisers, and he and Fulton did not get along. Connelly said years later that on that first day, April 13, after riding with Truman to the White House, Fulton had tried to take control of writing a speech the new president was scheduled to deliver, and that Connelly and others had threatened to quit over it.

According to Connelly, Truman called Fulton in and said, "Hugh, I want you to do something for me. I want you to go back to New York and stay there until I send for you." And that, Connelly, said, "was the departure of Hugh Fulton."[8]

Yet another version of the rift attributes it to some accidental bad timing on Fulton's part. That he sent out notices advertising his new firm and calling himself "former counsel of the Truman committee," but that the card arrived in the days after Roosevelt had died and as Truman was sworn in as president. This may have looked to the new president like Fulton was trying to capitalize on his name and may have seemed unseemly coming so soon after Roosevelt's death. Newspapers reported this story in May. Jonathan Daniels relates it in his book *The Man of Independence*, and Harold Robinson cites it in his oral history with the Truman Library.[9]

Likely it was some combination of all of these things. Fulton was not a skilled politician, and apparently did not distinguish himself in the election campaign. And it is possible that in some way or another he rubbed Truman the wrong way at the wrong moment just as Truman was stepping into the presidency. Regardless of friendships and personal feelings, Truman in those early days had to make tough decisions amid many competing interests and may have simply decided Fulton was not the man for a political position.

Truman himself later put it this way to Merle Miller: "He did a very good job all the time he worked for me. But later... later he got too big for his breeches which as I've told you happens time and again around Washington."[10]

In 1948, just before the presidential election, Herbert Maletz, one of the committee's early investigators who left for the army, ran into Hugh Fulton on a plane from New York to Washington. They chatted for a couple of hours, and Maletz asked the question outright: Why was Fulton not at the White House? "I'm not at the White House," Fulton said, "because Mr. Truman never asked me to work there. It's as simple as that."

Whatever the reasons, Fulton focused his attention on building up his law practice into a very successful one. Among his early clients were the industrialist and aircraft maker Howard Hughes and, not surprisingly, Andrew Jackson Higgins and Henry J. Kaiser.

After Truman's presidency, the two men remained friends for the rest of Fulton's life. Truman made an effort to see Fulton whenever he was in New York, and they kept up a casual and open correspondence.

"Dear Harry," Fulton wrote the former president in December 1954, updating Truman on the status of the former senators on the committee. "It occurred to me that while it is still possible to do so, we ought to have a reunion."[11]

After a lot of back-and-forth, and an illness of Truman, the idea petered out. It was Truman who revived it just over two years later, in January 1957. "Dear Hugh," he wrote, "sometime back, as you remember, you and I discussed the idea of having the old crowd meet together." Truman noted that since then Harley Kilgore had died, and that Carl Hatch was unwell. "Sometime when I am in New York I'd like to have lunch with you."[12]

Fulton swung into action, writing to the other senators and looking for dates. Owen Brewster wrote from Maine that he was in New York regularly and would love to attend. Mon Wallgren replied from California to say he was in. Hatch, now a federal judge, was a yes, too, but said he could not make it before spring. Harold Burton, now a justice of the United States Supreme Court, said he too would have trouble getting away, but would try.

In the end, with all the scheduling conflicts and health issues, it was several months before a date was settled: September 13, in New York. Fulton made reservations at Leone's Restaurant on West 48th Street and sent out the final invitations. Tom Connally, Jim Mead, Owen Brewster and Hatch could not make it. But Homer Ferguson was there, along with Burton and Wallgren and Joseph Ball. Truman and Bess were there, and Margaret brought her husband, Clifton Daniel, a reporter for *The New York Times*. Robert Kilgore was there to represent his father, and George Meader, now a Republican congressman from Michigan, came too.

The *New York Herald Tribune* covered the event and ran a photo of Fulton with Senators Wallgren and Truman, above a wartime photo of the three men.

"Dear Hugh," Truman wrote Fulton afterwards, "You do not know how much Mrs. Truman and I enjoyed that wonderful luncheon you gave us. If everyone there enjoyed the meeting half as much as I did, they really had a very good time."

After the reunion, the two men kept up their correspondence. "Dear Hugh," Truman wrote in December 1960, "I will be in New York, I hope, on the 21st and will be most happy to have lunch with you on the 22nd."

There were other reunions as well. Charles Patrick Clark became a Washington lobbyist, and for several years in the late 1950s and early 1960s organized reunions of the Truman Committee at the Mayflower Hotel. A highlight was the 1961 event, attended by, among other luminaries, President John F. Kennedy and Vice President Lyndon Johnson. Truman, now seventy-six, was "visibly moved by the many tributes," reported the Associated Press, and said he was still ready to serve his country. "I'm going to do what I can," he said, "but I haven't much left."[13]

Hugh Fulton died of a stroke, at his desk in Rockefeller Plaza on October 23, 1962, at age fifty-two.

When he heard the news, Truman sent Jessie Fulton a note: "I was as sorry as I could be to hear of the death of Hugh. I was very fond of him and I had hoped I could learn when his funeral would be so that Mrs. Truman and I could show our respect for him."[14]

He must have been quite surprised to see Jessie Fulton's response. She was bitter and angry about whatever had come between the two men at the start of Truman's presidency, and the way her husband was treated by others during the 1944 campaign. The relationship between her and her husband was such that "any affront to the one cut deeply into the other," she wrote. "So you see that your 'respects' matter not at all now."[15]

Truman took the unusual step, for this stage of his life, of by-passing his secretaries and responding to her in his own hand:

> *Your letter of November 12 was quite a surprise to me. When I resigned as Chairman of the Committee of which Hugh was the legal adviser, he told me at the time he was quitting and he wanted nothing more to do with "political" lawyers and that he would, from that time on, practice law as a "real" lawyer. Well he did and he made good at it. I was always his friend and saw him every time I was in New York and it was possible. I'll never understand your letter.*
> *Sincerely & also sadly,*
> *Harry S. Truman*[16]

Marion Toomey, now Marion Baker, attended that twenti-eth anniversary reunion, organized by Clark, in March 1961. She kept her copy of the evening's menu—filet mignon, with baked Alaska for dessert—signed by Truman, Matt Connelly, and Hugh Fulton.[17]

Toomey had moved to New York in October 1944 when she left the committee to join Fulton's law firm and stayed there for several years. She deeply admired Fulton, and though she was a lifelong Democrat, like Jessie Fulton she never forgave Truman for leaving him out of the administration.

In 1948, she left Fulton's firm to return to Washington, and worked briefly for the Interstate Commerce Commission. That same year, Marion married Raymond Baker, a lawyer with General Electric, and left her job soon after to begin raising the first of their five children. They moved around a bit with Ray-mond's job, to Cleveland and to Syracuse, New York, eventu-ally settling in Lynchburg, Virginia.[18]

By 1974, "she'd had enough of making lunches every morning for the kids," said her son, Dylan Baker, "and decided, 'I can do something now.'"[19] She began volunteering as a paralegal with the Legal Aid Society office in Lynchburg. Two years later she was admitted to the Virginia State Bar and became a full-time lawyer, helping families in need with housing, financial troubles, and a host of other legal problems.

In 1981, the legal aid office, facing a budget crunch, had to lay off one of its attorneys. Though Marion had seniority and her job was secure, she chose to resign, allowing another lawyer who was a single mother to stay employed. "I did not need the money," she told a local reporter. "My husband made enough."[20]

That didn't mean, though, that she quit showing up for work every day. She continued practicing law there, without pay, for another twenty-three years, handling about twenty cases a month. In 1994, at age seventy-eight, she was awarded the Lewis F. Powell Jr. Pro Bono Award given by the Virginia State Bar. She finally retired in 2004, spending time with her children and grandchildren in New York and Virginia. She died in 2016 at age one hundred.

For years, Marion Baker kept up with her good friend Shirley Hehmeyer, sending Christmas cards and the like, but with raising children and the other demands of busy lives that took them far away from Washington, they eventually lost touch.

After leaving the Truman Committee in 1943, Shirley got a job at the American Can Company, but it wasn't the same. "The Truman Committee had spoiled me," she said.[21] She and Walter stayed in Washington, where their first son, Philip, was born in 1945; Hugh and Jessie Fulton were the godparents.

Walter stayed on with the committee through 1946. He also began working with Frank McNaughton, a congressional affairs correspondent with *Time*, on a book about the new president.

This Man Truman was published in 1945. In 1948 they wrote a second book, *Harry Truman—President*.

In 1952, the Hehmeyers moved to Memphis, Tennessee, where Walter went to work for the National Cotton Council, and where a second son, Christopher, was born in 1955. For years, Walter served on the board of directors of the Memphis symphony, and in 1974, he became its general manager.

After Walter retired in 1980, the couple moved to Oxford, Mississippi, where they lived until Walter's death in 1987. Shirley eventually moved back to Memphis, where she renewed an old friendship from her Truman Committee days, George Meader, and they remained close until Meader's death in 1994. In later years, she spent time with a group of good friends known as "Team Shirley," until her death in 2011 at age ninety-one.[22]

George Meader became executive assistant to Rudolph Halley on what was now called the Mead Committee. In October 1945, he became chief counsel when Halley left to join Fulton's law firm. After two more years in Washington, Meader returned to Ann Arbor and private practice, and also resumed his political career. He lost a Republican primary for Congress in 1948, and returned to Washington to serve on a Senate banking subcommittee investigation.

In 1950, he ran for Congress again in Michigan, and won this time, serving seven terms. In later years, he continued in private practice and also served on committees that sought to improve how Congress worked, until his retirement in 1975.

After his wife, Elizabeth, died in 1974, he divided his time between Michigan and Washington, spending time with his children and grandchildren. In the 1980s, he began working on his memoirs, compiling his wartime recollections and his experiences as a county prosecutor.

In a typewritten section, "My Four Years With The Truman Committee," Meader wrote that Hugh Fulton's "contribution to Truman's rise to the presidency has not been adequately recognized," and also that Truman was the "best chairman of a committee I have ever served under, or with." He treasured the photo that Truman had signed for him on August 1, 1944, the day he resigned as chairman: "Very best regards & best wishes to George Meader efficient, capable and an expert on Transportation from Harry S Truman U.S.S. Mo. Prospective VP USA?"[23]

Meader died in 1994 at age eighty-seven.[24]

Rudolph Halley served as chief counsel for a little over a year before resigning in September 1945 to become a partner in Fulton's law firm, which now became Fulton, Walter and Halley. In the 1950s, Halley returned to Washington and became nationally known for his role as chief counsel in another famous congressional investigation, the Kefauver Committee.

Officially called the Special Committee on Organized Crime in Interstate Commerce, and chaired by Senator Estes Kefauver of Tennessee, the committee held hearings over more than a year. They were nationally televised, and gave Americans an inside look at interstate gambling and organized mobs, becoming a national media phenomenon as more than 30 million people tuned in.[25]

As chief counsel, Halley "summoned 400 underworld, political and other witnesses in fourteen major cities before fascinated public scrutiny." One of the most dramatic moments came when Halley questioned mob boss Frank Costello, head of the Luciano crime family, in New York on March 14, 1951. Costello, who twice walked out of the hearings while he was being questioned, was later convicted of contempt of the Senate and sentenced to eighteen months in prison.[26]

Halley later served as president of the New York City Council, and later ran unsuccessfully for mayor. He died, suddenly, of a pancreatic condition at age forty-three in November 1956.[27]

★ ★ ★

Wilbur Sparks became the committee's chief investigator when Harold Robinson resigned, and stayed on for another year. In 1946, he asked George Meader for permission to compile a list of all the people who had worked for the committee since 1941, with their dates of employment and biographical information—a list that became a huge help in the writing of this book.

In 1946, Halley and Fulton needed another lawyer in their Washington office, and Wilbur joined the firm, where he worked for a decade. In 1956 he left to become a staff lawyer for the Senate Judiciary Committee's antitrust and monopoly subcommittee, remaining there until 1972.

Throughout his life, Wilbur was a passionate barbershop quartet singer, and he and Ibbianne were deeply involved in the Society for the Preservation and Encouragement of Barber Shop Quartet Singing in America (later renamed the Barbershop Harmony Society). It was his "life outside of work," said his daughter, Sallie, and the singing was a constant presence in their home in Arlington, Virginia. "If you've ever heard a barbershop quartet, when they do it right, the chords 'ring,'" she recalled, "and our house was always ringing!"[28]

Wilbur was a member of the organization's Hall of Fame, and in 1995, the society created the annual "Ibbianne and Wilbur Sparks Award."[29]

They had two daughters, Sallie and Nancy, and four grandchildren. Wilbur died in September 2002 of cancer at age eighty-three.[30] Ibbianne passed away in 2016.

Harold Robinson stayed with Fulton's firm for about a year, then moved to California with his wife, Charlotte, and their son, Harold Jr. There he continued his career as an investigator. From 1948 to 1950, he worked for the California commission on organized crime, and in 1950 he returned to Washington to

join Rudolph Halley, working as an investigator on the Kefauver Committee.

In 1948, when President Truman was visiting the state, Robinson wrote him a long letter reminiscing about their wartime
days. Truman responded warmly, "Dear Robby," inviting Robinson to visit with him in Berkeley on June 12.

After the Kefauver hearings, Robinson worked for the state
attorney general's office, and in 1956, ran unsuccessfully for
the California state senate. In later years he taught criminology
at the University of California.[31] He died in Sacramento, aged
seventy-one, in April 1974.

Morris Lasker, who left the committee in 1942 to go into
the army, where he served as a major in the air corps, served
for many years as a federal judge in New York and Boston. He
died in 2009.[32]

Herbert Maletz also left in 1942 to join the army, eventually
rising to the rank of lieutenant colonel. After the war he worked
in the antitrust division of the Justice Department, and then in
a variety of government positions in Washington. In 1967 he
was appointed by President Lyndon Johnson to be a judge in the
United States Customs Court in New York, and later was a federal district judge in Maryland. He died in 2002 at age eighty-
eight.[33]

Matt Connelly, who had left the committee in July 1944 to
join Truman's Senate office staff, served as executive secretary
to Vice President Truman, and then as appointments secretary
in the White House.

In 1955, Connelly was indicted along with two other men on a
charge of bribery as part of a scandal dating from 1948, in which
Connelly used his influence in the White House to persuade the
Internal Revenue Service not to pursue criminal charges in an
investigation into income tax evasion by a Missouri businessman. Connelly was convicted and later sentenced to two years in

prison.[34] Connelly served six months before being paroled, and in 1962 was pardoned by President John Kennedy. He died in 1976.

Joe Martinez stayed with the committee until November 1945. He later returned to New Mexico, and served as the state attorney general and later as a justice of the state supreme court. He died in 1998.[35]

James Mead of New York replaced Truman as chairman of the committee, and remained in the Senate until 1947. Owen Brewster, who succeeded Mead as chairman, represented Maine in the Senate until 1952. Harley Kilgore of West Virginia was a senator until his death in 1956.

Mon Wallgren left in 1945 to serve as governor of Washington state and was later named by President Truman to serve on the Federal Power Commission. In 1948, Senator Joseph Ball of Minnesota was defeated in his re-election bid by a Democrat, Hubert H. Humphrey. Homer Ferguson of Michigan remained in the Senate until 1955. Carl Hatch remained in the Senate until 1949, when President Truman appointed him to be a US district judge in New Mexico. Tom Connally retired from the Senate in 1953 and died in Texas in 1963.

When Supreme Court Justice Owen Roberts died in 1945, Harry Truman named his former Senate colleague Harold Burton—a Republican—to replace him. It's another one of those bipartisan gestures that seems inconceivable today, even more incredible given that the Senate approved Burton's nomination, by a unanimous vote, the very next day.[36]

Allen Drury, who had covered these men as a reporter in the Senate, went on to be a reporter for The New York Times. In his spare time, he worked on a novel based on his experiences covering Washington. Advise and Consent, published in 1959, won the Pulitzer Prize for fiction in 1960.

Despite having been the cause of so much trouble, George Dye remained in his job at the Irvin Works. After the Truman

Committee investigation, he was placed in charge of plate inspection at the plant, where he revamped the inspection and production teams and made sure that inspectors and testers "carried out my instructions to the letter." Many of the changes he had been recommending for so long were adopted.[37]

In September 1943, after the dust had settled, he wrote to Rudolph Halley to update him on the situation. "You no doubt are familiar with many of the corrective measures that have been taken since the day you walked off with the heat book."[38] Not surprisingly, much of his letter contained technical details far beyond Halley's understanding, and he forwarded the letter to LeRoy Whitney, the steel expert who had joined the original fact-finding trip to Pittsburgh in March.

By late 1944, though, Dye's supervisor had departed, and things had gone back to the old ways. The new head of quality inspection "was content to sit in his office and go along with the bad practices of the pre-Truman days."

In January 1945, Dye finally had enough. He resigned his position and wrote a long letter to US Steel President Benjamin Fairless, outlining again, with his usual thoroughness and technical detail, what happened.

"I am not interested in remaining at Irvin. I've resigned and wouldn't return unless the salary were more attractive than any I have received in the past."[39]

He concluded by reminding Fairless that his statements to the Truman Committee were not unjustified, and expressing his hope that "vengeance will not extend beyond the corporation."

And with that, George Dye, who had for a few moments in 1943 been at the center of the national stage, went on with his life, his contributions and his courage largely unnoticed. After the war, he and Alice moved to Seattle, where he found work as a steel inspector. He died on May 17, 1992, in Antioch, California.

And what of the SS *Schenectady*? Despite the massive rupture, the tanker was repaired in less than four months and entered service in April 1943.[40] By December, Captain R.B. Gallery reported, the ship had made one trip across the Pacific Ocean and another to the east coast by the Panama Canal, and from there to the coast of North Africa to participate in the invasion there, dodging submarine threats along the way.[41]

Long afterwards, the debate continued about what caused the ship, and other Liberty ships and tankers, to break up. Eight were lost, and four others had broken apart and were salvaged, including Schenectady. All told, in these breakups, twenty-six people lost their lives.[42] The various investigations into the Schenectady and other incidents led to new construction techniques for these welded ships, and after March 1944, the number of fractures declined.

In 1948, Schenectady acquired new ownership, an Italian company, and a new name, Diodato Tripcovich. The ship continued to carry fuel until it was broken up for scrap at Genoa, Italy, in 1966.[43]

Bob Irvin stayed with the committee through September, 1945. Watching his friend and roommate Walter Hehmeyer manage the media had given him an idea of what he wanted to do after the war. "I never was cut out to be a lawyer, honestly," he recalled. "I was so fascinated by what he was doing, and thought to myself that at some point I'm going to get into the public relations business."[44]

Irvin managed the Washington office of a Detroit PR firm for a while, and in 1947 moved west, to Long Beach, and set up his own company. In that capacity he later represented the City of Long Beach, the harbor commission and other clients.

In early 1950, his work with the city brought him back to Washington. In its budget proposal that year, the Truman administration had proposed deactivating the Long Beach naval shipyard, and Irvin was part of a delegation sent east to try to reverse the decision.[45]

He was in town for several days, and on January 4 rang up his wartime colleague Matt Connelly, who told Irvin to come over and say hello. "So I went down to the White House and we shot the breeze for a while."[46] While the two men talked, Connelly rose suddenly and went into Truman's office. He came back a moment later and left the door open: "Well, aren't you going in and say hello to the boss?"

Irvin responded that the president was scheduled to give his State of the Union speech that evening and must be too busy working on it. "Hell, I'm not going to bother him," he told Connelly.

"Well, he's expecting you to come in."

So Irvin went and chatted with Truman, who asked him: "What are you doing in Washington?"

"As a matter of fact," Irvin said, "we're back here to convince your administration not to close our shipyard in Long Beach." Truman laughed and said he didn't know anything about it, but noted that when budget cuts had to be made, "somebody's going to get hurt and somebody's going to yell." Irvin told him he had a meeting scheduled with a key official, and Truman said he would make sure they got a fair hearing.

Then, as they were finishing, Truman asked whether Irvin was going to attend the speech that night. Irvin said he didn't have a pass.

"Well, would you like to go?"

"Sure I would," Irvin said.

Truman made a call, and that night Irvin rode "all by myself" in Bess Truman's limousine up to Capitol Hill. "I felt silly as the devil, one guy in this huge old limousine going up there." That night was the last time he saw Truman.

Irvin, who had three children, later divorced, and in 1966 met a nurse and fellow University of Michigan graduate, Arleen Bryant, and they married in 1969. He and Arleen retired in 1984 and in later years lived north of Santa Barbara. He died on January 27, 2003.

In the late 1960s and early 1970s, Irvin was one of many of

Truman's associates from all walks of life who were contacted by the Truman Presidential Library to sit for oral history interviews. From the Truman Committee days, there are interviews with Shirley and Walter Hehmeyer, Wilbur Sparks, Harold Robinson, John Tolan, John Abbott, Herbert Maletz, and many others.

Hugh Fulton and Rudolph Halley were of course gone by this time. And while the Truman Committee files take up more than four hundred feet of shelf space in the National Archives, these records don't really tell the story of the people and the personalities. There are tens of thousands of documents in those records. There are George Dye's letters, and the entries in the heat book with the *F* notations, the transcripts of the hearings with Henry Kaiser and John L. Lewis. And the handwritten letters from so many people around the country. But those documents don't say much about Hugh Fulton's management style or his fourteen-hour workdays, or what a long cross-country train ride was like in the middle of a war.

It is these oral history interviews—of young people, many of them in their first jobs out of college, thrown together in the excitement of wartime Washington—that along with Truman's letters to Bess bring to life the story of the Truman Committee and its chairman in the days before he was president.

Irvin sat down for his interview with archivist James Fuchs in Long Beach on March 26, 1970. And he told the stories of Joe Martinez and the steam bath, of the sudden trip to Pittsburgh to meet with George Dye, of Andrew Higgins and the tank lighters, and of his feelings on the day Truman resigned and came down to Room 160 to shake everyone's hand.

Like many of the people Bob Irvin worked with, his experience on the committee was an adventure and an experience that shaped the rest of his life. Twenty-five years later, he was still amazed at how Truman and Fulton and the senators on the committee were able to set aside their personal and partisan interests to get the work done.

"This was very inspiring to me fresh out of law school, to see these men who were there because of their political ability, putting the interest of the nation ahead of their own political positions. A very, very inspiring thing for a young guy."

★ ★ ★ ★ ★

ACKNOWLEDGMENTS

It was while I was writing the final pages of this book, in August 2022, that an alert came over my phone telling me the historian David McCullough had died. I looked down at the floor to the scattering of books spread out around my small desk, where his *Truman* was open to the chapter on World War I. I have read this remarkable book several times and have three copies of it—the copy I first read in 1992, another hardcover copy I bought on eBay to use in researching this book (which has taken quite a beating along the way), and then a Kindle edition that helped make searching much faster.

His knack for detail and creating beautiful sentences was an inspiration and a model as I thought over the years that I might like to write a book someday, and *Truman* was of course a major source when it came to telling this story.

The other major biography that informed my knowledge of Truman's life was Alonzo Hamby's *Man of the People: A Life of Harry S. Truman*. While McCullough tells a riveting story and is a great fan of Truman's, Hamby's book is more analytical, and often more critical of Truman. I found his sections on Truman and race, and on Truman's later life, particularly helpful. I'd recommend either book, or both, to anyone who wants to learn more.

Like most biographers of Truman, neither author spends a lot of time on the Truman Committee. McCullough, for example, devotes forty-four pages to the weeks in the summer of 1944 that led to the selection of Truman as Roosevelt's running mate, but only thirty-nine pages to the three years that came before. Most biographies give the Truman Committee a chapter or so before moving on to his presidency, almost as if they're in a hurry to get to the good stuff.

Before this one, there have been two books about the Truman Committee—the first, written in 1947, is an admiring but hurried telling that draws very heavily on long excerpts from the committee's published reports. The second is an excellent book from 1964 by Donald H. Riddle, the historian and former head of John Jay College in New York, called *The Truman Committee: A Study in Congressional Responsibility*. Here too, my copy has become sadly worn from all the use I've put it to. Riddle's purpose was scholarly: asking, and answering, the question of whether congressional investigating committees accomplish anything, and using the Truman Committee as a case study of how they can get things right.

And so Riddle's approach, based on his doctoral thesis from Princeton University, was very different from my goal of telling the story of the committee and its many characters. For example, while Riddle has a chapter each on Canol and on the Curtiss-Wright cases, he barely mentions the fake steel investigation or the Hollywood probe or Truman's West Coast trip. Nevertheless, his writing is clear and sharp—and he actually got to talk with Truman and Hugh Fulton and Wilbur Sparks and others—and I relied on his book for a professional historian's analysis.

Other Truman books that contributed a lot to the story were Margaret Truman's colorful biographies of her father and mother; Jonathan Daniels's *The Man of Independence*; and Frank McNaughton and Walter Hehmeyer's *This Man Truman*, which has lovely detail and the benefits of being written so close to the events, by one of the actual participants in the story. Merle Miller's *Plain Speaking: An Oral Biography of Harry S. Truman* is of course lively and funny and in many ways delightful, but in his later years, Truman tended to embellish or oversimplify at times, and therefore needs to be read with a grain of salt.

Huge thanks to WordFire Press and its publisher, Kevin Anderson, and to the heirs of Allen Drury, Kenneth and Kevin Killiany, for permission to quote from Drury's wonderful book, *A Senate Journal, 1943-45*. It is still available from WordFire along with many of his other works, including his Pulitzer Prize-winning *Advise and Consent*.

Many other books helped in the writing of this one, and you can find them referenced in the endnotes, but I'll single out a few that might be of interest for readers who want to know more, without plunging too heavily into scholarly works. Mark Harris's *Five Came Back: A Story of Hollywood and the Second World War*, reads like a novel and informed the chapter on Darryl F. Zanuck and the Hollywood investigation. For the inspirational story of the US economic mobilization and the war on the home front, in no particular order: A.J. Baime's *The Arsenal of Democracy: FDR, Detroit, and an Epic Quest to Arm an America At War*; David Brinkley's *Washington Goes to War*; and Maury Klein's comprehensive *A Call To Arms: Mobilizing America for World War II*. Donald Nelson's *Arsenal of Democracy* provides another first-hand account from one of the key participants, but it is long out of print and hard to find.

For biographies or more about some of the key characters, I enjoyed and found useful the following: Jerry Strahan's *Andrew Jackson Higgins and the Boats That Won World War II*; Arthur Herman's *Freedom's Forge: How American Business Produced Victory in World War II*, which zooms in on the contributions of Henry Kaiser and William Knudsen; and John Kennedy Ohl's biography, *Supplying the Troops: General Somervell and American Logistics in World War II.* Joseph Lelyveld's *His Final Battle* brings to life the final days of Franklin Roosevelt.

Of course, the sources for so much of what happened on the Truman Committee from 1941 to 1944 are the documents and files and all that paperwork. On and off for more than four years, Adam Berenbak, archivist with the Center for Legislative Archives at the National Archives in Washington, was a guide and adviser and finder of treasures. His patient help was indispensable in making sense of more than four hundred linear feet of documents from the Truman Committee files, and from the thousands more pages of transcripts and hearings and published reports.

With my deadline approaching and the Harry S. Truman Presidential Library shut down by the pandemic, Samuel Rushay, Laurie Austin, and Tammy Williams made my visit there when it finally reopened in April of 2022 an enjoyable and productive experience. For the limited time I had available, they made sure I had access to everything I needed and, in one case long after I left, helped correct an oversight at the last minute. I'm also grateful to the staff there for their online offerings. So much of what I needed, notably those amazing oral histories and Truman's correspondence with Bess and Margaret and many photos, is accessible online, which made it possible to do a lot of the work during the two years when travel and in-person research were not an option.

Independence was quiet on the spring day in April when I visited Harry and Bess's home on North Delaware Street, and I was the only one on the tour that afternoon. As the National Park Service guide, whose name I regretfully did not note, reminded me, it's pretty rare to get a private tour of a presidential home, and it was a memorable experience. I have a vivid picture in my mind of Truman's overcoat and hat hanging on the hook there, right where he left them.

The staff at the Bentley Historical Library at the University of Michigan in Ann Arbor were helpful, too, in pulling George Meader's papers out of deep storage and making them available.

Next to Truman's letters to Bess, Meader's letters home to his wife in Michigan are the closest thing to a diary from anyone on the Truman Committee, at least that I know of. And so it was the friends and descendants of some of the key players who helped bring these characters to life, and I have spent many pleasurable evenings over the past few years on phone and Zoom calls with people who knew the people I was writing about.

Christopher Hehmeyer gave generously of his time to tell me all about Walter and Shirley and what he knew of their lives during the war and after. Imagine my pleasure, at opening an envelope he sent me, to find his dad's wartime photo album, with pictures of the Fulton farm, and Hugh Fulton by his pool, and Shirley and Wilbur Sparks and Marion Toomey, and Bob Irvin outside his apartment in Washington, and those honeymoon photos (!) from New Orleans. There is Robby Robinson clowning around outside the Old Absinthe Bar with Shirley and Frank Parks, with Walter unseen behind the camera. And there, too, was the menu from their dinner at Restaurant Antoine. Chris also introduced me to Frank Jackson and Susan Carr Oppenheimer, who shared recollections of their friends Walter and Shirley.

PHOTO BY WALTER HEHMEYER, COURTESY OF CHRISTOPHER HEHMEYER.

Franklin Parks, Shirley Hehmeyer and Harold Robinson in the French Quarter in New Orleans, February 1943.

Sallie Sparks told me all about her dad, Wilbur, and her mom, Ibbianne, and their lives together, and also shared many wonderful photos.

In October 2021 I met with Dylan Baker, Lisa Horner, and Greg Baker on a long Zoom call, and they told me about their mother, Marion Toomey Baker, and her remarkable life and career. I had been thinking about this book for years, and working on it seriously since 2018, and so it was sad to learn that their mom had passed away in 2016. Like Chris Hehmeyer and Sallie Sparks and others, they've cheerfully and patiently answered my many follow-up questions, and shared family photos and mementos.

Teri Ferrieri reached out to several members of her family to help me learn more about her grandfather, Robert Irvin. Her mom, Carol Irvin Ferrieri, shared photos and documents, and thanks as well to Arleen Irvin and James Irvin, and to Bob Irvin's friend Peter Guttman, who shared helpful details and recollections.

After a couple of years of noodling around on the idea, I was beginning to think this book might not happen when Gillian MacKenzie wrote to say she was interested, and with her as agent, things went quickly uphill from there. Gillian shaped a rough idea into a concrete proposal, and I've benefited greatly from her expertise, her support, and the resources of her agency.

Everyone needs an editor, and I am lucky enough to have a great one. Peter Joseph at Hanover Square Press saw the potential in the proposal and took a chance on it. Over the course of the writing, he has shaped and molded the story and provided razor-sharp feedback. It's a much better story for it.

Jennifer Stimson's excellent copy editing corrected errors of style and substance, and helped untangle the places where I'd written myself into a knot. And Editorial Assistant Eden Railsback managed a hundred different details with calm efficiency.

Having friends and colleagues who've written books and who

think a lot about writing and storytelling, it turns out, is a big help when it comes to trying something like this. I'm lucky enough to have both. For many years in the old NPR building, where our cubicles were kitty-corner from each other, and then in her current life as a writer and author, Barbara Bradley Hagerty told me enough times that I should write a book someday that at some point I started to believe her. She's been willing many times to talk through problems or roadblocks.

Edith Chapin, my boss for much of this time, provided encouragement and insightful criticism, and her suggestions on the early draft identified some key fixes. Nishant Dahiya offered suggestions and feedback several times along the way that were extremely valuable in shaping the narrative. Pam Fessler shared with me the proposal for her excellent book, *Carville's Cure*, and talked me through her writing and research process. Ron Elving gave it an early read, bringing his vast knowledge of Washington to bear. Other friends and colleagues who've listened and offered help and inspiration along the way include Frank Langfitt, David Kidd, Mary Louise Kelly, Noah Adams, Neenah Ellis, Charlie Gofen, Leah Donnella, Ulrich Boser, Gene Demby, and Jack Lessenberry. And I should thank my colleagues on NPR's education team and the *Code Switch* podcast for their patience and support, as well as my current bosses (and friends), Terry Samuel and Vickie Walton-James.

Having said that, the work, and any mistakes or errors it contains, are of course mine alone.

Finally, for more than four years now, Mary Ellen Murphy has, with boundless patience and a sharp eye, offered solid guidance, insightful criticism, gentle suggestions and enthusiastic support, and for those things I am grateful and lucky.

ENDNOTES

Author's note: The sources of all quotations are cited in the endnotes. I have shortened or condensed some quotes, without using ellipses, and cleaned up spelling and punctuation, for clarity and brevity. Many of the conversations reported are drawn from later recollections, notably the oral histories on file in the Truman Library, but I have used quotation marks around dialogue only where the subject described the comments as such.

Introduction

1. "No. 1 Tanker," *The Bos'n's Whistle*, Nov. 5, 1942. Oregon Historical Society Research Library.

2. *The Oregonian*, Nov. 6, 1942.

3. FBI, Report of Special Agent Julius H. Rice, Jan. 20, 1943, from author's FOIA request.

4. *The Oregonian,* Jan. 18, 1943; *The Sunday Oregonian*, Jan. 17, 1943.

5. "Final Report of a Board of Investigation Convened by Order of the Secretary of the Navy to Inquire into the Design and Methods of

Construction of Welded Steel Merchant Vessels, July 15, 1946," (Washington: Government Printing Office, 1947), 29.

6. *The Oregonian*, Jan. 18, 1943.

7. *The Oregonian*, Jan 19, 1943.

Chapter One

1. Frank McNaughton and Walter Hehmeyer, *This Man Truman* (New York: McGraw-Hill, 1945), 90-91.

2. Jonathan Daniels, *The Man of Independence* (Philadelphia: J.B. Lippincott, 1950), 215.

3. Daniels, 197.

4. Wesley McCune and John R. Beal, "The Job That Made Truman President," *Harper's Magazine*, June 1945, 616.

5. Rick Atkinson, "Ten Things Every American Should Know About Our Army in World War II," Foreign Policy Research Institute, May 28, 2009, https://www.fpri.org/article/2009/05/ten-things-every-american-student-should-know-about-our-army-in-world-war-ii/.

6. Walter Reuther, radio broadcast Dec. 28, 1940, accessed Mar. 25, 2022, http://reuther100.wayne.edu/pdf/500_Planes_Speech.pdf.

7. The US Air Force would not be established as a separate military branch until 1947.

8. Tim Trainor, "How Ford's Willow Run Assembly Plant Helped Win World War II," *Assembly*, Jan. 3, 2019, https://www.assemblymag.com/articles/94614-how-fords-willow-run-assembly-plant-helped-win-world-war-ii.

9. Merle Miller, *Plain Speaking: An Oral Biography of Harry S. Truman* (New York: Berkley Medallion, 1974), 172.

10. David McCullough, *Truman* (New York: Simon & Schuster, 1992), 255.

11. Arthur Herman, *Freedom's Forge: How American Business Produced Victory in World War II* (New York: Random House Trade Paperbacks, 2013), 96.

12. William P. Helm, *Harry Truman: A Political Biography* (New York: Duell, Sloan and Pearce, 1947), 163-164.

13. Miller, *Plain Speaking*, 175.

14. Harry Truman, *Memoirs by Harry S. Truman, Vol. 1, 1945: Year of Decisions* (1955; repr. New York: Smithmark Publishers, 1995), 165 (hereafter cited as *Memoirs, Vol. 1*).

15. McNaughton and Hehmeyer, 91.

16. The exact dates and the route covered on this road trip are unclear, as there are several versions of the story. The most detailed account, and the one written most closely after the event, is that of McNaughton and Hehmeyer in 1945 (91), which says "he drove from Washington straight and unannounced to the fort," and then continued on from there. (Walter Hehmeyer, in his oral history on file at the Truman Library, says the details came from Truman himself.) This version also matches the version Truman told Merle Miller in *Plain Speaking*. The notion that he drove 30,000 miles on this trip, as Margaret Truman (*Harry S. Truman*, 138) and later Truman himself (*Plain Speaking*, 175) claimed, are, as David McCullough notes, "preposterous."

17. McNaughton and Hehmeyer, 92.

18. *St. Louis Post-Dispatch*, Feb. 3, 1941.

19. Helm, *Harry Truman*, 152.

20. *Congressional Record*, Vol. 87, Part 1, Feb. 10, 1941, 830, 837.

21. *Congressional Record*, Feb. 10, 1941, 830.

22. *St. Louis Post-Dispatch*, March 2, 1941.

Chapter Two

1. McCullough, 57.

2. Miller, *Plain Speaking*, 46.

3. Miller, *Plain Speaking*, 52.

4. McCullough, 52.

5. Daniels, *The Man of Independence*, 59.

6. Daniels, 58.

7. McCullough, 78.

8. Harry Truman, "Remarks to Members of the National Guard Association," Oct. 25, 1950, Public Papers, Truman Library.

9. McCullough, 73.

10. Harry Truman, letter to Bess Wallace, May 9, 1911, Truman Library.

11. Harry Truman to Bess Wallace, June 22, 1911, Truman Library.

12. Harry Truman to Bess Wallace, July 12, 1911, Truman Library.

13. Miller, *Plain Speaking*, 70.

14. Harry Truman, *Memoirs, Vol. 1*, 128.

15. Margaret Truman, *Bess W. Truman* (New York: MacMillan, 1986), 58.

16. Harry Truman to Bess Wallace, July 14, 1917, Truman Library.

17. Harry Truman to Bess Wallace, Mar. 20, 1918, Truman Library.

18. Harry Truman to Bess Wallace, May 26, 1918; June 2, 1918, Truman Library.

19. McCullough, 119.

20. Daniels, 96-97.

21. Harry Truman to Bess Wallace, Sep. 1, 1918, Truman Library.

22. Harry Truman to Bess Wallace, Sep. 8, 1918, Truman Library.

23. Harry Truman, *Memoirs, Vol. 1*, 131; Harry Truman to Bess Wallace, Nov. 11, 1918, Truman Library; McNaughton and Hehmeyer,

24. Margaret Truman, *Harry S. Truman*, 61.

25. Fifteen presidents, including Truman, are known to have been Masons, from Washington to Gerald Ford. History.com, "This Day in History: August 04, 'George Washington Becomes a Master Mason,'"

accessed July 3, 2022, https://www.history.com/this-day-in-history/washington-becomes-master-mason.

26. Daniels, *The Man of Independence*, 77.

27. Daniels, 109.

28. Harry Vaughan, oral history, Truman Library.

29. McCullough, 188.

30. Alonzo Hamby, *Man of the People: A Life of Harry S. Truman* (New York: Oxford University Press, 1995), 120.

31. Hamby, 117.

32. Hamby, 122.

33. Hamby, 145.

34. Daniels, 146.

35. Hamby, 159, 152-3.

36. Hamby, 159-160.

37. Hamby, 163.

Chapter Three

1. McCune and Beal, "The Job That Made Truman President," *Harper's Magazine*, June 1945, 618.

2. Margaret Truman, *Harry S. Truman*, 139.

3. Matthew Connelly, oral history, Harry S. Truman Library.

4. McCune and Beal, *Harper's Magazine*, June 1945.

5. Merle Miller, *Plain Speaking*, 175.

6. *St. Louis Star-Times*, Dec. 31, 1940.

7. Hugh Fulton letter to Harry Truman, Mar. 17, 1943, Senatorial and Vice-Presidential papers (hereafter referred to as SVP Papers), Truman Library; Jonathan Daniels, *The Man of Independence*, 224; Marquis W.

Childs, unidentified magazine article, "Truman's Right Hand Man" June 2, 1945, Fulton collection, Truman Library.

8. Alexander Hehmeyer, letter to Walter Hehmeyer, Nov. 30, 1971, Truman papers, Truman Library.

9. George Meader, oral history, Truman Library.

10. McCune and Beal, *Harper's Magazine*, June 1945.

11. Harry Truman to Bess Truman, Mar. 17, 1941, Truman Library.

12. Harry Truman to Bess Truman, Mar. 19, 1941, Truman Library.

13. Harry Truman to Bess Truman, Mar. 21, 1941, Truman Library.

14. George Meader, "My Four Years With The Truman Committee," typescript, George Meader Papers, Bentley Historical Library, University of Michigan.

15. Stephen K. Bailey and Howard D. Samuel, *Congress at Work* (New York: Henry Holt and Company, 1952), 296.

16. Miller, *Plain Speaking*, 174.

17. Miller, *Plain Speaking*, 173-174.

18. Donald H. Riddle, *The Truman Committee: A Study in Congressional Responsibility* (New Brunswick, NJ: Rutgers University Press, 1964), 15.

19. *Harry S. Truman*, by Margaret Truman, 139.

20. McCune and Beal, *Harper's Magazine*, June 1945.

21. Bailey and Samuel, *Congress at Work*, 297.

22. Bailey and Samuel, 298.

23. Harold G. Robinson, oral history, Truman Library.

24. Wilbur D. Sparks, oral history, Truman Library.

25. Robinson, oral history.

26. "Duquesne Spy Ring," FBI.gov, accessed July 9, 2022, https://www.fbi.gov/history/famous-cases/duquesne-spy-ring#.

27. Robinson, oral history.

28. Robinson, oral history.

29. Shirley Key Hehmeyer, oral history, Truman Library.

30. Shirley Key Hehmeyer, oral history; Walter Hehmeyer, oral history.

31. Shirley Key Hehmeyer, oral history; Harold Robinson, oral history.

32. Walter Hehmeyer, oral history, Truman Library.

33. Shirley Key Hehmeyer, oral history.

34. Walter Hehmeyer, oral history.

35. Walter Hehmeyer, oral history.

Chapter Four

1. Eugene Schmidtlein, "Truman the Senator" (PhD diss., University of Missouri, 1962), 248.

2. *The Washington Post*, Apr. 16, 1941.

3. *Chicago Daily Tribune*, Apr. 16, 1941.

4. *The New York Times*, Apr. 16, 1941.

5. *The New York Times,* Apr. 16, 1941.

6. *The New York Times*, Apr. 16, 1941.

7. "Hearings Before A Special Committee Investigating the National Defense Program, Part I" (Washington: US Govt. Printing Office, 1941), Apr. 15-17, 1941.

8. *The Washington Post*, Apr. 25, 1941.

9. "She's Lawyer at 20," unidentified newspaper clipping, 1936, from the files of Dylan Baker, Lisa Horner, and Gregory Baker.

10. Dylan Baker, Lisa Horner, and Greg Baker, in conversation with the author, Oct. 25, 2021.

11. "She's Lawyer at 20," unidentified newspaper clipping, 1936.

12. McNaughton and Hehmeyer, *This Man Truman*, 125.

13. Harry Vaughan, oral history, Truman Library; and Harry Truman, *Memoirs Vol. 1*, 195.

14. Edgar C. Faris, oral history, Truman Library.

15. Hugh Fulton, memorandum, June 15, 1942, Truman Committee files, National Archives.

16. Hugh Fulton, memorandum to staff, "Office Procedure," May 14, 1941, RG-46, AD-1 General Records, Truman Committee files, National Archives.

17. Walter Hehmeyer, oral history, Truman Library.

18. Miller, *Plain Speaking*, 175.

19. "Additional Report of the Special Committee Investigating the National Defense Program" (hereafter referred to as the First Annual Report), Jan. 15, 1942 (Washington: US Govt. Printing Office, 1942), 167.

20. Harry Truman to Bess Truman, June 17, 1941, Truman Library.

21. Harry Truman to Bess Truman, June 18, 1941, Truman Library.

22. Harry Truman to Bess Truman, June 19, 1941, Truman Library.

23. Medical records, 1917–1955, Military Personnel File of Harry S. Truman, Truman Library.

24. Harry Truman to Bess Truman, June 30, 1941, Truman Library.

25. Harry Truman to Bess Truman, July 3, 1941. Truman Library.

26. Medical records, 1917–1955, Military Personnel File of Harry S. Truman, Truman Library.

27. Truman Committee, "Report on Aluminum Investigation," June 26, 1941, included as an appendix to the First Annual Report (Washington: US Govt. Printing Office, 1942), 201.

28. "Report on Aluminum Investigation," appendix to the First Annual Report, 205.

29. "Report on Aluminum Investigation," appendix to the First Annual Report, 202.

30. *St. Louis Post-Dispatch*, June 27, 1941.

31. *Knoxville News-Sentinel*, Knoxville, TN, July 23, 1941.

32. Sister M. Patrick Ellen Maher, "The Role of the Chairman of a Congressional Investigating Committee: A Case Study of the Special Committee of the Senate to Investigate the National Defense Program 1941-1948," (PhD diss., Saint Louis University, 1962), 82.

33. Maher, 82.

34. Appendix to the *Congressional Record*, 77th Congress, Volume 87—Part 13 (Washington: US Govt. Printing Office, 1941), A3629-30.

35. *Tacoma News-Tribune*, June 30, 1941.

36. *Wisconsin State Journal*, June 30, 1941.

37. *Greenwood* (MS) *Commonwealth*; *Times* (Munster, IN); *Sayre* (OK) *Daily Headlight-Journal*; June 30, 1941.

38. Wilbur D. Sparks, oral history, Truman Library.

39. Sparks, oral history.

40. Sallie Sparks, email to the author, Aug. 2, 2021.

41. Charles Clark letter to Hugh Fulton, July 19, 1941, Truman Committee files, National Archives.

42. Shirley Key Hehmeyer, oral history, Truman Library.

43. Walter Hehmeyer, oral history.

44. McNaughton and Hehmeyer, *This Man Truman*, 110.

45. *Congressional Record*, Aug. 14, 1941.

46. *Congressional Record*, Aug. 14, 1941.

47. Investigation of the National Defense Program, "Report on Camp and Cantonment Investigation," Aug. 14, 1941, reprinted as appendix

to the First Annual Report, Jan. 15, 1942 (Washington: US Govt. Printing Office, 1942), 240.

48. "Report on Camp and Cantonment Investigation," appendix to First Annual Report, 243, 245.

49. Appendix to First Annual Report, 240.

50. Appendix to First Annual Report, 249, 254–255.

51. *Congressional Record*, Aug. 14, 1941.

52. Appendix to First Annual Report, 243, 245.

53. Appendix to First Annual Report, 241.

Chapter Five

1. *Los Angeles Times*, Aug. 18, 1941.

2. Harry Truman to Bess Truman, Aug. 15, 1941, Truman Library.

3. Harry Truman to Bess Truman, Aug. 16, 1941, Truman Library.

4. Harry Truman to Bess Truman, Aug. 17, 1941, Truman Library.

5. *Los Angeles Times,* Aug. 18, 1941.

6. Bess Truman to Harry Truman, Aug. 20, 1941, Bess Truman Papers, Truman Library; Harry Truman to Bess Truman, Aug. 20, 1941, Truman Library.

7. Eugene Schmidtlein, "Truman the Senator," (PhD diss., University of Missouri, 1962), 309.

8. Harry Truman to Bess Truman, Aug. 20, 1941, Truman Library.

9. *Los Angeles Times*, Aug. 17, 1941.

10. Harry Truman to Bess Truman, Aug. 21, 1941, Truman Library.

11. Harry Truman to Bess Truman, Aug. 21, 1941.

12. Harry Truman to Bess Truman, Aug. 21, 1941.

13. Bess Truman to Harry Truman, Aug. 30, 1941, Bess Truman Papers, Truman Library.

14. Harry Truman to Bess Truman, Aug. 31, 1941, Truman Library.

15. Harry Truman to Bess Truman, Aug. 24, 1941, Truman Library.

16. *Spokesman-Review*, Spokane, WA, Aug. 26, 1941.

17. *Spokesman-Review*, Aug. 26, 1941.

18. Truman, Margaret: *Harry S. Truman*, 141.

19. Harry Truman to Margaret Truman, Aug. 27, 1941, Truman Library.

20. Harry Truman to Bess Truman, Aug. 31, 1944.

21. Maher, PhD diss., 21.

22. Donald Riddle, *The Truman Committee*, 9.

23. Hamby, *Man of the People*, 254.

24. *The Washington Post*, Jan. 3, 1942.

25. *Congressional Record*, Feb. 10, 1941, 838.

26. Memorandum: "Preliminary conference on racial discrimination," June 25, 1941, Truman Committee files, National Archives.

27. *Pittsburgh Courier*, March 1, 1941.

28. *Cleveland Call and Post*, July 12, 1941.

29. Schmidtlein, PhD diss., 248.

30. Roosevelt in 1941 appointed Byrnes to a seat on the Supreme Court, a seat he held for only fifteen months before resigning in October 1942 to rejoin the administration as head of the Office of Economic Stabilization. He became one of Roosevelt's top advisers, and President Truman would make him secretary of state.

31. *Pittsburgh Courier*, July 5, 1941.

32. *Pittsburgh Courier*, July 5, 1941; Walter White telegram to Harry Truman, June 27, 1941, Truman Committee files, OP-45 Race Discrimination,

National Archives; Randolph did postpone the march after Roosevelt issued an executive order, 8802, on June 25, which banned discrimination in federal work training programs.

33. *Pittsburgh Courier*, July 5, 1941, July 12, 1941; *Philadelphia Tribune*, July 10, 1941.

34. *Pittsburgh Courier*, July 12, 1941.

35. For example, C.A. Franklin letter to Harry Truman, Nov. 13, 1940, SVP Papers, Truman Library.

36. Alfred Steinberg; *The Man from Missouri* (New York: Putnam, 1962), 171.

37. Hamby, *Man of the People*, 239.

38. Harry Truman to Bess Truman, Sep. 24, 1941, Truman Library.

39. Harry Truman to Bess Truman, Dec. 21, 1941, Truman Library.

40. Harry Truman to Bess Truman, Sep. 18, 1941, Truman Library.

41. *Kansas City Times*, Sep. 19. 1941; Harry Truman to Bess Truman, Sep. 20, 1941, Truman Library; *Springfield Daily News*, Springfield, MO, Sep. 20, 1941.

42. Harry Truman to Bess Truman, Sep. 24, 1941, Truman Library.

43. *St. Louis Post-Dispatch,* Sep. 30, 1941; Harry Truman to Bess Truman, Oct. 3, 1941.

44. *Detroit Free Press*, Oct. 26, 1941.

45. *Detroit Free Press*, Oct. 23, 1941; *Pittsburgh Press*, Oct. 23, 1941; *St. Louis Post-Dispatch*, Oct. 29, 1941.

46. *Congressional Record*, Oct. 29, 1941, 8303–8304.

47. Wilbur Sparks, oral history.

48. Robert Irvin, oral history; author interview with Dylan Baker, Greg Baker, and Lisa Horner, Oct. 25, 2021.

49. *Kenosha News*, Kenosha, WI, Nov. 25, 1941.

50. Margaret Truman, *Bess W. Truman* (New York: MacMillan, 1986), 206.

51. Harold Robinson, oral history, Truman Library.

52. *Indianapolis Star,* "Washington Merry-Go-Round," Nov. 15, 1941; Harry Truman to Bess Truman, Nov. 16, 1941, Truman Library; Margaret Truman, *Letters from Father* (New York: Arbor House, 1981), 38.

53. Margaret Truman, *Bess W. Truman,* 207.

54. Harry Truman to Bess Truman, Dec. 7, 1941, Truman Library.

55. Truman, Margaret, *Harry S. Truman,* 144-145; Margaret Truman, *Bess W. Truman,* 207.

56. Harry Truman letter to Ethel Noland, Dec. 14, 1941, Truman Library.

57. Harry Truman to Ethel Noland, Dec. 14, 1941.

58. Harry Truman to Ethel Noland, Dec. 14, 1941; Margaret Truman, *Harry S. Truman,* 145.

Chapter Six

1. David Brinkley, *Washington Goes To War* (New York: Knopf, 1988; repr. New York: Ballantine, trade edition, 1996), 89.

2. Gordon W. Prang, *At Dawn We Slept* (New York: McGraw-Hill, 1981; repr. Penguin Books, 1982), 539.

3. Christopher Hehmeyer, telephone interview with the author, June 30, 2020; Donald M. Nelson, *Arsenal of Democracy: The Story of American War Production* (New York: Harcourt, Brace and Co., 1946), 6; *The Washington Post,* Dec. 9, 1941.

4. *The Washington Post,* Dec. 10, 1941.

5. Margaret Truman, *Harry S. Truman,* 148; Harry Truman to Ethel Noland, Dec. 14, 1941, Truman Library.

6. *The Washington Post,* Dec. 9, 1941.

7. Margaret Truman, *Harry S. Truman,* 145.

8. Investigation of the National Defense Program, "Additional Report," Dec. 10, 1941, 1.

9.   Fulton memo to staff, Dec. 15, 1941, Truman Committee files, National Archives.

10. Harry Truman to Bess Truman, Dec. 20, 1941, Truman Library.

11. Memorandum, "HST appointments with FDR, 1934-1945," Nov. 7, 1963, SVP Papers, Truman Library.

12. William Helm, *Harry Truman: A Political Biography* (New York: Duell, Sloan and Pearce, 1947), 53.

13. Harry Truman to Bess Truman, Dec. 31, 1941, Truman Library.

14. *The Washington Post*, Jan. 13, 1941.

15. *Congressional Record*, Jan. 15, 1942, 371-372.

16. McNaughton and Hehmeyer, *This Man Truman*, 113.

17. Donald Riddle, *The Truman Committee*; 65; *Congressional Record*, Jan. 15, 1942, 381.

18. McNaughton and Hehmeyer, 114; *The Washington Post*, Jan. 16, 1942.

19. *Congressional Record*, Jan. 15, 1942, 386.

20. *The Washington Post*, Jan. 15, 1942; Harry Truman, *Memoirs, Vol. 1,* 180.

21. *Congressional Record*, Jan. 15, 1942, 385.

22. First Annual Report, 55.

23. Some pilots found that despite its shortcomings, the P-40, if flown properly, could compete at lower altitudes with German and Japanese fighters. Later versions of the plane, with better engines and armaments and longer range, served in frontline duty throughout the war, in virtually every theater, with British, Canadian, Australian, New Zealand, and Soviet forces. In the US forces, however, it was largely phased out in 1943 and 1944, replaced by the P-51 Mustang, P-47 Thunderbolt, and P-38 Lightning.

24. First Annual Report, 56.

25. First Annual Report, 58.

26. First Annual Report, 52.

27. *The New York Times*, Jan. 16, 1942.

28. Harry Truman to Margaret Truman, Jan. 3, 1942, Truman Library.

Chapter Seven

1. *Pittsburgh Press*, Feb. 2, 1942.

2. *Pittsburgh Press*, Jan. 26, 1942.

3. *Pittsburgh Press*, Jan. 27, 1942.

4. George E. Dye, letter to Harry Truman, Feb. 2, 1942, Truman Committee files, OP-31 Steel, National Archives.

5. McCune and Beal, *Harper's Magazine*, June 1945, 619.

6. Aaron N. Sadoff, letter to Harry Truman, Sep. 1, 1942, Truman Committee files, OP-31, Steel, National Archives.

7. Wilbur Sparks, oral history, Truman Library.

8. Rudolph Halley, letter to Aaron Sadoff, Sep. 9, 1942, Truman Committee files, National Archives.

9. Sparks, oral history.

10. Robert Irvin, oral history, Truman Library.

11. Henry W. Jonkhoff, letter to Harry Truman, Jan. 29, 1942, Truman Committee files, OP-20 Patents and Inventions, National Archives.

12. Charles Clark, letter to Henry W. Jonkhoff, Feb. 9, 1942, Truman Committee files, National Archives.

13. Charles Clark, letter to George Dye, Feb. 26, 1942, National Archives.

14. George Dye, letter to Harry Truman, Feb. 17, 1942, National Archives.

15. George Dye, letter to Harry Truman, Feb. 17, 1942, National Archives.

16. George Dye to Harry Truman, Feb. 17, 1942.

17. George Dye, letters to Harry Truman: Feb. 17, 1942; May 5, 1942; Charles Clark to George Dye, May 20 and May 22, 1942, National Archives.

18. "Campaign Summaries of World War 2: Battle of the Atlantic—Its Development," Naval-History.net, accessed Jan. 12, 2022, https://www.naval-history.net/WW2CampaignsAtlanticDev.htm.

19. Nelson, *Arsenal of Democracy*, 60.

20. Nelson, *Arsenal of Democracy*, 63.

21. Harry Truman, *Memoirs, Vol. 1,* 179.

22. *The New York Times,* Jan. 29, 1942.

23. *The Washington Post,* Jan. 29, 1942.

24. *The New York Times,* Jan. 29, 1942.

25. Nelson, *Arsenal of Democracy*, 224.

26. Maury Klein, *A Call to Arms* (New York: Bloomsbury Press, 2013), 405, 304.

27. *Minneapolis Star Tribune,* May 27, 1942; *The New York Times,* May 27, 1942.

28. *Congressional Record,* May 26, 1942, 4543.

29. Christopher Hehmeyer, telephone interview with the author, June 30, 2020.

30. Dylan Baker, Lisa Horner, and Greg Baker, interview with the author over Zoom, Oct. 25, 2021.

31. Irvin, oral history.

32. Irvin, oral history; Harry Truman, *Memoirs, Vol. 1,* 173.

Chapter Eight

1. Shirley Key Hehmeyer, oral history, Truman Library.

2. This section is drawn from Shirley Key Hehmeyer, oral history, Truman Library.

3. Nelson, *Arsenal of Democracy*, 246.

4. Harry Truman, speech over Radio Station KMOX, St. Louis, May 31, 1942, Harry Truman Papers, SVP Papers, Truman library.

5. Klein, *A Call To Arms*, 180.

6. Arthur Herman, *Freedom's Forge,* 40.

7. Herman, 44, 49.

8. Nelson, *Arsenal of Democracy*, 245.

9. Klein, *A Call To Arms*, 186.

10. Unsigned memo, June 24, 1942, AD-5 staff assignments, Truman Committee files, National Archives.

11. Hugh Fulton letter to Eagle Parachute Company, June 3, 1942, Truman Committee files, National Archives.

12. Harry Craddock, letter to Harry Truman, June 25, 1942, OP-6 War Department Matters, Complaints file, Truman Committee files, National Archives.

13. Harry Truman, undated note, Truman Committee files, OP-6 War Department Matters, Complaints file, National Archives.

14. Matthew Connelly, memo to staff, Sep. 8, 1943, AD-3 Office procedure, Truman Committee files, National Archives.

15. The documents referenced in this section are in the files of the Truman Committee, OP-6, War Department Matters, Complaints, Box 205, National Archives.

16. First Annual Report, 4.

17. Riddle, *The Truman Committee*, 39.

18. First Annual Report, 3.

19. Irvin, oral history.

Chapter Nine

1. Jerry E. Strahan, *Andrew Jackson Higgins and the Boats That Won World War II* (Baton Rouge: Louisiana State University Press, 1994; repr. Louisiana Paperback Edition, 2013), 10.

2. Stephen Ambrose, *D-Day: June 6, 1944: The Climactic Battle of World War II* (New York: Simon & Schuster, 1994), chap. 2, Kindle.

3. Strahan, 102.

4. Victor H. Krulak, *First to Fight: An Inside View of the U.S. Marine Corps* (Annapolis: Bluejacket Books, Naval Institute Press, 1984), 97, Kindle.

5. Herbert Maletz, memorandum to Hugh Fulton, July 10, 1942, OP-3 Interoffice Memoranda, Truman Committee files, National Archives; Truman Committee, Third Annual Report (Washington: US Govt. Printing Office, 1944), 162.

6. Walter Hehmeyer, oral history, Truman Library.

7. Harold Robinson, oral history, Truman Library.

8. Third Annual Report, 144.

9. Third Annual Report, 145.

10. Third Annual Report, 145.

11. Third Annual Report, 146.

12. Third Annual Report, 167.

13. *Richmond Times-Dispatch* (Richmond, VA), Aug. 6, 1942.

14. Third Annual Report, 133.

15. Third Annual Report, 133.

16. *The Washington Post*, Sep. 22, 1942.

17. Irvin, oral history.

18. Knox did not receive the results of the internal investigation he had ordered until Nov. 7 (Third Annual Report, 133).

19. *Congressional Record*, Sep. 14, 1942.

20. Maury Klein, *A Call to Arms*, 190.

21. Margaret Truman, *Harry S. Truman*, 141.

22. Harry Truman to Bess Truman, June 13, 1942, Truman Library.

23. *The Washington Post*, March 8, 1942.

24. Helm, 189.

25. Bess Truman to Harry Truman, June 16, 1942, Truman Library.

26. *Courier Journal* (Louisville, KY), June 25, 1942.

27. *The Washington Post*, July 8, 1942.

28. Harold Robinson, oral history, Truman Library.

29. Robinson, oral history.

30. Matthew Connelly, oral history.

31. This account is drawn from Connelly's oral history in the Truman Library.

32. *Congressional Record*, July 16, 1942; *Courier Journal* (Louisville, KY), Aug. 9, 1942.

33. Connelly, oral history.

34. McCullough, *Truman*, 284.

35. McCullough, 308.

36. Margaret Truman, *Bess W. Truman*, 203, 213; Bess Truman to Harry Truman, Aug 13, 1942, Truman Library; Harry Truman to Bess Truman, Apr. 30, 1942.

37. Harry Truman to Bess Truman, June 23, June 25, June 28, 1942, Truman Library.

38. Harry Truman to Bess Truman, June 27, 1942, Truman Library.

39. Harry Truman to Bess Truman, June 28, 1942, Truman Library.

40. Bess Truman to Harry Truman, June 28, 1942, Truman Library.

41. "The Talk of the Town," *The New Yorker*, Nov. 23, 1987.

Chapter Ten

1. George Dye to Harry Truman, May 5, 1942, Truman Committee files, OP-31 Steel, National Archives.

2. Dye to Truman, May 18, 1942.

3. Dye to Truman, May 19, 1942.

4. Dye to Truman, July 2, 1942.

5. Hugh Fulton memorandum to Rudolph Halley, July 6, 1942, Truman Committee files, OP-31 Steel, National Archives.

6. Hugh Fulton to Carnegie Illinois Steel, July 6, 1942, Truman Committee files, National Archives.

7. George Dye to Hugh Fulton, July 15, 1942.

8. Robert Irvin, oral history.

9. Harry Truman to Bess Truman, July 1, 1942, Truman Library.

10. *Dear Bess: The Letters from Harry to Bess Truman, 1910-1959,* ed. Robert Ferrell (New York: W.W. Norton, 1983), 475.

11. Margaret Truman, *Harry S. Truman,* 149.

12. Harry Truman to Bess Truman, July 25, 1942, Truman Library.

13. Shirley Key Hehmeyer, oral history; Marquis Childs, "Truman's Right Hand Man," undated magazine article, Hugh Fulton papers, Truman Library.

14. Sparks, oral history.

15. Harry Truman letter to Judge Lewis Schwellenbach, July 29, 1942, Harry Truman, SVP Papers, Truman Library; Harry Truman to Bess Truman, Aug. 21, 1942, Truman Library.

16. Harry Truman to Bess Truman, Aug. 8, 1942, Truman Library; Alonzo Hamby, *Man of the People,* 277.

17. There are two versions of how Truman came to sign off on the draft. In one account, which comes from Senator Harley Kilgore, a "girl" from the magazine showed up in Truman's office and pulled a fast one on him, "rushing into his office" and sweet-talking him into thinking he didn't need to look at the pages and "begging" him to sign them right away. Then there is Walter Hehmeyer's version, from his oral history in the Truman Library, which has the author of the piece get-

ting Truman's approval, then persuading Hehmeyer and Fulton that Truman had seen the revised version and signed off. The Kilgore account is found in Alfred Steinberg, *The Man From Missouri: The Life and Times of Harry S. Truman* (New York: G.P. Putnam's Sons, 1962), 195-196, and also appears in Margaret Truman, *Harry S. Truman*, 161-162. Steinberg says Truman "initialed each page." Hehmeyer was asked about this in his oral history interview in 1969: "Did he initial every page, by any chance?" Hehmeyer responded, "No. He did not, no, he did not, he just wrote his name across the title page. I can see what happened. The writer just said, 'This is fine. Everybody on the staff says this is fine.' So Senator Truman said, 'Fine,' and signed his name on it."

18. Margaret Truman, *Harry S. Truman*, 161-162; Hamby, *Man of the People*, 277; Walter Hehmeyer, oral history.

19. Harry Truman to Bess Truman, Sep. 27, 1942, Truman Library.

20. Walter Hehmeyer, oral history.

21. Harry Truman to Bess Truman, Oct. 2, 1942, Truman Library.

22. Harry Truman, "We Can Lose The War In Washington," *American Magazine*, Nov. 1942; Margaret Truman, *Harry S. Truman*, 162; Alfred Steinberg, *Man of the People*, 196.

Chapter Eleven

1. George Dye, letter to Harry Truman, Nov. 14, 1942, OP-31 Steel, Truman Committee files, National Archives.

2. George Dye to Harry Truman, Nov. 11, 1942; Dye letter to Benjamin Fairless, Jan 6, 1945, OP-31 Steel, Truman Committee files, National Archives.

3. *Pittsburgh Post-Gazette*, Dec. 15, 1938; *Pittsburgh Press*, Apr. 10, 1981.

4. "Preliminary Report Concerning Faking of Inspections of Steel Plates by Carnegie-Illinois Steel Corporation," typescript, Apr. 1943, OP-31 Steel, Truman Committee files, National Archives.

5. Dye to Truman, Nov. 14, 1942.

6. *Pittsburgh Post-Gazette*, Sep. 15, 1942; George Dye to Harry Truman, Aug. 4, 1942.

7. George Dye to Harry Truman, Oct. 5, 1942, OP-31 Steel, Truman Committee files, National Archives.

8. George Dye, handwritten statement signed March 16, 1943, OP-31 Steel, Truman Committee files, National Archives.

9. *Pittsburgh Post-Gazette*, Nov. 14, 1942.

10. Hugh Fulton, handwritten note to Jeanne Campbell, undated (approx. Nov. 1942), Truman Committee files, National Archives.

11. Jeanne Campbell, memo to Hugh Fulton, Nov. 5, 1942, Truman Committee files, National Archives.

12. Wilbur Sparks, telegram to Hugh Fulton, Dec. 24, 1942, OP-3, Interoffice Memoranda, Truman Committee files, National Archives.

13. Author correspondence with Sallie Sparks; *Savannah Reporter and Andrew County Democrat* (Savannah, MO), Dec. 25, 1942, and Jan. 1, 1943; *St. Joseph Press* (St. Joseph, MO), Dec. 27, 1942, and Jan. 3, 1943, *The Kansas City Star*, Dec. 29, 1942;

14. Riddle, *The Truman Committee*, Appendix IV, 185.

15. *Business Week*, June 26, 1943.

16. McCune and Beal, *Harper's Magazine*, June 1945.

17. *Business Week*, June 26, 1943; *St. Louis Post-Dispatch*, Apr. 25, 1943.

18. McCullough, 282.

Chapter Twelve

1. Truman Committee, Second Annual Report (Washington: US Govt. Printing Office, 1943), 1.

2. Second Annual Report, 1.

3. Encyclopedia of Detroit, "Model T," detroithistorical.org; accessed June 14, 2022, https://detroithistorical.org/learn/encyclopedia-of-detroit/model-t.

4. A.J. Baime, *The Arsenal of Democracy: FDR, Detroit, And an Epic Quest*

to Arm an America at War (New York: Houghton Mifflin Harcourt, 2014), 90-91.

5. Baime, *The Arsenal of Democracy*; 191.

6. *Times Herald* (Port Huron, MI), Feb. 19, 1943.

7. Baime, *The Arsenal of Democracy,* 191; *Times Herald* (Port Huron, MI), Feb 19. 1943; *St. Louis Globe-Democrat*, Feb. 23, 1943.

8. Telegram, Hugh Fulton to Henry Bishop, Feb. 17, 1943, Truman Committee files, National Archives.

9. *St. Louis Star and Times*, Feb. 18, 1943, 3.

10. George Meader, oral history, Truman Library.

11. Harry Truman to Bess Truman, Feb. 19, 1943, Truman Library.

12. Author interviews with Christopher Hehmeyer, Frank Jackson, Susan Oppenheimer; *The Washington Post*, Feb 20, 1943.

13. Harold Robinson, oral history, Truman Library.

14. Robinson, oral history.

15. Robinson, oral history.

16. Menu in the possession of Christopher Hehmeyer.

17. Strahan, 49-50, 64, 72.

18. Shirley Key Hehmeyer, oral history, Truman Library.

Chapter Thirteen

1. The account of Kaiser's testimony is drawn from "Verbatim Record of Proceedings of the Senate Committee Investigating National Defense Program," Tuesday, March 8, 1943, National Archives.

2. Frederick C. Lane, *Ships for Victory: A History of Shipbuilding Under the U.S. Maritime Commission in World War II* (Baltimore: Johns Hopkins University Press, 1951; repr. paperback ed. 2001), 544-545.

3. Irvin, oral history.

4. George Dye to Harry Truman, Jan. 6, 1943; OP-31 Steel, Truman Committee files, National Archives.

5. Rudolph Halley, letter to George Dye, Jan. 13, 1943; Hugh Fulton, letter to George Dye, Feb. 14, 1943, OP-31 Steel, Truman Committee files, National Archives.

6. Irvin, oral history; George Dye, undated memo, handwritten in pencil, to Rudolph Halley, National Archives.

7. Deposition by Rudolph Halley: "Grand Jury Investigation of Alleged Falsification of Records At Irvin Works, of Carnegie Illinois Steel Corporation; Vol. 1." US District Court of the United States for the Western District of Pennsylvania, Apr. 12, 1943, OP-31 Steel, Truman Committee files, National Archives.

8. Halley deposition, 14, 11.

9. "Preliminary Report Concerning Faking of Inspections of Steel Plates by Carnegie-Illinois Steel Corporation," typescript, Apr. 1943, OP-31 Steel, Truman Committee files, National Archives.

10. Halley deposition, 15.

11. Irvin, oral history.

12. Halley deposition, 21.

13. Halley deposition, 22-24; Irene Pasternak, handwritten statement, March 16, 1943, OP-31 Steel, Truman Committee files, National Archives.

14. Halley deposition, 27.

15. Halley deposition, 28.

16. Halley deposition, 33.

17. George Dye, photostat of handwritten affidavit, March 16, 1943, Truman Committee files, OP-31 Steel, National Archives.

18. Halley deposition, 36.

19. Halley deposition, 40-41.

20. Halley deposition, 46-4;, Irvin, oral history.

Chapter Fourteen

1. "Hearings Before a Special Committee Investigating the National Defense Program," March 23, 1943, National Archives.

2. "Hearings," March 23, 1943, 7149, National Archives.

3. Hearings, March 23, 1943, 7152.

4. Hearings, March 23, 1943, 7168.

5. Hearings, March 23, 1943, 7179.

6. Hearings, March 23, 1943, 7184.

7. Hearings, March 23, 1943, 7171, 7189

8. Hearings, March 23, 1943, 7215.

9. *Time*, March 8, 1943.

10. Truman quotes Schwellenbach's telegram in a letter to Senator Sherman Minton, March 13, 1943; James Byrnes, letter to Harry Truman, March 6, 1943; Harry Truman to James Byrnes, March 13, 1943; Senatorial and vice-presidential papers, Truman Library.

11. Harry Truman to Henry Luce, March 13, 1943; Henry Luce to Harry Truman, March 13, 1943; SVP Papers, Truman Library.

12. Second Annual Report, March 11, 1943.

13. Press release, Apr. 19, 1943, OP-31 Steel, Truman Committee files, National Archives.

14. *Pittsburgh Post-Gazette*, Apr. 16, 1943.

15. Truman Committee, "Additional Report–Concerning The Faking Of Inspections Of Steel Plate By Carnegie-Illinois Steel Corporation" (Washington: US Govt. Printing Office, 1943), Apr. 19, 1943.

16. *Christian Science Monitor*, May 3, 1943.

17. *Christian Science Monitor*, May 4, 1943.

18. Erwin D. Canham to Owen Brewster, May 25, 1943, OP-31 Steel, Truman Committee files, National Archives.

19. *Dayton Herald* (Dayton, OH), May 15, 1943; *Pittsburgh Press*, Aug. 13, 1943; *Morning News* (Wilmington, DE), Sep. 13, 1943; *The Cincinnati Enquirer*, Oct. 5, 1943.

Chapter Fifteen

1. Mark Harris, *Five Came Back: A Story of Hollywood and the Second World War* (New York: The Penguin Press, 2015; repr. Penguin Books, paperback, 2015), 89-90; *San Francisco Examiner*, Sep. 10, 1941.

2. Harris, *Five Came Back*, 148.

3. Harris, 113.

4. "List of Walt Disney's World War II productions for Armed Forces," Wikipedia, accessed Jan. 12, 2022, https://en.wikipedia.org/wiki/List_of_Walt_Disney%27s_World_War_II_productions_for_Armed_Forces.

5. Harris, 113.

6. Peter Ansberry, memorandum to Hugh Fulton, Oct. 23, 1942, OP-6, War Department Matters, Truman Committee files, National Archives.

7. Ansberry memo to Fulton, Sep. 17, 1942, OP-6 War Department Matters, National Archives.

8. Ansberry to Fulton, Sep. 17, 1942; Ansberry to Fulton, "Summary of Movie Investigation," RG46, Restricted Documents, SEN79A–F30, Truman Committee Files, National Archives; Ansberry to Rudolph Halley, Oct. 28, 1942, OP-3 Interoffice Memoranda, Truman Committee files, National Archives.

9. Ansberry memo to Fulton, Feb. 8, 1943, RG46, Restricted Documents, SEN79A–F30, Truman Committee Files, National Archives.

10. Ansberry to Fulton, Feb. 8, 1943.

11. Memorandum, Hugh Fulton to members of the committee, Feb. 16, 1943, Truman Committee files, National Archives.

12. Robert Patterson, letter to Harry Truman, Feb. 15, 1943, RG46, Restricted Documents, SEN79A–F30, Truman Committee Files, National Archives.

13. "Verbatim Record of Proceedings of Senate Committee Investigating National Defense Program," Thursday, Feb. 14, 1943 (Washington: Bureau of National Affairs, 1943), in OP-42 The Motion Picture Industry, Truman Committee Files, National Archives.

14. "Verbatim Record of Proceedings," Feb. 14, 1943.

15. Published hearings, Special Committee Investigating the National Defense Program, Part 17, Feb. 16, 1943, 6877.

16. *Los Angeles Times*, Feb. 17, 1943.

17. *Time*, March 15, 1943.

18. Mimeograph typescript: "Statement of Honorable Robert P. Patterson, Undersecretary of War," Apr. 3, 1943, OP-42 The Motion-Picture Industry, Truman Committee files, National Archives.

19. *The Baltimore Sun*, Apr. 4, 1943.

20. Harry Truman, letter to Lewis Schwellenbach; Apr. 8, 1943; SVP Papers, Truman Library.

21. Harris, *Five Came Back*, 220.

Chapter Sixteen

1. Hugh Fulton, "Memorandum to Members of the Committee," March 26, 1943, AD-1 General Correspondence, Truman Committee files, National Archives.

2. *Courier-News* (Bridgewater, NJ), March 24, 1943.

3. *Pittsburgh Post-Gazette*, March 24, 1943.

4. *Time*, Apr. 5, 1943, 14.

5. The account and dialogue of this hearing are drawing from "Hearings, Special Committee Investigating the National Defense Program," Part 18, March 26, 1943, National Archives.

6. *Time*, Apr. 5, 1943.

7. "The Fight For Quality Production," speech by Senator Harry Truman,

delivered over the Blue Network, Shenandoah, IA, Oct. 4, 1943, online, Truman Library.

8. "Investigation of the National Defense Program, Additional Report: Aircraft," July 10, 1943, included as an addendum to: Truman Committee, Third Annual Report, 359.

9. "Additional Report: Aircraft," July 10, 1943, 358-366; Harry Truman, *Memoirs, Vol. 1*, 184.

10. Additional Report: Aircraft, 360.

11. Flight data recorders, or "black boxes" did not become common in airplanes until the 1960s. Wikipedia.org, "Flight Recorder," accessed July 22, 2022.

12. "Additional Report: Aircraft," 358-366.

13. McCullough, 286.

14. Lynne Olson, "Too Little, Too Late, The people and politics leading to president Roosevelt's belated decision to help rescue Jews in Europe," *The New York Times*, Nov. 8, 2015, A39.

15. *South Bend Tribune* (South Bend, IN), Apr. 15, 1943.

16. Harry Truman, "Speech To Be Delivered Before the United Rally to Demand Rescue of Doomed Jews," press release, Apr. 15, 1943, PR-2, Copies of Speeches by Members and Staff of the Committee, Truman Committee Files, National Archives.

17. Bess Truman to Harry Truman, Apr. 21, 1943, Truman Library; handwritten notes, Hugh Fulton to Matt Connelly, Apr. 19, 1943, OP-31 Steel, Truman Committee files, National Archives.

18. Truman Committee, "Additional Report: Shipbuilding and Shipping," Apr. 22, 1943, in Third Annual Report, 251.

19. *Evening Sun* (Baltimore, MD), Apr. 22, 1943.

20. *The New York Times*, Apr. 23, 1943, 3.

21. *The Washington Post*, Apr. 28, 1943, 1; *The New York Times*, Apr. 28, 1943, 1.

22. Hugh Fulton, letter to Edward Polhamus, May 6, 1943, OP-20 Patents and Inventions, Truman Committee files, National Archives.

23. Frederick Rentschler, United Aircraft Corporation, letter to Hugh Fulton, June 24, 1943, OP-30 Aviation, Truman Committee Files, National Archives.

24. Hugh Fulton to Igor Sikorsky, June 21, 1943, AD-1 General Records, Truman Committee files, National Archives; Drew Pearson, "Merry Go-Round: Navy Slow in Making Use of Helicopters," *The Washington Post*, May 7, 1943, B11.

25. *The New York Times*, May 25, 1943.

Chapter Seventeen

1. This section is drawn from Robert Irvin, oral history, Truman Library.

2. Irvin, oral history

3. Harry Truman to Bess Truman, June 25, 1943, Truman Library.

4. *St. Louis Star-Times*, July 9, 1943, 1.

5. "HST Appointments with FDR, 1934-45," memorandum sourced from the papers of Franklin Roosevelt, in the FDR Library in Hyde Park, NY, dated Nov. 4, 1963, in SVP Papers, correspondence files, Truman Library.

6. *St. Louis Star-Times*, July 9, 1943, 1.

7. Harry Truman to Bess Truman, July 9, 1943, Truman Library.

8. *St. Louis Daily Globe-Democrat*, July 11, 1943, 4b.

9. Fulton memo to Margaret Buchholz, May 27, 1943, Truman Committee files, National Archives.

10. George Meader, "Initiation to Washington: My Four Years With the Truman Committee," undated typescript, George Meader Papers, University of Michigan, Bentley Historical Library, Ann Arbor.

11. Truman Committee, "Additional Report: Aircraft," July 10, 1943, reprinted as an appendix in Third Annual Report, 344.

12. "Additional Report: Aircraft," in Third Annual Report, 345.

13. "Additional Report: Aircraft," 347.

14. "Additional Report: Aircraft," 357.

15. The Helldiver was indeed faster and more modern than the Douglas SBD Dauntless, which had proven so effective and reliable at Midway and other battles early in the war. By 1945, more than seven thousand Helldivers were built, and the plane saw widespread use in the US Navy, and by other countries. Wikipedia.org: "Curtiss SB2C Helldiver," accessed March 28, 2022.

16. "Additional Report: Aircraft," 367.

17. "Additional Report: Aircraft," 370.

18. St. Louis Post-Dispatch, July 11, 1943, 6a.

19. The New York Times, July 11, 1943, 1.

20. The Cincinnati Enquirer, July 12, 1943, 11.

21. The New York Times, July 12, 1943.

22. The New York Times, July 13, 1943, 9; PM (New York, NY), July 13, 1943 (clipping in Wilbur Sparks papers, Truman Library); The Philadelphia Inquirer, July 19, 1943, 9.

23. Cincinnati Post, Aug. 20, 1943, clipping in Wilbur Sparks scrapbook, Truman Library.

24. The account of this hearing that follows is drawn from "Hearings, before a Special Subcommittee Investigating the National Defense Program," Part 20, Aug 20, 1943 (Washington: US Govt. Printing Office, 1943), 8363-8415.

25. The New York Times, Sep. 1-3, 1943.

26. PM (New York, NY), Sep. 2, 1943, in scrapbook, Wilbur Sparks papers, Truman Library.

27. The Washington Post, Sep. 5, 1943.

28. The New York Times, March 7, 1943, scrapbook, Wilbur Sparks Papers, Truman Library.

Chapter Eighteen

1. McCullough, 292.

2. Harry Truman to Bess, July 12, 1943, Truman Library.

3. Harry Truman to Harry G. Waltner, Jr., Feb. 5, 1944. Truman Papers, Truman Library.

4. Memorandum, Nov. 4, 1963: "HST appointments with FDR, 1935–1945," SVP Papers correspondence files, Truman papers, Truman Library.

5. *Christian Science Monitor*, Apr. 30, 1943.

6. *Christian Science Monitor*, Apr. 30, 1943.

7. *Wall Street Journal*, Dec. 28, 1943, 6.

8. McCullough, 294.

9. *The New York Times*, July 27, 1943, 19.

10. Robert L. Riggs, "Wallace Can Run With Roosevelt—If He Makes Good," *Courier-Journal* (Louisville, KY), Aug. 1, 1943, 33.

11. Correspondence File, Invitations, Oct. 1943, SVP Papers, Truman papers, Truman Library.

12. Margaret Truman, *Bess W. Truman*, 219.

13. Margaret Truman, *Bess W. Truman*, 219.

14. Harry Truman to Bess Truman, June 21, 1943, Truman Library; Harry Truman to Bess Truman, July 10, 1943; Margaret Truman, ed., *Letters from Father* (New York: Arbor House, 1981), 48.

15. Harry Truman to Bess Truman, July 16, 1943, Truman Library.

16. Harry Truman to Bess Truman, July 17, 18, 1943, Truman Library.

17. Margaret Truman, Bess W. Truman, 219.

18. Harry Truman to Bess Truman, July 9, 10, 15, 16, 1943, Truman Library; Margaret Truman, *Bess W. Truman*, 219-220; Margaret Truman, *Letters from Father*, 48.

19. George C. Marshall, "Memorandum for General Strong," June 14, 1943; *The Papers of George Catlett Marshall,* Vol. 4, *"Aggressive and Determined Leadership," June 1, 1943–December 31, 1944* (Baltimore and London: The Johns Hopkins University Press, 1996), 11–12.

20. "Conversation on the Manhattan Project and Secrecy," Henry Stimson, telephone conversation with Harry Truman, June 17, 1943, on the website nuclearfiles.org, accessed Apr. 11, 2022, http://www.nuclear files.org/menu/library/correspondence/truman-harry/corr_truman_ 1943-06-17.htm.

21. Harry Truman to Lewis Schwellenbach, July 15, 1943, Truman Library.

22. Harry Truman to Bess Truman, Sep. 7, 1943, Truman Library.

23. Harry Truman to Bess Truman, Oct. 5, 1943, Truman Library.

24. Harry Truman to Bess Truman, Oct. 13, 1943, Truman Library.

25. Klein, *A Call to Arms,* 620.

26. "Losses during the Battle of the Atlantic," Wikipedia.org, accessed Apr. 15, 2022, https://en.wikipedia.org/wiki/Losses_during_the_ Battle_of_the_Atlantic.

27. Harry Truman, "Speech Before the National Association of Secretaries of State at St. Louis, Missouri," Oct. 18, 1943, SVP Papers, Truman Library.

28. "Additional Report: Outlines of Problems of Conversion From War Production," Special Committee Investigating the National Defense Program, Nov. 5, 1943, published as addendum to Third Annual Report, 389.

29. "Additional Report: Outlines of Problems of Conversion From War Production," in Third Annual Report, 391-392.

Chapter Nineteen

1. Allen Drury, *A Senate Journal 1943-1945* (Monument, CO: WordFire Press eBook Edition, 2021), Kindle, 12.

2. Drury, *A Senate Journal,* 13.

3. Frank N. Schubert, "Mobilization: The U.S. Army in World War

II," U.S. Army Center of Military History, accessed Apr. 11, 2022, https://history.army.mil/documents/mobpam.htm.

4. John Kennedy Ohl, *Supplying the Troops: General Somervell and American Logistics in WWII* (Northern Illinois University Press, 1994; repr: Plunkett Lake Press and Cornell University Press, eBook, 2020), Kindle, 13.

5. Drury, 47.

6. Ohl, *Supplying the Troops*, 127.

7. Matthew Connelly, oral history, Truman Library.

8. "Department of Defense Coordination and Control," hearing before the Senate Military Affairs Committee, March 6, 1942 (Washington: US Govt. Printing Office, 1942), 7.

9. Ohl, 41.

10. "Memorandum for the Chief of Staff, Subject: The use of negro man power in war," Oct. 30, 1925, Franklin Roosevelt Library, accessed Apr. 13, 2022, https://www.fdrlibrary.org/documents/356632/390886/tusk_doc_a.pdf/4693156a-8844-4361-ae17-03407e7a3dee.

11. Daniels, *The Man of Independence*, 218; Ferrell, ed., *Dear Bess: The Letters from Harry to Bess Truman*, 479.

12. Riddle, 75-76; Daniels, 218; Ohl, 41.

13. Ohl, 127; Riddle, 102.

14. Riddle, 102.

15. Ohl, 128.

16. "Additional Report: Canol," Investigation of the National Defense Program, Jan. 8, 1944, published as an addendum to Third Annual Report (Washington: US Govt. Printing Office, 1944), 457.

17. Riddle, 103.

18. Riddle, 118, 105.

19. Canol report, 458.

20. Riddle, 119.

21. Ohl, 130.

22. Ohl, 131.

23. Ohl, 131, 134; Riddle 109.

24. Ohl, 136.

25. "Hearings Before a Special Committee Investigating the National Defense Program, Part 22, The Canol Project" (Washington: US Govt. Printing Office, 1944), 9588.

26. "Hearings, Part 22, Canol," 9596.

27. "Hearings, Part 22, Canol," 9606-9607.

28. "Hearings, Part 22, Canol," 9618.

29. "Hearings, Part 22, Canol," 9623.

30. Ohl, 136.

31. Donald Nelson to Hugh Fulton, Dec. 11, 1943, Hugh Fulton Papers, Truman Library.

32. Drury, 47.

33. Drury, 48.

34. Drury, 48.

35. Drury, 47.

36. Third Annual Report: "The Canol Project," 459.

37. "Additional Report, The Canol Project" in Third Annual Report, 461.

38. Ohl, 140.

Chapter Twenty

1. John Abbott, oral history, Truman Library.

2. Abbott, oral history; John H. Tolan Jr., oral history, Truman Library.

3. Abbott, oral history.

4. Tolan, oral history.

5. Tolan, oral history; John A. Kennedy, oral history, Truman Library.

6. Tolan, oral history.

7. Tolan, oral history.

8. Tolan, oral history.

9. Irvin, oral history.

10. Irvin, oral history; Homer Ferguson, "You Can't Fool Us Senators," *Liberty*, Dec. 22, 1945, 100.

11. Tolan, oral history.

12. *Congressional Record*, Jan 22, 1945, 384; *Liberty*, Dec. 22, 1945.

13. Irvin, oral history.

14. Tolan, oral history.

15. George Meader, letters to Elizabeth Meader, Nov. 17, 25, 28, 1943, George Meader Papers, Bentley Historical Library, University of Michigan, Ann Arbor.

16. Memo, Harold Robinson to Mildred Dryden, Dec. 3, 1943, Truman Committee files, National Archives.

17. McCullough, 290.

18. Margaret Truman: *Bess W. Truman*, 213; *Harry S. Truman*, 141.

19. Harry Truman to Bess Truman, July 25, 1942, Truman Library.

20. Margaret Truman, *Harry S. Truman*, 159.

21. *The New York Times,* Jan. 30, 1943, 26.

22. Harry Truman to Edward O'Keefe, Feb. 2, 1944, SVP Papers, Truman Library.

23. *The New York Times*, Jan. 30, 1944, 26; Memorandum, "Tentative

Launching Program: U.S.S. Missouri," SVP Papers, Truman Library. In later years, both Margaret and her father would claim the navy forced him to rush his speech on purpose. "The admirals on hand were busy revenging themselves on Dad for previous humiliations," she wrote in her biography of her father, *Harry S. Truman* (159). "He had about three minutes to deliver a fifteen-minute speech. I never heard him talk so fast in my life." Yet Truman, in the letter on Feb. 2, also said that, "They pushed the launching up on account of the tide" (letter to Edward O'Keefe, Feb. 2, 1943, SVP Papers, Truman Library). And in the days leading up to the ceremony, Admiral Kelly had informed Truman in writing that he would have just three minutes to speak. "I will be pleased to speak for three minutes at the launching," he responded (Harry Truman to Admiral Monroe Kelly, Jan. 24, 1943, SVP Papers, Truman Library). Whatever the case, it is clear from all accounts that he had to rush through his remarks.

24. Margaret Truman, *Harry S. Truman*, 159.

25. *The New York Times*, Jan. 30, 1943, 26; Margaret Truman, *Harry S. Truman*, 159-160.

Chapter Twenty-One

1. *The New York Times*, March 27, 1944, 12.

2. Truman Committee, Third Annual Report, 9.

3. Klein, *A Call To Arms*, 677-679.

4. *The Washington Post*, Feb. 19, 1944, 1.

5. Third Annual Report, 6.

6. Third Annual Report, 10-11.

7. *The New York Times*, March 5, 1944, 1.

8. Drury, *A Senate Journal*, 151-152; *Montgomery Advertiser*, March 9, 1944, 1.

9. Drury, 151-153.

10. Drury, 177.

11. *The New York Times*, March 27, 1944, 12.

12. *The New York Times*, March 27, 1944, 12.

13. *Palladium-Item* (Richmond, IN), March 28, 1944, 2; *Buffalo Evening News*, March 28, 1944, 7.

14. Drury, 177.

15. Drury, 177.

16. Drury, 257.

17. Hugh Fulton, letter to John Cahill, Nov. 18, 1943, Truman Committee papers, AD-1 General Records, Correspondence, National Archives.

18. George Meader, letter to Elizabeth Meader, June 30, 1944, Meader papers, Bentley Library, University of Michigan, Ann Arbor.

19. George Meader, "Initiation to Washington: My Four Years With the Truman Committee," typescript, George Meader Papers, Bentley Library, University of Michigan, Ann Arbor.

20. Meader, letters to Elizabeth Meader, Apr. 15, 1944, May 16, 1944; Meader papers, Bentley Library, University of Michigan.

21. George Meader, letter to Bobby Meader, Apr. 27, 1944, George Meader papers.

22. Meader, letter to Elizabeth Meader, Apr. 15, 1944, Meader papers.

23. Rudolph Halley, memorandum, Mar. 21, 1944, Truman Committee papers, General Records, Correspondence, National Archives.

24. Hearings, Investigation of the National Defense Program, May 25-26, 1944, 10520.

25. "Court Gives Corrigan 1 1/2 Years in Navy Deal," *New York Daily News*, June 17, 1947, 43.

26. John H. Tolan Jr., oral history, Truman Library.

27. Tolan, oral history.

28. Tolan, oral history.

29. Tolan, oral history.

30. Tolan, oral history.

31. This section is drawn from "Hearings, Investigation of the National Defense Program, May 25-26, 1944" (Washington: US Govt. Printing Office, 1944), 10505-10591.

32. "Hearings," 10516.

33. "Hearings," 10517.

34. "Hearings," 10550.

35. "Hearings," 10561.

36. Abbott, oral history.

37. "Hearings," 10544.

38. "Hearings," 10585.

39. Abbott, oral history.

40. *The Washington Post*, May 27, 1944, 1. Corrigan was not court-martialed—as Admiral Gatch had predicted, he was later tried in federal court. He was convicted in 1947, sentenced to eighteen months in prison and fined $5,000, but the conviction was overturned on appeal in May 1948. The federal appeals court "held that 'evidence was sufficient to sustain the verdict,' reached in June 1947, but that certain reports were accepted as evidence 'in error,'" acccording to the *New York Daily News* from May 29, 1948.

Chapter Twenty-Two

1. Harry Truman, letter to Scott Loftin, March 8, 1944, SVP Papers, Truman Library.

2. *Kansas City Times*, Feb 23, 1944, 1.

3. *The New York Times*, Nov. 21, 1942, 1.

4. Memo, "HST appointments with FDR, 1935-1945," Nov. 4, 1963, Truman papers, Truman Library.

5. Joseph Lelyveld, *His Final Battle: The Last Months of Franklin Roosevelt* (New York: Alfred A. Knopf, 2016), Kindle, 155.

6. *Salt Lake Tribune*, May 8, 1944, 5.

7. McCullough, 296; Daniels, *Man of Independence*, 242–243.

8. *St. Louis Post-Dispatch*, Oct. 8, 1944.

9. McCullough, 299; Lelyveld, 162.

10. Lelyveld, 162.

11. *New York Daily News*, July 12, 1944, 1.

12. Drury, *A Senate Journal,* 304.

13. Lelyveld, 166.

14. McCullough, 301. As with many events surrounding the choice of Roosevelt's running mate in 1944, and the dramatic events of the Chicago convention, there are many differing versions of this meeting and different accounts of who said what. Among the key disagreements about these weeks is whether Roosevelt passively, uncaringly accepted Truman on the word of his advisers, or whether, as Ed Flynn said afterwards, he steered it towards Truman. This version is drawn primarily from the accounts of Truman biographers David McCullough and Alonzo Hamby, and Joseph Lelyveld's account of Roosevelt's final months, and from Jonathan Daniels's *The Man of Independence.*

15. There is much confusion about when this letter was written: that night, after the dinner meeting broke up, or in the following days in Washington, or possibly in Chicago when Roosevelt met briefly with Hannegan on his way to the West Coast. See, for example, McCullough, 306; Hamby, 280–281; Lelyveld, 170–171; Margaret Truman, *Harry S. Truman,* 172–173.

16. Lelyveld, 161; Hamby, 280.

17. Margaret Truman, ed., *Letters from Father,* 55.

18. Hamby, 282.

19. McCullough, 303.

20. Truman, *Memoirs, Vol. 1,* 191. The request from Byrnes would later lead to a feud between the two men after Byrnes left Truman's presidential administration, with Truman claiming Byrnes must have asked him

this favor in an attempt to get around Roosevelt's selection of Truman, according to Alonzo Hamby (page 282).

21. *The South Bend* (IN) *Tribune*, July 15, 1944, 1; McCullough, 302; *La Crosse* (WI) *Tribune*, July 16, 1944, 1.

22. *Memoirs, Vol. 1*, 191.

23. Margaret Truman, *Bess W. Truman*, 227-228.

24. Hamby, 283. It is possible that this is the note that Hannegan obtained after the meeting on July 11, and that the more formal letter was written on the train in Chicago.; "I still could not be sure..." from *Memoirs, Vol. 1*, 191.

25. Some accounts say this happened on Wednesday the 19th. Truman, in his memoirs, 192, puts it on Thursday, "the day before the Vice-President was to be nominated." Daniels, 233, says "Truman and [Postmaster General Frank] Walker remember the time as late Thursday afternoon. Others are not so sure."

26. Margaret Truman, *Harry S. Truman*, 174.

27. *Memoirs, Vol.1*, 192

28. Lelyveld, 173

29. Lelyveld, 173, Memoirs, Vol. 1, 192-193. Jonathan Daniels, in *The Man of Independence*, has Truman saying, "My God."

30. Margaret Truman, *Bess W. Truman*, 230.

31. Margaret Truman, *Bess W. Truman*, 231; *Harry S. Truman*, 182-183.

32. *Memoirs, Vol. 1*, 193.

33. George Meader to Elizabeth Meader, July 22, 1944, Meader Papers, Bentley Historical Library, University of Michigan.

34. Telegram, Hugh Fulton to Harry Truman, July 25, 1944, Truman Committee papers, National Archives.

35. McNaughton and Hehmeyer, *This Man Truman*, 137.

36. Harry Truman to Bess Truman, Aug. 4, 1944.

37. Harry Truman to Henry Wallace, Aug. 3, 1944, Truman Committee papers, National Archives.

38. Drury, *A Senate Journal*, 326.

39. Drury, 344.

40. *Congressional Record*, Vol. 90, Part 5, Aug. 7, 1944, 6476-6478.

41. Walter Hehmeyer, oral history, Truman Library.

Chapter Twenty-Three

1. Daniels, *The Man of Independence*, 227.

2. Harry Truman to Bess Truman, Aug. 4, 1944, Truman Library.

3. *Plain Speaking*, 211.

4. McCullough, 340-341; McNaughton & Hehmeyer, 207-209.

5. Hamby, 290.

6. *Harper's Magazine*, June 1945, 616.

7. Daniels, 228.

8. Riddle, 154.

9. *Time*, Mar. 8, 1943, 13.

10. McCune and Beal, *Harper's Magazine*, June 1945, 620.

11. Memphis *Commercial Appeal*, Apr. 23, 1944, 36.

12. Truman Committee, Third Annual Report, 40-42.

13. *Time*, Mar. 8, 1943, 13.

14. Riddle, 146.

15. Hamby, 257-258.

16. *Afro-American* (Baltimore, MD), Aug. 5, 1944, 10.

17. Klein, *A Call To Arms*, 298.

18. *Christian Science Monitor,* Jan. 13, 1944, 1.

19. Hamby, 258; Truman Committee, "Additional Report, Outlines of Problems of Conversion From War Production," Oct. 25, 1943, addendum to Third Annual Report, 390.

20. *Harper's Magazine,* June 1945, 621.

21. *Harper's Magazine,* June 1945, 618.

22. *Plain Speaking,* 178–179

23. *Harper's Magazine,* June 1945, 619.

24. Sparks, oral history.

25. *A Senate Journal,* 344.

26. Riddle, 155.

27. John Duggan Jr., letter to Harry Truman, Mar. 29, 1943, Truman Committee files, OP-31 Steel, National Archives.

Epilogue

1. Hugh Fulton, letter to G.B. Cole, Aug. 7, 1944, Hugh Fulton Papers, Truman Library.

2. Walter Hehmeyer, oral history, Truman Library.

3. *The Washington Post,* Apr. 23, 1945, 4.

4. Miller, *Plain Speaking,* 216.

5. Mildred Dryden, oral history, Truman Library.

6. "Merry-Go-Round," *The Washington Post,* Apr. 19, 1945.

7. "Merry-Go-Round," *The Washington Post,* Apr. 20, 1945.

8. Matthew Connelly, oral history, Truman Library.

9. *Wichita Falls Times* (Wichita, KS), May 27, 1945, 24; Harold Robinson, oral history, Truman Library.

10. Miller, *Plain Speaking,* 176.

11. Hugh Fulton, letter to Harry Truman, Dec. 6, 1954, Hugh Fulton Papers, Truman Library.

12. Harry Truman to Hugh Fulton, Jan. 16, 1957, Hugh Fulton Papers, Truman Library.

13. *Pottsville Republican* (Pottsville, PA), Mar. 10, 1961.

14. Harry Truman to Jessie Fulton, Nov. 6, 1962, Post Presidential Papers, Name File, Hugh Fulton, Truman Library.

15. Jessie Fulton to Harry Truman, Nov. 12, 1962, Post Presidential Papers, Name File, Hugh Fulton, Truman Library.

16. Harry Truman to Jessie Fulton, Nov. 24, 1962, Post Presidential Papers, Truman Library.

17. Menu in the possession of Gregory Baker.

18. "Marion Baker: Serving the Public Good," *Virginia Lawyer*, May 1994, clipping provided by Gregory Baker.

19. Author interview with Dylan Baker, Greg Baker, and Lisa Horner, Oct. 25, 2021.

20. *News & Advance* (Lynchburg, VA), May 30, 1994, A-2, clipping provided by Gregory Baker.

21. Shirley Key Hehmeyer, oral history, Truman Library.

22. *Commercial Appeal* (Memphis, TN), Feb. 2, 2011, 21.

23. George Meader, typescript, "My Four Years With The Truman Committee," George Meader papers, Bentley Historical Library, University of Michigan, Ann Arbor, 11, 26-27.

24. *Detroit Free Press*, Oct. 18, 1994.

25. "Special Committee on Organized Crime in Interstate Commerce." United States Senate website, accessed Aug. 20, 2022, https://www.senate.gov/about/powers-procedures/investigations/kefauver.htm.

26. *The New York Times,* Nov. 20, 1956; *Daily News* (New York, NY), Mar. 15, 1951; *The New York Times*, July 19, 1952.

27. *The New York Times*, Nov. 20, 1956, 37.

28. Sallie Sparks, email to the author, Dec. 11, 2021.

29. Website: harmonizers.grouporganizer.com, accessed Aug 20, 2022, https://harmonizers.groupanizer.com/system/files/attachments/16610/No.%2012%20%E2%80%93%201970%20Mr.%20President,%20Mr.%20Barbershopper%20.pdf.

30. *The Washington Post*, Sep. 7, 2002.

31. Campaign brochure, 1956, Harold Robinson Papers, Truman Library.

32. *Boston Globe*, Dec. 27, 2009.

33. *Baltimore Sun*, Jan. 9, 2002.

34. *St. Louis Post-Dispatch*, Dec. 1, 1955; *Kansas City Star*, Mar. 5, 1957; *St. Louis Globe-Democrat*, Nov. 23, 1962.

35. *Albuquerque Tribune*, Jan. 31, 1998.

36. *The New York Times*, Sep. 20, 1945.

37. George Dye, letter to Benjamin Fairless, Jan. 6, 1945, OP-31 Steel, Truman Committee Files, National Archives.

38. George Dye to Rudolph Halley, Sep. 1, 1943, OP-31 Steel, Truman Committee Files, National Archives.

39. George Dye to Benjamin Fairless, Jan. 6, 1945.

40. Website: "Auke Visser's Famous T-Tanker's Page," accessed Aug. 21, 2022, http://www.aukevisser.nl/t2tanker/id411.htm.

41. *Oregonian*, Dec. 26, 1943, 17.

42. "Final Report of a Board of Investigation To Inquire Into The Design and Methods of Construction of Welded Steel Merchant Ships," July 15, 1946 (Washington: US Govt. Printing Office, 1946), 3.

43. Website: "Auke Visser's Famous T-Tanker's Page," accessed Aug. 21, 2022, http://www.aukevisser.nl/t2tanker/id411.htm.

44. Robert Irvin, oral history, Truman Library.

45. *Long Beach Press-Telegram*, Jan. 11, 1950.

46. Robert Irvin, oral history, Truman Library.

INDEX

Page numbers in *italics* indicate illustrations.